The Battle of Lake Erie and Its Aftermath

The Battle of Lake Erie and Its Aftermath

A Reassessment

David Curtis Skaggs,
editor

THE KENT STATE UNIVERSITY PRESS
Kent, Ohio

Frontis: Perry departs the *Lawrence*. Sketch by Dean Mosher; property of David Curtis Skaggs.

Library of Congress Catalog Card Number 2012048782
ISBN 978-1-60635-179-6
Manufactured in the United States of America

LIBRARY OF CONGRESS CATALOGING-IN-PUBLICATION DATA
The Battle of Lake Erie and its aftermath : a reassessment / David Curtis Skaggs, editor.
pages cm
Sequel to: War on the Great Lakes, (1991)
Includes bibliographical references.
ISBN 978-1-60635-179-6 (hardcover) ∞
1. Lake Erie, Battle of, 1813. 2. Lake Erie, Battle of, 1813—Influence.
I. Skaggs, David Curtis.
E356.E6B285 2013
973.5'254—dc23
2012048782

17 16 15 14 13 5 4 3 2 1

Contents

Introduction

DAVID CURTIS SKAGGS

Few naval battles in American history have left a more enduring impress on our national consciousness than the Battle of Lake Erie, 10 September 1813. Master Commandant Oliver Hazard Perry's battle flag emblazoned with the message "Don't Give Up the Ship," now enshrined at the U.S. Naval Academy, has become a naval maxim. His succinct after-action report—"We have met the enemy and they are ours"—constitutes one of the more memorable battle summaries in our national history. The 352-foot Doric column at the Perry's Victory and International Peace Memorial on South Bass Island, Ohio, is one of the tallest memorials in the world and constantly reminds those sailing on this Great Lake of not only the naval engagement but also the two centuries of peace that followed. Often sailing on these waters is the Pennsylvania Historical and Museum Commission's U.S. brig *Niagara,* a replica of the relief flagship of Perry's squadron. It, too, keeps the memory of the U.S. Navy's first squadron-to-squadron victory alive among the general public, and it also keeps alive the skills so necessary in a sailing navy.

It is appropriate, therefore, to celebrate the bicentennial of the American victory with a review of the battle and its consequences with a series of essays on a variety of topics related thereto. Twenty-five years ago Jeff Welsh and I gathered essays from a scholarly conference into a book entitled *War on the Great Lakes: Essays Commemorating the 175th Anniversary of the Battle of Lake Erie* (Kent State University Press, 1991). The time has come to update this collection and to incorporate new scholarship of the past quarter-century.

Assembled here are contributions dealing with events leading up to the naval battle, the battle itself, and its immediate and long-term consequences. Also, there are two essays dealing with the memory of the Battle of Lake Erie through the maintenance and exhibition of Perry's famous battle flag and the flagship *Niagara*'s role in letting us better understand aspects of the engagement on the lake.

While several of these essays bring to light new insights relating to this era, others provide summaries of current scholarship about the battle and its consequences. Collectively they provide the general reader, the military history enthusiast, and the professional historian new looks at this naval engagement and its impact on subsequent historical events. The reader will find each chapter a self-contained approach relative to a common subject—the Battle of Lake Erie and its consequences.

Larry Nelson sets the stage by describing the Maumee Valley and its importance in the campaigns of 1812. This river, today virtually unknown except to residents of northeast Indiana and northwest Ohio, brings a larger volume of water into the Great Lakes than any other watercourse. In a world of waterborne transportation, it was a critical route to the lakes, since the Black Swamp that lay to its south obstructed overland transportation northward from Cincinnati toward Detroit. With British naval dominance on Lake Erie, Americans were forced to either move through the swamp, as General William Hull did, or around it down the Maumee, as General Anthony Wayne had done nearly two decades earlier. The failure of General James Winchester's campaign to exploit the Maumee route in 1812 eventually led to his rash advance toward Frenchtown (Monroe, Michigan) the following January and his disastrous defeat there in the River Raisin Massacre. This defeat contributed to the decision to concentrate on gaining naval dominance on Lake Erie before advancing toward Detroit. Control of the lake would not only allow a more convenient means of logistically supporting ground troops; it would also permit an invasion of Canada without having to utilize the vulnerable ground transportation link between the Maumee Rapids and Detroit that had contributed to General William Hull's surrender of Detroit in August 1812.

That effort is summarized in my brief essay on the Lake Erie campaign. The successful labors of Oliver Hazard Perry, along with those of shipbuilder Noah Brown and their sailors and workmen at Presque Isle Bay (Erie, Pennsylvania), created a squadron larger and with much more firepower than that of the British. Given his advantages, Perry should have easily won the Battle of Lake Erie. The inexperience of the U.S. Navy officers in squadron tactics hampered their conduct during the battle. As the captain of the *Lawrence,* Perry proved a resolute and effective commander; as the commodore of the American squadron he was less capable. Mike Palmer, a distinguished scholar of naval command and control problems during the age of fighting sail, criticizes Perry's failure to signal his subordinates and communicate his intentions as the situation his squadron faced changed during the course of the three-hour battle. This failure made what should have been a relatively easy U.S. Navy triumph into one whose outcome was in doubt.

Despite his inadequacies during the battle, Perry proved a most cooperative and effective leader of the navy's support of the army's campaign to gain control of southeastern Michigan and southwestern Upper Canada (modern Ontario). My essay on the unity of effort between Perry and Major General William Henry Harrison during the subsequent retaking of Detroit and the Thames River campaign demonstrates how the army and navy could mutually support one another without a single command authority. Elsewhere during the War of 1812 one finds interservice rivalries, personality clashes, and Washington headquarters directives adversely affecting the conduct of joint operations.

Most American studies of the war in the Great Lakes region claim that Perry and Harrison were "saviors of the Old Northwest" and devote little attention to subsequent campaigns north of a line from Detroit to Chicago. But as far as military efforts go, their triumphs in the autumn of 1813 left nearly half the region's territory in the hands of a few redcoats, more numerous fur traders and their voyageurs, and Indian allies. From Prairie du Chien to Fort Mackinac, these three groups fought a gallant delaying action that failed not on the battlefield but at the negotiating table. Brian Dunnigan, who has spent most of his summers on Mackinac Island, uses his accomplished scholarly skills to describe the American inability to retake Fort Mackinac nearly a year after Perry's victory. He demonstrates how the tactical inadequacies of the American attackers combined with the determined defense of British lieutenant colonel Robert McDouall, his soldiers, and their native allies frustrated the American efforts. An important observation of Dunnigan's essay is whether this expedition was strategically misplaced and Commodore Arthur Sinclair's vessels would have been more useful in supporting the more critical campaign on the Niagara peninsula.

Collectively, these five essays set the scene for the Battle of Lake Erie and its military consequences. But this battle and its impact on Harrison's successful ground campaign that eventually resulted in the American victory at the Battle of the Thames and the victorious British defense of Mackinac Island are only part of the story. Far more important than these encounters by themselves are the short- and long-term consequences of military operations. It is these that the second section of essays explores.

Everyone studying the War of 1812 concludes that the biggest losers were the Native Americans. As Dan Barr incisively describes, the Delawares' attempt to preserve their identity by observing neutrality during the conflict did not exempt them from eventual expulsion from the woodlands of Indiana to the grasslands of Kansas. Caught between the rush of American frontiersmen anxious to claim the lush soils of the Wabash Valley and the millenarian nativist revivalism of Tenskwatawa, the Shawnee Prophet, the Delawares' search for a "middle ground," as scholar Richard White calls it, failed them in the long run.

One of the consistent charges by Americans prior to the War of 1812 was that British fur traders and Indian agents, especially Matthew Elliott at Amherstburg, Upper Canada (modern Ontario), encouraged and abetted Native American opposition to the United States. John Bowes demonstrates that this British specter haunted Americans in the Old Northwest into the early 1830s; even though the American victories on Lake Erie and at the Thames should have caused all Native Americans east of the Mississippi to forego such expectations. But a few, including the Sauk chief Black Hawk, vainly hoped for a return of support from His Majesty's government. Bowes makes clear that American fears and Black Hawk's hopes had some basis in fact. One must always remember that conservative Canadian officials in the early 1830s feared an alliance between the United States manifest destiny advocates and opposition Upper Canada politician William Lyon Mackenzie that may have contributed to their encouragement of Black Hawk.

Few midwesterners profited more from the American victories in the Old Northwest than John Tipton of Indiana, who exemplifies the most successful American settlers who exploited the opportunities arising out of the American victories in the Old Northwest. As Ginette Aley writes, by 1814 he had risen from private to colonel in the Indiana militia as a consequence of his military exploits at the Battle of Tippecanoe in 1811 and afterward. He benefited greatly from land dealings in the Wabash Valley in the years following the war and yet tried to preserve some semblance of fairness toward the Native Americans living there. Despite his opposition to those who wanted to expel the Indians, Tipton was elected to the United States Senate. Tipton exemplifies those for whom the battles at Tippecanoe, Lake Erie, and the Thames allowed them to exploit the fruits of victory to their own advantage.

Like Barr does in his study of the Delawares, Aley concentrates on the demise of the middle ground in Indian-white relations.

Readers will note the interaction between Aley's essay and that by Phyllis Gernhardt on Fort Wayne's development following the war. The transformation of Fort Wayne from a frontier outpost to a thriving commercial and agricultural center typifies the way by which Euroamericans exploited the opportunities that arose from the military and naval victories in the Old Northwest. What was once a valley filled with forests and Native American fields of corn and gourds became a center of land speculation, farming, commerce, and transportation to markets from Buffalo to New Orleans. Gernhardt's story was replicated throughout the Old Northwest as warfare changed the political situation and expanded the economic opportunities for white settlement.

Often forgotten in the study of military affairs is the impact of service on subsequent careers of individuals engaged in particular battles. Charles Brodine's examination of the career of Thomas Holdup Stevens chronicles the consequences of the Battle of Lake Erie on the subsequent promotion and assignments of the youngest and boldest of Perry's vessel commanders. Undoubtedly, Perry's early death adversely affected Stevens's career prospects, but his achieving the rank of captain (the highest rank in the U.S. Navy prior to the Civil War) and the desire of his namesake son and grandson to continue the family tradition of naval service constitute stunning testimony of the lasting effect of this battle.

The final section contains two essays on the historical legacies of Perry's victory. In the first of these Deborah Lee Trupin and Scott Harmon collaborate on the efforts to conserve the famous battle flag that flew on 10 September 1813. Their explanation of previous work at conservation and current technology regarding the latest endeavor in restoring this treasured flag should be most enlightening to those of us unfamiliar with modern fabric preservation techniques. This artifact of American naval history is a most dramatic reminder of Perry's victory, and its preservation is an important mission for the navy for which its message of "Don't Give Up the Ship" has become a virtual service motto.

The final essay by Walter Rybka of the flagship *Niagara* concerns one of the most exciting memorials to Perry's victory. The reconstruction of the *Niagara* by the Pennsylvania Historical and Museum Commission allows modern Americans an opportunity to better comprehend the world of fighting sail. No one is more familiar than Rybka, the longtime master and commander of this vessel, with the problems of navigation of Perry's relief flagship during the engagement on western Lake Erie. His description of the sailing characteristics of the various American vessels also provides an important understanding of the battle itself.

Collectively, these essays allow those interested in this engagement to review its place in the strategy and tactics of warfare on the upper Great Lakes during the War of 1812, to examine its consequences on the Natives and Americans affected by it, and to understand how its memory is preserved for generations to come.

Facing page: The Great Lakes region. Reprinted with permission from David Curtis Skaggs and Larry L. Nelson, eds., *The Sixty Years' War for the Great Lakes, 1754–1814* (East Lansing: Michigan State University Press, 2001).

Map 4. Great Lakes Region, 1795–1814

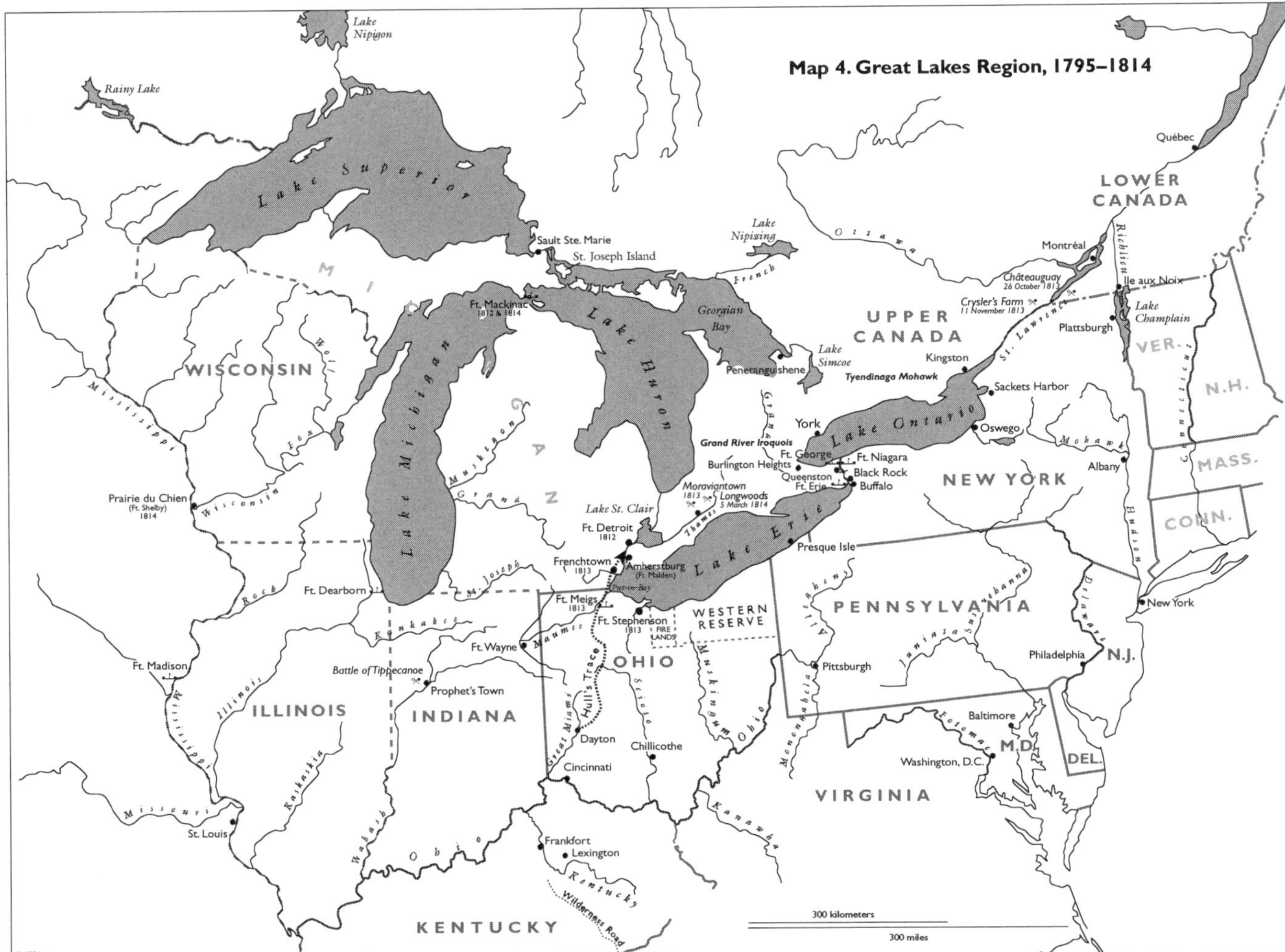

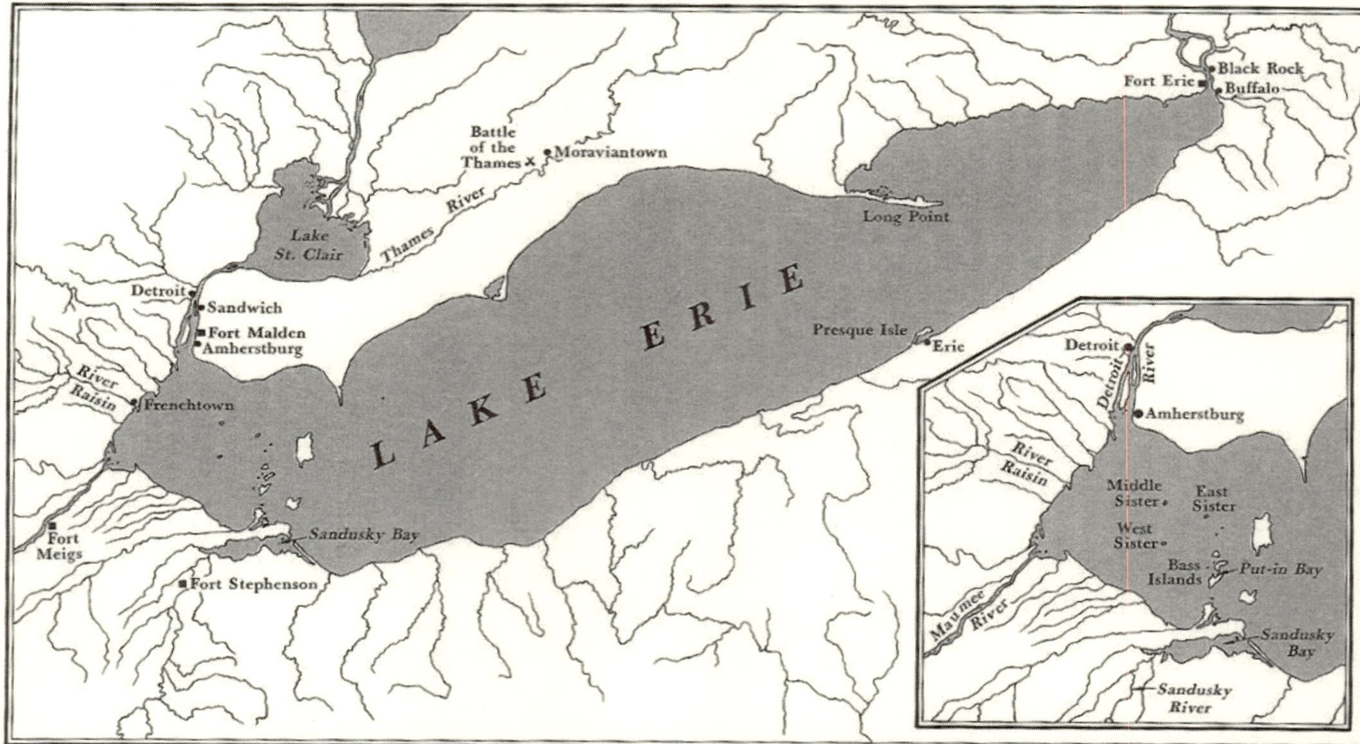

Lake Erie. Reprinted from William S. Dudley, ed., *The Naval War of 1812: A Documentary History*, vol. 2 (Washington, DC: Naval Historical Center, 1992).

PART I

Military Operations

The Maumee River Campaign, 1812–1813

LARRY L. NELSON

During the opening months of the War of 1812, the most important factor shaping the strategic environment within the Detroit theater was British naval control of Lake Erie. Control of Lake Erie permitted the British to move men and supplies easily from the Niagara theater to Detroit, Michilimackinac, and, indeed, throughout most of Upper Canada at will. Further, British control necessarily denied access and use of the lake to the Americans. There was simply no easy way for the United States to move men or supplies to Detroit or its environs without a long and arduous journey either directly through Ohio's Great Black Swamp, a nearly impenetrable morass extending some 40 miles north and south and 140 miles east and west laying along the southern border of the Maumee Valley, or by submitting to an equally tedious trek that circumvented the swamp to the south and west to Fort Wayne, then traveled down the Maumee River, and finally ended in a march of some 50 miles from the foot of the Maumee rapids in present-day Maumee to Detroit.[1]

If Lake Erie was the lock, Maumee Bay was one of the most important doors secured by the British Navy, for flowing into it from the west lay the Maumee River, at the time one of the most strategically important rivers in northern Ohio. The Maumee or its tributaries provided access into Ohio, Michigan, and the interior of Indiana. Those moving westward on the river found the Maumee rapids—a fourteen-mile-long series of shallow rapids extending from present-day Grand Rapids, Ohio, to present-day Maumee and Perrysburg (on the river's left and right bank, respectively) in which the river drops fifty-five feet—the last obstacle to a generally unimpeded journey to the Auglaize River at Defiance and, with it, access to southern Ohio. Or, if so inclined, travelers could continue all the way to the river's headwaters at

Fort Wayne. From there, after a short portage to the Wabash River, journeyers could then ride that stream to the Ohio River and then to the Mississippi River and, from there, to the Gulf of Mexico.

The key to controlling the Maumee was command of the foot of the rapids where lay a strategic intersection of land and water routes. By directing events at the rapids, both belligerents could protect or interdict supplies, arms, materials, and troops destined either for Ohio or Sandwich (present-day Windsor, Ontario) and also guarantee access and use of the traditional land routes of invasion leading both to the United States or Canada. Even before the declaration of war, American officials had decided to use the Maumee Valley as the primary corridor through which to deliver men, materials, and provisions to Detroit.[2]

Secretary of War William Eustis named the governor of the Michigan Territory, William Hull, a brigadier general in the U.S. army in the spring of 1812. Eustis ordered Hull to lead a force of 2,000 Ohio militia and U.S. regulars to Detroit and, should circumstances warrant, then carry the war to Canada. Mustering in Urbana, Ohio, in early June, Hull's army marched northward, traversing the Great Black Swamp and arriving at the foot of the Maumee rapids on 29 June, where it lingered for two days while Hull rested and consolidated his force. Renewing the march on 1 July, the next day Hull learned of the 18 June declaration of war. Continuing the advance, Hull ordered a detachment of Ohio militia commanded by Captain Henry Brush to man a small blockhouse and stockade built originally during the 1790s Wayne campaigns at Frenchtown (present-day Monroe, Michigan) on the River Raisin. The remaining Americans then pushed ahead to Detroit, reaching the city on 5 July and crossing into Canada on 11 July. But Hull's offensive lost momentum long before it could threaten Fort Amherstburg, the British stronghold in Malden (also called Fort Malden). Eventually, the American army reversed its course and retreated back to Detroit. On 16 August, when faced with an enterprising and intrepid counteroffensive mounted by the commander of British military forces in Upper Canada, Isaac Brock, Hull surrendered his army, his post at Detroit, and the remainder of the Michigan Territory to the British.[3]

The articles of capitulation demanded that all American troops at Detroit surrender themselves and their arms to the British. The surrender also included troops not actually in Detroit but nonetheless attached to Hull's army and within the Michigan Territory. Specifically, the surrender included two small garrisons, the detachment of Ohio militia at Frenchtown on the River Raisin, and a second, smaller detachment of Ohio militia occupying a small blockhouse and stockade recently erected at the foot of the Maumee rapids.[4]

William Hatch, a War of 1812 veteran who served under Hull at Detroit and who was with the general as his army marched through northwest Ohio, explained in his memoir that in 1812, "only the eastern and southern parts of Ohio were settled, and that even these portions of the state were but thinly peopled. By drawing a line from near Cleveland on Lake Erie to the Falls of the Ohio River, all north and west of that line, with the exception of a few old French posts, with their feeble settlements, was, as it respects our race, an unbroken wilderness, an untouched forest, occupied only by powerful Indian tribes with no other defenses that what the feeble, stockaded posts known as Forts Wayne, Dearborn, Harrison, and the really strong fort of Detroit afforded." Hatch's description was apt. Very few Europeans lived in the state's northwest quadrant, a region largely ceded to native peoples by the 1795 Treaty of Greenville. But one of the few populated areas in northwest Ohio in 1812 lay at the foot of the Maumee rapids, directly along Hull's avenue of approach. Indeed, the foot of the Maumee rapids in 1812 was the site of a long-established, populous, and thriving community, Port Miami, established in 1805.[5]

Congress established Port Miami on 18 January 1805, when it created the District of Miami and authorized the establishment of a port of entry at the rapids. Port Miami was a sizable community. Centered around a small cluster of homes and farms built along both sides of the Maumee River at the rapids, the district stretched like a narrow ribbon from Swan Creek (Toledo) westward to present-day Napoleon, Ohio. Although a few settlers had moved to the locale in 1805, fewer than twenty-five families lived within five miles of the Maumee rapids in 1807. But by 1812 Port Miami had grown into a substantial, bustling community of seventy families made up of as many as 600 people. Resident Lewis Bond claimed that farms near the town contained "an immense quantity of corn standing in the fields, potatoes, oats, and some wheat in stock, with large droves of cattle and hogs." Edward Dewar, deputy assistant quartermaster general at Fort Amherstburg, noted likewise that the settlement contained a large number of cattle, was surrounded by fields yielding approximately 8,000 bushels of corn, and was able to provide 300 men to the local militia. These substantial economic resources, when combined with the village's considerable population and strategic location, would make Port

Miami a particularly vulnerable target of opportunity for British offensive actions in the days immediately following the declaration of war.[6]

Hull's army had passed directly through Port Miami while on its way to Detroit. When the army crossed the Maumee on 29 June, it camped directly below the Fallen Timbers battlefield a few miles above the village. The following day the army paraded in full dress uniform and then marched through Port Miami, led by a band of music and a corps made up of the army's massed fifes and drums. According to William Kennedy Beall,

> From my situation, I could see the entire army on its march. The two front regiments were smartly uniformed. The army marched in sections, forming a line of near two miles in length. The day was clear and favorable to their muskets, which reflected the brilliancy of the sun. The light dragoons, elegantly uniformed, formed the advance guard. The 4th Regiment U.S. Infantry was in front of Col. Cass's and Col. Findlay's Regiments. And Col McArthur brought up the rear. The rifle companies formed a flank guard, and marching by single file at some distance from each other, extended to the rear on each side of the army. The view was grand and inspiring, and the general was in fine spirits.

John Hunt remembered that as the army passed through the town they were saluted by the village's militia company, commanded by Captain Lewis Bond. According to Hunt, Bond's company was uniformed in round stovepipe hats decorated with a buck's tail placed conspicuously in front. The admiration was mutual. In a later recollection of the same incident, Bond claimed that Hull's troops were well armed, provided with good music, and made a martial appearance. They were, he thought, "fine looking, well disciplined, and fit for any service."[7]

Hull's arrival was a godsend for the village's residents, all of whom were growing increasingly concerned as the United States and England edged toward war. After meeting with village leaders, Hull, who had built a series of blockhouses along his route from Urbana, consented to building a small blockhouse and stockade for the settlement's protection and to garrisoning it with a detachment of thirty men, perhaps supplemented with invalids or others deemed unable to complete the journey to Detroit. A company of Ohio militia led by Lieutenant Samuel Davidson was to build the post and then place it under the command of Lieutenant John Caris.[8]

No account survives that describes what went on at the Maumee garrison in the days between the declaration of war and Hull's surrender. But we do have a good idea of the state of affairs at the small outpost manned by Ohio militia at the River Raisin. Samuel Williams, who was stationed there, kept a diary and wrote a series of letters to family and friends in Ohio. In a diary entry dated 9 July, he recorded that the military defenses at the site consisted of a single line of pickets, made of round logs with sharpened tops about 12 inches in diameter, set close together and standing 7 or 8 feet above the surface. Two log blockhouses about 18 feet square and 12 feet high commanded the fort's diagonal angles. These blockhouses projected 6 feet beyond the pickets, and the stockade had been built so that portholes in the blockhouses could enfilade two sides of the enclosure. But he also observed that the blockhouse and stockade, now nearing twenty years of age, were "so much decayed that they formed a very poor defense against musket or rifle balls, and none against cannon."[9]

In a letter to Ohio governor Edwin Tiffin dated 11 August, Williams recorded that "it is certain that our affairs on this frontier wear a very serious and gloomy aspect. All communication between us and Detroit has been for several days wholly cut off by the enemy. The express mail, which, until lately, always succeeded in getting through, has entirely failed. We are, therefore, without any advices from Detroit and the army and know nothing of its movement, nor whether, nor when relief will reach us. We are at a loss what to think of these things. Our position is a most perilous one. We are liable at any time to be overwhelmed by the vastly superior force of the enemy." And in a letter to his wife dated 14 August, two days before the American surrender, he wrote that "all thought of being able to proceed to Detroit is now abandoned; and our attention is turned exclusively to fortifying our position and putting it in the best state of defense we can. If the enemy should bring their field artillery to the attack—which if they come, they will surely do—our rotten stockade will be battered to the ground in ten minutes. What our fate will be I cannot tell. But if we fall, we shall sell our lives as dearly as we can. We have lost all confidence in General Hull." Williams's comments reflect the plight of a lonely and isolated garrison where morale was spiraling dangerously downward and confidence, resolve, and even hope itself had evaporated almost entirely.[10]

Immediately after occupying Detroit, the British dispatched a small detachment to Frenchtown to take possession of the American stockade. The garrison's advanced guard stopped the delegation about half a mile from the fort and escorted them, disarmed and blindfolded, into the stockade. Unaware of the American capitulation, Brush accused the party of being spies and even went so far as to assemble his command on the post's parade ground for the purpose of hanging the envoys before one of his junior officers convinced the commander to abandon his rash and reckless plan. Indeed, the confrontation between Brush and his subordinates became so heated that Brush was dissuaded only after his second-in-command threatened to shoot him if he persisted. But later, two American soldiers who had fled from Detroit straggled into the post and verified the details surrounding Hull's defeat. At an officer's meeting held late that evening, the Americans decided to disregard their orders to surrender and instead retreat to Ohio. Failing to destroy a significant quantity of military stores housed at the garrison and leaving a few sick American soldiers who were unable to travel behind in the stockade, Brush and his command abandoned their post at 11:00 that night. The withdrawal was so wild and undisciplined that a witness, Frederick Folley, described the Americans as "panic struck." They "flew in all directions," he claimed, "some climbing over the pickets of the stockade," others making their escape as best they could "without leave or order," "loosing their shoes, packs, and some flung away their arms, ammunition, and equipment; some stealing any horse they could," and riding away "full chase."[11]

Two days later, a British force led by Captain Peter Chambers of the Welsh 41st Regiment of Foot, augmented by a large force of Indians led by the Shawnee Tecumseh and the Wyandot Roundhead, arrived at the Raisin to take possession of the American post. Frenchtown was the first objective in an extended campaign in which Chambers was to secure the surrender of the American garrisons on the Raisin, at the Maumee rapids, and, if circumstances permitted, at Fort Wayne. Brush had abandoned a substantial supply of arms, rations, and materials at the post, including a brass howitzer, 19 "shot" howitzers, 114 muskets and bayonets, 12 pistols, 64 cartridge boxes, 7 rifles, 6 swords, 46 barrels of flour, 9 barrels of pork, 1 barrel of whiskey, and 2 wagons. Chambers seized the cache of American weapons and then destroyed the stockade and blockhouses. But as Chambers's soldiers completed the seizure, his native allies also destroyed several private homes and looted the trading posts of merchants John Anderson and George Knaggs.

Anderson, who had lived at the Maumee rapids for many years during the 1790s, claimed that when he returned to his home following the raid, "I found the house knee-deep in feathers, straw, china, queen's ware, and my writing-desk chopped to pieces with tomahawks; all my papers scattered with the feathers or carried away, also my books. The reader may form his mind as to my feelings on this occasion, for I am destitute of language to express it." Soon after, the destruction became generalized. According to Chambers, the village became "one universal scene of desolation."[12]

The violence outraged Chambers, who was utterly unprepared to deal with it or its consequences. He and Charles Askin, Chambers's second-in-command who led a small number of Canadian militia, repeatedly asked Matthew Elliott, the head of the British Indian Department at Malden who had also accompanied Chambers to Frenchtown, to come to the scene of the violence and intervene. But, according to Askin, Elliott, "for all the good he did, he might as well have stayed where he was." Eventually Tecumseh, with help from Chambers, put a stop to the pillaging.[13]

Chambers and Askin were convinced that though quelled for the moment, the Indian violence would reignite if the mission continued as planned to the Maumee rapids. Despite the fact that he had been ordered to proceed to the American garrison at Port Miami, Chambers was actually considering abandoning the mission entirely and simply returning to Malden when a French informant came forward and told the British officer that 180 American soldiers still remained at the Port Miami blockhouse.[14]

Moments later, William Fairfield, a physician from Port Miami, arrived under a flag of truce. According to Lewis Bond, rumors of Hull's surrender had placed Port Miami under a "dreadful suspense." The settlement at Port Miami had sent Fairfield to Frenchtown to tell the British that the American military had evacuated its post and to ask that the British come to the rapids and take possession of any military stores still remaining there. By doing so, the Port Miami settlers hoped to prevent the type of uncontrolled Indian depredation that had already brought Frenchtown to ruination. Fairfield also told Chambers that only a few sick American soldiers remained at the rapids, not the 180 claimed by the Frenchman. But the information, even if confused and contradictory, was enough for Chambers, who was anxious to mitigate his disappointing performance at the Raisin. The British officer ceased his dithering and immediately drew up plans for a strike against the American settlement the next day.[15]

Lieutenant John Caris, who commanded the blockhouse at the Maumee rapids, learned of Hull's surrender as Brush's men passed through the settlement hours before dawn on 21 August. Caris reacted immediately. Assembling his command before sunup and the town at daybreak, he informed the Port Miami settlers that he and his detachment were preparing to leave. He urged the town to gather what they could, leave what they could not carry, and make their way to safety under the protection of his company. A few families accepted the offer, and quickly thereafter Caris abandoned his post and made his way to central Ohio.[16]

Chambers and his party arrived at the rapids early in the afternoon. To his dismay, his earlier prediction was correct. The Indians were aggressively plundering the town. They had already stolen most of the community's horses and livestock, destroyed many houses, and set the American blockhouse on fire. Lewis Bond remembered that the arrival of the Indians and the British caused "confusion and dismay" throughout the community. According to Bond, "Some were for making a stand at this place. A fine blockhouse was completed, but the stockade was not finished; but it was said what can two hundred or three hundred men do if General Hull's army were obliged to surrender and the attempt may operate against the inhabitants? This place was therefore evacuated."[17]

Hester Purdy Green, who lived at the rapids as a child in 1812, remembered that when the Indians arrived, "all was fright and confusion. We, and most of the others, excepting the soldiers, gathered what we could handily and left. We stopped at Blalock's a short time, and an Indian messenger arrived telling us to come back, as they would not kill us, but only wanted some of our property; looking around until he found Blalock's gun, he took it, went out and got a horse my mother had ridden to this point, and departed. We went back and remained three days, in which time the Indians were pretty busy in driving off our live stock (we lost sixteen head), and plundering the houses of such as had not come back." And Mrs. Philothe Clark, also a child in 1812, recalled that "the Indians plundered a few houses, took all the horses and mules they could find, and left."[18]

Because the looting and destruction was so widespread, Chambers was able to commandeer only a small amount of supplies. The British gunboat *Chippewa* and two other large vessels under the command of Lieutenant Benoit Bender arrived at the settlement in late afternoon. Soon after his arrival, Bender confiscated five additional canoes that had been abandoned at the rapids and began to load a small quantity of soap and candles, 77 barrels of pork, 18 barrels of flour, 2 barrels of salt, a musket bayonet, a cartridge box, and about 9 barrels of whiskey into his boats for the trip back to Detroit.[19]

Late in the evening, Indians began to plunder the boats. After nightfall, they also shot and scalped one of Bender's French-speaking boatmen and wounded another. Once again, Chambers was unable to restore order. But unlike the incident at Frenchtown, here the violence escalated. Chambers left no detailed account of what transpired that night. But what is certain is that the situation continued to deteriorate to such an extent that the officer felt compelled to gather his command at midnight and flee the rapids. Indeed, Chambers left so precipitously, and the events of the evening had proven so physically and emotionally draining, that the small fleet found it necessary to pull ashore only a few miles downriver from the rapids so that the exhausted men and crews could sleep until morning. Moreover, the following day, before the flotilla had reached the mouth of the Maumee, the British were hailed by a Canadian member of Bender's crew who was running down the river after them crying. He claimed that Chambers had left in such great haste that the captain had inadvertently left him and another crew member at the rapids and that, as the two men passed through an Indian village earlier in the day trying to catch up with Chambers and his party, the Indians had detained and murdered his companion.[20]

Britain's first foray into the Maumee Valley, then, had destroyed two minor American supply posts and netted the British a small quantity of provisions and weapons. But the expedition had been characterized by disturbing violence directed against civilians, the wholesale destruction of private homes and property, and an astonishing level of ineptitude demonstrated by the officer commanding the mission. Moreover, although the force had never encountered a single American soldier beyond the small number of incapacitated invalids left at the Raisin and the rapids, it had also suffered two dead and one wounded. Within a few days of Chambers's return to Detroit, Colonel Henry Procter, Chambers's commanding officer, sent a letter to Brock noting that he was taking it upon himself to "permit" Chambers to transfer to Niagara, believing that his abilities might be put to better use in that theater.[21]

In the days following the raid, Lewis Bond recollected that "the inhabitants now determined to leave the place as fast as possible. Those who had boats went towards Cleveland taking with them one sick officer of the Ohio militia and two soldiers who had been left behind sick when the evacuation took place and which the British and Indians did not know. But these unfortunate people were obliged to leave much of their property behind. Others went by land towards Urbana and also left much property, some nearly all."[22]

As Chambers and his force returned to Detroit, a second large native expedition led by Potawatomi headman Winamac was descending on the small American garrison at Fort Wayne. American forces had occupied the headwaters of the Maumee since September 1794, when troops commanded by Anthony Wayne began construction on a small post a short distance from the confluence of the St. Joseph's and St. Mary's rivers. In 1800 the post commander, Colonel Thomas Hunt, replaced the original facility with a new fort composed of four blockhouses and a log stockade enclosing six log barracks and a brick powder magazine. Further, the post was surrounded by a sizable village occupied by French *habitants* and marked by simple log homes, orchards, fenced fields, an Indian "factory" (trading post), and a large, two-story log council house used by government officials and the region's Indians.[23]

Relations between the American garrison and the region's native peoples had always been tense. In 1807, when the United States and Great Britain nearly came to blows as a result of the *Chesapeake-Leopard* Affair, distrust between Fort Wayne's soldiers and the area's Indians was particularly high. Those mutual suspicions reemerged forcibly following the November 1811 Battle of Tippecanoe. Only a few months after the engagement, an informant had told Fort Wayne's commanding officer, Captain James Rhea, that he was convinced that the Indians were determined to commence hostilities in the spring. And in March Rhea wrote to a fellow officer that "from the best information I can get, I have every reason to believe we shall have an Indian war this spring, whether we have a British war or not."[24]

Rhea's worst fears were realized after learning of the of Fort Dearborn massacre. In early July 1812 General Hull ordered Fort Dearborn's commander, Captain Nathan Heald, to abandon his post (located at present-day Chicago) and retreat with his garrison to either Detroit or Fort Wayne. After receiving his orders in early August, Heald complied; but on 15 August a large group of hostile Potawatomis attacked the retreating column, comprised of some 54 regulars, 12 militia, 9 women, and 18 children, only a short distance from the fort. Heald survived the assault, but 26 regulars, all of the militia, 2 adult women, and 12 children lost their lives.[25]

Rhea learned of the disaster on 19 August and dispassionately reported the incident to Secretary of War Eustis and Ohio governor Return Jonathan Meigs. But, in a third letter to his friend John Johnston, the Indian agent at Piqua, Ohio, Rhea revealed a sense of anxiety that bordered on panic. "My dear friend, do all you can to give us some assistance," begged Rhea. "From the best information I can get, they are determined on this place . . . *For God Sakes!* Call on Gov. Meigs for to assist us in sending more men . . . You know our situation here, & do all you can. Shall start all our families from this (place) tomorrow. *For God Sakes!* Try in some way to get some (provisions) forwarded to us. I expect if there is not something done, we must fall a-prey." The following day, 20 August, the garrison learned of Hull's surrender. On 22 August Winamac's force, comprised of approximately 260 Ottawas and Potawatomis, surrounded the American post. "What their intentions are is uncertain," reported Rhea, "but we have some reason to suppose from their appearance and conduct that little *good* is intended."[26]

Antoine Bondie, a Fort Wayne trader and habitant, told the post's Indian agent, Benjamin Stickney, that a friendly Potawatomi had warned him that British agents had urged the Indians to attack the American outpost, promising them that British troops from Detroit would join them shortly to assist in the fort's destruction. When Stickney informed Rhea of this intelligence, the captain, perhaps in a show of false bravado or perhaps because he was becoming increasingly incapacitated by fear, dismissed the warning. But Rhea's private concerns for the safety of his garrison were not misplaced. After observing the garrison for a while, the Indians began to kill livestock near the fort, steal horses, and commit "many other minor depredations." On 28 August the Indians assaulted two soldiers who were away from the stockade to drive in some cattle and took one prisoner; Indians attacked and killed Stephen Johnston, John Johnston's brother and the assistant factor, or Indian agent, at Fort Wayne, a few miles from the post; and on 29 August Indians plundered and destroyed the gardens and fields near the fort. On 3 September Rhea placed the garrison on full alert and ordered every man to his post. Then he got as drunk as could and stayed that way until he was relieved of command nine days later.[27]

The following day, Winamac came to the garrison to meet with Rhea under a flag of truce. When an intoxicated Rhea asked Winamac what his intentions were, Winamac replied "You know that Fort Mackinac is taken, Detroit is in the hands of the British, Fort Dearborn has been taken, and you must expect to fall next, probably in a few days." Rhea made no reply, but he invited Winamac to his quarters where he continued to drink. Eventually, the parlay ended when the captain suddenly exclaimed to Winamac that "my good friend, I love you; I will fight for you; I will die by your side! You must save me!" The astonishing outburst convinced Winamac that the officer was pathetically ill-prepared to defend his post. Before dawn the following morning, Winamac and his forces began a general assault against the American garrison.[28]

According to Lieutenant Daniel Curtis, Rhea's second-in-command, when the attack began, Rhea was "drunk as a fool" and "incapable of exercising rationality on any subject whatever." Indeed, Curtis subsequently claimed that "the fears and apprehensions which arose from the disorder and confusion he created among the men were among our greatest troubles." But Curtis and his fellow officer Lieutenant Phillip Ostrander made plans to, if need be, "silence his noise and clamor by coercive measures" and then mounted a spirited and vigorous defense of the post. Over the course of the next eight days, Winamac's forces launched two direct assaults against the outpost, harassed the garrison with small-arms fire, unsuccessfully attempted to set the fort's stockade on fire, burned all of the buildings within the town surrounding the garrison, killed or carried off all of the village's livestock, and destroyed the crops in the nearby fields. Curtis, Ostrander, and the remainder of the garrison, though, stood their ground and successfully repelled every assault. Fort Wayne did not surrender.

William Henry Harrison, the governor of the Indiana Territory, learned of Hull's surrender and the Fort Dearborn disaster on 28 August. Harrison, who, as governor, commanded the Indiana Militia and who had also been appointed by Kentucky governor Charles Scott a major-general in the Kentucky Militia, immediately marshaled a force of about 2,200 men at Georgetown and prepared to reinforce Fort Wayne. As the American army moved northward, intelligence slowly made its way to Harrison revealing that the garrison was already under attack. Harrison hastened his advance and on 11 September wrote Eustis that although he had received no certain information concerning the post since 3 September, he expected to reach the fort the following day, but not without "a severe contest." The battle, though, never came. As the American column neared the beleaguered garrison, the attackers gave up the siege and Harrison entered the outpost unopposed.[29]

After taking possession of Fort Wayne, Harrison rested for a day and then made a series of punitive raids against the Indian villages in the surrounding region. Eventually, Harrison's forces destroyed Potawatomi settlements on the Elkhart and St. Joseph's rivers, Miami villages on the Wabash near Fort Wayne, and Ottawa towns on the Blanchard River in Ohio.[30]

As these expeditions concluded, Harrison turned command of the army at Fort Wayne over to his subordinate, Brigadier General James Winchester, and returned to Piqua, Ohio. On 24 September he learned that President James Madison had appointed him to command the North Western Army, a substantial force comprised of some 10,000 men consisting of federal troops deployed in Ohio, Indiana, and Illinois along with volunteer and militia units within the region from Kentucky, Ohio, Pennsylvania, and Virginia. With the upper–Maumee Valley pacified, and now a potent army at his disposal, Harrison offered a bold plan that would bring all of the Maumee River under American control and thus pave the way for the repatriation of Detroit. Harrison intended to deploy his army into three divisions, or wings. The right wing, consisting of militia units from Pennsylvania, Ohio, and Virginia, would escort artillery and munitions from Pittsburgh to Upper Sandusky. The center wing, consisting of Kentucky mounted volunteers and Ohio militia, would advance northward over Hull's Road accompanying provisions and supplies to the Maumee Valley. Both of these divisions would then converge at the Maumee rapids while the third wing, consisting of the troops now commanded by General Winchester at Fort Wayne, would advance directly down the Maumee to rendezvous with the first two divisions.[31]

Winchester put Harrison's plan into action on 23 September, leading some 2,200 troops down the north bank of the Maumee. But what Winchester did not know was that as he moved eastward, a strong force of British and Indians was also moving westward up the Maumee. On 14 September British authorities at Fort Malden had ordered a detachment of 150 regulars accompanied by three pieces of artillery, 100 militia, and nearly 800 Indians to assist in the siege of Fort Wayne. Led by Major Adam Muir, the expedition had advanced by boat as far as the site of Fort Defiance (at the confluence of the Maumee and Auglaize rivers) and then by land an additional twelve miles, moving cautiously along the Maumee's south bank.[32]

On 25 September Muir's Indian scouts encountered Winchester's forward guard and learned of the advancing American army. Soon after, other minor skirmishes between the advanced elements of both armies alerted each force to the other's presence. Muir understood at once that if Winchester advanced aggressively along the north bank, he could cut off Muir's line of retreat. The British officer, therefore, abandoned his advance to Fort Wayne, withdrew to about three miles above the site of Fort Defiance, and attempted to deploy his men to meet the Americans. Winchester, though, unsure as to the size and composition of the British force, halted his advance and raised a temporary earthen and log breastwork around his position. In the lull that followed, as each army waited for the other to act, Muir's native allies began to question the placement of his troops and the deployment of his artillery. Indeed, the disagreement became so heated that Indians from Mackinac and Saginaw abandoned the mission altogether. Further, an American prisoner told Muir that the American force consisted of over 3,000 men, including cavalry and artillery. Short of supplies, abandoned by his allies, and believing that he was facing a vastly superior force, Muir concluded that he had not the "smallest chance of success or even escaping" and retreated back to Detroit.[33]

Winchester eventually renewed his advance, arriving at the site of Fort Defiance unmolested on 29 September. At the site he refortified the position, building a new post, Fort Winchester, a short distance from the one built by Anthony Wayne in 1794. Although unscathed by combat, Winchester's troops were woefully undersupplied and underprovisioned and his men universally malnourished. Disease, including pneumonia, ague, and dysentery, swept through the army, and by mid-October inclement weather virtually halted the army's advance. Discipline and subordination collapsed nearly entirely, and only the personal intervention of Harrison himself prevented a general mutiny among the troops.[34]

Although circumstances had, for the moment, halted the American advance, Muir's retreat, and with it confirmation of an American offensive, stirred the British at Fort Amherstburg into motion. Procter ordered Matthew Elliott to organize the area's Indians and lead them to the Maumee rapids to retrieve an estimated 8,000 bushels of corn and 200 cattle (the abandoned crops and livestock of Port Miami) that remained in the vicinity. By so doing, Procter hoped to provision a growing number of displaced natives who were appearing daily in Malden and to deny these substantial resources to the Americans. Elliott arrived at the rapids on 7 November.[35]

The Americans, too, were aware of these assets and the British attempt to recoup them. In early November Harrison ordered Ohio Militia brigadier general Edward Tupper, who commanded Harrison's left wing, to march to the rapids from Fort McArthur, disperse the British, and claim the supplies. Tupper's spies captured a British officer, Andrew Clark, who told them that more than 500 natives and 50 militia were at the rapids on the north side of the river accompanied by gunboats, bateaux, and a schooner. Tupper's main force of approximately 650 volunteers advanced quickly from the south, but when the Americans attempted to cross the Maumee to engage the British, they were turned back by the swift current. A second attempt to ford the river by carrying all the men on horseback also failed. On 14 November Tupper paraded his army on the river bank directly opposite the British encampment, hoping to entice the enemy cross the river en masse where they could then be engaged and destroyed. [36]

But the plan failed. Few Native Americans and no British crossed the river. Moreover, reinforcements that Tupper had requested from Winchester failed to rendezvous with the American column. Tupper, virtually out of provisions, was forced to retreat back to Fort McArthur. During the withdrawal, a large force of Indians led by Split-log attacked Tupper's main column at some distance from the rapids but was driven away without inflicting American casualties. At about the same time, a small group of American soldiers, contrary to orders, followed some hogs into a cornfield and were attacked by a party of mounted Indians. Four Americans died in the ambush, the only Americans killed during the entire expedition. Although Tupper failed to secure the provisions waiting at the rapids, the raid nonetheless convinced the British to abandon Port Miami. On 8 December the British force retreated from the rapids, for the moment tacitly ceding the Maumee Valley from Fort Wayne to Port Miami to Harrison and the Americans.

In the wake of the Tupper expedition, Winchester renewed his advance down the Maumee on 1 January 1813. The army arrived at the rapids on 13 January, where, within a few days, Winchester expected to rendezvous with Harrison, who was commanding the right wing of the American advance. Here, Winchester halted his army while his men gathered corn from the fields that once surround Port Miami and built a small stockaded blockhouse on the north bank of the Maumee, near the one destroyed by Chambers the previous August.[37]

On the evening of 13 January, two men from Frenchtown arrived at the American camp. They told Winchester that British authorities were aware of the American advance and that British troops and their Indian allies were arresting American sympathizers in the River Raisin settlement, confiscating supplies and provisions stored at the community, and preparing to burn the entire village. Other refugees from the Raisin arrived at the rapids over the course of the next two days and confirmed the original reports. All of the informants urged Winchester to advance to Frenchtown, take possession of the settlement, and thus protect the pro-American contingent there and secure the badly needed provisions for his own use. Their arguments were compelling, and on the evening of 16 January Winchester sent Lieutenant

Colonel William Lewis and 550 men to secure Frenchtown. Shortly thereafter, Winchester also sent Lieutenant Colonel John Allen with more than 100 additional soldiers to reinforce Lewis.[38]

The American detachment arrived at Frenchtown on 18 January and easily dispersed a small force of British and Indians occupying the village. With the town under American control, Winchester advanced with the remainder of his force and joined Lewis at the Raisin on 21 January. But the American advance prompted British authorities to go on the offensive. Procter quickly assembled nearly 1,300 troops reinforced by several small artillery pieces and moved against the Americans. At dawn on 22 January, the British force attacked the American encampment. Although the ensuing engagement was hard fought, the British and their native allies destroyed Winchester's army and eventually took Winchester prisoner and either captured or killed all but thirty-three of the Americans.[39]

Harrison, who had been following Winchester with supplies and reinforcements and who had advanced a few miles north of the Maumee rapids, learned of Winchester's defeat from survivors fleeing the disaster shortly after noon on the 22nd. Convinced that Winchester's defeat was complete and believing that British forces might follow up their victory by advancing on his force, which was badly dispersed along the route from Ohio, Harrison elected to retreat to the Portage River in Ohio and consolidate his force. On 1 February 1813 he advanced from the Portage to the foot of the Maumee rapids and began to construct Fort Meigs. Although Harrison's offensive had stalled, his occupation of the rapids allowed American forces to retain control of the Maumee River from Fort Wayne to Fort Meigs. Further, the construction of a strong post at the rapids allowed American forces to again threaten Detroit once Harrison accumulated the men, provisions, and supplies necessary to reattempt the postponed offensive.[40]

For the Americans and British alike, the campaigns to control the Maumee Valley in 1812 were characterized by the lack of a focused strategic plan for the region, tactical misjudgments, logistical inadequacies, and failures of leadership at both the command and operational levels. These deficiencies continued to define operations in the Maumee Valley through the spring of 1813.

Seven months into the War of 1812, the campaign for Detroit had reached an impasse. In early spring 1813, the tactical situation along the Maumee River resembled that which had existed before the war. Harrison had managed to maintain a tenuous control of the Maumee Valley from the river's headwaters at Fort Wayne to the rapids. Yet, British control of Lake Erie, and with it control of the Maumee River from its mouth to the head of navigation at the rapids, denied the stream's full potential to either side. But Winchester's defeat at River Raisin clearly revealed that when American forces moved beyond the Maumee Valley, they were vulnerable to Great Britain's superior numbers and logistical flexibility. The stalemated advance along the Maumee underscored to American military planners the absolute necessity of U.S. naval dominance on Lake Erie if the United States hoped to successfully repatriate Detroit and the Michigan Territory. In fact, as David Skaggs points out in this volume, the campaign to secure the Maumee had proven so ineffective that, by early 1813, American leaders were openly suggesting that Harrison remove his army from the Maumee Valley to the southern shore of Lake Erie, where it would serve a mere supporting role in an intensive naval campaign that would secure the lake and then wrest Detroit from the British.

Although British and American actions to secure the Maumee River had failed to come to fruition, the valley bore the scars of nearly six months of vigorous combat. As American troops made their way down the valley to the rapids in the early spring of 1813, many noted the widespread destruction found along their route. "Along the river is the handsomest country I ever saw," claimed one soldier from Virginia. "There have been several fine plantations in the vicinity of the camp, but all is a scene of desolation. After Hull's surrender, the whole country was laid waste by the Indians; every half mile there has been a house—the only indication of a habitation that now remains is their ruins that cover the ground where they once stood." Likewise, Sergeant Greenbury Keen from Pennsylvania noted that as his company moved down the Maumee Valley, they "passed some delightful cornfields with the corn on the stocks. These fields lay low, the bottoms are but narrow, the banks high, and the country level back. The improvements have been pretty good, though all (now) burnt." Unfortunately, in February 1813 the violence had not ended. The tragic loss of Winchester's army at Frenchtown would be followed by two British offensives directed against Fort Meigs at the Maumee rapids, the siege of Fort Stephenson at Lower Sandusky, and Perry's dramatic naval victory on Lake Erie before American authorities could utilize the Maumee Valley effectively in the campaign against Detroit.[41]

NOTES

1. David Curtis Skaggs and Gerard T. Altoff, *A Signal Victory: The Lake Erie Campaign, 1812–1813* (Annapolis, MD: Naval Institute Press, 1997), 5–32.

2. Charles Elihu Slocum, *History of the Maumee River Basin* (Defiance, OH: Charles Slocum, 1905), 443–511.

3. Skaggs and Altoff, *A Signal Victory*, 5–32.

4. "Articles of Capitulation of Detroit, 16 August 1812," Ernest A. Cruikshank, *Documents Relating to the Invasion of Canada and the Surrender of Detroit, 1812* (Ottawa, Canada: Government Printing Office, 1912), 146; "William Hull to the Officer of the Block House on the Miami, 17 August 1812," *Michigan Pioneer and Historical Collections*, 40 vols. (Lansing: Michigan Pioneer Historical Society, 1877–1929), 40:454 (hereafter cited as *MPHC*); Alexander Clark Casselman, ed., *Richardson's War of 1812, with Notes and a Life of the Author* (Toronto: Historical Publishing Co., 1902), 47–92. See also Skaggs and Altoff, *A Signal Victory*, 5–32; Alec R. Gilpin, *The War of 1812 in the Old Northwest* (East Lansing: Michigan State University Press, 1958), 44–125; Sandy Antal, *A Wampum Denied: Procter's War of 1812* (Ottawa, Canada: Carleton University Press, 1997), 67–110. For general studies, consult Donald R. Hickey, *The War of 1812: A Forgotten Conflict* (Urbana: University of Illinois Press, 1989), 72–99; and John K. Mahon, *The War of 1812* (Gainesville: University Presses of Florida, 1972), 29–106.

5. William Stanley Hatch, *A Chapter of the History of the War of 1812 in the Northwest* (Cincinnati: Miami Printing and Publishing Co., 1872), 56–57.

6. Lewis Bond, "Journal of Battle and Massacre of River Raisin January 22 & 23, and of the War of 1812," Richard C. Knopf, ed., *Document Transcriptions of the War of 1812 in the Northwest*, 10 vols. (Columbus: Anthony Wayne Parkway Board and Ohio State Historical Society, 1956–62), vol. 19, pt. 1:190; "Edward Dewar to Colonel M'Donal, October 19, 1812," *MPHC*, 15:169–71; Slocum, *History of the Maumee River*, 512–15; Hezekiah Hosmer, "Amos Spafford," Charles Whittlesey, *Early History of Cleveland, Ohio* (Cleveland: Fairbanks, Benedict, & Co., 1867), 347–52; Henry Howe, *Historical Collections of Ohio* (Cincinnati: Bradley & Anthony, 1848), 523–24; Patrick M. Tucker and David M. Stothers, "The Amos Spafford Farm and the War of 1812 in Ohio: A Case of Historic Memory Loss," *Northwest Ohio History* 78, no. 1 (2010): 17–47.

7. Harrison Scott Baker II, ed., *Journal of William Kennedy Beall: Assistant Quartermaster under General William Hull, War of 1812* (Columbus: Society of the War of 1812 in the State of Ohio, 1999), 1–2; Richard J. Wright, ed., *The John Hunt Memoirs: Early Years of the Maumee Basin, 1812–1835* (Maumee, OH: Maumee Valley Historical Society, 1975), 6–7; Bond, "Journal," 182.

8. William Hull, *Memoirs of the Campaign of the North Western Army of the United States* (Boston: True & Greene, 1824), 35, 118–19; Bond, "Journal," 182; Slocum, *History of the Maumee River*, 272; "John Harmon to E. Whittlesey, January 25, 1858," *Western Reserve Historical Society War of 1812 Collection*, 1:33; Robert B. McAfee, *History of the Late War in the Western Country* (Lexington, KY: Worsley & Smith, 1816), 68–69.

9. Samuel Williams, "Expedition of Captain Henry Brush with Supplies for General Hull, 1812," *Ohio Valley Historical Series Miscellanies* (Cincinnati: Ohio Valley Press, 1871), 25. In a later writing Williams also noted that "the site had been very injudiciously selected for defense. It had no elevation whatever above the surrounding plain and the ground having a considerable descent from the garrison toward the rear, the greater part of the parade ground inside the picketing could have been easily and effectually annoyed over the tops of the rear line of pickets from a thick forest about a furlong (*i.e.* about an eighth of a mile—LLN) in the rear." See Samuel Williams, "Interesting Topography of Ohio, June 9th, 1813," *Niles Weekly Register*, 7 July 1813.

10. Williams, "Expedition of Captain Henry Brush," 30–32.

11. Charles Askin, "Extract from an Original Journal of Charles Askin, in the Canadian Archives," Cruikshank, *Documents,* 242–245; "Captain William Elliott to Henry Procter, 22 August 1812," William Wood, ed., *Select British Documents of the Canadian War of 1812* (Toronto: Champlain Society, 1920), 1:500–501; "Henry Brush to William Eustis, August 25, 1812," Knopf, *Document Transcriptions of the War of 1812 in the Northwest,* vol. 6, pt. 3:64–65. Folley's comments are found in "Frederick Folley to Eustis, August 31, 1812," ibid., 92–93

12. Askin, "Journal," 244–45; "Chambers to Procter, 24 August 1812" and "Return of Arms and Stores Found at the River Au Raisin 20th August 1812," Wood, *Select British Documents,* 1:499; Richard C. Knopf, ed., *A Short History of the Life of John Anderson* (Columbus: Anthony Wayne Park Way Board, 1956), 26–28; "Diary of Wm. McCay," Wood, *Select British Documents,* 1:554–555. For Chambers's expedition, see Tucker and Stothers, "The Amos Spafford Farm and the War of 1812."

13. "Chambers to Procter, 24 August 1812"; Askin, "Journal," 244–245. See also Reginald Horsman, *Matthew Elliott, British Indian Agent* (Detroit: Wayne State University Press, 1964), 196–197.

14. Askin, "Journal," 244–245.

15. Ibid.; Bond, "Journal," 187–188.

16. Bond, "Journal," 187–188.

17. "Chambers to Procter, 24 August 1812"; Bond, "Journal," 187–88; Askin, "Journal," 246.

18. Slocum, *History of the Maumee River,* 514–15. See also, Howe, *Historical Collections,* 523–24.

19. "Return of Provisions Found at the Foot of the Miamis Rapids," Cruikshank, *Documents,* 1:177; "Chambers to Procter, 24 August 1812"; Askin, "Journal," 246.

20. "Chambers to unaddressed, 17 January 1815," *MPHC,* 16:45; Askin, "Journal," 244–45; Bond, "Journal," 187–88; "Chambers to Procter, 24 August 1812."

21. "Henry Procter to Isaac Brock, August 26th, 1812," Cruikshank, *Documents,* 180–81.

22. Bond, "Journal," 188.

23. Charles Poinsatte, *Outpost in the Wilderness: Fort Wayne, 1706–1828* (Fort Wayne: Fort Wayne Historical Society, 1976), 27–50; Paul Woehrmann, *At the Headwaters of the Maumee: A History of the Forts of Fort Wayne* (Indianapolis: Indiana Historical Society, 1971), 59–257; Gerard T. Hopkins, *Mission to the Indians from the Indian Committee of Baltimore Yearly Meeting to Fort Wayne in 1804* (Philadelphia: T. Ellwood Zell, 1862), 50; McAfee, *History of the Late War,* 126.

24. "Robt. Forsyth to Rhea, 10th March 1812," Knopf, *Letters to the Secretary of War, 1812,* 1:83; "Rhea to Captain John Whistler, March 14th, 1812," ibid., 94. See also Woehrmann, *Headwaters of the Maumee,* 171–218.

25. "Rhea to R. J. Meigs, August 19th, 1812," and "Rhea to Eustis, August 20th, 1812," Knopf, *Letters to the Secretary of War, 1812,* 3:40, 48. See also Alec R. Gilpin, *The War of 1812 in the Old Northwest* (East Lansing: Michigan State University Press, 1958), 126–28.

26. "Rhea to R. J. Meigs, August 19th, 1812," Knopf, *Letters to the Secretary of War, 1812,* 3:40; "Rhea to Eustis, August 20th, 1812," ibid., 48; "Rhea to John Johnston, August 19th, 1812," Knopf, *Document Transcriptions of the War of 1812 in the Northwest,* 2:27; "Rhea to Meigs, August 22nd, 1812," ibid., 32. See also "Extract of a Letter from Daniel Landon to Charles Peltier, Contractor's Agent, Fort Wayne, August 24, 1812," Knopf, *Document Transcriptions of the War of 1812 in the Northwest,* vol. 5, pt. 1:234.

27. The events surrounding the siege of Fort Wayne are found in "Lt. Daniel Curtis to Kingsbury, September 21, 1812," Northwest Territory Collection, Indiana Historical Society, Indianapolis; "Lt. Daniel Curtis to Friend Cullen, October 4, 1812," Slocum, *History of the*

Maumee River Basin, 275–79; "Mann Butler's Account of the Siege of Fort Wayne," *Fort Wayne Times,* 27 May 1852; "A Soldier's Letter at the Siege of Fort Wayne, 1812," *Fort Wayne Sentinel,* 17 September 1879; Benjamin Stickney's account is found in Slocum, *History of the Maumee River Basin,* 279–82. See also Woehrmann, *Headwaters of the Maumee,* 230–35.

28. For this and the following paragraph, see "Curtis to Kingsbury" and "Curtis to Friend Cullen"; Edgar B. Wesley, ed., "A Letter from Colonel John Allen to Judge William Logan, October 2, 1812," *Ohio State Archaeological and Historical Quarterly* 36 (July 1927): 332–39.

29. "William Henry Harrison to William Eustis, August 28, 1812," Knopf, *Document Transcriptions of the War of 1812 in the Northwest,* 1:23–24; "William Henry Harrison to William Eustis, September 11, 1812," ibid., 30; "William Henry Harrison to William Eustis, September 21, 1812," ibid., 31–32; McAfee, *History of the Late War,* 135–45.

30. "Harrison to Eustis, September 21, 1812"; McAfee, *History of the Late War,* 145–48; Elias Darnell, *A Journal Containing an Accurate and Interesting Account of the Hardships, Suffering, Battles, Defeat, and Captivity of the Kentucky Volunteers and Regulars Commanded by General Winchester in the Years 1812–1813* (Philadelphia: Lippincott & Grambo, 1854), 14–15.

31. For Harrison's appointment to command the North Western Army, see "Eustis to Harrison, September 17, 1812," Knopf, *Document Transcriptions of the War of 1812 in the Northwest,* 8:85–86; for his Maumee Valley strategy, see "Harrison to Eustis, September 21, 1812."

32. James Winchester, *Historical Details Having Relation to the Campaign of the Northwestern Army Under Generals Harrison and Winchester During the Winter of 1812–13* (Lexington, KY: Wersley & Smith, 1818), 18; Askin, "Journal," 545; "Brock to Prevost, September 18, 1812," Wood, *Select British Documents,* 1:593; W. H. Merritt, "Military Journal of Events Principally on the Detroit and Niagara Frontiers," ibid., 3:566–67. See also "Expedition to Fort Wayne," Casselman, *Richardson's War of 1812,* 93–103.

33. "Muir to Procter, September 26, 1812," and "Muir to Procter, September 30, 1812," *MPHC,* 15: 148–49, 151–52.

34. "Winchester to Eustis, October 7, 1812," Knopf, *Letters to the Secretary of War, 1812,* 4:18; Darnell, *Journal,* 26, 37–39; McAfee, *History of the Late War,* 146. See also Charles E. Slocum, "The Origin, Description, and Service of Fort Winchester, with Mention of Some of the Persons and Events Connected with It," *Ohio Archaeological and Historical Quarterly* 9, no. 1 (1901): 253–77.

35. "Dewar to McDonnell, October 19, 1812"; "Elliott to Claus, October 28, 1812"; "Procter to Sheaffe, October 30, 1812"; and "Procter to Sheaffe, November 9, 1812," all in *MPHC,* 15:169–70, 173–75, 178–79.

36. For this and the following paragraph, see "Tupper to Harrison, November 16, 1812," Knopf, *Document Transcriptions of the War of 1812 in the Northwest,* vol. 5, pt. 1:278–80; "Harrison to Eustis, November 15, 1812," Knopf, *William Henry Harrison and the War of 1812,* 49–52; McAfee, *History of the Late War,* 187–91; "Elliott to St. George, November 11, 1812," *MPHC,* 15:182–83.

37. Darnell, *Journal,* 41–43; Winchester, *Historical Details,* 21–22.

38. "Isaac Day to Harrison, January 12, 1813," and "Winchester to Harrison, January 17, 1813," Knopf, *Document Transcriptions of the War of 1812 in the Northwest,* vol. 7, pt. 1:23, 33.

39. "Lewis to Winchester, January 20, 1813," ibid., 42–43; "Winchester to Harrison, January 19, 1813," ibid., 41; "Winchester to Harrison, January 21, 1813," ibid., 49; "Procter to Sheaffe, January 13, 1813," Wood, *Select British Documents,* 2:3; Darnell, *Journal,* 54–56. For accounts of the Battle of the River Raisin, see Dennis M. Au, *War on the Raisin: A Narrative Account of the War of 1812 in the River Raisin Settlement, Michigan Territory* (Monroe, OH: Monroe County Historical Commission, 1981); Gilpin, *The War of 1812 in the Old Northwest,* 147–72; Antal, *A Wampum Denied,* 161–90.

40. "Harrison to [blank], January 24, 1813," *William Henry Harrison and the War of 1812,*

77–79; "McClenahan to Harrison, January 26, 1813," *Letters to the Secretary of War, 1813*, 1:61–62; "Harrison to [blank], January 26, 1813," ibid., 81–82. For the construction of Fort Meigs, see Harlow Lindley, ed., *Fort Meigs and the War of 1812: Orderly Book of Cushing's Company, 2nd U.S. Artillery April 1813–February 1814 and Personal Diary of Captain Daniel Cushing October 1812–July 1813* (Columbus: Ohio Historical Society, 1976); Larry L. Nelson, *Fort Meigs: War of 1812 Battleground* (Columbus: Ohio Historical Society, 1999); "The Mapping of Fort Meigs," *Northwest Ohio Quarterly* 58, no. 4 (1986): 123–42; and "A Mysterious and Ambiguous Display of Tactics: The Second Siege of Fort Meigs, July 21–28, 1813," *Ohio History* 120 (2013): 5–28.

41. Entry for 2 February 1813, Sally Young, ed., "To the Rapids: Journal of a Tour of Duty in the Northwestern Army under the Command of Major-General W. Henry Harrison, by Sergeant Greenbury Keen, First Regiment, Second Brigade, Pennsylvania Militia," typescript, Ohio Historical Society, Columbus; "Picture of a Soldier's Life, from a Private in the 'Petersburg Volunteers' to His Friend in That Place," *Niles Weekly Register*, 8 May 1813.

Gaining Naval Dominance on Lake Erie

DAVID CURTIS SKAGGS

In the summer of 1812 the surrender of Detroit and the defeat of American forces on the Niagara frontier forced Washington to realize that naval control of Lakes Ontario and Erie were essential components to victory in the Old Northwest and Upper Canada (modern Ontario). The navy sent Commodore Isaac Chauncey to Lake Ontario with instructions to build the vessels necessary to gain control there and on Lake Erie. Soon Chauncey began what became a shipbuilders' war between his own construction operations at Sackets Harbor, New York, and those of the British at Kingston, Upper Canada. By the end of 1814 both sides were constructing vessels of over 100 guns, yet neither was able to maintain naval superiority on Lake Ontario.[1]

On Lake Erie the situation became quite different. The British dominated the lake in the summer of 1812 with the ship *Queen Charlotte* (18 guns), the brig *General Hunter* (10 guns), the schooner *Lady Prevost* (12 guns), and a brig owned by the British fur trading North West Company named *Caledonia* (3 guns). With the capture of Mackinac Island and Detroit in the summer of 1812, the British received the American commercial sloop *Friends Good Will* (renamed *Little Belt*) and the U.S. Army supply brig *Adams* (renamed *Detroit*), both of which were unarmed at the time of their capture. All the Americans had on the lake were a few unarmed commercial vessels at Buffalo, of which two sloops would be armed and fight at Lake Erie as *Trippe* and *Somers*.[2]

For the Americans to change the naval situation on this lake, they would have to construct, arm, and man a squadron of vessels above Niagara Falls. Commodore Chauncey gained naval superiority on Lake Ontario in the fall and spring of 1812–13, and this allowed the American forces to secure control of the British Niagara River posts of Fort George and Fort Erie at both ends of the river. Now the Americans dominated the logistical line between the lower and upper lakes, thereby allowing them to send naval equipment, weaponry, and men from the eastern seaboard to the lakes. For the British, however, the loss of the Niagara portage meant that what few supplies and men they might spare from Lake Ontario had to use the primitive road net from Burlington Bay on the lake's northwest side to Port Dover at Long Point on Lake Erie. This meant that construction of new Lake Erie warships at Amherstburg, Upper Canada, at the southern end of the Detroit River would have to be done with materials and shipwrights available there and not with equipment or men obtainable from the lower lake.

The British would soon suffer a loss to their Lake Erie squadron when U.S. Navy lieutenant Jesse Duncan Elliott conducted a nighttime cutting-out raid in the fall of 1812 that captured the *Detroit* (formerly *Adams*) and *Caledonia* from their anchorage at Fort Erie. Although the *Detroit* ran aground in the Niagara River and had to be burned to save it from recapture, Elliott's bold enterprise subtracted two vessels from the British inventory and added one to the American. The balance of naval power on Lake Erie had begun to shift. British major general Isaac Brock warned his superior, Lieutenant General Sir George Prevost, that the Americans were "making every exertion to gain naval Superiority on both Lakes which if they accomplish I do not see how we retain the Country."[3]

Meanwhile, at Presque Isle Bay (Erie, Pennsylvania) Great Lakes mariner Daniel Dobbins supervised the initial construction of four gunboats for the navy—*Ariel, Scorpion, Tigress, Porcupine*—from November until the following March. Commodore Chauncey visited the Erie shipyard in January and approved its selection for the construction of a new brig despite the sandbar at Presque Isle Bay. He also disliked the size of the gunboats and ordered the enlargement of two that were not in frame. Above all he contracted with New York shipbuilder Noah Brown to bring his well-known talents and skilled shipwrights from the East Coast to build these vessels. Brown and his workers began arriving in early March.[4]

The Great Lakes commodore needed someone he trusted to supervise the shipbuilding, someone who would see that the necessary ship components arrived—sails, cordage, iron, cannons, shot, etc.—someone to see that the rigging was set, the ships launched, the sailors trained, and someone to ensure that British dominance of Lake Erie was eliminated. He needed someone used to working with civilian shipwrights, public contractors, and military bureaucracy; he wanted someone used to command. This was a tall order,

Captain Oliver Hazard Perry. Reprinted from Benson J. Lossing, *Pictorial Field-Book of the War of 1812* (New York: Harper Brothers, 1869).

especially since naval personnel were stretched from the high seas to the Great Lakes; few wanted to serve on the lakes when it was perceived that saltwater service elicited greater fame and prize money.

Languishing in Newport, Rhode Island, commanding the gunboats was twenty-seven-year-old Master Commandant (equivalent to modern commander) Oliver Hazard Perry. Besmirching his experience and record was his captaincy of the U.S. schooner *Revenge*, which was lost in a fog off Watch Hill Reef, Rhode Island, on 9 January 1811. Although a board of inquiry exonerated him in the incident and placed the blame on the sailing master, the loss of the *Revenge* ruined Perry's reputation with Navy Department headquarters. But Perry had been the supervisor of the construction of several gunboats, and he had also commanded a schooner and a gunboat squadron.

So when Perry's request for a saltwater billet went unheeded and, in desperation, he finally asked for a lakes billet by writing directly to Chauncey. The Great Lakes commodore responded enthusiastically, and Perry received orders to report to him at Sackets Harbor before going on to Presque Isle Bay. Perry brought with him more than 140 officers and men from his Rhode Island station, including Sailing Masters Stephen Champlin (a cousin) and Thomas C. Almy, both of whom would command ships in the Lake Erie squadron, and William V. Taylor, who would be Perry's sailing master. Chauncey expected Perry to supervise the construction, rigging, provisioning, and manning of the Lake Erie squadron, but the commodore anticipated that he would himself command it when it was ready. However, that depended on him maintaining naval dominance on Lake Ontario, something not achieved when the fleet at Presque Isle Bay was ready to sail.[5]

The emphasis on gaining naval dominance on Lake Erie was a consequence of the failure of the 1812 land campaign to retake Detroit, as described by Larry Nelson in his essay. For 1813, the national command authorities determined to regain the initiative through naval superiority and an amphibious landing on the Canadian shore near Amherstburg. To this end, General William Henry Harrison received orders to halt his ground operations at the Maumee Valley. Secretary of War John Armstrong ordered Major Thomas S. Jesup to Cleveland, where he was to issue contracts for the construction of dozens of landing craft (Schenectady boats) to transport ground troops to Canada after the navy had won control of Lake Erie's waters. It was assumed that all this would be accomplished by early summer.[6]

Noah Brown and Oliver Hazard Perry, with their shipbuilders and sailors, accomplished feats of extraordinary speed and quality in the ensuing months and finished two identical brigs—*Lawrence* and *Niagara*—and four gunboats. With the addition of *Caledonia, Somers,* and *Trippe* from the Niagara River, Perry now had a clear advantage over the Royal Navy squadron provided he could bring his two brigs over the sandbar at the mouth of Presque Isle Bay. When British commander Robert H. Barclay temporarily lifted his loose blockade of the bay, Brown, Perry, their workers, and crews brought the brigs and gunboats into the lake, 1–4 August 1813. This was perhaps the decisive event in the Americans' quest for naval dominance on Lake Erie.[7]

While the Americans built two brigs and four gunboats at Erie, the British attempted to construct the largest warship on the upper lakes at Amherstburg. With a limited number of workmen and with the absence of logistical support after the capture of the Niagara portage, construction of a ship named the HMS *Detroit* (not to be confused with the vessel of the same name that Elliott's raid destroyed) slowed. Cannibalization from vessels no longer fit for use assisted in its construction, but it was not launched until the end of July and was still not ready to sail when Perry's squadron entered the lake. Because Perry now had the dominant squadron on the lake, Barclay withdrew to Amherstburg to await the *Detroit*'s completion. Arming the *Detroit* with different caliber cannons from the walls of Fort Malden, Barclay was not able to sail until the second week of September.

By that time the British squadron carried 64 guns throwing 905 total weight of metal and 496 pounds in broadside. The American squadron mounted 54 guns with a total weight of metal of 1,536 pounds and a broadside of 936. Barclay's advantage was the *Detroit*'s long guns with an effective range of approximately a mile. His best opportunity lay in having his flagship disable one of the American brigs before shifting to the other. Unfortunately for him, his second vessel, the *Queen Charlotte,* was armed with short-range carronades (like Perry's two brigs). How to fight with two dissimilarly armed men-of-war presented the Royal Navy commander with a difficult battle plan. Historian Fred Drake concludes that "Barclay was damned if he fought a close action, damned if he ranged in a running fight, and damned if he had not fought at all."[8]

For both commanders the advantage lay in having the weather gage—being to the windward of one's opponent. For Barclay it meant his long guns might eliminate one of the American brigs before it came into carronade range; instead, Barclay allowed Perry to close with the long-gunned *Detroit* before it inflicted too much damage on the *Lawrence.* The shift in the winds from Barclay's to Perry's advantage had much to do with the engagement's outcome.

When Perry's squadron sailed out of Presque Isle Bay in early August, it was woefully undermanned. Commodore Chauncey was supposed to provide Perry with sufficient seamen, but because the Lake Ontario squadron was also increasing in size, the Great Lakes commander refused to send sufficient personnel to meet Perry's needs on Lake Erie. Thus, Perry could not attack Barclay at Amherstburg because he did not have enough trained sailors to maneuver his ships in the Detroit River. If the HMS *Detroit* was ready, he could not fight Barclay on the lake because of an inability to fight his vessels given the shortage of skilled seamen and experienced officers. Had he been fully manned in early August, Perry might well have caught the British Army and its Indian allies on the lake during a retreat after failed attacks on Fort Meigs (Perrysburg, Ohio) and Fort Stephenson (Fremont, Ohio). He had two possible sources for sailors. One was to cull the militia and regular army units in the area, and the other was to pressure Chauncey to forward needed tars from Lake Ontario.

Perry required approximately 600 sailors to fully man his nine combatants. Most of the men Perry had brought with him from Newport were held by Chauncey at Sackets Harbor—out of approximately 150, only 40 ended up on Lake Erie—which was not critical in the spring since Perry's fleet was under construction. Slowly Chauncey allowed a few sailors to dribble into the Lake

Erie squadron. Because Chauncey expected to secure naval dominance of the lower lake and to bring men with him when he assumed command on the upper lake, all this was reasonable. But as such dominance was not achieved by midsummer and the shipbuilding race between Chauncey and British commodore Sir James Lucas Yeo demanded more and more sailors for the expanding Lake Ontario squadron, the few original men Perry brought with him were seldom augmented. By mid-June Perry wanted to fully man his vessels and initiated an acrimonious series of letters to Chauncey about the failures to send men for service above the Niagara Falls. He said that General William Henry Harrison desired naval assistance to drive British ground forces from northwest Ohio and that he, Perry, could not comply. Between May and mid-July Chauncey received more than 500 men but forwarded only 55 to Lake Erie. Finally, in late July, the Great Lakes commodore sent 122 junior officers and bluejackets to Perry.[9]

Not all of these personnel were from the navy. Like some of Chauncey's crews, they contained soldiers from four army units: the 9th and 14th U.S. Infantry, the 1st U.S. Light Dragoons, and the 3rd New York Artillery. Perry impetuously wrote to Chauncey that one group he had sent was "a motley set, blacks, Soldiers, and boys, I cannot think that you saw them after they were selected." To this the commodore bluntly replied, "I have yet to learn that the Colour of the skin, or the cut and trimmings of the coat, can affect a man's qualifications or usefulness." Perry began recruiting from the militia in northwest Pennsylvania.

Still short of officers and men and with no one capable of commanding the *Niagara,* Perry received his last complement of tars from Chauncey on 9 August: Master Commandant Jesse Duncan Elliott, eleven officers, and ninety-one men. Elliott had been the flag captain of Chauncey's flagship, and he now became the captain of the *Niagara.*

When Perry sailed from Erie for the last time on 6 August 1813, he had approximately 450 men with him, including a number of soldiers. From General Harrison's army he had acquired another 130. Death, desertion, and illness decimated the ranks from Lake Ontario and Presque Isle Bay, and illness at Put-in-Bay further reduced the number that would participate in the battle. Approximately 40 percent of Perry's sailors were really soldiers. The greatest percentage of soldiers served as marines on various ships, with army captain Henry Brevoort commanding the soldiers-turned-marines on the *Niagara* and marine lieutenant John Brooks commanding those on the *Lawrence.* Soldiers also dominated the gunboat crews, a fact that might partially explain their inability to close with the enemy during the first hours of the battle. Perry had two weeks to convert the last group of landsmen into sailors before facing the horrors of ship-to-ship combat.[10]

Jesse Duncan Elliott remains one of the most enigmatic characters in the early U.S. Navy, and his conduct at the Battle of Lake Erie is one of the most controversial aspects of his contentious career. Recently acclaimed a hero for his conduct in the raid that brought the *Caledonia* into American hands and destroyed the first *Detroit,* Elliott's attitude toward Perry at this point is unknown. His personality defies complete analysis, and the information regarding his emotional stability is inconclusive. Naval historian Christopher McKee calls Elliott "a complex, strange, and possibly sick man."[11] He was a skilled sailor and ambitious officer whose experience as a flag captain made him familiar with squadron maneuvers and signaling; he had more experience in this regard than Perry. But neither of them had engaged in ship-to-ship combat.

Serving under the two master commandants commanding the two identical brigs that constituted the main strength of the American squadron was a mixed bag of officers. The seven captains of the smaller vessels in Perry's flotilla were young and inexperienced—at least one was under twenty-one—and some had personality deficiencies. Daniel Turner, commander of Perry's third-largest vessel, the *Caledonia,* had acquired a reputation as a genial companion with temperate drinking habits but a hard disciplinarian. Captaining the *Scorpion* was twenty-four-year-old Sailing Master Stephen Champlin, a man of modest talent and simple taste who had commanded a commercial vessel before the war. Lieutenant John Packet of the *Ariel* was about twenty-three years old and had been in grade only six weeks. He had been a midshipman on the *Constitution* in two of its battles and was the only commanding officer with combat experience. Packet's efficiency report of 1815 described him as a "gentlemanly officer of sober habits—wanting in professional acquirements, and the industry to attain them." Augustus H. M. Conkling of the *Tigress* was "an elegant officer in appearance, but too convivial even for the navy." (One really had to be a consumer of very large amounts of alcohol to be "too convivial" for the early U.S. Navy.) Another hard drinker was Midshipman George Senat of the *Porcupine.* This Louisianan would be killed in 1814 in his second duel with Midshipman James McDonald. His commander wrote after the incident that Senat "was an extremely intemperate young man, and will be of no loss to the Service." Thomas Holdup of the *Trippe* was only eighteen but was considered "the very soul of chivalry, generous, high-minded, gallant and heroic." His distinguished naval career would be followed by that of a son and grandson who became admirals. Sailing Master Thomas Almy of the *Somers* had merchant experience before the war and died of pneumonia three months after the battle. Surgeon Usher Parsons described him as an "active, efficient officer, and much esteemed by his brother officers." Elliott claimed that Almy was drunk during the battle; if true, it may partially account for the lagging performance of his vessel, the lead among the four gunboats bringing up the squadron's rear.[12]

Because of the frequent changes in personnel coming from Lake Ontario, command of and personnel on board various vessels changed often, contributing to a lack of cohesion between officer and crew. The two American brig commanders were slightly older than their opponents, but most of the others were significantly younger, and all lacked combat experience when compared with their opposite numbers. Theirs was not a Nelsonian "band of brothers."

At a commanders' conference shortly before the battle, Perry issued two somewhat conflicting orders to his subordinates: "commanding officers are particularly enjoined to pay attention to preserving their stations in Line" and "engage your designated adversity, in close action." A line of battle could not be broken without good reason, and this restriction on maneuver could be limiting if enemy ships changed their battle stations. But if a foe did change its position in the enemy line, what was the captain of the opposing vessel to do? Perry made no provision for changing positions or for closing with the enemy in a melee that might occur in the course of an engagement. Paraphrasing Lord Nelson, Perry admonished his commanders, "If you lay the enemy close alongside you can't be out of place."

During this meeting, Perry showed his senior officers the "fighting flag" recently sewn in Erie, inscribed with Captain James Lawrence's last order, "Don't Give Up the Ship." They were to keep it a secret from their crews until the day of battle; its hoisting would be his signal for action.[13]

Knowing that his naval dominance of the lake choked not just the military logistical line but also the food supply line for the soldiers and Indians in the Detroit River region, Perry anchored his fleet at Put-in-Bay on South Bass Island and awaited Barclay's arrival. On the morning of 10 September 1813, his lookout sighted the British leaving the mouth of the Detroit River, and Perry weighed anchor. Initially the wind favored Barclay, but it suddenly changed and in a light breeze gave Perry the weather gage. The British hove to and in

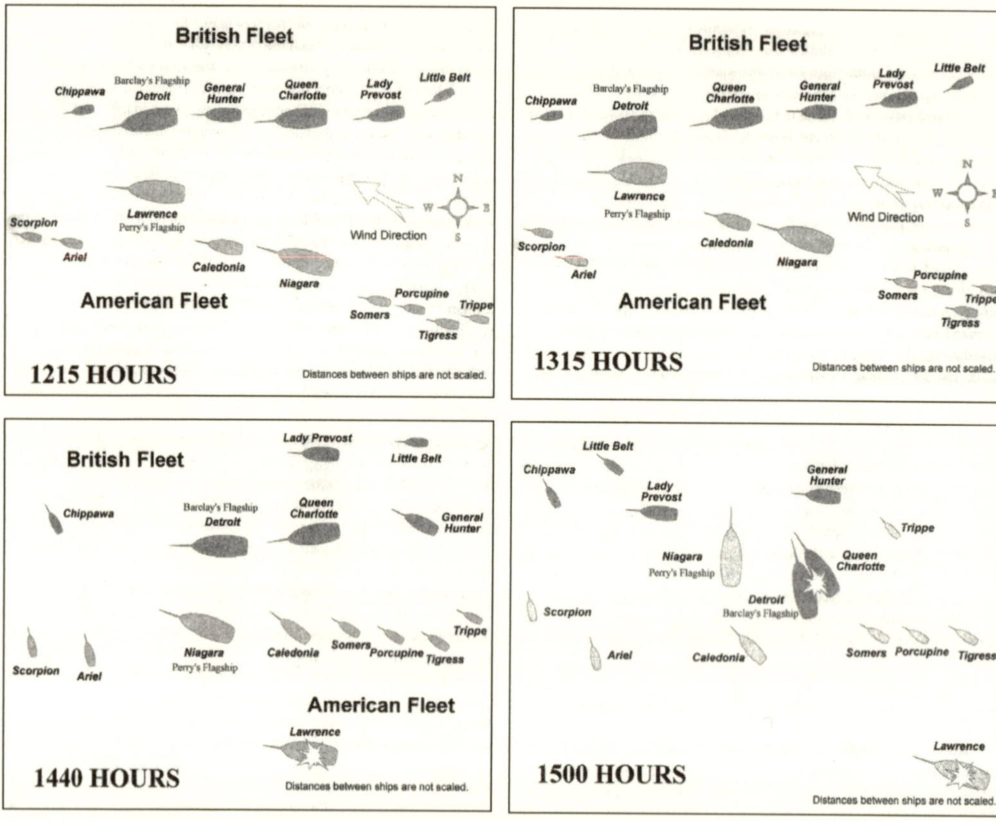

Phases of the battle of Lake Erie. From Skaggs and Altoff, *A Signal Victory: The Lake Erie Campaign, 1812–1813* (Annapolis: Naval Institute Press, 1997).

a compact line awaited the American attack. Perry advanced slowly, but his square-rigged brigs soon outdistanced the slower sloop-rigged gunboats, which eventually trailed two miles behind the flagship.

The first Royal Navy shot against the *Lawrence* fell short. But instead of waiting for his line to close up, Perry immediately headed for the *Detroit* and began a duel that would last nearly three hours. Trailing him and focusing on the *General Hunter,* the thin-hulled *Caledonia* opened fire with its long guns and Elliott in the *Niagara* trailed behind, even though his carronades could not engage the *Queen Charlotte.* When the *Queen Charlotte*'s captain saw he could not fight the *Niagara,* he moved forward of the *General Hunter* and began attacking the *Lawrence,* which now fought the two largest British brigs. The

Niagara kept its place in line rather than moving forward. It did not engage its designated foe as Perry directed but did keep its place in the line of battle.

For over two hours the *Lawrence* fought off the *Detroit* and the *Queen Charlotte,* the *Caledonia* engaged the *General Hunter,* and the *Niagara* remained in line with no opponent. The gunboats disabled the trailing British vessel but did not close with either the *General Hunter* or the *Queen Charlotte* with their long guns. Up to this point Perry had fought the *Lawrence* gallantly but had been delinquent as commodore in not communicating to his subordinates his desires regarding the changing situation. Meanwhile, Elliott refused to support his commander by leaving his position in the line of battle.

Finally, and almost simultaneously, Perry decided to leave the helplessly damaged *Lawrence* (two-thirds of its crew were now casualties) by long boat, and Elliott, believing Perry was either dead or severely wounded, decided to come forward. On boarding the *Niagara,* Perry ordered Elliott to command the gunboats while he directed his relief flagship. The gunboats delivered devastating fire with their long guns against the *General Hunter* and the *Queen Charlotte* while Perry maneuvered the *Niagara* through the British line, forcing the two largest British ships to surrender. Soon the entire British squadron lowered their flags.[14]

The drama of transferring his flag from one vessel to another—the famous "we have met the enemy and they are ours" message to General Harrison and

Perry's battle flag. Reprinted from Benson J. Lossing, *Pictorial Field-Book of the War of 1812* (New York: Harper Brothers, 1869).

the theatrical "Dont Give Up the Ship" battle flag—made Perry a national hero overnight. The Royal Navy's loss of an entire squadron gave Americans great pride in a triumph over the "mistress of the seas." Shortly thereafter Perry assisted General Harrison with an amphibious invasion of the Canadian shore that resulted in the recapture of Detroit and the defeat of the British and Indians at the Battle of the Thames on 5 October 1813. Lake Erie and the Ohio Valley were free from British and Indian depredations.

Jesse Duncan Elliot was both furious and envious. Outraged at what he thought was Perry's less-than-supportive report of his decision to bring the *Niagara* forward without orders, and envious of his commander's acclaim while he was ignored in the battle's aftermath, he engaged in a thirty-year battle with Perry and his supporters that eventually ended with Elliot's reputation in tatters.[15] Although one can criticize Perry's command and control during the battle, one must never forget his determination, enterprise, and leadership in building a superior fleet on Lake Erie, in getting his brigs over the bar at the mouth of Presque Isle Bay, in molding and training a disparate and inexperienced group of officers and men into a reasonably cohesive fighting force, and in courageously commanding the *Lawrence* and resolutely transferring his flag so that he might win America's first naval squadron triumph.

NOTES

1. For a solid analysis of the war on Lake Ontario, see Robert Malcomson, *Lords of the Lake: The Naval War on Lake Ontario, 1812–1814* (Toronto: Robin Bass Studio, 1998).

2. The standard secondary study of the strategic and tactical aspects of the Battle of Lake Erie is David Curtis Skaggs and Gerard T. Altoff, *A Signal Victory: The Lake Erie Campaign, 1812–1813* (Annapolis, MD: Naval Institute Press, 1997).

3. Brock to Prevost, 11 Oct. 1812, William S. Dudley and Michael J. Crawford, eds., *The Naval War of 1812: A Documentary History*, 3 vols. (Washington, DC: Naval Historical Center, 1985–), 1:331–33.

4. Chauncey to Perry, 15 Mar. 1813, ibid., 2:422–23.

5. Perry to Sec/Navy Paul Hamilton, 28 Nov. 1812, ibid., 1:354; Chauncey to Perry, 20 Jan. 1813, and Chauncey to Sec/Navy William Jones, 21 Jan. 1813, ibid., 2:422.

6. Monroe to Harrison, 26 Dec. 1812, and Armstrong to Harrison, 3 Apr. 1813, Douglas E. Clanin et al., eds., *The Papers of William Henry Harrison, 1800–1815*, 10 microfilm reels (Indianapolis: Indiana Historical Society, 1993–99), 7:63–69. Jones to Chauncey, 3 July 1813, in Dudley and Crawford, *Naval War*, 2:4509–12.

7. W. A. B. Douglas says, "Barclay's one lapse was to let Perry and his ships escape out of Erie and into the lake." See Douglas, "The Honor of the Flag Had Not Suffered: Robert Heriot Barclay and the Battle of Lake Erie," William Jeffrey Welsh and David Curtis Skaggs, eds., *War*

on the Great Lakes: Essays Commemorating the 175th Anniversary of the Battle of Lake Erie (Kent, OH: Kent State University Press, 1991), 33.

8. Frederick C. Drake, "Artillery and Its Influence on Naval Tactics: Reflections on the Battle of Lake Erie," Welsh and Skaggs, *War on the Great Lakes,* 29. Perry to Jones, 19 Jun. 1813, Dudley and Crawford, *Naval War,* 2:481–82.

9. Jones to Chauncey, 26 June, 3 July 1813; Perry to Chauncey, 27 July 1813; Chauncey to Perry, 30 July 1813; Harrison to Perry, 4 Aug. 1813; Perry to Jones, 19 June, 4 Aug., 10 Aug. 1813; Jones to Perry, 3 July, 18 Aug. 1813, all in Dudley and Crawford, *Naval War,* 2:481–546.

10. The most thorough discussion of the manpower Perry had available is found in Gerard T. Altoff, *Deep Water Sailors, Shallow Water Soldiers: Manning the United States Fleet on Lake Erie, 1813* (Put-in-Bay, OH: Perry Group, 1993). For the Royal Navy side see D. L. Hendry, C. C. Morrisey, and D. C. Skaggs, "British Personnel at the Battle of Lake Erie," *Inland Seas* 54 (Winter 1998): 298–314.

11. Christopher McKee, "An Aerial View of Put-in-Bay: United States Historians Scrutinize a Campaign," Welsh and Skaggs, *War on the Great Lakes,* 90. Lawrence J. Friedman and David Curtis Skaggs are kinder toward Elliott's "sickness" than McKee is in "Jesse Duncan Elliott and the Battle of Lake Erie: The Issue of Mental Stability," *Journal of the Early Republic* 10 (Winter 1990): 497–516.

12. On the American squadron's officer corps see David Curtis Skaggs, *Oliver Hazard Perry: Honor, Courage, and Patriotism in the Early U.S. Navy* (Annapolis, MD: Naval Institute Press, 2006): 94–98. On Holdup, see Charles Brodine's essay in this collection.

13. Perry Order Book, 20 Aug. 1813, and Daniel Turner Affidavit, 2 July 1818, Perry Papers, William L. Clements Library, University of Michigan, Ann Arbor; W. W. Dobbins, *History of the Battle of Lake Erie* (Erie, PA: Ashbury Printing, 1913), 68–69; Skaggs, *Oliver Hazard Perry,* 98–101. On the preservation of the battle flag see the chapter by Deborah Trupin and Scot Harmon in this collection.

14. Perry to Harrison, 10 Sept. 1813; Perry to Jones, 10 Sept. 1813; Barclay to Yeo, 12 Sept. 1813; Perry to Jones, 13 Sept. 1813; Wm. Taylor to wife, 15 Sept. 1813; U. Parsons to Wm. Parsons, 22 Sept. 1813, all in Dudley and Crawford, *Naval War,* 2:553–65.

15. For the commander's after-action report see Perry to Jones, 13 Sept. 1813, ibid., 2:557–59. An extended discussion of the Perry-Elliott controversy may be found in Skaggs, *Oliver Hazard Perry,* 136–42, 191–98, 219–44. For a counterargument criticizing Perry's leadership in the battle, see Mike Palmer's essay in this collection.

"It Is Better to Make a Signal Than to Curse One's Subordinates"

Oliver Hazard Perry and the Battle of Lake Erie

MICHAEL A. PALMER

At its bicentennial, the Battle of Lake Erie remains one of the most famous military engagements in American history. Oliver Hazard Perry's message announcing his victory—"We have met the enemy, and they are ours"—has become an unforgettable passage, and the commodore, so often pictured being rowed, upright and fully exposed, from the battered *Lawrence* to the *Niagara,* is a recognized hero of a nearly forgotten war.[1]

Nevertheless, despite Perry's victory, almost as soon as the battle ended it became a topic of controversy. The Americans had secured a total triumph, but Perry's chief subordinate, Master Commandant Jesse Duncan Elliott, and several of his supporters questioned Perry's handling of the squadron and, in a more subtle fashion, challenged the commodore's personal behavior. James Fenimore Cooper, who served in the early navy himself (1807–11), knew many of the individuals engaged at Lake Erie and wrote one of the first histories of the U.S. Navy. Cooper, while he addressed many of the controversies surrounding the battle in his narrative, avoided direct criticism of Perry and concluded: "The personal deportment of Captain Perry, throughout the day, was worthy of all praise."[2] Nevertheless, Cooper had his private doubts, as he expressed in a letter to a friend in 1839: "The testimony, given in the shape of letters and affidavits, ten years after the affair, is so contradictory that I will defy any man to make head or tail of it. Without knowing the characters of the witnesses thoroughly, no man can say who ought to be believed and who not."[3]

The record of the battle indicates that Perry, as Cooper wrote, was steadfast and heroic throughout a brutal engagement. He was fortunate to have survived the day given the devastation of his flagship, the brig *Lawrence,* by British fire. Postbattle suggestions to the contrary issued by Elliott and his supporters were groundless, reckless, and petty and undermined the more serious of their charges: Perry's handling of the squadron, his service as commodore, had not equaled his handling of the *Lawrence* as its captain.

When Perry took command of the American squadron on Lake Erie, he had the tools of victory thrust into his hands. His two brigs alone, the *Lawrence* and the *Niagara,* designed and constructed by Noah Brown, outgunned the entire British squadron on the lake by almost 50 percent.[4] To win, Perry had to avoid a battle in which the British, who held a two-to-one superiority in long guns, would hold the wind gauge and be able to control the range of the engagement. If Perry could manage that and keep the two Brown-built brigs with their thirty-six 32-pounder carronades together in the battle line, *he could not lose.*[5] A rather fortunate shift of wind handed Perry the wind gauge as the battle commenced, but he failed to keep his well-armed brigs together in line. The fault lay with Perry's prebattle instructions, and their impact on the course of the engagement was marked.

Captain Perry clearly fought his own ship very well, but *Commodore* Perry unnecessarily placed his squadron at risk before the battle began, and once it commenced he failed to direct the movements of his squadron, other than the *Lawrence,* during the engagement. Perry's mishandling of the American flotilla turned an easy victory into a hard-fought contest that could have ended as easily in defeat as in victory.

Command and control during the age of fighting sail took one of two basic forms. Most navies, including those of the United States and Great Britain, relied on centralized methods of numerary flag systems to manage communications between ships.[6] Such systems were in their heyday in the early nineteenth century.

There were problems with centralized signaling systems, however. Poor visibility, the smoke of battle, damage to the masts and rigging of the flagship, a change in the direction of the wind, or the physical extent of an engagement usually made communication problematic. A commander who could not see the entirety of the battlefield was hardly well placed to exercise control over it. This, and a variety of other problems, often made it impossible for a commander to bring his entire force into action. Admiral Richard Lord Howe, who won a great victory at the Glorious First of June in 1794, signaled for his fleet to pass through the enemy line of battle. Only seven of his twenty-six ships responded as he had hoped.[7]

Common doctrine, training, and a commitment to the exercise of initiative by subordinates provided an alternative style of command. Vice Admiral Horatio Lord Nelson, generally considered the epitome of a naval commander during the age of fighting sail, was the foremost practitioner of what could be termed a decentralized approach.[8] Nelson understood the problems inherent in reliance on signal flags in the midst of battle. He used them sparingly, if at all, once an engagement began and trusted the initiative of his subordinates to fight and win the battle. Nelson maximized the fighting power of his fleets and brought a higher percentage of his ships into action through reliance on doctrine and inspiration, not through the use of visual signals. We rightly associate Nelson with his "band of brothers," the "Nelson touch," and signals that detailed not a plan of battle but an exhortation to duty.

American naval officers during the late eighteenth and early nineteenth centuries, the formative period for their nascent service, were well aware of the experiences of their contemporaries in the British and the French navies. During the American Quasi-War with France, 1798–1801, the U.S. Navy first adopted a signaling system based on French models but soon, in part to facilitate cooperation with the Royal Navy, adopted British methods.[9] Stephen Decatur Jr. and other young American naval officers serving in the Mediterranean during the Tripolitan War (1801–5), sought to emulate Nelson's style and method. As a result, both decentralized and centralized approaches to command were known to American naval officers when war began in 1812.

The American signaling system in use in June 1812 was based on British examples and American experience.[10] Authored by Captain John Rodgers, this quasi-official signal manual was printed privately by Thomas Kirk in Brooklyn, New York.[11] It listed signals alphabetically and left them unnumbered. A commander could take the book and number the signals listed as he saw fit. Assuming he did so in a nonconsecutive manner, he possessed a personalized and fairly secure signaling manual for his squadron.

There were, of course, problems with such an approach. Since signals were arranged alphabetically, and not by type, random numbering made incoming messages difficult to locate. To avoid this problem, American commodores numbered the signals consecutively and unimaginatively. For example, the eleventh signal on the list became Signal #11.

The navy used the "Rodgers system" from the outbreak of war in June 1812 until June 1813. On 1 June 1813, Captain Philip Bowes Vere Broke, commanding His Majesty's frigate *Shannon*, captured Captain James Lawrence's American frigate *Chesapeake* and along with it a copy of one of the Thomas Kirk signal books.[12] Secretary of the Navy William Jones and the senior captains of the service immediately recognized that they needed to develop a replacement. Service captains drafted a new signal manual by July 1813.[13]

The signal book occasionally reputed to be the one used by Perry at the Battle of Lake Erie is a pre-1813 manual.[14] The notation on the title page—"Commodore O H Perry USN Lake Erie"—is written in the same hand as that which made note of the presentation of the book: "H. F. Moffat USN, Aug. 19, 1868." Several signals printed in the book refer to Long Island (#89), Jersey (#90), and Governor's Island (#95), and other notations handwritten into the book mention other locales around New York City—for example, #104, "Run up to Amboy (NJ)." The book may well have belonged to Perry, but if it did he used it in New York and perhaps later when he commanded gunboats at Newport, Rhode Island. By the summer of 1813 the book was no longer in use by the U.S. Navy.

On 10 July 1813 Secretary Jones sent eleven copies of the new signal book to Lake Erie for Perry's squadron.[15] Copies of these signal books have thus far eluded researchers, though their possession would not make much difference to the history of the battle. Oliver Hazard Perry made no use of the new signal book once the engagement began.

Since Perry chose not to rely on signals, by default he embraced a decentralized approach to the command of his squadron.[16] Decentralized systems, although often superior to centralized varieties, worked best when two elements were present. First, a commander had to create a general vision of how he wished an engagement to unfold *and* possess the charisma and leadership ability to communicate that vision to his subordinates *before* the battle. Second, a commander needed at least a few battle-experienced subordinates able to operate on their own initiative and to whom he could empower to do so.

Exercising command in a decentralized fashion without such preparations was a recipe for disaster. French admiral Pierre-André de Suffren, who earned fame in command of the French squadron in the Indian Ocean during the 1778–83 war with Britain, was perhaps the most energetic and aggressive French admiral of the age of fighting sail. Nevertheless, an examination of Suffren's Indian Ocean campaigns demonstrates the failure of decentralized command approaches without "a significant degree of commitment and comprehension throughout the chain of command."[17]

That is not to say that Commodore Perry could not have made a decentralized system work, especially given the numerous advantages he possessed. Commodore Thomas Macdonough, the victor of the Battle of Plattsburgh Bay on Lake Champlain on 11 September 1814, faced a situation somewhat comparable to Perry's on Lake Erie the previous year.[18] Macdonough, unlike Perry, devised a clear plan of action meant to maximize American advantages and communicated that plan clearly to his inexperienced subordinates. Macdonough chose to meet the British with his squadron moored in the bay, much as French vice admiral François-Paul Brueys d'Aiguïlliers had met Nelson at Aboukir Bay ("the Nile") in August 1798. Brueys made innumerable errors. He failed to anchor both fore and aft along the five fathom line, to run springs from the ends of his ships so they could pivot, and to discuss before the battle how he intended to fight—at anchor or under sail—should the British appear on the horizon. Macdonough, despite his youth and inexperience, did all of the above: he laid out his line to its maximum advantage; his ships were moored on springs and could pivot in battle and could not be doubled, as the British had doubled the Brueys's line; before the battle he met often with his captains and explained how he intended to fight the battle; and when the engagement began, he issued a Nelsonian prebattle exhortation to his crew.

No such clear plan of action emerges in accounts of Perry's preparations for battle in September 1813. Perry's subordinates on Lake Erie were no more, and in some ways were less, unseasoned commanders than Macdonough's. Master Commandant Jesse Duncan Elliott was the most skilled of Perry's subordinates, a man already tested in battle. Unfortunately, Elliott had expected to be given the command on Lake Erie and was thus somewhat disgruntled. The other commanders of Perry's ships were mostly unseasoned, and Perry had not worked to turn them into anything approaching a "band of brothers."

Oliver Hazard Perry was not a Nelsonian figure. At twenty-eight he was not as young for responsible command as it sounds to twenty-first-century ears; nevertheless, Perry lacked both squadron and battle experience. Unlike Macdonough, Perry had never been under fire and was at best unseasoned. He had served during the Quasi-War in the frigate *General Greene* under his father, Captain Christopher Raymond Perry.[19] However, the ship saw little sea action.[20] During the Tripolitan War, he saw somewhat less service than many of his contemporaries; he was not among Commodore Edward Preble's

"Boys" but was a favorite of the lackluster and unfortunate John Rodgers. Yet after the war, Perry gained a reputation as one of the finest young commanders in the service, despite his loss of the *Revenge* off the New England coast in 1811, and his crews were happy, well-disciplined, and well-trained.[21]

With the outbreak of war in June 1812, William Jones's predecessor as secretary of the navy, Paul Hamilton, ordered Perry to take command of the dozen gunboats laid up at Newport, Rhode Island. Perry's first task was to outfit and man the vessels, a task Perry performed adequately, although not without administrative difficulty. While Perry got along well with his men, his tenure was marked by disagreements with the Navy Department and growing personal dissatisfaction: Perry longed for and lobbied for a seagoing command.

Perry's pre-1813 commands had not prepared him for squadron command. Six months commanding gunboats at Newport was hardly a test. And while Perry's careerism was marked, the same cannot be said for his professionalism. Advanced navigation—for example, the ability to determine longitude as well as latitude—was unknown to Perry.[22] As John Rodgers, Perry's mentor, wrote later in the war, "Captain Perry, as you well know, is a good officer but, I do not believe, has ever paid so much attention to naval science as to qualify him for such a situation [a position on the Board of Navy Commissioners]."[23] While most historians praise Perry for drilling his crews in guns and musketry, Cooper, quoting Daniel Dobbins, noted that during the 10 September engagement the *Lawrence*'s carronades had been overshotted "with grape and canister, and sometimes with langrage over all!"[24] Carronades had short barrels and lacked sufficient muzzle velocity to propel more than a single shot—grape, canister, or langrage, but not all three in combination—over any distance with effect. Nor, the historical record shows, did Perry attempt to master the new signal books sent to him by Secretary Jones or the old ones, had Perry chosen to use them. And when the engagement opened on 10 September in a fashion not in accord with Perry's prebattle assumptions, the commodore made virtually no effort to control his squadron by signals, despite the fact that his subordinates were not supporting the *Lawrence* in the battle.

Perry was never satisfied with the Lake Erie command. His acceptance from the start was a Hobson's choice. He had lobbied for the position, using his contacts in Washington, and had written directly to the naval commander on the lakes, Commodore Isaac Chauncey. While a lake command was better than gunboats in Newport, the young Rhode Islander much preferred command of a single ship—a corvette or a frigate. His eyes remained fixed on the Atlantic and the "real" blue-water naval war where fellow officers such as Isaac Hull, William Bainbridge, and Stephen Decatur Jr. were gaining fame. As soon as he secured the laurels of victory on 10 September, he immediately used them as currency to secure his transfer from the lakes. Secretary Jones wrote that "there is much of importance yet to be done upon the Upper Lakes, which I should like you to bring to maturity." Perry's primary thought was not the promising land campaign made possible by his victory, but a seagoing command in the Atlantic. Perry requested a transfer on 20 September, and on the 29th Jones acquiesced, with obvious disappointment.[25]

The assignment to the Lake Erie command left Perry dissatisfied. He struggled with the tedious administrative details related to the construction, outfitting, and manning of his flotilla. He quickly grew disgruntled and continued to press for an Atlantic command.[26] He complained incessantly about his superior (Commodore Chauncey), his subordinates, and his men.[27] As the campaign on the lakes reached its climax in the late summer of 1813, Perry wrote to Secretary of the Navy Jones requesting relief.[28]

There were few secrets in the U.S. Navy of the early nineteenth century; Perry's feelings were most likely known throughout the squadron. His attitude did nothing to forge a relationship of mutual trust between himself and his captains or his men. He appealed over the head of Commodore Chauncey directly to the secretary of the navy. When Chauncey responded to one of Perry's requests for reinforcement, with a detachment that included black sailors, Perry demeaned their service.[29] A "mortified" Chauncey replied, "I regret that you are not pleased with the men sent you . . . for to my knowledge a part of them are not surpassed by any seamen we have in the fleet, and I have yet to learn that the Colour of the skin, or cut and trimmings of the coat, can affect a mans qualifications or usefulness—I have nearly 50 Blacks on board of this Ship and many of them are amongst my best men."[30] Perry's evident distaste for his command also outraged his second-in-command, Jesse Duncan Elliott. Elliott, unlike Perry, had wanted the command on the lake and, had Perry not been given it, probably would have had it.

Time limitations and a surly attitude left Perry unable to turn his mostly inexperienced subordinates into anything approaching a "band of brothers." Given that command reality, Perry ought to have been prepared to rely on signals to direct his squadron in battle. On 10 July Jones sent Perry drafts of the new signal books. The revised editions came out in August; these probably never reached Perry, but the July draft did.[31] But if Perry distributed the preliminary signal books to his captains, he did not make use of them once the engagement commenced. The commodore instead devised a short list of his own signals for the squadron.[32] His abbreviated June 1813 list was too simplistic to address the situations what would develop during the engagement that began on the morning of 10 September 1813. All of his signals were made with the ensign or a pair of colored flags variably placed at the mastheads, gaff, or in the rigging, a method that would be difficult and ultimately impossible to employ once the *Lawrence* came under heavy British cannonade and was damaged aloft. His primitive system demonstrated that he had little grasp of the numerary systems that had dominated naval signaling since the 1770s.

Perry did share with his subordinates his expectations for battle. He distributed various sailing orders and met with his captains on the nights of 6 and 9 September. The sailing orders are interesting but ultimately confusing. Perry discussed the possibility of employing his ships in two separate lines, each led by one of the brigs, or in a single line led by the *Lawrence*. In the unitary line of battle, he placed the sloop *Somers* between the two brigs. In yet another order of battle the *Lawrence* and *Niagara* led. Perry also stressed the importance of fighting in close order at close range, a critical point given the American superiority in short-range carronades.[33] At the meeting on the 9th he reviewed the possibility of a surprise attack against the British at anchor.[34] In this situation, the last discussed before the battle, the *Niagara* would lead the line. Thus, when the battle began, Perry's captains were not sure which order of battle they would be employing as they weighed anchor.

Perry's major blunder was to assign "a designated foe" to each of his ships.[35] That decision left the actual order of the American line in the engagement to the determination of the British commander, Commodore Robert Heriot Barclay. If Barclay's fleet did not arrive in the expected order, Perry might well find the *Lawrence* and *Niagara* separated in the American line.

Perry's last-minute efforts to impart to his subordinates a concept for the battle were well intentioned and laudable, but they were also inadequate and, to a degree, confusing. Would the American squadron fight in a single or a dual line? Where would the two brigs be placed? Had these questions been addressed before the battle, the squadron could have been anchored accordingly. As it was, when the British appeared on the horizon, the Americans had to scramble to form their single line, but with the slow and weak *Caledonia* sandwiched between the *Lawrence* and the *Niagara* because of Barclay's dispositions, not Perry's desires. Nor did Perry have the means at hand to signal his intentions to his inexperienced and confused subordinates.

To further the sense of bewilderment among the Americans, on the morning of 10 September the British caught the Americans at anchor. Alert American lookouts sighted the enemy, preventing a surprise attack, but as they made their reports on the British order of battle, it became clear that Barclay's line was not in the order expected by Perry. Worse yet, as the Americans struggled to get under way, the wind was light and from the southwest. Barclay held the weather gage and could determine the range, long or short, at which the engagement would be fought. This was exactly what he wanted, since he knew he had to keep the battle beyond the carronade reach of Perry's two brigs. Barclay had every expectation that he would hold the windward position throughout the battle. Normally, during the course of the day, the wind backs (follows the movement of) the sun across the horizon in a clockwise fashion.[36]

For Perry, starting the battle without the wind gage, given the respective positions of the two squadrons, meant fighting the engagement at a severe disadvantage. Nevertheless, since the American squadron was totally unprepared to battle it out at anchor with the British, as was Macdonough at Plattsburg, Perry had little choice but to accept battle under sail, despite the unfavorable wind. The Americans struggled to get under way and into their respective positions vis-à-vis the British. In response to Barclay's sailing order, the *Lawrence* led the squadron instead of the *Niagara,* which followed in the third slot behind the much slower and weaker *Caledonia.* For the Americans, the battle couldn't have begun under less auspicious circumstances.

But Oliver Hazard Perry was a lucky man on 10 September 1813. At about 10 o'clock the wind unexpectedly began to haul toward the southeast. Now the Americans, as they formed their line, held the weather gage and could control the range.[37] Perry passed the order to his ships to close their order to a half-cable length (360 feet), half the standard close order for battle.[38]

At 11:45 the British opened the action with their long guns; ten minutes later the Americans responded. The two lines slowly converged. The *Lawrence,* in the lead, bore most of the British fire and was initially unable to respond with its short-range carronades. Perry sensed that he needed to close the range more quickly and bring up the rest of his ships. According to his official report, he "made sail and directed the other vessels to follow for the purpose of engaging with the enemy."[39]

Unfortunately, despite Perry's intentions, the *Lawrence* remained unsupported and was battered for several hours. Perry's decisions made between the first sightings of the morning and noon, when he attempted to close the range between the two squadrons, were inconsistent with his prebattle instructions to his confused subordinates. Perry had drummed the need for a close action into the heads of his captains, yet he had accepted battle when the British held the windward position and could determine the range. Only a fortuitous and uncharacteristic change of the wind, and not some maneuver on Perry's part, provided the Americans with the weather gage. Nor did Perry initially adopt an approach toward the British that would close rapidly the range between the two flotillas. Rather than direct his line to turn as a unit toward the British and then reform its own line abreast the enemy, Perry had led his slowly forming line on an angled approach toward Barclay's squadron while ordering his own ships to close rank. This maneuver, termed "concentration" in the era, maximized the fire of one's own line against a portion of the enemy's but was effective only if both lines were in contact along their entire length. This was not the case at Lake Erie.

Perry did have a problem with the mix of his fleet, although he knew that before the battle. His sloops and schooners were mostly armed with long guns and could best engage the British at long range; given their lightness, they were vulnerable in a close engagement. The brigs *Lawrence* and *Niagara* carried about two-thirds of Perry's firepower, but they needed to be employed at close range. Perry was right, before the battle, to have insisted on a close engagement; but his decision to form his line of battle in response to the British order forced the separation of the two brigs and left the slower and weaker *Caledonia* in between, with Perry himself leading the line. All of these factors increased the uncertainty among Perry's subordinates. What was their commodore planning to do?

Perry's actions at noon only furthered these uncertainties. He decided to close the range with Barclay as quickly as possible. There were three ways to do so. Perry, holding the windward position, could lead his line across the head of Barclay's squadron. To do this he needed to head a point or two toward the British off a parallel course, increase sail, and reach ahead of them. Second, he could adopt an even sharper approach and lead his line through Barclay's squadron—that is, "break" Barclay's line. This was a common tactic in the age of sail and one that frequently bore decisive results. Third, Perry could have each of his ships simultaneously turn toward the British and approach Barclay's line until the range had closed. At that point, a subsequent signal would bring the Americans back into a line ahead formation along a closer parallel course.

Historians of the battle had mostly concluded that Perry planned to adopt the first approach: he increased the *Lawrence*'s sail and turned toward his enemy, expecting that his subordinates would follow him in the line ahead. This is, however, only an assumption. We do not know from the testimony exactly what Perry intended. We do know from his postbattle report that, when he later boarded the *Niagara,* he "determined to pass through the enemy's line."[40] This could mean that he had planned to do the same at noon when he was on the *Lawrence.*

Whatever Perry's intentions, from the ships trailing the *Lawrence,* all three maneuvers would have looked more or less identical. From the *Caledonia,* immediately behind the *Lawrence,* an observer would have seen the flagship increase sail and turn toward the British line. But it would have been hard to gauge from behind, based on the sharpness of Perry's turn toward the British, whether he intended to pass ahead or through the British formation. Alternatively, the captain of the *Caledonia* could conclude that he ought to mimic the movements of the *Lawrence* along with the rest of the squadron.[41] Indecision and uncertainty in warfare lead to paralysis.

Perry's responsibility as commodore was to make sure that his intentions, whatever they were, were understood and acted on by the rest of the ships in his squadron. The normal procedure in the age of fighting sail would have been for Perry to make the proper *visual* signal from his flagship. The problem, of course, was that his short signal list did not include anything appropriate to the situation, nor had he prepared his subordinates to watch for signals from the manual sent to Perry from Secretary Jones. According to Perry's official report, he "directed the other vessels to follow," which itself is an ambiguous statement. Did he mean to follow in line? Or did he mean to mimic his movements and turn toward the British?

And just how did Perry "direct" his subordinates? Usher Parsons described the critical moment in the *Lawrence:* "The commodore was on the quarter deck with two young officers, Thomas Brown and his own brother Alexander Perry, whose duty it was to run with his orders to every part of the ships, for in the din and uproar of battle no officer can be heard ten feet off."

Naval battles in the age of sail were, indeed, cacophonic. Nevertheless, Commodore Perry, who could not be heard "ten feet off," directed his squadron to "follow" when he "ordered the word to be passed by [speaking] trumpet to the vessels astern."[42] Here we have a commodore who has to use his brother to give orders to the various divisions on the *Lawrence* because they cannot be heard at a distance beyond ten feet ordering the critical signal of the Battle of Lake Erie to be made by speaking trumpet to the *Caledonia* trailing the *Lawrence* by 300–400 feet![43]

Lieutenant Daniel Turner commanded the *Caledonia*, which, because of Perry's decision to allow Barclay to determine the American order of battle, followed the *Lawrence* and was sandwiched between it and the *Niagara*. There's no evidence among the records of the battle that Turner ever received (heard) Perry's "signal." The inexperienced Turner left without direction, having no clue what he should do as he saw his commodore angle toward the British. The *Caledonia* sailed on but continued to fall further behind, either because Turner failed to increase sail or because the *Caledonia* was slow, or perhaps a combination of the two. As the *Caledonia* fell behind, so did the next-in-line *Niagara*, until Elliott ordered Turner to turn away from the battle and allow the *Niagara* to pass ahead.

Confusion in battle wastes time. The ships in the American line were making about two knots—that is, 12,000 feet per hour. At the time Perry changed course, Elliott was about a quarter-mile behind the *Lawrence* (about 1,500 feet, or seven or eight minutes). If Turner and Elliott responded promptly to Perry's signal—if they had been able to hear it (which was physically impossible)—by the time the *Caledonia* increased sail and changed course, the *Niagara* would have fallen even further behind and several more minutes to the rear, because as Perry turned toward the British and further off the wind, his speed was increasing and he was pulling ahead of the ships to his rear. The only maneuver that would have prevented this from happening would have been for the entire American line to mimic the *Lawrence*'s movements with a simultaneous turn toward the British.

The *Caledonia*, Turner's brig, was known to be a poor and unhandy sailor and was simply too slow to keep pace with the *Lawrence*. For that reason, Perry should never have adopted an order of battle that could leave the *Caledonia*, or any of the other ships, in line between the two Americans brigs.

As a result, as Perry turned toward the British and closed the range he was unsupported for the better part of two hours. Lack of support in sailing age battles was, unfortunately, the norm. It is a constant refrain in the naval record. Subordinate admirals were always failing "to come up" in myriad battles. But in the case of the battle of Lake Erie, remarkably, at no point did Commodore Perry make any effort to signal his intentions to his subordinates. For two hours Captain Perry was so engrossed fighting his own battle that he made no effort to direct the movements of his own squadron. In recalling the old adage, "It is better to light a candle than to curse the darkness," one might say of Perry at Lake Erie that "it is better to make a signal than to curse one's subordinates."

Ultimately, with the *Lawrence* battered into near submission, Perry left his brig in a cutter and made his way to the *Niagara,* according to accounts recorded a full half-mile from the action.[44]

Was Elliott actually so far behind when Perry left the *Lawrence?* Usher Parson's diary entry and the published log of the *Lawrence* provide some significant time checks.[45] At 2:30 P.M. the *Lawrence*'s last gun was dismounted, and Perry shortly thereafter left the flagship. Ten minutes after Parsons saw Perry reach the Niagara, the *Lawrence* stuck.[46] At 2:50 the *Detroit* and the rest of the British van struck, fifteen minutes after Perry took the *Niagara* under his command and ran down on the British. If the *Detroit*'s striking came fifteen minutes after Perry reached the *Niagara,* he reached the brig at 2:35, which means that Perry spent at the most five minutes getting into and out of the cutter and rowing to the *Niagara.* If Elliott was, as Perry and his supporters claimed, a full half-mile behind the *Lawrence,* the men who rowed the commodore to the *Niagara,* after fighting a horrific battle for over two hours, managed to propel the cutter through the water at a speed better than seven knots. A good rowing speed in the cutter would have been about half that, or something over three knots. Consider also that as the men in the boat rowed, the *Niagara* was moving toward them; Elliott's brig was probably within a quarter-mile of the *Lawrence,* which at that point was dead in the water. This was about the same distance that had separated the brigs at noon. Elliott had fallen further behind, perhaps as much as a half-mile, because of the slower *Caledonia.* But once he ordered Turner out of the way, the *Niagara* began to make up the distance that separated it from the *Lawrence.* One can certainly fault Elliott for not ordering Turner out of the way sooner; or, one can fault Perry for leaving the determination of the American order of battle in Barclay's hands.

The Battle of Lake Erie, examined in a larger context of engagements during the age of fighting sail, is at once atypical and typical. It is atypical because of the American victory. Enemy fleets were rarely "wiped out" in the age of sail. Even Macdonough failed to capture the entire British force that attacked him at Plattsburgh. But the behavior of Perry's subordinates was all too typical of sailing age engagements. In most battles, large numbers of the ships poised for battle never engaged in combat. And subordinates rarely demonstrated initiative, let alone outright heroism. Clearly, Jesse Duncan Elliott was no Horatio Nelson. In fact, few sailing age captains would have even shown the initiative Elliott demonstrated when he directed Turner to get the plodding *Caledonia* out of his way.

The inadequacies of Perry and his captains were shared, unfortunately, by many of the early historians who attempted to explain the details of the battle. When a naval historian familiar with the engagements of the age, notably C. S. Forester, addressed the details of the battle, the events of 10 September 1813 took on an all-too-familiar form: they represented "the infernal problem which had plagued attacking fleets ever since they were first formed in line."[47]

Elliott *could* have reacted more quickly and come to Perry's support. Of that there can be no doubt. The very vehemence of Elliott's defense, which lasted for decades, suggested that he knew and regretted the fact that he had not done more. He had, after all, missed a great opportunity to make himself the U.S. Navy's Horatio Nelson. But Elliott was no Nelson; he was a better-than-average officer for the American service, but that was all.

But Elliott was not the man in charge; Perry was. And the fact remains that Perry failed to make any use of signals during the entire time he was under fire. Nor had Perry prepared his subordinates adequately for what was coming. Yes, he had stressed the need for close action, but he accepted battle when the British held the weather gage, and he allowed his opponent to determine the line of battle for the American flotilla.

Given Perry's responsibilities as commodore, his command of his fleet on 10 September 1813 must be judged a failure. Commodore Perry failed to properly exercise command. His initial dispositions—the slow *Caledonia* wedged between his brigs—complicated maneuvers. He failed to make use of the available signals to communicate his intentions to his squadron during the approach. He became immersed in his private single-ship engagement for over two hours, never once even considering the possibility of signaling his squadron. He was fortunate to be saved by Captain Perry and the hard-fighting officers and men of the *Lawrence* and by Jesse Duncan Elliott, who did rally the rear of the squadron during the final stage of the engagement.

To criticize Perry as commodore is not to justify or overlook the short-comings of Elliott, however. Perry may have been a second-rate commander in chief, but he was a good captain, a fine officer, and a gentleman. His fighting qualities and perseverance ultimately won the day. As James Fenimore Cooper wrote, "Captain Perry's merit was an indomitable resolution not to be conquered, and the manner in which he sought new modes of victory, when the old ones failed him."[48] Nevertheless, the Americans owed their victory on Lake Erie to a fortuitous change of wind, more heavily armed and manned ships, and tough crews, especially that of the *Lawrence.* Lake Erie was a battle almost lost by Commodore Perry but then won by Captain Perry. Elliott, while certainly no coward, allowed the opportunity to win the battle in a Nelsonian fashion slip through his fingers, and his post-battle campaign to silence what were exaggerated criticisms of his conduct became so vigorous and negative that they ultimately proved counterproductive. But historians ought not criticize Elliott too harshly for his failure to use the *Niagara,* as had Nelson the *Captain* at the battle of Cape St. Vincent. On 10 September 1810, Elliott confronted his own mediocrity and began a long, unsuccessful struggle to vindicate himself, probably more in his own than in the public mind.

NOTES

1. For the "forgotten war" theme, see Donald R. Hickey, *The War of 1812: A Forgotten Conflict* (Urbana: University of Illinois Press, 1989). For the most recent scholarship on Lake Erie, see David Curtis Skaggs, *Oliver Hazard Perry: Honor, Courage, and Patriotism in the Early U.S. Navy* (Annapolis, MD: Naval Institute Press, 2006); and David Curtis Skaggs and Gerard T. Altoff, *A Signal Victory: The Lake Erie Campaign, 1812–1813* (Annapolis, MD: Naval Institute Press, 1997).

2. James Fenimore Cooper, *History of the Navy of the United States of America,* 2 vols., 3rd ed. (Cooperstown, NY: H. & E. Phinney, 1848), 2:197. Hickey writes in *The War of 1812:* "Perry's victory on Lake Erie was a tribute to his courage and coolness under fire and to the effective use of his superior resources" (133).

3. James Fenimore Cooper to James De Peyster Ogden, 11 June 1839, James Franklin Beard, ed., *The Letters and Journals of James Fenimore Cooper,* 6 vols. (Cambridge, MA: 1960–68), 3:385–87. For a further examination of the Cooper-Perry-Elliott triangle, see David Curtis Skaggs, "Aiming at the Truth: James Fenimore Cooper and the Battle of Lake Erie," *Journal of Military History* 59 (Apr. 1995): 237–56.

4. Skaggs, *Perry,* 92.

5. In the machine age, multiple weaker ships hold an advantage over a single stronger ship because of the limitations of range finders, which do not permit ships to engage more than one or two targets simultaneously. For example, at the Battle of the River Platte, the German pocket battleship *Admiral Graf Spee,* with its 11-inch guns, could not manage the attack along divergent approaches of the Royal Navy heavy cruiser *Exeter* (8-inch guns) and the light cruisers *Ajax* and *Achilles* (6-inch guns). In the age of sail, range finding was not an issue, and a single

powerful ship could easily overwhelm multiple lighter vessels. For example, on 20 February 1815 the U.S. Navy frigate *Constitution* easily captured the British corvettes *Cyane* and *Levant*, despite the fact that their combined weight of broadside was slightly greater. If Perry had kept the *Lawrence* and *Niagara* together in line, they alone had sufficient firepower to devastate the entire British squadron at close range.

6. For a discussion, see Michael A. Palmer, *Command at Sea: Naval Command and Control since the Sixteenth Century* (Cambridge, MA: Harvard University Press, 2005).

7. Ibid., 165–68.

8. Michael A. Palmer, "Lord Nelson: Master of Command," *Naval War College Review* 41 (Winter 1988): 105–16.

9. Michael A. Palmer, *Stoddert's War: Naval Operations during the Quasi-War with France, 1798–1801,* 2nd ed. (Annapolis, MD: Naval Institute Press, 2000), 77.

10. Captains Thomas Truxtun, James Barron, John Barry, Edward Preble, and John Rodgers contributed to the development of American signaling systems between 1779 and 1812.

11. John Rodgers, *Signals to Be Used by the Squadron under the Command of Commodore John Rodgers* (Brooklyn, NY: Thomas Kirk, 1812).

12. The copy of the *Chesapeake*'s signal book is held by the National Maritime Museum, Greenwich, England. George Budd to William Jones, 18 June 1813, Letters from Officers below the Rank of Master Commandant, 1813, Record Group 45, National Archives, Washington, DC (hereafter cited as Captains Letters).

13. Jones to William Bainbridge, 30 June 1813, Captains Letters, 1813.

14. The 1812 signal book, a copy of which is held by the Erie County Historical Society, was superseded by a new signal book by September 1813 and definitely was not used by the squadron during the battle.

15. Jones to Perry, 10 July 1813, Letters from Master Commandants, 1813, RG 45, National Archives (hereafter cited as Master Commandants Letters).

16. My focus here is on Perry as squadron/flotilla commander and not on his other duties, among them administrative matters. The latter tasks he performed admirably. As Theodore Roosevelt wrote, "[Perry's] claim to fame rests much less on his actual victory than in the way in which he prepared the fleet that was to win it." Theodore Roosevelt, *The Naval War of 1812* (New York: G. P. Putnam Sons, 1897), 274.

17. Palmer, *Command,* 157–61.

18. For a recent scholarly biography of Macdonough, see David Curtis Skaggs, *Thomas Macdonough: Master of Command in the Early U.S. Navy* (Annapolis, MD: Naval Institute Press, 2003), 109–39.

19. For the elder Perry's troubles during the Quasi-War, see Palmer, *Stoddert's War,* 170–72.

20. The *General Greene* spent most of its time in the West Indies supporting the cause of San Domingue (Haitian) revolutionary Toussaint Louverture. After it returned to the United States in 1800, the elder Perry, a Republican, was the subject of a court of inquiry. Damning testimony led President John Adams and Secretary of the Navy Benjamin Stoddert to suspend the Rhode Islander for three months. Many of the charges leveled against Perry were considered substantiated, among them the mistreatment of subordinates. Stoddert never recalled Perry to duty, nor did the Republican administration of Thomas Jefferson following its electoral victory in 1800. Christopher Raymond Perry was hardly a model commander for a young midshipman.

21. Richard Dillon, *We Have Met the Enemy: Oliver Hazard Perry, Wilderness Commodore* (New York: McGraw-Hill, 1978), 47–57; Skaggs, *Perry,* 25–48.

22. Later in the war, when Perry prepared for a wartime cruise to European waters, he had to write his father for instructions on how to determine longitude. Perry to Wederstandt, 14 Oct. 1814, Oliver Hazard Perry, Miscellaneous Manuscripts Collection, Library of Congress,

Washington, DC. The U.S. Navy did not start using chronometers until the 1820s. The determination of longitude by observation was a complex mathematical process, mastered among U.S. Navy officers by Captain Thomas Truxtun, who wrote the first American treatise on the method in 1794.

23. Quoted in Christopher McKee, *A Gentlemanly and Honorable Profession: The Creation of the U.S. Naval Officer Corps, 1794–1815* (Annapolis, MD: Naval Institute Press, 1991), 214.

24. Dillon, *We Have Met the Enemy,* 36; Cooper, *History,* 2:196n. Roosevelt also mentioned that inexperienced American commanders during the War of 1812 often "overcharged carronades" (*War of 1812,* 262–63).

25. Skaggs, *Perry,* 130; Jones to Perry, 29 Sept. 1813, William S. Dudley and Michael J. Crawford, eds., *The Naval War of 1812: A Documentary History,* 3 vols. (Washington, DC: Naval Historical Center, 1985–), 2:577.

26. Perry to Jones, 29 Jan. 1813, Master Commandants.

27. Perry to Christopher Raymond Perry, 9 Aug. 1913, Oliver H. Perry Papers, William L. Clements Library, University of Michigan, Ann Arbor; Perry to Jones, 19 June 1813, Area Files 7, RG 45, National Archives. Perry to Chauncey, 27 July 1813; Perry to Jones, 30 July 1813; Perry to Jones, 8 Aug. 1813; Perry to Jones, 2 Sept. 1813, Master Commandants.

28. Perry to Jones, 10 Aug. 1813, Dudley and Crawford, *Naval War,* 2:532–33.

29. Perry to Chauncey, 27 July 1813, ibid., 529–30.

30. Chauncey to Perry, 30 July 1813, ibid., 530–31.

31. For the July draft of the signal book, see Jones to Perry, 10 July 1813, Letters to Officers, Ships of War, 1813, RG 45, National Archives. See also U.S. Navy Department, *Signals for the Use of the United States Navy; as adopted by Order of the Navy Department, August 1813* (Washington, DC: Department of the Navy, 1813). The evidence suggests that the August signal books did not reach Perry in time for the battle.

32. Perry's order of sailing and signals, 11 June 1813, Daniel Dobbins Papers, Buffalo Historical Society, Buffalo, NY. Perry listed a dozen signals:

> To get underway
> To form the order of sailing ahead
> To form the order of sailing abreast
> To form the line of battle on the starboard tack
> To form the line of battle on the larboard tack
> To close more the present order
> To open more the present order
> Tacks
> To follow the motions of the commodore
> To engage the enemy
> To chase
> To repair on board the Commodore all commanders.

33. Alexander Slidell Mackenzie, *The Life of Commodore Oliver Hazard Perry,* 2 vols. (New York: Harper & Brothers, 1840), 1:221–22.

34. Affidavit of H. B. Brevoort, 7 Nov. 1818, *Review of a Pamphlet Purporting to be Documents in Relation to the Differences Which Subsisted between the Lake Commodore Oliver H. Perry and Captain Jesse D. Elliott* (Boston: H. B. & J. Brewster, 1834): 45–46.

35. Skaggs, *Perry,* 100.

36. Barclay considered the loss of the weather gage a severe handicap: "The weather gage gave the enemy a prodigious advantage as it enabled them, not only to choose their position, but their distance also, which they did in such a manner as to prevent the carronades of the

Queen Charlotte and the *Lady Prevost,* from having much effect, while their long guns did great execution particularly against the *Queen Charlotte.*" It is apparent from the British accounts of the engagement that Barclay commanded an unwieldy mix of vessels undermanned and officered by men of little experience and that, like Perry, he also had difficulty bringing all his ships into action. Robert Heriot Barclay to James Lucas Yeo, Dudley and Crawford, *Naval War,* 2:555–56.

37. Cooper, *History,* 2:189–90.

38. Usher Parsons, *Battle of Lake Erie: A Discourse* (Providence, RI: Benjamin T. Albro, 1854), 10; William V. Taylor to Alexander Mackenzie, 16 Jan. 1841, William V. Taylor Papers, Newport Historical Society, Newport, RI. Standard close order was one cable's length.

39. Perry to Jones, 13 Sept. 1813, Dudley and Crawford, *Naval War,* 2:557–59.

40. Perry to Jones, 13 Sept. 1813, ibid.

41. In his report Perry mentions that he increased sail but does not actually state that he turned more toward the British line. Ibid.

42. Parsons, *Discourse,* 10; Mackenzie, *Perry,* 1:233; the affidavit of William V. Taylor, ibid., 2:263–66. The only firsthand accounts of the battle that mention Perry's verbal instructions passed by speaking trumpeter are those written by men of the *Lawrence,* who all stated that Elliott acknowledged the signal, though how he could have heard it remains a mystery. The accounts written by the men of the *Niagara,* not surprisingly, make no mention of any order being passed by trumpet. Daniel Turner, commander of the *Caledonia,* the vessel sandwiched between the *Lawrence* and the *Niagara,* in his affidavit written in support of Perry, acknowledged the receipt of the commodore's earlier visual signal to engage but mentioned no order passed by trumpet. Affidavit of Daniel Turner, Mackenzie, *Perry,* 2:253–55.

43. There were techniques to ensure that hoisted signal flags were visible in low-wind conditions. I would note that none of the accounts of the battle mentions the wind in relation to any inability to hoist flag signals.

44. Mackenzie, *Perry,* 2:245, wrote that Perry took fifteen minutes to cross the half mile separating the two American brigs. Those figures for time and distance have been accepted by most American historians. See John K. Mahon, "Oliver Hazard Perry: Savior of the Northwest," in *Command Under Sail: Makers of the American Naval Tradition, 1775–1850,* ed. James Bradford (Annapolis, MD: Naval Institute Press, 1985,) 136; Gerard T. Altoff, "The Battle of Lake Erie: A Narrative," in *War on the Great Lakes: Essays Commemorating the 175th Anniversary of the Battle of Lake Erie,* ed. William Jeffrey Welsh and David Curtis Skaggs (Kent, OH: Kent State University Press, 1991), 13–14. David Skaggs does not speculate about the amount of time Perry spent in the boat either in his biography of Perry or in *A Signal Victory.*

45. 10 Sept. 1813, John C. Fredriksen, ed., *Surgeon of the Lakes: The Diary of Dr. Usher Parsons, 1812–1814* (Erie, PA: Erie County Historical Society, 2000), 48–51; Charles Oscar Paullin, ed. *The Battle of Lake Erie* (Cleveland: Rowfant Club, 1918), 57–58; log of the *Lawrence,* Newport Historical Society.

46. Perry, in his official report, stated that he was on the *Niagara* when he saw the *Lawrence* strike.

47. C. S. Forester, *The Age of Fighting Sail: The Story of the Naval War of 1812* (Garden City, NY: Doubleday, 1956), 182.

48. Cooper, *History,* 2:197n.

Invading Canada

Joint Operations Across Lake Erie

DAVID CURTIS SKAGGS

On 10 September the sound of guns echoed across Lake Erie, the rumble heard from Detroit to Cleveland. But the outcome of the long-expected naval engagement was unknown to those on shore. The next day General William Henry Harrison ordered his troops garrisoned at Camp Seneca (modern Old Fort, Ohio) to march to Lower Sandusky, even though no one knew the result of the naval engagement. But before the arriving troops had time to pitch their tents, a boat came up the river "with all the speed oars could give her." Shortly after the officer commanding the vessel reached Harrison's headquarters at Fort Stephenson, the troops "heard a tremendous shout and hurrahing, and then the booming of cannon. All eyes were turned in that direction, knowing that something glorious had occurred, what, we could not guess." Soon, recalled Supply Sergeant Alfred Brunson, a man came "running down the hill at a break-neck speed" and announced to the anxious soldiers the news of the American victory on the lake. There ensued a universal shout and rejoicing. Everyone knew the consequences of the destruction of the British squadron on the lake—the invasion of Canada was about to begin.[1]

The 1813 invasion of Canada by General Harrison's North West Army with the assistance of Perry's squadron constitutes the most immediate consequence of the Battle of Lake Erie.

The need to invade Canada was the end result of American military defeats, miscues, surrenders, and leadership incompetence in 1812. The most serious of these mistakes in the western theater was the surrender of Detroit. General Isaac Brock of Upper Canada (modern Ontario) exploited British control of Lake Erie to transfer troops from the Niagara frontier to Fort Malden on the Canadian side of the Detroit River. American brigadier general William Hull

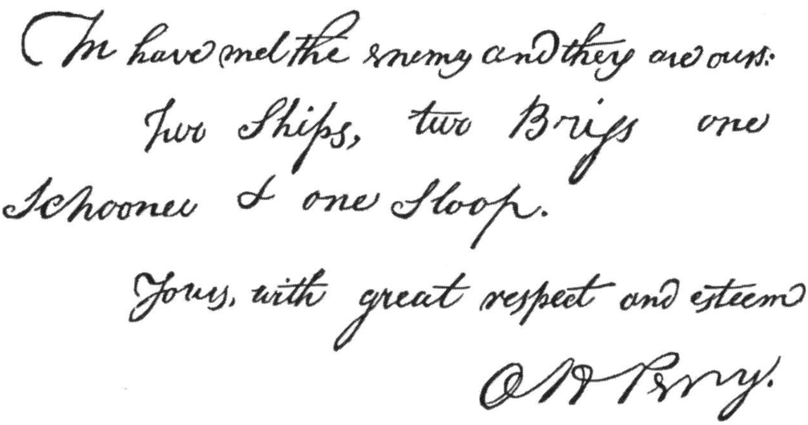

We have met the enemy and they are ours:
Two Ships, two Brigs one
Schooner & one Sloop.
Yours, with great respect and esteem
O H Perry.

Perry's message. Reprinted from Benson J. Lossing, *Pictorial Field-Book of the War of 1812* (New York: Harper Brothers, 1869).

allowed Brock's troops to land on the Michigan shore without opposition. Using the threat of an Indian massacre if the Americans resisted, which had been used elsewhere by the British, Brock demanded the capitulation of the territorial capital. Hull surrendered on 16 August without firing a shot.[2]

In his earliest 1812 planning, Harrison never sought naval assets in the quest for military dominance of the Old Northwest. In the summer and fall of 1812 he concentrated on the retaking of Detroit without any naval assistance; this was predicated on the obvious conclusion that there was no way an American naval force could be constructed, armed, and manned before the end of the shipping season. Only gradually did he envision the necessity of naval superiority on Lake Erie as a requirement for the reconquest of Detroit. His first intimation of any Navy Department effort on the Great Lakes came in a letter from Secretary of War William Eustis dated 1 September.[3]

Meanwhile, Harrison's close ally, Governor Isaac Shelby of Kentucky, concluded that to try to retake Detroit without taking Fort Malden first was the wrong course. In a letter to the new secretary of war, John Armstrong, the governor advised that "a decisive step" be employed to "secure the superior command of Lake Eire, which being effected would prevent the Enemy from reinforcing his troops in that quarter & the forwarding of supplies for their use." At the same time, American use of waterborne transport would dramatically cut transportation costs by reducing the need for wagons and their drivers, artillery horses, pack horses, pack horse masters and their drivers, and the necessary forage to support them.[4] By early 1813 it had become apparent to those in Washington that the accomplishment of the objective of retaking and holding Detroit and of subduing hostile Native Americans within the United States necessitated two missions be achieved: first, secure naval dominance of Lake Erie, which would isolate the British and Indians on the Detroit River from sources of supply and reinforcements; and second, conduct a military campaign from the Ohio Valley into southern Michigan and what is now southwestern Ontario that would destroy the British-Indian alliance and the British Army in the region. To accomplish the latter, the United States committed itself to a cross-lake amphibious operation involving both army and navy forces cooperating toward a common objective.

To achieve optimum results in joint army-navy operations, the American military currently seeks unity of command, whereby an officer from one service commands all military forces in a particular region. But an organizational arrangement that has been successful since World War II was not in vogue in the early republic. In the early nineteenth century there was no way the Navy Department was going to allow a War Department general to have operational command over its officers, ships, or crews. Instead, interservice synchronization required a "unity of effort" between cooperating generals and commodores to achieve the desired "coordination and cooperation toward common objectives, even if the participants are not necessarily part of the same command or organization."[5]

Harrison wrote Secretary Eustis on 12 December that an "Army advancing to Detroit along a line of Operation passing so near" Fort Malden risked being logistically cut off as General Hull had been by interruptions of the supply lines from Ohio. Consequently, he argued, "the attack ought not to be directed against Detroit, but against Malden." But Harrison sought to accomplish this task not through naval operations but by attacking across Lake Erie or the Detroit River when they were frozen.[6]

In December 1812 acting Secretary of War James Monroe concluded, "It is obvious that the Command of Lake Erie would dissipate many difficulties which now weigh heavy on" the ground forces.[7] But the type of coordination in the first instance was logistical, not command; in the second it involved the navy gaining dominance on the lake, not any direct army effort. Therefore, the degree of cooperation, coordination, and interdependence that existed between Major General William Henry Harrison and Master Commandant

Oliver Hazard Perry merits special attention for its level of mutual effort and operational success.

On 3 April 1813 Secretary of War John Armstrong issued a long directive to Harrison. In it he listed several objectives. Obtaining command of the lakes was the first priority, which he insisted would be achieved by early June. Land operations would be curtailed until naval superiority became reality. Second, the approach to Malden should be achieved by a waterborne operation using the flat-bottomed Schenectady bateaux, which the secretary authorized Major Thomas Jesup to build in Cleveland for the purpose of transporting army troops across the lake after the navy secured control, rather than engaging in a "difficult, dangerous and enormously expensive" overland campaign out of Fort Meigs.[8]

Third, since the Malden force was estimated to be no larger than 2,000 men, Harrison could raise no more than 7,000 for his campaign. This limit was imposed for more than military reasons; the increasingly limited resources of the Treasury Department constrained troop and logistical expenditures. The secretary cautioned Harrison not to order up new drafts of militia. Instead, he was to rely on the 17th and 19th U.S. Infantry regiments already formed and the newly authorized 24th, 26th, 27th, and 28th Infantry regiments and the Regiment of Light Dragoons being raised in Ohio and Kentucky. Armstrong noted that the first two were not fully manned and that the others were in their infancy, but he expected Harrison to "promote" enlistments in regular army units.[9]

Secretary Armstrong's plans immediately fell apart. Regular army recruitment in Missouri, Ohio, and Kentucky lagged far behind the unit authorizations. Secretary Armstrong expected the seven regiments raised in the west would constitute all the offensive forces Harrison would need. But the secretary gave the general a loophole in militia limitations. "Should the recruiting Service go on less fortunately in the patriotic states of Kentucky and Ohio, than in other parts of the Union," Harrison received permission to call out militia units to make up the difference between the regular force authorization and its actual strength. By early July it became apparent that Secretary Armstrong's hopes for a regular army corps at the center of the North West Army had failed; only 2,000 answered the call to join the seven regiments. The secretary of war reluctantly gave the general the option to call on state militias to augment his force.[10]

While the shipbuilding at Erie, Pennsylvania, proceeded only slightly behind schedule, the navy's inability to man Perry's squadron produced delay after delay in operational activities on the lake. Nonetheless, the new secretary of the navy, William Jones, summarized the Washington expectations of the midwestern campaign in early July:

> The consequences of cutting off . . . [the enemy's] Naval force on Erie would be incalculably great, and probably would be immediately followed by his abandonment of Malden, and the upper country; which would immediately induce the desertion of the Savages, and release of a great part of General Harrison's army, which might immediately have been transported, by our fleet, to Niagara, and produce a decisive blow in that quarter also.[11]

In the midst of all this intraservice rivalry, interservice cooperation received a blow when Secretary of War Armstrong and Secretary of the Navy Jones issued joint regulations on 8 April specifically limiting command relationships between army and navy commanders in the field. Army officers found themselves prohibited from commanding any naval vessel and navy officers forbidden from commanding any army units.[12] This regulation prohibited Perry from using in a command position army captain Henry Brevoort, who had previously commanded the army supply brig *Adams* on Lakes Erie and Huron and was a far more experienced ship master and commander than many of Perry's very junior subordinates. Besides, Brevoort was the only officer in the U.S. forces to have sailed in Lakes Huron and St. Clair. Concerning ground troops on naval vessels, Harrison and Perry soon violated this order so as to fill empty billets on Perry's ships. They found that some "volunteers" would not become sailors unless their junior officers commanded them.[13]

In early July Harrison and Perry began exchanging letters, from which blossomed a spirit of cooperation. The army commander suggested Put-in-Bay on South Bass Island as an ideal port for Perry's use, one that would also provide security for Harrison's forces in northern Ohio. Harrison further noted that it would take some time to assemble enough troops for a cross-lake invasion. One of Harrison's staff officers wrote of the general's "perfect conviction, that no exertion will be omitted on [Perry's] part to give the Crisis an issue of Profit and Glory to the arms of our Country."[14]

That "Profit and Glory" were delayed until Perry dominated the lake. It was not until August that Commodore Chauncey directed his flag lieutenant, newly promoted Master Commandant Jesse Duncan Elliott, and 101 seamen and one Marine to join Perry. Some of Harrison's soldiers filled the remaining billets in the navy ships. Finally, in mid-August, Perry dominated Lake Erie, but the Royal Navy squadron remained at Amherstburg on the Detroit River. With Perry controlling the lake, Major Jesup began forwarding to Sandusky Bay the Schenectady bateaux whose construction he had supervised in Cleveland.

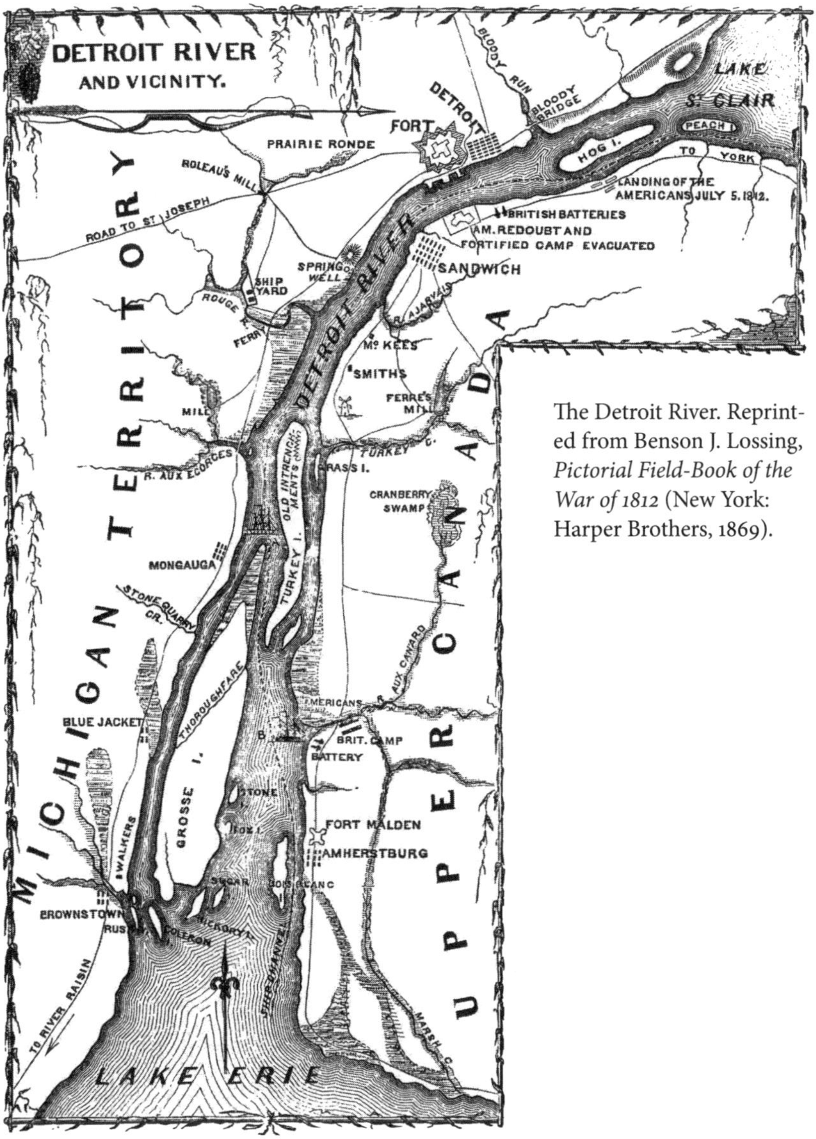

The Detroit River. Reprinted from Benson J. Lossing, *Pictorial Field-Book of the War of 1812* (New York: Harper Brothers, 1869).

It was in Sandusky Bay on 19 August that Harrison first met Perry. The commanders, their senior commanders, and their staffs consulted for three days, shaping the operational planning for the next several weeks with a series of decisions. First, Perry would try to entice Barclay and his squadron out of the Detroit River and the protection of Fort Malden's guns to defeat the Royal Navy force. Second, Harrison would begin moving most of his forces to the mouth of the Portage River (modern Port Clinton, Ohio), where they would be joined by Jesup's boats. Third, Harrison would solicit Kentucky governor Isaac Shelby to send volunteers to reinforce Harrison's regular regiments, which were woefully undermanned. Fourth, Harrison would provide enough volunteer militia and regular army troops to fill the still-vacant billets in Perry's vessels. (Eventually, 40 percent of Perry's sailors were either regular soldiers or volunteers, mostly from Pennsylvania and Kentucky.[15]) Finally, once Perry captured, destroyed, blockaded, or reduced to insignificance the British naval squadron, Perry's vessels would escort and tow the Schenectady landing craft to the Canadian shore. Theirs would be the most complex, sophisticated, and integrated joint operation in the brief history of American warfare.

On 10 September Commander Robert H. Barclay brought his Royal Navy flotilla out of the Detroit River and onto Lake Erie. With approximately 130 of Harrison's soldiers on board his vessels, Perry won a dramatic victory that resulted in the capture of the entire Royal Navy squadron. Both the militiamen and regulars who fought with Perry constituted an important segment of his manpower during the battle that achieved extraordinary fame for the navy. One Kentuckian recalled Perry saying "that had it not been for the [army] volunteers the battle would have been lost."[16]

Along the Detroit River the British waited anxiously to learn the results of the naval engagement. Looking through the smoke they could not determine the outcome. But on the morning of 11 September, the ships sailed away toward South Bass Island and no small vessel returned carrying Barclay's expected victory message. Soon it dawned on them that not only had the Royal Navy been beaten, but the entire squadron was lost. Such an unexpected outcome completely changed the situation for the right wing of His Majesty's forces in Canada and its native allies. As a new reality confronted the residents of the Detroit River Valley, they reacted in different ways.

Native Americans were split in their response. Some sent word to Harrison that they were willing to negotiate; in fact, they might even support American forces. Others quietly left and returned to their homes to the north or defiantly stayed with their families in southern Michigan. Some of this was undoubtedly a consequence of a lack of vessels to transport their families and baggage across the Detroit River. Led by Tecumseh, several hundred warriors remained with the British, the last remnants of the coalition that Tecumseh and Tenskwatawa (the Prophet) had formed just a few years before.

Among the Canadians there were obvious misgivings. Few rallied to the British flag; most went home, and, for the most part, the militia units of the Western District of Upper Canada went unmustered. Their livelihoods, property, and families were in jeopardy. For the Americans living inside British-occupied Michigan, there was an anxiety that they might be ravaged by the retreating natives before their countrymen arrived. They awaited the advancing North West Army with expectation that their year-long nightmare was about to end.

General Procter faced a dilemma. He had long promised the natives that he would never yield a foot of Canadian soil. Militarily, it was obvious that his staying at Fort Malden and Detroit was no longer tenable. Much of the fort's artillery had been stripped to equip the Royal Navy's *Detroit*, which had been lost in the Battle of Lake Erie. However, the British feared that retreat might bring on the wrath of the Indians. Consequently, he delayed making a decision and acting decisively. That would prove to be catastrophic for the 41st Regiment of Foot and the British Indian Department.

While he moved his headquarters northward to Sandwich (modern Windsor, Ontario), Procter did not issue the order to withdraw up the Thames River Valley and move his army toward the central wing of the British Army on the Niagara Peninsula.[17] Perhaps this lingering along the Detroit River was a consequence of a speech made by Tecumseh on 18 September in which the Shawnee warrior reminded him that the British had twice before given "the hatchet to his red children" and twice before they had betrayed them at a peace conference from which the natives were excluded. For a third time "our British father" gave the natives "the tomahawk and told us that he was then ready to strike the American; that he wanted our assistance; and that he would certainly get us our lands back." Tecumseh wanted to remain at Amherstburg and fight to the end. Then, if "they defeat us, we will then retreat." In the dramatic moment of this speech, Tecumseh turned toward Procter and condemned his plans to withdraw, comparing the general's conduct to that of "a fat dog, that carries its tail upon its back, but when affrighted, it drops it between its legs and runs off."[18]

Implicit in Tecumseh's address was the threat that the natives might turn on their outnumbered British allies if a stand were not made. It took Indian agent Matthew Elliott's most persuasive diplomacy to convince Tecumseh to bring his men and their wives and children up the Thames River to a point where they might make a stand. Still, many natives withdrew from the retreating column, especially the Miamis, Potawatomis, Chippewas, and Ottawas.

Tecumseh's once-proud confederation dwindled to approximately a thousand warriors. The British and their native allies began moving out of Sandwich on September 27, more than two weeks after the Americans had gained control of Lake Erie. The delay provided General Harrison time to assemble the watercraft and troops necessary to land on Canadian soil. The question was whether the British and their allies, burdened with women, children, supply boats, and wagons, could move fast enough to elude the advancing Americans. On the same day that Procter left Sandwich, Harrison's army landed on the Detroit River shore south of Amherstburg, and that evening they raised the American flag over the smoldering ruins of Fort Malden.

Once the news of Perry's victory reached Harrison, the Eighth Military District commander began issuing orders to subordinates to concentrate their forces at the mouth of the Portage River (modern Port Clinton, Ohio). Major Jesup's Schenectady boats had been concentrated in Sandusky Bay and were pulled across the narrow Marblehead peninsula dividing that body of water from the mouth of the Portage. General Duncan McArthur reduced the fortifications at Fort Meigs into a small stockade and then moved his men toward the rendezvous point. At Fort Meigs only Colonel Richard M. Johnson's mounted infantrymen remained, with orders to wait until the invasion fleet was launched before they would march to Detroit.

Harrison directed that supplies accumulating at Upper Sandusky and Camp Seneca be forwarded downstream and brought across the narrow isthmus, thereby avoiding over forty miles of navigation that might make the goods vulnerable to the hazards of Lake Erie storms. Pennsylvania, Ohio, and Kentucky volunteers arrived, although many of the Pennsylvanians had "constitutional scruples" about invading a foreign country and refused to cross the lake. By far the most important component of the assemblage was the mounted Kentucky unit commanded by Governor Isaac Shelby.

A key ingredient in Harrison's strategy was to engage friendly natives in the American cause and to dissuade hostile Indians from supporting the British. The general urged friendly Wyandot, Shawnee, and Seneca Indians in the vicinity join him in the enterprise, and approximately 260 did. At this conference

Harrison told the natives that they "must conform to our mode of warfare. You are not to kill defenceless prisoners, old men, women, or children."

The general subsequently sent some of these Wyandot allies to meet with disgruntled fellow tribesmen north of the River Raisin to see if they would remain neutral during an American advance in the Detroit Valley. Instead of just the Wyandots, however, British Indian agent Matthew Elliott saw to it that representatives of the most hostile tribes were also present. Reputedly, Wyandot war chief Walk-in-the-Water secretly sent a message to Harrison that he would try to keep his people out of the pending fight. Though Harrison remained skeptical of this possibility, he proved to be pleasantly surprised.[19]

Following the naval victory that had been assisted by army troops, it was Perry's turn to assist Harrison. For the cross-lake operation, Perry directed his efforts in five different areas. First, the navy transported most of Harrison's army from the mouth of the Portage River for an attack on Fort Malden. The mounted units built a strong fence of brush and fallen timber across the two-mile-wide isthmus between the Portage and Sandusky rivers and turned their horses loose to graze and await their owners' return. Thus, Governor Shelby's mounted Kentuckians now became infantrymen.[20]

Second, Perry planned for supporting naval gunfire during the Canadian landing (though it was unneeded because there was no British opposition). Third, his gunboats supported the ground forces in their advance up the Thames River. Fourth, his vessels brought supplies from eastern Lake Erie to the Detroit River area to supplement the limited agricultural provisions and military equipment available in the region. Finally, he maintained naval superiority on the Detroit River and Lake St. Clair—a relatively minor task given the capture of most of the Royal Naval vessels on Lake Erie a few days before.[21] Perry's actions constituted a degree of naval support for army operations unequalled in the War of 1812.

General Harrison consulted Perry on joint operational matters and heeded the naval officer's technical advice. An early instance of this came when the two officers and their staffs sailed on the *Ariel* up the Detroit River to reconnoiter a landing site for the ground forces being brought across the lake. Theirs was more than a cursory survey of the coast; Harrison's subsequent invasion order indicated a solid understanding of the geographic complexity and potential enemy situation he confronted.

Nowhere is this level of cooperation more apparent than in the operational order General Harrison issued on the eve of the amphibious attack on the Canadian shore. The minutely detailed order attempted to cover all expected exigencies. Harrison's initial landing parties were to be led by some of his most experienced officers. The general's directions for the navy were much less specific. The order merely required that the "arrangements for landing the troops will be made entirely under the direction of an officer of the navy whom Commodore Perry has been so obliging as to offer for that purpose. The debarkation of the troops will be covered by the cannon of the vessels." Given this latitude and trust, Perry assigned each warship to tow several of the bateaux during the approach toward the shore. Perry would superintend the squadron's fire support; Master Commandant Jesse D. Elliot would manage "the debarkation of the troops."[22]

A few of Perry's directives provide additional evidence of their cooperative efforts in the days following. He directed the commanders of two of his smaller vessels to "proceed to the Portage river . . . & take on board as many of Col. [Thomas] Smith's Reg. of Riflemen, as [your vessels] will carry & land them at Malden. If you are not able to bring them all, you will return to the river for the remainder." To Lieutenant Thomas Holdup he wrote, "You will keep as near the Army with the *Caledonia* as possible, that you may be enabled to deliver them provisions as called for." Lieutenant George Senat of the *Porcupine* received a directive to "proceed to the Lake St. Clair, and join me at the mouth of the river Thames, where the baggage you have on board for the army will be landed." During the pursuit of Procter, Master Commandant Elliott sailed up the Thames with the *Scorpion*, *Tigress*, and *Porcupine* providing artillery and logistical support plus river-crossing transportation for Harrison's rapidly advancing ground troops while Perry (now a captain) served the general as an aide-de-camp. As Perry informed Secretary Jones, "Every possible exertion will be made by the officers & men under my command to assist the advance of the Army, and it affords me great pleasure . . . to say, that the utmost harmony prevails between the Army and Navy." General Harrison confirmed this in a letter to Secretary Armstrong in which he noted that "Commodore Perry gives me every assistance in his power."[23]

A second instance of Harrison heeding Perry's counsel involved the pursuit of Procter, which could have gone either along the Thames or via water to a point on the north shore of Lake Erie where a short march would have placed the Americans in a blocking position capable of capturing the whole of Procter's force. Taking Perry's advice to use the land option rather than risk the fall storms on the lake, Harrison marched his combined columns east from Sandwich with Perry's gunboats supporting him.[24]

A third example of their mutual consultation involves the planned attack on Mackinac Island. After the victory at the Thames, Harrison and Perry planned to carry out the return of Fort Mackinac to American control that Secretary of War Armstrong desired. Eventually this plan was abandoned due to Perry's concerns regarding weather conditions on Lake Huron in the fall.[25]

While all these joint army-navy efforts ensued, stationed at the much-reduced Fort Meigs and apprehensive about their being used in the campaign, Colonel Richard M. Johnson's Kentucky mounted riflemen finally received orders to advance northward. Harrison sequenced the mounted soldiers' movement at a slower pace than the amphibious one so that the natives would learn of the capture of Fort Malden before Johnson's men came to their vicinity. Consequently, the mounted Kentuckians found little opposition as they moved toward Detroit, which they reached on 30 September.[26]

After landing south of Amherstburg, Harrison's amphibious forces marched toward Sandwich; Perry's armada moved up the Detroit River along with them. On 29 September the army entered the Canadian town, and Perry immediately began ferrying General McArthur's brigade across to Detroit. Perry also sent Master Commandant Elliott with the *Niagara, Lady Prevost,*

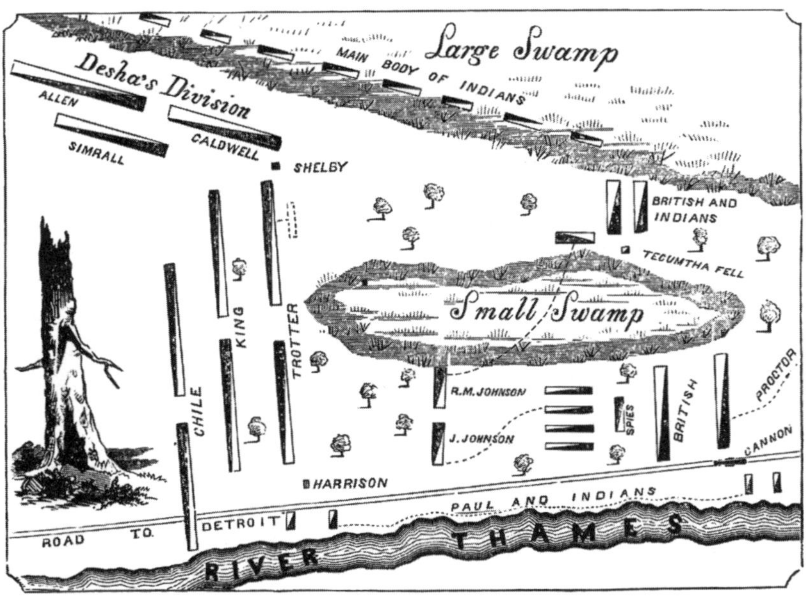

The Battle of the Thames. Reprinted from Benson J. Lossing, *Pictorial Field-Book of the War of 1812* (New York: Harper Brothers, 1869), as modified by Bill Nelson Maps.

Scorpion, and *Tigress* up the river and into Lake St. Clair in an unsuccessful attempt to capture the British vessels loaded with baggage and weaponry. On 30 September and 1 October, Perry's sailors ferried Colonel Johnson's mounted infantrymen and their horses across the river to Sandwich. Once he knew Harrison would pursue Procter by land, Perry proceeded with the *Ariel* and *Caledonia* to the mouth of the Thames River. The *Porcupine* joined them shortly thereafter, and the three gunboats crossed the Thames bar into the river. Under Elliott's command, the *Scorpion, Tigress,* and *Porcupine,* carrying army supplies, proceeded up the river for several miles until it became clear that the steep river banks would not allow their artillery to be useful, and then they were left behind under army guard. Perry joined Harrison's staff as a volunteer aide-de-camp. For the next several miles some bateaux and captured canoes carried supplies for the army until it neared Moraviantown. Throughout the campaign Perry kept his pledge "to cooperate with the Army," with his other vessels being "employed in the transportation of troops, provisions &c for the Army."[27]

While Perry's sailors ferried Johnson's men and horses across the River on 1 October, Harrison held a conference with Governor Shelby. The two concluded that Procter's force might be caught in less than four days if they followed the British along the southern shore of Lake St. Clair and then eastward along the Thames River. They also considered the option of having Perry's squadron tow the Schenectady boats loaded with his soldiers and their baggage to a point on Lake Erie's Canadian shore where a short march northward would interpose his forces between Procter's and the Niagara peninsula. Many thought that Procter's three-day head start made the success of the land option unlikely. Perry doubted that the winds would allow a timely movement out of the Detroit River and along the lakeshore to intercept Procter. There were also apprehensions that Procter might pick up Canadian militia reinforcements as he withdrew. The two options were presented to a meeting of general officers. Eventually, Harrison indicated his and Shelby's preference for the land route, and this became the route of advance. Speed now became the most important aspect of the ensuing operation.[28]

Harrison's allocation of forces under his command seems almost deliberately done to incite the disgust and opposition of Secretary of War Armstrong. The regular army infantry brigade of General McArthur remained in Detroit, where they protected the residents from the natives and the natives from the Kentuckians. It was feared that the Miamis and Potawatomis who remained in Michigan might attack Detroit during Harrison's pursuit. For the secretary of war, this force allocation was an affront to his emphasis on employing regulars over volunteers when possible. As it was highly probable that the pursuit might result in an encounter with British regulars, Armstrong feared the volunteers lacked the discipline and training necessary for formal combat. General Harrison determined that his Kentuckians had more combat experience and military zeal than the recently recruited regulars. Harrison took with him only 150 regulars from the 27th U.S. Infantry plus about 200 natives in a force numbering near 3,000.

At sunrise on 2 October the Americans began their march. With Colonel Johnson's horsemen in the lead, the army troops set a rugged pace and covered twenty-five miles the first day and encamped only nine miles from the mouth of the Thames. The primitive roads were lined with trees in the full bloom of fall color, and the barns were filled with the plenty from the recent harvest. It took great restraint on the officers' part to curb looting. It appears that General Procter did not expect a land pursuit. He left bridges intact and during the first couple of days appears not to have had a rear guard of scouts to ascertain Harrison's actions. The Americans covered over forty miles in two days and moved along the south banks of the River Thames. Procter learned that Harrison was no more than a day behind him and that the Americans lacked the burdensome logistical train and families that accompanied the British and natives. He was going to be compelled to stand and fight the opponent that deeply detested him personally.

Both armies were hampered by an incessant rain that slowed their progress. The rains had made the roads so impassable that along the primitive wilderness trail the British abandoned military and personal baggage and wagons. Although Tecumseh's warriors harassed the American advance parties, they caused no significant delay.[29]

As they neared the hamlet of Moraviantown (where Moravian missionaries had established a settlement for the Christian Delawares), there was evidence of the hasty and obviously overencumbered British-Indian retreat. A schooner containing military stores was left burning in the river, and a house had been torched in an effort to destroy hundreds of shoulder weapons (many of which were rescued from the flames). After a march of a few more miles the Americans found another vessel in flames and near it a distillery containing ordnance and naval stores on fire. The British abandoned the last of their supply bateaux, including approximately 174 wounded and sick men who surrendered. The Americans used these vessels to cross the river to its north bank, where the British and their allies were assembled.[30]

They were about three miles short of the Moravian mission. By anchoring his line on the Thames and the swamp, General Procter exploited the terrain as much as he could. Except for the area in the vicinity of the road, the battlefield was lightly to heavily wooded, making it difficult to determine the actions of friend or foe. The woods would make it impossible for advancing American infantry to maintain their formations. Thus, the redcoats "silently awaited" the attack, "each determined to do his duty, but very few with any doubt as to the result."[31] Needless to say, the morale of the British troops was at low ebb.

As was his wont, General Harrison conducted his prebattle arrangements with caution. Finally, at 2:30 P.M., Harrison signaled for Colonel Richard Johnson's mounted riflemen to attack, crying, "Charge them, my brave Kentuckians!" A bugle sounded on the right, and its call was soon echoed by others along the American line. Lieutenant Colonel James Johnson's mounted battalion dashed forward and soon drove through the left wing of the British infantry, causing the remainder to flee to the second line. The Kentuckians soon surrounded them, and the British quickly surrendered. It was all over in less than ten minutes.

As soon as he noted the American penetration of his line, General Procter, Indian agent Matthew Elliott, and their cavalry escort fled to the rear, dashing past the column of wagons, women, and children along the road and disappearing into the woods. Both Procter and Elliott knew full well that no prisoner of war legalisms could spare them from the wrath of the Kentuckians who wanted revenge on the men they felt were the architects of the River Raisin massacre and other frontier atrocities. There was no doubt, wrote one contemporary observer, that while the Kentuckians would spare the British who surrendered, there was the exception of Procter and Elliott—"these, neither the authority of Harrison nor of Shelby could have saved."[32]

But the rout of the British line did not end the battle. From the trees on the American left, the native allies put up a withering fire. Not joining his brother in the charge against the main British line, Colonel Richard Johnson's men struggled through a small swamp. Soon most of them were dismounted by the dense underbrush and native gunfire. Even so, the Kentuckians hit the left flank of the natives and the few British troops located at this position. Tecumseh's voice could be heard giving orders to his warriors as they attacked the ragged line of Kentuckians, but soon one of these riflemen cut him down.

Colonel Johnson was wounded five times, and several of his men were killed. Whether or not the Kentucky colonel killed the native chieftain will remain a controversy, but there is little doubt that Tecumseh died from a bullet fired by someone from Johnson's regiment. The remnants of Tecumseh's defiant confederacy withdrew into the large swamp, not pursued by the Americans. It was over in less than half an hour. For these natives the era of serious armed resistance to American advance into the Ohio Valley and Great Lakes was over. According to Harrison, Perry's presence and conduct during the battle "cheered and animated every breast."[33] The Battle of the Thames, or Moraviantown, as the Canadians call it, was the first major American land victory of the war.

Throughout the campaign, the navy provided logistical support to the army, especially in bringing supplies from Erie and Cleveland to the rapidly moving North West Army as it advanced deep into the Western District of Upper Canada. Finally, after the Battle of the Thames, Perry's squadron transported regular army elements of Harrison's army from Detroit to the Niagara frontier. Perry acknowledged that the Canadian invasion did not allow his officers and men "to shew gallantry" in combat, but, he told Secretary of the Navy Jones, "they evinced throughout, the greatest disposition to be serviceable in transporting the Army and rendering it, every assistance in their power."[34]

The Harrison-Perry cooperation constitutes one of the few successful joint efforts in early American military history. Seldom had commanders from different services worked together more closely and efficiently than these young commanders (Harrison was just forty and Perry twenty-eight years old). Harrison and Perry achieved that unity of effort that was critical to the attainment of the national objective. In the often ignored aftermath of Perry's naval victory, they overcame interservice ambitions and operational biases to focus on a common goal. Undoubtedly, some of this was because of Perry's deference to Harrison's rank, experience, and professionalism. But Harrison also exhibited a degree of respect toward his junior colleague in his laudatory reports regarding the naval commander's actions. Perhaps the best example of this mutual admiration came when Harrison allowed Perry to cosign a proclamation establishing government in the recently conquered area of Upper Canada. Such an honor was indeed singular, especially since none of the general officers under Harrison's command signed the document.[35] Theirs was an excellent example of how coordination may be achieved by cooperation without vesting command authority in a single individual. Such joint operational activity requires cooperative personal relationships between each service commander and a willingness to subordinate particular service preferences for a common objective. Or, as Secretary Jones wrote, commanding officers from different services should "cherish harmony, rather than punctilio."[36] Harrison and Perry exemplified the implementation of that credo.

NOTES

1. Alfred Brunson, *A Western Pioneer,* 2 vols. (Cincinnati: Hitchcock & Walden, 1872): 1:121. Similar sentiments are found in Eleazer Wood, "Journal of the Northwestern Campaign of 1812–13," in *Campaigns of the War of 1812–15,* ed. George W. Cullum (New York: James Miller, 1879): 404–7; and Robert B. McAfee, *History of the Late War in the Western Country* (Bowling Green, OH: Historical Publications Co., 1919), 304–5, 390.

2. Primary sources on the Detroit campaign are in E. A Cruikshank, ed., *Documents Relating to the Invasion of Canada and the Surrender of Detroit, 1812,* Publications of Canadian Archives, No. 7 (Ottawa: Government Printing Bureau, 1913); Milo M. Quaife, ed., *The John Askin Papers,* 2 vols. (Detroit: Detroit Library Commission, 1931): 2:708–23. Among the better secondary accounts are Robert S. Quimby, *The U.S. Army in the War of 1812: An Operational and Command Study,* 2 vols. (East Lansing: Michigan State University Press, 1997), Alec R. Gilpin, *The War of 1812 in the Old Northwest* (East Lansing: Michigan State University Press, 1958), George F. G. Stanley, *The War of 1812: Land Operations* (Toronto: National Museums of Canada and Macmillan, 1983).

3. Eustis to WHH, 2 Sept. 1812, Douglas E. Clanin et al., eds., *The Papers of William Henry Harrison, 1800–1815,* 10 microfilm reels (Indianapolis: Indiana Historical Society, 1993–99), 6:56.

4. Shelby to Armstrong, 21 Feb. 1813, Richard C. Knopf, ed., *Document Transcriptions of the War of 1812 in the Northwest,* 10 vols. (Columbus, OH: Anthony Wayne Parkway Board and Ohio State Historical Society, 1956–62), vol. 7, pt. 1:685–86.

5. U.S. Department of Defense, Dictionary of Military and Associated Terms, Joint Pub 1–02, (Washington, DC: Department of Defense, 2001), 295; available online at www.dtic.mil/doctrine/jel/doddict; Maurice Matloff, ed., *American Military History* (Washington, DC: Office of the Chief of Military History, 1969), 9. The current army definition of "unity of command" reads: "For every objective, ensure unity of effort under one responsible commander. Applying a force's full combat power requires unity of command. Unity of command means that a single commander directs and coordinates the actions of all forces toward a common objective. Cooperation may produce coordination, but giving a single commander the required authority is the most effective way to achieve unity of effort. The joint, interagency, intergovernmental, and multinational nature of unified action creates situations where the commander does not directly control all organizations in the operational area. In the absence of command authority, commanders cooperate, negotiate, and build consensus to achieve unity of effort." Department of the Army, *Operations,* FM 3–0 (Washington, DC: Department of the Army, 2008), A-3. See also U.S. Department of the Army, *Operations,* FM 100–5 (Washington: Department of the Army, 1976), 2–6–2–8. For early-nineteenth-century doctrine on service command distinctions, see War Department Regulation, 8 Apr. 1813, Knopf, *Document Transcriptions,* 8:141.

6. WHH to Eustis, 12 Dec. 1812, Clanin, *WHH Papers,* 6:791.

7. Circular, Hamilton to Selected officers, 20 June 1812, William S. Dudley and Michael J. Crawford, eds., *The Naval War of 1812: A Documentary History,* 3 vols. (Washington, DC: Department of the Navy, 1985–), 1:140; Monroe to WHH, 26 Dec. 1812, Clanin, *WHH Papers,* 7:63–69.

8. Shelby to Armstrong, 21 Feb. 1813, Jesup to Armstrong, 27 Mar. 1812, Knopf, *Document Transcriptions,* vol. 7, pt. 1:122–23, 198; Jesup to Armstrong, 11 and 12 Apr., 5 and 14 June, 1 Aug. 1813, ibid., pt. 2:25, 31, 158, pt. 3:51. See also Armstrong to WHH, 5 Mar. 1813, Clanin, *WHH Papers;* Armstrong to Jesup, 9 Mar. 1813, *American State Papers: Military Affairs,* 7 vols. (Washington, DC: Gales & Seaton, 1832–), 1:452. Secondary sources include Frederick C. Drake, "Loss of Mastery: The British Squadron on Lake Erie, May–September 1813," *Journal of Erie Studies* (Fall 1989): 54–57; and Howard S. Miller and Jack Alden Clarke, "Ships in the Wilderness: A Note on the Invasion of Canada," *Ohio History* 71 (July 1962): 124–28.

9. Armstrong to WHH, 3 Apr. 1813, Knopf, *Document Transcriptions,* 8:138–39.

10. McAfee, *History,* 360.

11. Jones to Perry, 3 July 1813, Dudley and Crawford, *Naval War,* 2:487–88.

12. Regulations, 8 Apr. 1813, Knopf, ed., *Document Transcriptions,* 8:141.

13. John Norris to A. S. Goodman, 27 Mar. 1869, ibid., 10:157. In one case Lieutenant James Coburn of Captain John Paine's troop of Kentucky cavalry led fifteen of his men on the *Caledonia.* These "horse marines" later brought the British ship *General Hunter* to Put-in-Bay. The best discussion of the composition of Perry's crews is found in Gerard T. Altoff, *Deep Water Sailors, Shallow Water Soldiers: Manning the United States Fleet on Lake Erie—1813* (Put-in-Bay, OH: Perry Group, 1993).

14. WHH to Perry, 5 July 1813, and A. H. Holmes [for WHH] to Perry, 23 July 1813, Clanin, *WHH Papers,* 8:506–7, 597.

15. Altoff, *Deep Water Sailors,* 40. A close look at Altoff's extensive list indicates that most of the hands on the four trailing gunboats were soldiers. The *Trippe,* for instance, had a crew of thirty-five, of whom only eleven were sailors. Ibid., 33.

16. Perry to WHH, 10 Sept. 1813, to Jones, 10 September 1813, Dudley and Crawford, *Naval War,* 2:553–54; John Norris to A. T. Goodman, 7 Apr. 1869, Knopf, *Document Transcriptions,* 10:158. On the Battle of Lake Erie, see David Curtis Skaggs and Gerard T. Altoff, *A Signal Victory: The Lake Erie Campaign, 1812–1813* (Annapolis, MD: Naval Institute Press, 1997), 118–48; Michael A. Palmer, "It Is Better to Make a Signal than to Curse One's Subordinates: Oliver Hazard Perry and the Battle of Lake Erie" and Walter R. Rybka, "Observations on the Sailing Characteristics of the U.S. Brig *Niagara,*" David Curtis Skaggs, ed., *The Battle of Lake Erie and Its Aftermath* (Kent, OH: Kent State University Press, 2013).

17. James Cochrane, "The War in Canada, 1812–1814" (unpublished manuscript, ca. 1840, Welsh Regimental Museum, Cardiff Castle, South Wales, UK), 55–59; Horsman, *Elliott,* 212.

18. McAfee, *History,* 400–404.

19. Ibid., 375.

20. Brunson, *Western Pioneer,* 1:129; McAfee, *History,* 391–95.

21. Perry to Jones, 24 and [ca. 28] Sept. 1813, Dudley and Crawford, *Naval War,* 2:269; General Orders, 27 September 1813, directing the joint landings on the shore south of Ft. Malden, Clanin, *WHH Papers,* 9:273–79.

22. General Orders, 27 Sept. 1813, Clanin, *WHH Papers,* 9:273–79; Perry to Officers in Charge of Prime Vessels, 22 Sept. 1813, Order Book, Lake Erie, 1813, Perry Papers, William L. Clements Library, University of Michigan, Ann Arbor; McAfee, *History,* 391–400.

23. Perry to J. E. McDonald, to Thomas Holdup, and to Senate, 2 Oct. 1813, Order Book, Lake Erie, 1813, Perry to Jones, 20 Oct. 1813, Perry Papers; WHH to Armstrong, 22 Sept. and 9 Oct. 1813, Clanin, *WHH Papers,* 9:256, 323–34; Perry to Jones, 24 Sept., 7 Oct. 1813, Dudley and Crawford, *Naval War,* 2:569–70.

24. McAfee, *History,* 411–12; Harrison's after-action report to Armstrong, 9 Oct. 1813, Clanin, *WHH Papers,* 9:323–34.

25. WHH to Armstrong, 10 and 16 Oct. 1813, and WHH to Meigs, 11 Oct. 1813, Clanin, *WHH Papers,* 9:344, 357, 410–11.

26. McAfee, *History,* 406–10.

27. Perry to Jones, [ca. 1 Oct.], 7 Oct. 1813, Dudley and Crawford, *Naval War,* 2:570; WHH to Armstrong, 9 Oct. 1813, Clanin, *WHH Papers,* 9:323–34.

28. McAfee, *History,* 411–12.

29. Ibid., 413–18; Cochrane, "War in Canada," 59–61.

30. McAfee, *History,* 417–18.

31. Cochrane, "War in Canada," 63.

32. Samuel R. Brown, *Views of the Campaigns of the North-Western Army* (Troy, NY: Francis Adancourt, 1814), 74. Colonel Johnson's claim to have personally killed the Indian chieftain would lead to the most inane campaign slogan in American history: "Rumpsey dumpsey, rumpsey dumpsey, Colonel Johnson killed Tecumseh."

33. For the Thames campaign, see Alexander Clark Casselman, ed., *Richardson's War of 1812* (Toronto: Historical Publishing, 1902), 204–42; Lowell H. Harrison, ed., "Nat Crain and the Battle of the Thames," *Filson Club History Quarterly* 64 (July 1990): 377–83; WHH to Armstrong, 9 Oct. 1813, in Clanin, ed., *WHH Papers,* 9:323–34 (also in Dudley and Crawford, *Naval War,* 2:570–76); Procter to de Rottenburg, 23 Oct. 3 and 16 Nov. 1813, Wood, *Select British Documents,* 2:323–27, 331–32, 338–41; McAfee, *History,* 419–32; Cochrane, "War in Canada," 62–66. Secondary sources include Sandy Antal, *A Wampum Denied: Procter's War of 1812* (Ottawa: Carleton University Press, 1997), 297–353; Stanley, *War of 1812,* 201–14; Quimby, *U.S. Army in the War of 1812,* 1:270–92; Cleaves, *Old Tippecanoe,* 188–205; Gilpin, *War . . . in the Old Northwest,* 214–34; John Sugden, *Tecumseh: A Life* (New York: Henry Holt, 1997), 355–80, Anthony J. Yanik, *The Fall and Recapture of Detroit in the War of 1812: In Defense of William Hull* (Detroit: Wayne State University Press, 2011), 153–75.

34. Perry to Jones, 24 Sept. 1813, Dudley and Crawford, *Naval War,* 2:569.

35. A Proclamation, 18 Oct. 1813, Clanin, *WHH Papers,* 9:435–36.

36. Jones to Chauncey, 8 April 1813, Dudley and Crawford, *Naval War,* 2: 434.

“No One Acquired Any Military Glory in This Affair”

The American Attempt to Retake Mackinac, 1814

BRIAN LEIGH DUNNIGAN

Humphrey H. Leavitt was cold, wet, sick, and dispirited as he sailed down Lake Huron aboard the U.S. schooner *Caledonia* in the second week of August 1814. The moaning of injured soldiers and the stench of their wounds had driven the eighteen-year-old aide-de-camp from shelter below deck to sleep in the open air. There “the chilling atmosphere, and drenching fogs of August nights” caused him to awaken each morning “thoroughly chilled, and my blankets saturated with water from the dense fogs.” Young Leavitt was one of the officers and men of William Cotgreave’s regiment of Ohio Volunteers who had been crammed aboard the *Caledonia* since mid-July. Sick for much of this time, he had been dosed heavily by the surgeon with “narcotic medicines” and had thus been unable to land and fight the British and Indians on Mackinac Island on 4 August. His fellow soldiers were repulsed in that battle and withdrew to the ships. “Thus ended the ill-directed and disastrous expedition against Mackinac,” opined Leavitt as the high mass of the island dropped below the horizon on 6 August.[1]

Leavitt and his naval and military comrades in arms had participated in an ambitious but strategically unsound and ultimately unsuccessful amphibious operation that had been made possible by Oliver Hazard Perry’s Lake Erie victory of September 1813. With naval control of the upper Great Lakes firmly in the hands of the U.S. Navy, it had been feasible to transport a military force into distant and poorly charted Lake Huron in an attempt to retake the strategic northern post of Michilimackinac, which had been captured by the British at the very outset of the War of 1812. Although the operation dealt a blow to the North West Company's fur-trading establishment at Sault St. Marie and destroyed the abandoned Fort St. Joseph and the lone, armed British vessel on the upper lakes, it proved unable to dislodge the stubborn garrison of Michilimackinac. Lackluster leadership of the American force coupled with the difficult terrain of Mackinac Island and the determination and resilience of its British and Native American defenders ensured that Michilimackinac would not be regained by force of arms in 1814.

The objective of the 1814 expedition was a military and fur-trading post situated some 300 miles north of Detroit on a steeply elevated, 2,400-acre island at the eastern end of the Straits of Mackinac, the connecting body of water between Lake Huron and Lake Michigan. Mackinac Island was strategically located where it could influence the trade in furs that moved through Lake Michigan and Lake Superior to the north. The island was also a convenient resort of the northern Indian nations, particularly the Ottawas and Ojibwes of the nearby region as well as groups from as far west as Wisconsin and the upper Mississippi River. Michilimackinac, as one correspondent noted in the summer of 1812, "owes its consequence entirely to Indian trade."[2]

Overlooking the town and harbor from a 120-foot-high bluff on the south shore of the island stood Fort Mackinac, a fortification originally constructed by the British in the early 1780s and finally relinquished to the Americans in 1796 in fulfillment of the 1783 treaty that ended the War for Independence and established a boundary between the United States and British North America. The former British garrison withdrew about fifty miles to the northeast, where it established a new fort on St. Joseph Island near the mouth of the St. Mary's River and just inside their territory.

The chief strength of Fort Mackinac was its commanding position atop the bluff, where it had been laid out to protect the harbor below and cover the traders' village that lined the shore. Cobbled together from stonework, earth, and logs, it was not particularly impressive as a fortification. Worse, at a distance of only a few hundred yards to the north, Fort Mackinac was dominated by higher ground where well-placed artillery would soon pound it to rubble. Considering this enormous defect in the fort's position, any significant improvements to the fortifications would have been futile. Instead, Fort Mackinac's American garrison had done its best, in 1798–99, to make the place tenable against an attack by Indians or troops possessing only small arms. Pickets were erected on the walls and three blockhouses were constructed as strong points and positions for light cannon. There was neither the money nor the manpower to fortify the high ground behind the fort.[3]

The declaration of war in June 1812 found the condition of Fort Mackinac unchanged and its garrison composed of a single company of artillery numbering sixty-one men. Despite rising tensions in the West since the autumn of 1811, Lieutenant Porter Hanks and his officers remained unaware of the outbreak of hostilities as late as the third week of July. The British commandant of Fort St. Joseph was more promptly informed, and, gathering his even smaller garrison, Captain Charles Roberts enlisted the aid of several hundred Canadian fur traders and double that number of native warriors to descend on Mackinac Island on the night of July 17. Landing on the far western end of the island, they marched along a rough track through the woods, placed a single 6-pounder cannon on the rising ground behind the fort, and called on Hanks to surrender. Heavily outnumbered and faced with the implied threat of Roberts's likely inability to control his Indian allies, the American officer promptly complied.[4]

For the British, this was a signal victory with both military and commercial benefits. Not only was the influence of the United States removed from the northern Great Lakes, but Britain's commercial and diplomatic ties with the Indians were also strengthened. The British would fight to defend this advantage. "The Island and Fort of Michilimackinac is of the first importance, as tending to promote our Indian connexion and secure them in our interest," Governor General Sir George Prevost wrote in the summer of 1814. Michilimackinac's influence was felt across a vast region, and it provided "security to the great trading establishments of the North-West and Hudson's Bay Companies, by supporting the Indians on the Mississippi."[5] The collapse of American forces at Detroit and Chicago in August 1812 further cemented Britain's influence over the northern nations.

For the United States, the fall of Michilimackinac was the first in a series of humiliating defeats that would not be fully reversed until Perry's victory on Lake Erie on 10 September 1813, the subsequent recovery of Detroit, and the decisive defeat of British and Native American forces at the Battle of the Thames in October 1813. This resurgence of American arms suddenly exposed Michilimackinac to the possibility of attack at a time when it was particularly vulnerable, for the capture of the place had not been followed by reinforcement of its British garrison. Few resources had, in fact, been devoted to the post, and its commandant had not even been able to fortify the higher ground behind the fort that had been the instrument of British victory in 1812.[6]

The Michilimackinac garrison was fortunate to survive 1813 without a fight, for the Americans had every intention of making an attempt on the place. As early as July, Commodore Isaac Chauncey had ordered Perry to follow up success on Lake Erie by moving against the British on Lake Huron. He was authorized to cut Michilimackinac's communications with Canada and then take the post, which, Chauncey noted, "ought to be garrisoned and kept."[7] An immediate strike might have been successful, but the difficulties of logistics and weather in the northern lakes favored the British. Although naval vessels and troops were promptly assembled at Detroit in early October, a shortage of provisions and violent autumn storms had ended any hopes for an operation by the middle of the month.[8] A week later, Canadian fur trader and Indian agent Robert Dickson expressed confidence from Michilimackinac that, since the Americans were now unlikely to appear until spring, "with the proper support we will be able to baffle any attempt of the Enemy for the next season."[9]

Support was indeed forthcoming during the winter and spring of 1814, although the size of the reinforcement was not large. Two companies of the Royal Newfoundland Regiment, a few artillerymen, and a detachment of Royal Navy sailors were sent overland from Kingston by way of Lake Simcoe to the Nottawasaga River at the southern end of Georgian Bay. After a difficult winter march, the men constructed boats and embarked with supplies for Michilimackinac on 22 April. Negotiating fields of floating ice and severe late winter weather, they reached their destination on 18 May, much to the relief of the garrison. Leading the reinforcements was Lieutenant Colonel Robert McDouall of the Glengarry Light Infantry Fencibles, who assumed command of Michilimackinac.[10] McDouall was, in many ways, the most valuable part of the reinforcement, and his energy and determination would do much to preserve the British position on the northern lakes.

McDouall immediately set about preparing for the anticipated American assault. The old fort was strengthened, and, most important, the troops constructed a redoubt and blockhouse on the island's highest point overlooking Fort Mackinac and the lake below. By 17 July the second anniversary of the capture of Michilimackinac, the fortification, dubbed Fort George, was nearly complete, and McDouall could boast that its position was "one of the strongest in Canada" and that "no force that the Enemy can bring will be able to reduce it."[11] McDouall also acted to supplement his small body of regular troops with local manpower. Although large numbers of voyageurs were not available as they had been in 1812, in part because of the diversion of some of them on 28 June to counter the occupation by the Americans of Prairie du Chien on the Mississippi River, some militia were summoned from Sault Ste. Marie and considerable numbers of Native Americans responded to the colonel's call to face the Americans. By the time U.S. naval vessels appeared in late July, McDouall could count his available forces as about 200 regulars and local fencibles, 100 militia, and around 350 native warriors.[12] This was a force to be reckoned with, particularly when alert, well led, and in possession of the formidable terrain of Mackinac Island.

For the Americans, Michilimackinac represented unfinished business from the 1813 campaign and the humiliating events of 1812. The strategic necessity of taking it back from the British was less apparent. The post was acknowledged to be of importance to the fur trade, and its possession aided the British in the maintenance of their Indian alliances that had been strained by the loss of Detroit and Malden and the death of Tecumseh in the autumn of 1813. But the Americans were also planning a major campaign on the Niagara River, and the naval vessels and troops that would be sent against Michilimackinac might be better used to support operations on eastern Lake Erie. The northern lakes were far from the areas where a decisive blow could be struck against British forces in Canada. As Secretary of War John Armstrong advised President Madison, operations on Lake Ontario would have a more telling effect, but "take Mackinaw, and what is gained but Mackinaw itself?"[13]

The justification for launching the expedition against Michilimackinac seems to have come, ironically enough, from the British attempt to secure the post by building boats on Georgian Bay and transporting reinforcements to Fort Mackinac. Intelligence suggested to the Americans that the British effort was more substantial than it actually was and that it was possible that new naval vessels were to be constructed for service on Lake Huron. On 1 June the secretary of the navy ordered Commodore Arthur Sinclair, now commanding on the upper lakes, to undertake a full attempt against Michilimackinac to break up this supposed establishment. The military component was to be drawn from troops at Detroit and the new Fort Gratiot at the head of the St. Clair River, and Lieutenant Colonel George Croghan was entrusted with the command of the land forces. In ordering him on this duty, Secretary of War Armstrong reminded him that the "safety of Detroit, the command of the lakes, the general security of that frontier depends upon it." Armstrong ordered Croghan to embark as many men as could be accommodated aboard Sinclair's squadron. Surgeon Usher Parsons, serving aboard the brig *Lawrence* during the expedition, understood its purpose to be "to retake Mackinac by storm and also destroy any shipping there may be on the upper lakes."[14]

Commodore Sinclair's naval component included Perry's two heavily armed brigs, *Niagara* and *Lawrence;* the schooners *Caledonia, Tigress,* and *Scorpion;* and three small supply vessels. The ships and troops gathered at Fort Gratiot at the entrance to Lake Huron, where the military force was fully embarked and the squadron sailed on 14 July. The soldiers included five companies of regular infantry drawn from the 17th, 19th, and 24th regiments; a detachment of the Corps of Artillery with a few light field guns; and Colonel William Cotgreave's regiment of Ohio Volunteer Infantry. Altogether, the troops numbered between 750 and 800. Conditions aboard the vessels were crowded and uncomfortable. The *Lawrence* carried more than 300 of the regulars, while the same number of Ohio troops was squeezed into the *Caledonia.*[15] Presumably the balance of the regulars embarked on the *Niagara.*

Sinclair led his squadron directly for Georgian Bay and the shipbuilding establishment he supposed to be located on Matchedash Bay. His effort was soon frustrated, however, by the difficulties of navigating the treacherous waters with their myriad islands and channels. Croghan later reported that "the Commodore, from the want of Pilots acquainted with that unfrequented part of the Lake, despair'd of being able to find out a passage through the Islands into that Bay." Although Croghan claimed that the search for a way to Matchedash Bay consumed a week, Surgeon Parsons's diary makes it clear that Sinclair searched for only two days before giving up and that the squadron turned north toward Michilimackinac on 16 July. Near the conclusion of the hunt for an entrance, a sail was sighted in the distance. This was presumed to be the North West Company's schooner *Nancy,* the only armed British vessel of any size on the lake; but after an initial order by Sinclair to give chase, the pursuit was called off, probably because of the difficulty of finding a way through the islands.[16]

By the evening of the 19th, Sinclair's squadron had arrived at the northern end of Lake Huron, negotiated the Detour Passage, and sighted Fort St. Joseph, which it found abandoned. The men stripped its buildings of useful items and set it afire the next day. On 21 July a sail appeared in the river, the small North West Company schooner *Mink* with a cargo of flour. It was promptly taken and added to the U.S. flotilla. Efforts to disrupt the British position on the St. Mary's River continued with the 22 July dispatch of boats under Lieutenant Daniel Turner of the *Scorpion* and soldiers led by Major Andrew Hunter Holmes, Croghan's second-in-command. They proceeded to Sault Ste. Marie, where they destroyed the North West Company establishment and took a Lake Superior trading schooner found above the rapids. Turner's men saved the vessel from destruction by its own crew only to see her fatally bilged when they attempted to bring her down the river. They left the *Scorpion* at St. Joseph to await the return of Turner and Holmes and rejoined the fleet off Mackinac Island on 30 July. [17]

In the meantime, most of the squadron had sailed toward its ultimate goal, the post of Michilimackinac, where Croghan and Sinclair reported that they arrived on the 26 July. This was the first that most of the Americans had seen of the place, and they were struck by its dramatic topography. Sinclair later described the island as "a perfect Gibraltar, being a high inaccessible Rock on every side except the west" from which the only approach to the fort was through thick woods and underbrush, the route used by the British in 1812.[18] Fort Mackinac overlooked the harbor and likely landing places on the southeast end of the island, while the new redoubt, Fort George, stood on the hill behind it more than 300 feet above the lake. The terrain and the fact that the British had "strongly foretified" the dominating heights deeply impressed Colonel Croghan, and he later admitted to Secretary Armstrong, "I at once despair'd of being able, with my Small force, to carry the place by storm."[19]

Croghan's attitude was apparent to many of the naval and military officers. He had disapproved of the operation in the first place, believing, as he told his superior, General Duncan McArthur, "if it be taken, we are not at all benefitted."[20] Moreover, he thought his force too small for the task, particularly after having observed the island and its defenses. He also believed that the British and Indians outnumbered him, which they did not, although the two land forces were not much different in actual numbers, a fact that favored the defenders and gave some substance to Croghan's concern. A pair of local French residents of Point St. Ignace, located on the mainland to the west of Mackinac Island, confirmed on 31 July, with only slight exaggeration, that the British had 400 regulars and militia and as many Indians.[21]

Sinclair and Croghan had limited options for approaching the British position, but they at least enjoyed the mobility afforded by the vessels and could select their landing place. Their choices were essentially the relatively level ground behind the village of Michilimackinac and below Fort Mackinac or the lengthier and much rougher uphill route from the low, western end of the island. The first possibility allowed the troops to land and advance under cover of the heavy guns of the warships. This was apparently the preferred approach, as it would not permit the Indians to operate as effectively as they could in the woods. The problem was Sinclair's discovery that, because of the height of Fort Mackinac above the lake, the ships' guns "could not when near enough to do him [the enemy] an injury elevate sufficiently to batter" the fort. Fort George was even more inaccessible, "commanding every point of the Island, and almost perpendicular on all sides." This discovery probably took place on 27 July when the *Niagara* exchanged fire with one of the fort's blockhouses, although Sinclair pointed out that his vessels drew enemy shot on "several instances." Islander Samuel Lasley recalled having watched a large brig trade fire with the fort only to have its 24-pounder ball fall short and merely plough up a potato patch on the lower ground.[22]

By 30 July, with most of the squadron having hung off the island for four days, Surgeon Parsons heard that Croghan was talking of not landing. It was time for a decision, made even more imperative by the fact that the expedition, through some oversight, was seriously short of provisions. By 27 July, Parsons reported in his diary, the army was entirely out of food and was being supplied by the navy. By the following day the sailors were on three-quarter rations, while the soldiers were receiving only half. Humphrey Leavitt pointed out that the problem had been discovered soon after entering Lake Huron and that the shortage was due to a "villainous omission" by those who provided for the "military part" of the expedition.[23] It was apparent that action had to be taken, for there was no way to obtain additional provisions on northern Lake Huron.

On 31 July Colonel Croghan and "other officers" gathered aboard the *Lawrence* for a council of war. They heard the estimate of the enemy force from the prisoners taken at St. Ignace, and Croghan left the meeting "with the determination to fight."[24] It was probably at this time that he formulated or agreed to a plan to land on the low, western end of the island and establish his troops "on some favorable position, whence I could be enabled to annoy the enemy by gradual and slow approaches, under cover of my artillery, in which I should have the superiority in point of metal." He argued that this passive approach, accomplished under cover of the guns of the ships, would cause the British to either attack him or risk the defection of their Indian allies, who accounted for half their numbers. Croghan had been informed by "individuals who had lived many years on the Island" that such a position could be found not far from the beach.[25]

The local informants were John Dousman and Ambrose Davenport, who had left Mackinac Island in 1812 after having refused to take the British oath of allegiance. The position they recommended was a cleared area of some 200 acres of farmland and orchard occupied by Dousman's brother, Michael. Through this land ran the rough road from the beach to Fort Mackinac about a mile and a half to the southeast. It offered open space for a lodgment by Croghan's troops, but the land tended steeply upward toward the fort in a series of terraces, and young, second-growth forest and brush ringed the open farmland. Along the side of the clearing nearest the fort was a substantial ridge or terrace, an ancient glacial lake beach that ran the full width of the open ground and into the woods on either side.

Although Croghan reported that he "immediately" made preparations to disembark his forces, it would be several more days before the opposing forces met in battle. Surgeon Parsons, who had watched Croghan leave the *Lawrence* resolved to fight, commented the next day about the "strange dallying" of fleet and army. The fault apparently lay with assembling the scattered warships, which had been posted at different stations on opposite sides of the island and could only concentrate by sailing around the northwest end, as the guns of Fort Mackinac denied them passage past the harbor and town. Wind and weather conspired to delay a landing on 2 August, and the army's desire to get ashore on the 3rd was frustrated when the *Mink* could not be found. The army's field guns, an essential part of Croghan's plan, had been transferred to the prize schooner, which had become separated in the fog because of a defective compass. The *Mink* rejoined the fleet during the course of the day but too late for the operation to proceed.[26] The landing and battle would have to wait until the next day, 4 August.[27]

Having observed the movements of the fleet for more than a week, Colonel McDouall had, by this time, little doubt where a landing would come, and he took measures to oppose the Americans long before they could approach the forts. He left some gunners and 25 militiamen in each of them and then marched his disposable forces, which amounted to 140 regulars and uniformed fencibles, some 50 militia, and about 350 Indian warriors, to the place he had selected for opposing any advance.[28] He considered the position "excellent but at an unavoidable and too great a distance from the

Forts," but it proved to be a fortuitous decision for frustrating Croghan's plan. McDouall's choice was the long, elevated ridge that cut across the end of Dousman's farm. Although he thought the position too extensive for his forces, he was pleased that "the ground was commanding & in front clear as I could wish it." The spot had another useful characteristic, described by both McDouall and Bulger as a "natural Breast work" that "protected my men from every shot." This feature, visible today, was the ridge itself. Standing in the hollow behind it, the troops were almost completely covered and could fire over the top of the ridge. The regulars and militia were disposed in this position, while the Indians took their places in the woods to either side. McDouall's field artillery, a 6-pounder and a 3-pounder, were placed in the road at the top of the ridge.

The British commander hoped that the Indians would prevent the Americans from moving through the woods around his flanks, which would force them to remain in the open ground in front of his position. To his troops he ordered that "on the close approach of the Enemy they were to pour in a volley and immediately charge, numerous as they were."

The U.S. squadron was finally ready to act by the morning of the 4th, although the dallying seems to have continued and the movements of fleet and army were slow and deliberate. Surgeon Parsons reported that the vessels were ordered to get under way at about 9:00 A.M. and by 11:00 had formed a line of battle facing the landing place. At 1:00 P.M. the troops began to disembark into their boats, and at 2:00 the ships opened fire with a bombardment that "cleared the shore." British lieutenant Andrew Bulger reported that after "sweeping the landing place by a heavy fire," the troops disembarked onto the beach. By 3:00, according to Parsons, the soldiers were formed on the shore and beginning their advance into the island.

The American column had to pass up the road through several hundred yards of woods and brush before the expanse of Dousman's farm opened before them. Croghan recognized this as the area where he had planned to establish his fortified enclave, and he realized that the British had beaten him to it. He could see the enemy line in a position that he considered "well selected," extending along the top of the ridge at the edge of the woods on the far side of the field some 500 yards ahead. He also noted that the British had the advantage of a "temporary breast work." As Croghan's force debouched from the woods, the British artillery opened fire. Parsons heard them commence at 3:15. McDouall complained that his cannon had little effect because he had no artillery officer to direct them, but their fire must have been rapid, because Croghan estimated that the British had four guns. The range was long, at any rate, and the firing had little effect.

From his distant position on the ridge, Lieutenant Bulger thought that the Americans "halted, and for some time, (as we imagined) appeared undetermined what to do." He speculated, probably correctly, that they "had not expected to meet with any opposition before reaching the Fort." The halt, accompanied by a cessation of firing, lasted some twenty minutes before the Americans advanced in two lines, with 250 Ohio volunteers in the front rank and 480 regulars forming the second. A reserve of 80 regulars and marines was posted at the rear of the flanks.[29] Their progress across the farm was accompanied by a "constant irregular fire" that was easily heard from the ships.

British and American accounts of the battle diverge somewhat at this point. McDouall thought that the enemy was advancing a party toward the woods on his right. He accordingly shifted the thirty men of the Michigan Fencibles to oppose them. Then came a message from the forts which reported that the two American brigs had slipped around the island behind McDouall's left flank and were landing troops to march directly to the forts. The information was incorrect, and it is clear from Surgeon Parsons's diary that the vessels remained off the landing place, but McDouall felt he had no choice but to retire to a position where he could protect the forts from this new threat.

At just about the same time, Croghan ordered his second-in-command, Major Andrew Hunter Holmes, to take part of the regulars from the second line and advance to the woods on their right in order to get around the left flank of the British line. Contemporary maps of the island show a rough track in that direction, the probable goal of Holmes and his men.[30] Many of the Indians had already begun to retire with McDouall, but a number of Menominees under Chief Thomas or Tomah had remained behind, had noted the movement, and were determined to oppose it. The Indians were, according to Croghan, posted in a "thick wood" on the American right, where they opened a destructive and accurate fire on the advancing Americans. At 4:10 Surgeon Parsons noted musketry of "considerable rapidity accompanied by yelling" that over the next few minutes became "very warm." This was probably the firing directed at Holmes and his men.

The effect was immediate and decisive. Holmes was killed and his next in command wounded, while the bulk of American enlisted casualties probably occurred at this time. "This unlucky fire," Croghan reported, not only cost several valuable officers but "threw that part of the line into Confusion, from which the best exertions of the officers were not able to recover it." Realizing that his effort to turn the British left had failed, Croghan ordered a charge by his remaining regulars against the front, which went as far as the position abandoned by McDouall, giving Croghan the impression that the enemy had been driven back. Throughout this time, Parsons described the sounds of musketry as "very frequent and irregular," while Croghan's men experienced "an annoying fire" from the Indians in the woods. This probably came from a force led by McDouall, who, hearing the firing by the Menominees on Holmes's party, had gathered his fifty militia and as many of the other retreating Indians as possible and turned back to support them.

By this time Croghan, in possession of the original British position, had discovered that "this disposition, from whence the enemy had just been driven, (and which had been represented to me as so high and Commanding) was by no means tenable, from being interspersed with thickets, and intersected in every way by ravines." He decided to abandon his original plan and no longer expose his force "to the fire of an enemy deriving every advantage which Could be obtaind from numbers, and a knowledge of the position." He ordered a retreat to the ships. Surgeon Parsons noted a change in the direction of the firing at 4:30, which indicated to him that the army was retiring. By 5:00 most of the troops were again on the beach and firing had ceased. Although McDouall reported that the Americans retreated "in the utmost haste and confusion," followed by his own troops, the operation was conducted in an orderly fashion. Commodore Sinclair credited Croghan with accomplishing the retreat in a "masterly manner." Writing in 1816, Robert B. McAfee described a deliberate retirement to the beach with Cotgreave's Ohio troops in line covering the regulars as they retreated across the field and then filed through the woods and down to the boats, hardly an operation conducted in confusion.[31]

American casualties were heavy, with a total of sixty-six killed and wounded, including Holmes and twelve privates killed on the field. Six officers and men later died aboard the ships. British and Indian losses were negligible. The body of Major Holmes had been left on the field, and on 5 August Croghan sent a request under a flag of truce for its return. Holmes's remains were recovered by the British and turned over to the Americans.[32]

The American squadron remained off Mackinac Island until 6 August. Croghan did not deem it prudent to make another attempt, and both he and Sinclair seem to have been thoroughly intimidated by the defensive situation presented by Mackinac Island. Both mentioned in their reports the "impenetrable thickness of the woods" and the uphill route from the landing place to the forts. The two combined to ensure, as Sinclair put it, "that no advantage gained could be profited by." The result of the battle seems to have been as Croghan had anticipated, convinced as he was that his force was too small and even outnumbered by the defenders. "Colo. Croghan would never have landed," Sinclair admitted, "could he have justified himself to his government, without having stronger proof than appearances that he could not effect the object in view."[33] The outcome of the action of 4 August had met his expectations. As Humphrey Leavitt summed it up, "Col. Croghan failed to sustain his previously-acquired reputation as a military man, and was evidently unfitted to command such an expedition. In truth, no one acquired any military glory in this affair."[34]

The remainder of the campaign was largely a naval operation. The U.S. squadron withdrew to Thunder Bay on the northeast coast of Michigan's lower peninsula, where Sinclair dispatched the *Lawrence, Caledonia,* and *Mink* to Lake Erie with the wounded, Cotgreave's regiment, and some of the regulars. He then set out with the *Niagara, Tigress,* and *Scorpion* in search of the *Nancy* and the British base at the mouth of the Nottawasaga River, the source of Michilimackinac's supplies. This time he was able to find his target. On 14 August, despite spirited and sustained resistance from a small body of sailors led by Lieutenant Miller Worsley of the Royal Navy, Sinclair and Croghan destroyed the *Nancy* and a blockhouse constructed for her protection.

Having done all that he could on Lake Huron, Sinclair's final concern was to prevent provisions from reaching Michilimackinac before the onset of winter. He ordered Lieutenant Daniel Turner to remain on the lake with the schooners *Scorpion* and *Tigress* to intercept British supply boats. The *Nancy*'s defenders would soon have their revenge, however. Lieutenant Worsley and his men had escaped the destruction of the *Nancy* and were able to slip past the blockading schooners and make their way to Michilimackinac. There, Colonel McDouall and Worsley organized a mixed force of sailors, soldiers, and Indians to attack the American vessels. This party, using small boats and canoes, surprised and captured the *Tigress* on 3 September and, two days later, used their prize, still under American colors, to take the *Scorpion*. The vessels were put to work moving supplies, and Michilimackinac remained firmly in British hands until returned to the United States in July 1815 following the conclusion of hostilities.[35]

The 1814 campaign on Lake Huron was a disappointing failure for American arms, and, as McAfee wrote in his 1816 history of the War of 1812 in the West, the year ended "with the results decidedly in favor of the enemy."[36] It had indeed, for not only had the British preserved their hold on Michilimackinac, they had gained, through capture, the naval vessels they had been unable to construct themselves. At the end of the navigation season, the British again had a small squadron operating on the upper lakes, a development that had been feared by the Americans and had served as an important motivation for launching the expedition against Michilimackinac in the first place.

Putting the best possible face on the undesirable outcome of the campaign, McAfee continued, "Colonel Croghan and Commodore Sinclair . . . conducted the expedition, as far as it depended on them, with great prudence, skill, and bravery, effecting every thing which it was possible to effect with the forces under their command." Had Lieutenant Turner been more fortunate in his blockade, McAfee maintained, Michilimackinac would have been deprived of supplies and would have become untenable that fall or early the following spring. That is probably true, but the unsuccessful blockade was made necessary by the inability of the naval and military force to take Mackinac Island earlier in the summer.

Despite this failure, the combined U.S. naval and military operation functioned well, for the most part, operating effectively on poorly known Lake Huron and enjoying successes at St. Joseph, Sault Ste. Marie, and Nottawasaga Bay against limited or no opposition. The navy efficiently transported, landed, and reembarked the troops of Croghan's command with no apparent friction between the two services. Faced with the strong position and nearly equal numbers of the enemy at Michilimackinac, however, the expedition and its commanders were unable to achieve the desired results.

This was due, in part, to circumstances and the inadequacy of the forces assigned for the task. Sinclair's naval vessels were powerfully armed but unable to neutralize the enemy's defenses because of the elevation of the forts above the water. The best they could do was transport and provide cover for the troops when they landed at the lower, western beach on 4 August. The navy carried out these tasks efficiently and well.

There is also much to be said in defense of George Croghan's performance, though he was unenthusiastic about the mission from the start and obviously conveyed his feelings to other members of the expedition. Only twenty-three years old, Croghan had made a name for himself by his determined defense of

Fort Stephenson in Ohio in 1813 but had relatively little experience commanding larger forces in the field. His conviction, from his first sight of Mackinac Island, that his forces were too few to take the place by storm was probably correct, as his disposable field force outnumbered that of his opponent by only about 200 men. Croghan landed his troops to at least make an attempt, but his passive strategy of establishing a fortified camp to discourage the Indian allies of the British foundered when his opponents seized the position first. From that point, Croghan had lost the initiative and was prudent enough to realize that he did not have the force to succeed in a long, uphill battle through the tangled woods and broken topography that lay between him and his goal.

"The Enemy formidable as they were in numbers have made so very poor a business of their attack" was British commander McDouall's dismissive summation of the American attempt on his post.[37] The Americans had indeed failed to retake Michilimackinac by force, but their numbers were not as formidable as McDouall supposed. George Croghan and Arthur Sinclair might not have gained any military glory in their attack on Michilimackinac, but, given the strength of the British position and the limited routes by which they could come to grips with their opponents, they and their troops and sailors conducted the operation with "prudence, skill, and bravery."

NOTES

1. Humphrey Howe Leavitt, *Autobiography of the Hon. Humphrey Howe Leavitt Written for his Family* (New York, 1893), 24–25, 22.

2. "North Western Country," *Niles Weekly Register,* 17 Oct. 1812, 105.

3. Brian Leigh Dunnigan, *A Picturesque Situation: Mackinac Before Photography, 1615–1860* (Detroit: Wayne State University Press, 2008), 64–68, 80–83.

4. For an account of the capture of Michilimackinac, see ibid., 101–2; and Brian Leigh Dunnigan, *The British Army at Mackinac, 1812–1815* (Mackinac Island, MI: Mackinac Island State Park Commission, 1980), 10–12.

5. Sir George Prevost to Earl Bathurst, 10 July 1814, [Andrew Bulger], *An Autobiographical Sketch of the Services of the Late Captain Andrew Bulger of the Royal Newfoundland Fencible Regiment* (Bangalore, India: Regimental Press, 2nd Battalion 10th Regiment, 1865), 9–10.

6. Dunnigan, *British Army,* 13–17.

7. Isaac Chauncey to Oliver H. Perry, 14 July 1813, Ernest A. Cruikshank, ed., *The Documentary History of the Campaign Upon the Niagara Frontier,* 9 vols. (Welland, Ontario: Lundy's Lane Historical Society, 1896–1908), 7:278–79.

8. William H. Harrison to Secretary of War, 16 Oct. 1813, ibid., 8:71–72.

9. Robert Dickson to Noah Freer, 23 Oct. 1813, *Michigan Pioneer and Historical Collections,* 40 vols. (Lansing: Michigan Historical Commission, 1877–1929), 15:423–24.

10. [Bulger], *Autobiographical Sketch,* 8–9.

11. McDouall to Gordon Drummond, 17 July 1814, *Michigan Pioneer Collections,* 15:616–19.

12. McDouall's preparations and available forces are described in Dunnigan, *British Army,* 18–22.

13. John Armstrong to President James Madison, 30 Apr. 1814, Robert B. McAfee, *History of the Late War in the Western Country, Comprising a Full Account of all the Transactions in that Quarter, from the Commencement of Hostilities at Tippecanoe, to the Termination of the Contest at New Orleans on the Return of Peace* (Lexington, KY: Worsley & Smith, 1816), 455–56.

14. McAfee, *History,* 456–57; John C. Fredriksen, ed., *Surgeon of the Lakes: The Diary of Dr. Usher Parsons, 1812–1814* (Erie, PA: Erie County Historical Society, 2000), 79.

15. Fredriksen, *Surgeon of the Lakes,* 82–84; Leavitt, *Autobiography,* 21.

16. Croghan to Armstrong, 9 Aug. 1812, Michael J. Crawford, ed., *The Naval War of 1812: A Documentary History,* Vol.3, *1814–1815* (Washington, DC: Naval Historical Center, 2002), 566; Fredriksen, *Surgeon of the Lakes,* 82–83.

17. Fredriksen, *Surgeon of the Lakes,* 84–87.

18. Sinclair to Secretary of the Navy Jones, 9 Aug. 1814, Crawford, *Naval War,* 569.

19. Croghan to Armstrong, 9 Aug. 1814, ibid., 566.

20. Croghan to Duncan McArthur, 3 July 1814, in McAfee, *History,* 459–60.

21. Fredriksen, *Surgeon of the Lakes,* 87.

22. Sinclair to Jones, 9 Aug. 1814, Crawford, *Naval War,* 569; Fredriksen, *Surgeon of the Lakes,* 86; Samuel Lasley account [ca. 1820], Charles Larned Papers, Burton Historical Collection, Detroit Public Library, Detroit.

23. Fredriksen, *Surgeon of the Lakes,* 86; Leavitt, *Autobiography,* 21.

24. Fredriksen, *Surgeon of the Lakes,* 87.

25. Croghan to Armstrong, 9 Aug. 1814, Crawford, *Naval War,* 566–67.

26. Fredriksen, *Surgeon of the Lakes,* 87–88.

27. Firsthand accounts of the Battle of Mackinac Island are limited. From the American side, Croghan's official report is Croghan to Armstrong, 9 Aug. 1814, Crawford, *Naval War,* 566–68. It gives a reasonable narrative of the course of the battle but no sense of time. Fortunately, Surgeon Parsons, who remained aboard the *Lawrence,* described the landing and then carefully timed the outbursts of firing and other sounds of battle that he could hear from his location. Fredriksen, *Surgeon of the Lakes,* 88–90. Humphrey Leavitt was too ill to land, so his *Autobiography* adds little detail other than what he heard from his comrades. Commodore Sinclair's report is Sinclair to Jones, 9 Aug. 1814, *Naval War,* 568–70, but his details of the battle are second hand and confused. The battle is also described in detail in McAfee, *History,* 462–64, using Croghan's report and some other unidentified sources. Extended descriptions from the British side include McDouall to Prevost, 14 Aug. 1814, *Michigan Pioneer Collections,* 25:591–94, and an undated, unsigned account probably by Lieutenant Andrew Bulger of the Royal Newfoundland Regiment, *Michigan Pioneer Collections,* 23:446–49. Bulger's *Autobiographical Sketch,* 11–12, gives a summary of the action that agrees in most details with McDouall.

28. For the composition of McDouall's forces, see Dunnigan, *British Army,* 22–23.

29. McAfee, *History,* 463.

30. See William S. Eveleth's 1817 "Map of the Island of Michilimackinac," reproduced in Dunnigan, *Picturesque Situation,* 125 fig. 4.7.

31. McAfee, *History,* 464.

32. Dunnigan, *British Army,* 26. Croghan's official return of casualties is printed in Roger Andrews, *Old Fort Mackinac on the Hill of History* (Menominee, MI: Herald-Leader Press, 1938), 141–42. Surgeon Parsons gives his own tabulation of casualties in Fredriksen, *Surgeon of the Lakes,* 90.

33. Sinclair to Jones, 9 Aug. 1814, Crawford, *Naval War*, 569.
34. Leavitt, *Autobiography*, 23.
35. The concluding naval activities are discussed in detail in Barry Gough, *Fighting Sail on Lake Huron and Georgian Bay: The War of 1812 and its Aftermath* (Annapolis, MD: Naval Institute Press, 2002), 103–12; and in Dunnigan, *Picturesque Situation*, 114–17.
36. McAfee, *History*, 472.
37. McDouall to Prevost, 14 Aug. 1814, *Michigan Pioneer Collections*, 25:593.

PART II

Consequences

Odyssey's End

The Battle of Lake Erie and the Failure of the Delaware Indian Struggle for Autonomy

DANIEL P. BARR

On 10 September 1813, Commodore Oliver Hazard Perry guided a small American naval squadron to victory over an even smaller British squadron near the Bass Islands at the western end of Lake Erie. It was a significant victory for the Americans during the War of 1812, one that was particularly important for its impact on the frontier. During the spring and summer of 1813, the British and their Indian allies, led by the indomitable Shawnee warrior Tecumseh, had invaded northwest Ohio twice in an effort to compromise American control of the Northwest Territory. But the Battle of Lake Erie essentially ended British offensive capability along the frontier. Perry's victory gave the Americans control of the lake, which in turn afforded them the ability to cut British supply and communication lines. The British and the Indian allies at Detroit were already low on provisions and supplies, and their threat to their supply lines compelled British general Henry Procter to abandon his defenses at the western end of Lake Erie and retreat into the Ontario peninsula. It was an unpopular decision with Procter's Indian allies. Tecumseh, who saw his dreams of an independent Indian nation crumbling, was particularly displeased. The Shawnee leader admonished the British for withdrawing, chastising them for acting like a "fat animal that carries its tail upon its back, but when affrighted, it drops it between its legs and runs off." Nonetheless, the Shawnee leader led his followers east with the British, bracing for a deciding fight with the Americans that would come a month later along the banks of the Thames River.[1]

Tecumseh was not the only Indian with a vested interest in the outcome of the naval engagement on Lake Erie. Many miles to the west, Delaware

Indians living along the White River in central Indiana also were affected by the American victory on the lake, albeit in a profoundly different manner than Tecumseh and his militant followers. The Delawares had chosen to remain apart from the conflict, but their neutrality titled heavily in favor of the Americans, for whom they often served as messengers and intermediaries. Perry's victory potentially portended good things for the Delawares, who hoped their amicable relationship with the Americans would pay dividends once Tecumseh and his British friends were beaten.

For the Delawares in Indiana, such hopes were grounded in decades of turmoil and struggle. For more than eighty years, from 1737 through 1818, the Delaware Indians had been locked in a determined struggle for autonomy, security, and survival that coincided with the birth and early expansion of the American nation. It was a lengthy process during which Delaware politics shifted from resistance to accommodation and back on multiple occasions as Delaware peoples struggled time and again to remake and reform themselves during a seemingly endless westward trek that took them from eastern Pennsylvania to the Mississippi River and beyond. It was a process marred by sociocultural uncertainty and political fragmentation, twin conditions imprinted on Delaware society by a nearly constant cycle of war. Beleaguered and besieged, Delaware headmen wrestled with one another over policies of accommodation and resistance, even as Christian missionaries preached the abandonment of traditional beliefs and customs while religious and political visionaries among the Delawares encouraged their followers to follow new paths into the future. But it was not an odyssey without end. Ultimately, the American victory at the Battle of Lake Erie would ensure that Delaware peoples found neither autonomy nor security within the confines of the rapidly growing United States. Confirmed in its control of the Old Northwest by Perry's victory, the United States soon expelled the Delawares and other native peoples from the region and forced them across the Mississippi River. They would survive, but their long odyssey in the East was over.

The origins of the Delawares' struggle for survival can be traced to the earliest European colonization of the mid-Atlantic seaboard. Prior to the arrival of European colonists, the Delawares, or Lenni Lenapes, as they were then known, inhabited sections of present-day eastern Pennsylvania, western New Jersey, and northern Delaware. They lived in a network of midsized villages along the banks of the Delaware River and its tributaries. The Delawares were not a politically centralized nation; rather, their semiautonomous village clusters were under the guidance of local or regional leaders. Moreover, Delaware communities were loosely organized around three phratries, often referred to as clans—turtle, turkey, and wolf—that were derived at least in part by linguistic variations within the Lenapes' Algonquian dialect. Daily life was governed by seasonal variations and a gendered division of labor, but a semisedentary mixture of hunting, fishing, and agriculture provided for a comfortable and fairly abundant existence.[2]

As was the case with most native inhabitants of the Americas, the arrival of European colonists brought rapid and profound change to the Delawares' traditional world. During the first half of the eighteenth century, initially amicable relations with colonists in Pennsylvania gradually gave way to contention and conflict, especially over land. The highly controversial 1737 Walking Purchase proved to be the breaking point. Using a curious and likely illegitimate 1686 treaty agreement, the Pennsylvania government swindled the Delawares out of over a million acres of prime land along the Delaware River. The agreement called for the Delawares to cede to the colony as much land as a man could walk in a day; but rather than engage in a leisurely walk as the treaty implied, Pennsylvania proprietor Thomas Penn and his agents hired a team of professional runners to mark off the cession. Aided by colonists who cleared the proposed path of timber and brush, the colony laid claim to a substantially larger tract of land than the Delawares expected. Exasperated Delaware leaders challenged the legitimacy of the Walking Purchase, but their claims were dismissed in 1742 when Pennsylvania enlisted the assistance of the Six Nations Iroquois as arbitrators. The Iroquois, who maintained a loose hegemony over the Delawares by virtue of a disputed conquest of all Pennsylvania Indians in the seventeenth century, ruled against the Delawares. Indeed, the Iroquois sachem Canasatego berated Delaware leaders for challenging the treaty, derided the Delawares as women, and ordered them to vacate the lands in question immediately.[3]

In the wake of the Walking Purchase and the Iroquois ruling, many Delawares migrated west across the Appalachian Mountains, where they established new communities along the upper Ohio–Allegheny River drainage. These Delawares were refugees, migrants forced from their homes in the East by the expanding tide of Euro-American settlement. As such, they adopted a militant posture regarding the defense and preservation of their new homeland, and when American colonists again threatened Delaware lands and autonomy during the 1750s, the Delawares fought furiously to maintain their territory and independence. During the Seven Years' War, commonly referred to as the French and Indian War in the American colonies, the Delawares waged a parallel war with the French in an effort to secure a treaty from the American colonists that would grant formal recognition of Delaware territory. Targeting frontier homesteads and isolated communities often situated on vacated Delaware lands east of the Appalachian Mountains, the Delawares waged war with the political aim of forcing the Pennsylvania government to recognize their landholdings in the Allegheny region. Striking quickly and often without warning, Delaware war parties ravaged the Pennsylvania frontier and displaced thousands of American colonists from their homes and farms. Finally in 1758, after three and half years of brutal war, several colonies and the British general John Forbes agreed to the Treaty of Easton, which did not explicitly recognize Delaware title to the Allegheny–upper Ohio region but did forbid colonial settlement west of the Appalachian Mountains under penalty of death.[4]

It was a stunning victory for the Delawares, one that provided de facto recognition of their rights to land in present-day western Pennsylvania. But it proved to be a short-lived success. American colonists violated the terms of the Easton agreement with impunity, and the British army was powerless to stop American encroachment on Delaware lands. As a result, many Delawares began shifting their villages west to the Muskingum River Valley in eastern Ohio. Then, in 1763, the Delawares joined in a pan-Indian uprising, known as Pontiac's War, in an effort to consolidate and confirm their control of their new upper Ohio Valley homeland. This time, however, the fortunes of war were not on their side. Following an initial wave of success, the Delawares were turned back after a hard-fought but indecisive battle at Bushy Run in August 1763. The next summer British colonel Henry Bouquet led a punitive expedition to the Muskingum and forced the Delawares to surrender. The British did not compel the Delawares to remove from the Muskingum River but, rather, attempted to subvert the independence of the Delawares and other Indian nations by asserting that they were now British subjects. Indeed, with the Proclamation of 1763, the British government erected a semipermanent boundary line between its American colonists and its new Indian subjects.[5]

The Delawares were not particularly pleased with this new arrangement, but the onset of the American Revolution provided them with an opportunity to assert their autonomy and secure recognition of their territorial rights. A new generation of Delaware leaders, in particular Newcomer and White

Eyes, attempted to gather together all the disparate bands of Delawares into a single polity, a unified Delaware nation that would comprise a powerful and persuasive Indian constituency in the Midwest. They established a capital at Coshocton on the Muskingum River, and the Delaware Council was created to serve as a national governing body. But White Eyes had even grander plans. He envisioned the Delawares becoming a westernized people, and he advocated the adoption of Christianity and Euro-American culture as a means of placing the Delawares on an equal footing with the Americans and the British. This became particularly important when the Revolutionary War began, as the Delawares found themselves caught between warring parties. The Delaware Council adopted a policy of neutrality, but White Eyes steered the Delawares toward an alliance with the Americans, an arrangement he hoped would culminate in the incorporation of the Delawares as the leading members of an Indian state in the new American nation. But that dream was shattered when White Eyes was killed in a dispute with American militia in 1778, which in turn caused many Delawares in Ohio to abandon their neutrality and fight alongside other British-allied Indians for the remainder of the war. A smaller number of Delawares maintained an alliance with the Americans, while others remained neutral, particularly those who had been converted to Christianity by Moravian missionaries. These divisions doomed the Delaware war effort. In 1780 Delaware scouts led an American army to Coshocton, which was burned, while the majority of the Delaware nation scattered throughout Ohio. But it was the peaceful Christian Delawares who suffered the cruelest blow of the war. In March 1782 American militia massacred ninety-two Christianized Delawares at the Moravian mission town of Gnaddenhutten in retaliation for assistance the Americans believed the Christian converts were providing hostile Indians.[6]

The 1783 Treaty of Paris ended the fighting between the British and Americans, but it did little to settle the situation on the frontier. Although some Delaware leaders agreed to treaties with the new United States government in 1784 and 1785, many Delaware warriors did not consider themselves beaten, and they strongly opposed any extension of American authority over the Midwest. But other Delaware leaders saw no prospect for success in renewed fighting. These internal divisions undermined Delaware resistance, and the Delawares found themselves superseded by other Indians, particularly the Miamis under Little Turtle and the Shawnees under Blue Jacket, in the struggle to defend the Old Northwest. A rising Delaware warrior faction under Buckongahelas fought with the Miamis and Shawnees in support of Indian rights during the wars of the early 1790s, but many other Delawares migrated west in an effort to escape the conflict. In 1795, following American victory at the Battle of Fallen Timbers, the United States government compelled the Indians of the Miami Confederation to sign the Treaty of Greenville. Under the terms agreed to at Greenville, the Delawares and other Indians relinquished most of present-day Ohio to the United States. In return for their lost villages and hunting territory, the Delawares were awarded a government annuity, an annual payment of $1,000 in goods that would become the economic lifeline of the nation. The annuity was guaranteed in perpetuity, as long as the Delawares promised never again to take up arms against the United States or to support any Indian nation that did. Accordingly, the renowned Delaware war captain Buckongahelas signed the treaty, remarking that "all who know me, know me to be a man and a warrior, and now I declare that I will for the future be a true and steady friend of the United States as I have heretofore been an active enemy."[7]

The Treaty of Greenville was a watershed event for the Delawares. For the better part of forty years, the Delawares had engaged the Americans—either in diplomacy or in war. They were worn down by the effort, divided politically, and in need of time to regroup. Following the Treaty of Greenville, many Delawares moved west to the White River in Indiana, accepting an invitation from the Miamis to settle there. Having ceded all claims to their own territory, the Delawares had little choice. Over the next five years, various bands of Delawares made their way west and established themselves in a string of nine villages along the west branch on the White River between present-day Muncie and Indianapolis. Other Delawares traveled even greater distances in an attempt to escape American influence. Several Delaware bands crossed the Mississippi River into Spanish Territory, settling at Cape Girardeau in Missouri, while groups of Christian Delawares crossed into British Canada. But the largest concentration of Delawares remained along the White River. By 1801 they had successfully recreated a semblance of the former Delaware nation in Indiana. All three major divisions were represented, with Buckongahelas retaining his role as war captain, while Tetepachsit (Tedpachsit), speaker of the Turtle clan, emerged as the principal chief. The Munsee/Wolf clan was present, although they remained somewhat aloof, as was their traditional custom, under their leader Hockingpomska. In an effort to resurrect the nation-building policies of Newcomer and White Eyes, the Delawares extended an invitation to Christian Delawares living at the Moravian mission town of Goshen, Ohio, to join the Delawares living in Indiana. The Delawares did not initially extend the invitation to the Moravian preachers, whom Buckongahelas distrusted, but in 1800 Tetepachsit sent word that the Moravian preachers, along with their Delaware converts, would be welcomed along the White River. Many Christianized Delawares chose to remain at Goshen, but by May 1801 a small group of Christian Delawares, along with two Moravian missionaries, John Peter Kluge and Abraham Luckenbach, were settled along the White River, where they established a new mission town.[8]

The major Delaware factions had converged along the White River, but rebuilding the Delaware nation proved difficult. The White River Delawares faced several challenges that undermined unity and fostered discord. Like their predecessors along the Allegheny–upper Ohio River, the Delawares in Indiana were refugees who once again had to rebuild their lives and communities. As they sought to reinvent themselves yet again, a strong inclination toward traditional beliefs and customs emerged. But the traditionalist mentality clashed with decades of Euro-American acculturation, undermining unity and commonality. A particular point of contention was economics. The Delawares resisted the efforts of the Moravian missionaries and the American government to install farming as the chief occupation among the Delaware men. Instead, they reverted to hunting and trapping, believing the abundance of game and fur-bearing animals in the Indiana forests would support a return to more traditional socioeconomic practices. But fur prices declined sharply during the early nineteenth century as white trappers saturated the market, leaving the Delawares and many other Indian peoples increasingly dependent on government annuities, which in many cases were designed to support an economic transition to farming. Yet, despite the decline of the fur trade and the economic troubles that accompanied it, the Delawares resisted conversion to farming, which Delaware men considered emasculating, and instead many men turned to alcohol to ease their anxiety and boredom. The situation deteriorated so rapidly that William Henry Harrison, governor of the Indiana Territory, forbade white settlers from hunting on Indian lands and outlawed the "selling or giving [of] any Spirituous Liquors" to the Indians. The measures provided little succor for the stresses plaguing Dealware society.[9]

Religion provided another source of discord. The presence of the Moravian missionaries was controversial, as the Delaware leadership in Indiana was pronounced in its anti-Christian attitude, barring Moravians from the Delaware Council and openly disregarding their advice. This anti-Moravian sentiment, which was sharp break from the nation-building policies of the Revolutionary era, grew in part from distrust over the role the Moravians played in the Gnadenhutten massacre of 1782. While there is little direct evidence that the Moravian missionaries had any culpability in the gruesome deed, many of the White River Delawares had relatives who had been killed at Gnadenhutten, and, understandably, they harbored harsh feelings toward the German missionaries. Indeed, some Delaware leaders accused the Moravians of preaching pacifism to their Delaware converts in order to make them easy targets for American settlers and militias, who could then "knock them over the head."[10] But more immediate problems also undermined support for the Moravians. The Moravians condemned alcoholism but could not stop white traders from bringing whiskey to the White River, undermining support for their mission. The Moravians accordingly won few converts along the White River, as suspicion and the inability of the Moravian preachers to combat pervasive alcoholism overwhelmed their religious message.[11]

Further compounding the situation was disease, which returned during the winter of 1804–5 to once again stalk the Delawares. Described by the Moravian missionaries in various terms as fever accompanied by coughing, nausea, and vomiting, the Delawares in Indiana likely suffered from a severe strain of influenza, which may have been made all the more deadly by a flare-up of smallpox. But regardless of what plagued the White River villages, the Delawares living there were dying, and neither native remedies nor the efforts of the Moravian missionaries proved effective in combating sickness. Indeed, the outbreak of disease further eroded the appeal of the Moravians and their Christian doctrine of an all-powerful benevolent god. Mary, a Christian Delaware sick with fever in April 1805, succinctly summarized the situation: "The Word of God does not heal my body," she remarked, "and that is what I want."[12]

Yet it was land that remained the greatest source of tension in Delaware society, just as it had for previous generations. In 1803 President Thomas Jefferson instructed Harrison to acquire as much Indian land as possible along the Ohio River, from the Indiana border to its confluence with the Mississippi. Accordingly, Harrison sent word to numerous Indian tribes that he would convene a council that June at Fort Wayne to finalize a tentative cession of lands around Vincennes that had been agreed on the year before. Many Indian leaders, including Delaware headmen, initially refused to attend, but Harrison made it known that only those tribes who had representatives at the council would receive their yearly government annuities. With economic returns from trapping and hunting declining rapidly, the Delaware leadership reluctantly agreed to attend the meeting. Not surprisingly, negotiations did not go smoothly. At one point, Buckongahelas, who had signed the Treaty of Greenville because he believed it would provide some measure of security for his people, became enraged at this latest push for Indian lands. He informed Harrison that the earlier agreements were irrelevant and that the lands around Vincennes belonged to the Delawares, who had been given them by the Piankashaws. The claim was tenuous at best, but it demonstrated the depth of frustration felt by the Delaware leader. Shawnee leaders, too, felt the pinch, at one point walking out of the proceedings, only to return later and demand that the matter be taken directly to President Jefferson in Washington. Nonetheless, a coalition of Harrison, Miami chief Little Turtle, and procession Potawatomis pressured the malcontent chiefs to relent, and ultimately Buckongahelas and Hockingpomska agreed to the treaty on behalf of the Delawares. The United States gained title to 1,800 square miles of land along the lower White River around Vincennes. But since the United States considered the agreement an extension of the 1795 Greenville treaty, the Indians received no increase in annuities.[13]

The following year Harrison wrestled an additional cession from Delaware leaders. In August 1804 the United States obtained title to all of the lands between the Wabash and Ohio rivers in return for a new annuity of $3,000 payable over ten years. The cession produced an immediate backlash among the Delawares. In January 1805 the Delawares asked the Moravian missionaries to translate the terms of the treaty, bringing into question whether their leaders fully understood what they had signed. That spring Buckongahelas and Hockingpomska complained to Indian Agent William Wells that the Delawares had not intended to sell any lands and had been deceived by Harrison. Besides, they argued, the Delawares were not the rightful possessors of the land in question, which they contended fell within the territory of the Piankishaws. But Harrison deftly maneuvered around their objections. The governor bribed the Piankishaws into confirming Delaware ownership of the ceded lands and chastised the Delawares for their apparent duplicity. Fortune favored the governor when the aged Buckongahelas succumbed to a lengthy illness and died in June 1805. Delaware resistance crumbled with him, as Hockingpomska turned to alcohol and Tetepachsit proved unequal to Harrison's strong-armed tactics. Indeed, when Harrison sent an emissary to inform the Delaware headman that the Piankashaws had confirmed the treaty, Tetepachsit "trembled and appeared very much agitated and confused." His agitation only intensified after Harrison held yet another council in August 1805, where enraged Miamis declared that the Delawares had no rights to any lands in Indiana whatsoever. Delaware leaders lamented that their Miami hosts might expel them from the White River and openly considered abandoning their villages and moving west of the Mississippi in search of Delawares who already had migrated beyond the river.[14]

By the middle of 1805, the situation along the White River had become dangerous. The frustration of the Delawares over their inability to sustain themselves independently of government annuities combined with mounting despair over the land cessions of 1803–5 to produce a climate of anger and fear. Not coincidently, the Moravian missionaries along the White River reported a dramatic increase in the frequency of visions and prophetic dreams, many of which offered explanations for the problems besieging Delaware society. The visions, which had begun to manifest in late 1803, were more often experienced by women than men. But regardless of who served as mystic, the dreams carried a strikingly similar message. The suffering of the Delawares, and Indian peoples in general, were the product of their own failings, not the work of land-hungry white settlers or the machinations of the American government. Indians had forsaken their traditional culture, the mystics preached, and the Creator was angry that the Delawares' acceptance and adoption of Euro-American culture, particularly Christianity, had transformed the Indians into something that they were never intended to be. In short, they were being punished by the Creator for their sins. But the visions also carried a message of hope. If the Delawares returned to traditional native lifeways, the Creator would end their suffering and undo all the wrongs that had befallen them.[15]

Foremost among the Delaware mystics in the White River villages was a woman named Beata. Nearly forty years earlier, in 1769, Beata's parents had asked the Moravians to baptize their infant daughter at the mission town of Friedenshutten along the Susquehanna River in Pennsylvania. Sometime thereafter Beata's family had abandoned Christianity, likely while Beata was still a child. After suffering numerous travails alongside her people, Beata was a resident of Tetapachsit's village along the White River when, in February 1805, she began experiencing powerful visions. In her dreams, the Creator told Beata that the Indians were being punished for their sins, particularly "drinking, fornication, stealing, murder, and the like." They had lost their Indian traditions and become too enamored with the Euro-American material and social culture. They had ceased to be Indians, at least in the sense that the Creator intended. The Delawares should refrain from such behavior immediately, she cautioned, for a savior was coming, a messenger from the Creator who would instruct the Delawares in what they must do to reclaim their lost traditions and rebuild their lives. But only the penitent and obedient would be saved. Beata warned that the faithful must follow her teachings, for she spoke with the voice of the Creator. The wicked, including secret witches whom Beata blamed for the disease and alcoholism plaguing Delaware society, would be severely punished.[16]

The rise of Beata and other Delaware mystics paralleled the increasing tension among the Delawares in 1804–5. The Moravians were aghast that "such and similar blasphemous things met with favor among the poor blind heathen," but they could not have been surprised.[17] The Indians were suffering. Years of economic distress had produced increased dependency on American annuities, but the annual funds were hardly enough to sustain the Delaware population living along the White River. More was needed, but the only readily available means to advance themselves economically was to sell more land. Yet that was hardly an ideal solution. Further reduction in Delaware territory would only make it more difficult for the Delawares to fend for themselves, as each land cession reduced the Delawares' available hunting and trapping territory. That could lead only to increased dependence on annuities and further erosion of traditional Delaware patterns of existence, the decline of which the mystics blamed for the social problems plaguing Delaware society. It was a downward spiral produced by decades of dispossession, migration, and cultural erosion, a lethal combination that left Delaware society in an uproar. Indeed, panicked Moravian missionaries lamented that the Indians "do not want to hear anything at all except what they learn through the extravagant visions." But the Moravians missed the meaning of the visions and failed to comprehend the appeal of the mystics. Theirs was a message of religious revitalization, a path to redemption and renewal. All that was wrong could be made right again, provided that anything that threatened the revitalization was eliminated.[18]

Given the heightened level of tension and stress, it is not surprising that Delaware society imploded during the summer of 1805. That June, the death of Buckongahelas provided the spark that set off a blaze of activity. Though the aged Delaware leader was perhaps eighty years old, many Delawares believed his death was the work of evil spirits. Others claimed he had been poisoned. Beata had preached that there were witches among the Indians, evildoers who used poisonous medicine bundles to make the Indians sick in order to bring about the downfall of their own people. Given the level of tension gripping Delaware society that summer and the fervor created by the mystics, it is understandable that some Delawares saw foul play in the death of a revered leader. Buckongahelas had been an important symbol of tradition and autonomy against the forces of change arrayed against his people. While Buckongahelas had participated in the unpopular land cessions of 1803–4, his later protests against those treaties indicate that he was never completely comfortable with selling Delaware lands in Indiana. Moreover, Buckongahelas had always been lukewarm in his relationship with the U.S. government and its agents, ever wary of negotiating with the Americans. He had fought the Americans on many occasions, and even in peace his was often a voice of caution and moderation with regard to the Delawares' erstwhile enemies and sometimes allies. And then there were the Moravians. Buckongahelas was a powerful voice among those Delawares who opposed the mission on the White River. Like many Delawares, he held the Moravians partly responsible for the massacre at Gnaddenhutten, and he especially opposed Moravian efforts to convert the Delawares into Christian farmers. He made his position clear in an 1803 oration to the Moravian missionaries along the White River: "We cannot drop our customs and teaching and sacrifices, for our forefathers too received them from God and left them to us. Every Indian must remain true to these things, and not let them go. Your teaching is only for white people." Throughout his long life, he never converted.[19]

In the wake of Buckongahelas's death, the Delawares began to search for the witches they believed were hexing their people. Many people were accused of witchcraft, including the principal chief, Tetepachsit. With the accusation of Tetepachsit, the religious revitalization movement of Beata clearly took on political overtones. Indeed, the Moravian missionaries Kluge and Luckenbach recorded that "never in all the time that we are here have the Indians been in such a state of revolution as they are at present."[20] Although he had been a civil chief among the Delawares since before the American Revolution, Tetepachsit had come to epitomize that which the mystics considered evil and degenerate in Delaware society. A former Moravian convert who had repatriated into traditional Delaware society, Tetapchsit nonetheless remained friendly toward the missionaries. It was he who had invited the Moravians to establish a mission along the White River in 1801, and it was to the Moravian mission that Tetapchsit fled for three days following his accusation. Moreover, although he publicly opposed the consumption of alcohol, Tetapachsit himself sold alcohol in the Delaware villages. Indeed, it appears that alcohol trading became his principal source of income. Tetapachsit's hypocrisy was not lost on him. Addressing his people during a feast celebration, he remarked: "My children you see how old I am, how gray my hair is; [but] I am still not on the right road as God desires it of us. We have often admonished you not to drink . . . We chiefs have now discovered why you have not changed either, because we ourselves do not do what we tell you to do." The chief's introspective remarks appear heartfelt, but they were not enough to blunt accusations that he bewitched his people with poisonous alcohol. That he continued to sell alcohol after being accused of witchcraft certainly did not help his standing. But politics, too, had aligned against Tetepachsit. Perhaps the darkest mark on the old chief's record was his involvement in land cessions. He had fixed his mark to numerous treaties with the Americans, including the Treaty of Greenville and the controversial cession of 1804. Like Buckongahelas, he afterward protested the 1804 treaty, but he was never able to endear himself to his people in the manner of Buckongahelas. Most importantly, Tetepachsit was unable or unwilling to carry on Delaware opposition to the land cession of 1804 after Buckongahelas's death. Thus, in July 1805 the Delawares removed Tetapachsit from his position as principal chief and placed him under arrest.[21]

This move was primarily political in nature and occurred within the established framework of Delaware governance. But accusing him of witchcraft was another matter entirely. This was a situation of great importance for the White River Delawares. It was a situation that required adjudication by individuals of standing and respect. With Buckongahleas dead and Hockingpomska lost to alcoholism, there was a generational gap in leadership within Delaware society. While the move against Tetepachsit was in many regards a political coup by a younger generation of Delawares who had become disenchanted with the leadership of their venerable statesman, these younger Delawares did not yet have the standing in their communities to condemn Tetepachsit for witchcraft without sparking civil strife. Even Beata refused to publically condemn Tetapchsit for witchcraft, insisting that she was "after all a woman" and lacked such authority. Yet perhaps the younger Delawares simply realized they did not need to make that bold of a power play. There was no need to potentially fracture Delaware society further, not when there was an individual of considerable power and prestige nearby, someone who could judge the merits of the witchcraft accusation against Tetepachsit and whose ruling would carry enough authority that Delaware society would not tear itself apart in contention. Thus, in March 1806 the White River Delawares invited Tenskwatawa, the Shawnee prophet, to visit their villages and expose the witches hiding within the Delaware communities.[22]

Tenkswatawa was a Shawnee who lived in a nearby village on the White River. Originally known as Lalawethicka, he was a brother of the influential Shawnee warrior Tecumseh. Yet despite his notable family affiliation, Lalawethicka had failed at most aspects of his life, eventually submitting to alcoholism and despondency. But in April 1805 he too began to experience powerful visions. After he fell into a trancelike state that left his relatives thinking he had died, he proclaimed himself the voice of the Creator, whom he called the Master of Life, and renamed himself Tenskwatawa, "the Open Door." His former life was over. No longer was he Lalawethicka the drunk; now he was a spiritual medium through which the Master of Life would teach his Indian children. His preaching was in many regards similar to that of Beata: the Indians had fallen into ruin because they had neglected their traditional rituals and customs; any return to prosperity must be preceded by a return to traditional customs and values, at least so far as this could be accomplished given their present state of affairs. Like Beata, he delivered a Christian-influenced message of an Indian afterlife, where oppressed but faithful Indians would be rewarded with an eternity in paradise while the wicked would be relegated to hell to be punished for their misdeeds. This message of hope resonated powerfully throughout the downtrodden Indian communities in the region. While Tenskwatawa made it clear that the Indians themselves deserved blame for their condition, he also revealed the existence of an evil spirit who was constantly working to bring Indian peoples to ruin. That spirit had its own Indian followers—Beata's witches, for instance—but its principal agents were the Americans, whom the Master of Life did not create. Instead, they were "the children of the evil spirit." Americans thus must be avoided, and Indians should rid themselves of American technology and material items. By naming the Americans as the servants of the evil spirit, Tenskwatawa put a common face on the enemy of all Indians, in the process ensuring that he would be the lead voice for the Indian revival. He became "the Prophet," and his teachings spread like wildfire through the Indian communities along the White River and throughout Indiana, quickly elevating him to a position of status and influence perhaps unrivaled by any other Indian leader on the frontier.[23]

Many Delawares from the White River traveled to Tenskwatawa's village to hear his message. The Prophet's warning against witches in Indian society resonated strongly with the Delawares, as Beata had issued the same message. Thus, the Delawares began to search for suspected witches in their midst; and when they found them, they summoned Tenskwatawa to confirm their suspicions and pass judgment, especially on the former chief, Tetepachsit. The Prophet arrived at the main Delaware village of Woapicamikunk (Wapicomekoke) in March 1806 to find that the proceedings had already begun. Impatient factions among the younger Delawares had been torturing Tetepachist with fire for two days, promising the old chief "that if he would surrender his poison and give up his bad art, he would be pardoned, but if he should refuse, he should be killed by tomahawk and have his body thrown into the fire." Under such extreme duress, Tetepachsit confessed to witchcraft and claimed to have hidden his poison at the Moravian mission. A delegation of young warriors, described by the Moravians as "seven wild Indians with their faces painted black," descended on the mission, where they arrested a Moravian convert, Joshua, who Tetepachsit had implicated in his witchcraft confession. Tetepachist recanted his confession once his torturers relented, but it was too late. The old chief, the Moravian convert Joshua, and approximately a dozen other accused were brought forth to face the Prophet.[24]

Tenskwatawa quickly named Tetepachsit and Hockinpomska, who had also now been accused, as witches. Joshua, the Moravian convert, was exonerated of witchcraft, but Tenskwatawa found him to be possessed of an evil spirit, so he too was condemned. An elderly woman, Caritas, a Moravian convert also known as Anne Charity, was the first to die. Delaware warriors tortured her by suspending her on a spit over a raging fire until she confessed, then lowering her into the fire. Tellingly, Caritas had adopted many Euro-American manners and customs of dress, which given the current climate along the White River doomed her perhaps as much as any other factor. Tetepachsit was next to go. Ten warriors with blackened faces dragged the old chief to the Moravian mission to locate the hiding place of Tetepachsit's poisons, but when they failed to discover anything, the warriors tomahawked Tetepachsit and threw his body into a hastily built fire. Joshua, the Moravian convert, was similarly tomahawked and burned alive, despite persistent pleas from Kluge and Luckenbach to spare him.[25]

The situation became complicated, and far more dangerous, following the departure of Tenskwatawa after the executions of Tetepachsit and Joshua. One of Tetepachsit's nephews, a Moravian convert and devout Christian named Billy Patterson, was accused and executed. But when the widow of Tetepachsit was condemned, an internal revolt against the witch hunt erupted. The brother of Tetepachsit's widow, a young warrior, intervened and prevented the execution of his sister, leading her away from the village while defying any among the Delawares to touch her. He soon returned and declared that it was Tenskwatawa who was in fact a witch. "An evil spirit has come among us," the young warrior intoned, "and we are killing each other." Perhaps emboldened by such bravery, warriors from Hockingpomska's village refused to allow the execution of their aged chief, despite his weakness for alcohol. Six warriors interceded as the old chief was prepared for execution and threatened to kill anyone who attempted to impose the sentence against Hockingpomska. Faced with this rebellion and the prospect of civil war in the White River villages, the mystics and the supporters of the Prophet backed down and released the eight remaining prisoners, including Hockingpomska.[26]

The witchcraft hysteria was an expression of the tension and suffering among the White River Delawares. The long years of war, dislocation, and deprivation erupted in a powerful expression of anguish and anxiety. The Delawares wanted to understand how they had been reduced to such a wretched condition. Their mystics told them that it was their own fault, that the Delawares had forsaken their traditional beliefs and become too much like their American counterparts. Yet, even within this generalized message of self-loathing there was a sliver of exoneration for the Delawares, for there were evil agents among them who sought to turn them from their rightful path. The witch hunts were intended to purge Delaware society of these forces, and thus they targeted those in their society who exemplified their tormentors, real or imagined. The accusation and execution of several Moravian converts during the witch crisis was a brutally symbolic rejection of the Moravians themselves. It proved effective. Sensing that the time when they were welcome along the White River had passed, the Moravian missionaries fled in September 1806. Similarly, the Delawares' attack against suspected witches within their communities was also a desperate backlash against the continued devastation that disease wrought among their people. The sickness that had plagued the Delawares through the winter of 1805–6 began to subside about the time the witch crisis hit its peak. It is uncertain how the

Delawares interpreted this development, but it is natural to surmise that it must have confirmed their suspicions and bolstered their confidence that they had done what was necessary. While these are important considerations, the witch crisis was at its core profoundly a political event. Buckongahelas, Tetepachsit, and Hockingpomska had directed the political and military fortunes of their people for three decades. In many regards, the death of Buckongahelas triggered the witch crisis, and by its end Tetepachsit had been condemned and executed. Hockingpomska barely escaped with his life, and he lost his position as head of the Wolf division. The witch crisis was a transition from an older established generation and pattern of leadership to something new. Thus, in many regards the Delaware witch crisis marked the end of an era. A younger generation rebelled and sought to assume leadership of the Delawares in Indiana, a new generation born to power in the heat of the witch crisis and the passions it had enflamed and determined to set their people back on the path to salvation and security.

If only it had been so simple. When the witch crisis subsided, the Delawares found themselves in the same precarious situation as before, hemmed in by the expanding American nation, under pressure to relinquish their remaining lands, and economically dependent on the very nation that seemed determined to dislodge them from Indiana. Indeed, the witch crisis brought a harsh warning from Governor Harrison, who admonished the Delawares for their actions and advised them to "let your poor old men and women sleep in quietness, and banish from your minds the dreadful idea of being burnt alive by their own friends and countrymen." The governor encouraged the Delawares to divorce themselves from Tenskwatawa, who would only lead them to "endless woe and misery." Harrison had become very concerned about the Prophet, who he increasingly considered a threat to American interests. But the Delawares stubbornly defended their actions, telling Harrison that "you white people also try your criminals, and when they are found guilty, you hang them or kill them, and we do the same among ourselves."[27]

The Delawares' response to Harrison was an expression of autonomy, a product of their determination not to be dominated by the Americans any longer. But reality was quickly setting in after the chaos of the witch crisis. While some Delawares certainly supported the Prophet, the majority of the Delawares were not adamant followers of Tenskwatawa. He had not sparked the witch crisis in their villages but, rather, had participated in a process already under way. Now the Delawares were caught in a difficult position. Harrison had warned them to disown the Prophet, yet to do so would be to go against the warnings of their own mystics, who counseled the Delawares to distance themselves from the Americans. Indeed, Tetepachsit was dead and Hockingpomska deposed in large part because younger Delawares believed they were too accommodating in their relationship with American officials. Still, most Delawares did not want to openly side with Tenskwatawa against the Americans for fear of losing their annuities. The mystics warned that allegiance to the Americans promised cultural ruin, but what other choice was there?

As they had for more than sixty years, the Delawares tried to chart their own course through the storm. In an unlikely twist, the Delawares, who had so recently overturned their old leadership for being too accommodating and too rooted in the past, reinstated elements of the that leadership. Kickthawenund, better known as William Anderson, became principal chief. While younger than Tetepchasit or Hokcinpomska, he was very much their contemporary. Under his leadership, the Delaware Council reached back into history and reasserted Delaware neutrality. They vowed to take no part in the escalating conflict between the Americans and Tenskwatawa. In the years after the witch crisis, the Delawares in Indiana began to distance themselves from Tenskwatawa and his growing legion of followers. It was a calculated process designed to insulate the Delawares from any forthcoming American military reprisal against the Prophet. In April 1808, when Tenskwatawa sought to establish a new village on the nearby Wabash River, the Delawares joined with the Miamis in an effort to block the Shawnee Prophet and his followers from settling along the Wabash. Having Tenskwatawa and his followers so close to their White River villages would possibly imperil the Delawares if the Americans decided to move against the Prophet. But Tenskwatawa ignored them and established his new village, Prophetstown, along the Wabash River so that he could "watch the Boundary Line between the Indians and the white people—and if a white man put his foot over it that warriors could easily put him back." Sensing the danger of being located so close to Tenskwatawa, the Delawares sent another delegation to the Prophet that summer asking him to dismiss his followers and live in peace. But a party of warriors under Tecumseh intercepted the delegation, dismissed their demands, and sent the Delawares back to the White River with "some indications of apprehension and terror."[28]

The pivotal moment for the White River Delawares perhaps came in September 1809, when Governor Harrison organized a meeting at Fort Wayne to discuss the cession of lands along the lower Wabash River. The Delawares were present, although their claim to the lands in question was debatable. Still, Harrison viewed them as important players in the drama unfolding along the frontier. The Delawares, for their part, seemed to be aware of their importance to Harrison and tried to use this to their advantage at the conference. Initially, the Delawares stayed neutral during the conference proceedings, but gradually they aligned themselves with Harrison and supported the sale against reluctant groups of Miamis. Harrison alluded that British agents must be at work among those Indians who would not sell, and the Delawares may have decided to throw their support behind the Americans if war was on the horizon. But ultimately it was the promise of additional annuities that prompted the Delawares and other Indians to agree to the cession. The Delawares secured a badly needed increase of $500 to their annuity, as well as a healthy share of $5,200 worth of goods Harrison distributed as gifts at the treaty signing. Both provided aid for the struggling Delaware communities along the White River, but their acceptance marked a reintegration of the Delawares into the American sphere of influence. Indeed, it appeared that the turmoil of 1805–6 had come full circle, as William Anderson, much like his former associates Tetepachsit and Hickingpomska, signed the treaty and accepted the annuities.[29]

The Treaty of Fort Wayne was an important and divisive event along the frontier in the years immediately preceding the War of 1812. In many ways it divided the Indian peoples who had accepted the treaty from those who did not. Indeed, for some Indians, particularly the supporters of Tenskwatawa and his brother Tecumseh, the Fort Wayne cession was a call to war. Tecumseh openly proclaimed that he would never allow the lands ceded at Fort Wayne to be surveyed or settled, while the Prophet warned Governor Harrison that "his people should not come any nearer to him . . . he smelt them too strong already." Tensions were high, as evidenced by a renewed witch crisis among the Delawares in 1810. As many as a dozen White River Delawares were reportedly condemned and executed as witches, but little else is known about the conditions that precipitated the crisis. Politics may again have been at the center of the turmoil. It is uncertain how many Delawares heeded the Shawnee brothers' call for war, but it is apparent that some young warriors left the White River villages for Prophetstown. However, the majority of the Delawares living in Indiana refused to join the militants and tried to remain apart from any potential conflict. Perhaps the Delawares still remembered their bitter defeat at Fallen Timbers, as well as the promise made by Buckongahelas at the Treaty of Greenville to never again make war against the Americans. Or the White River Delawares may have realized that their existence had become so heavily tied to American annuities that they simply could not risk the loss of their economic lifeline. Whatever their motivation, the bulk of Delawares resisted the overtures of Tenskwatawa and Tecumseh. The witch executions that spring may have been a purging of militants, as there was no visible turnover at the top of the Delaware political hierarchy. William Anderson remained as principal chief, despite having signed the Treaty of Fort Wayne, and the Delaware Council adopted policies that trended against the designs of Tecumseh and the Prophet.[30]

Accordingly, the spring following the Treaty of Fort Wayne was a dangerous time. Tenskwatawa and Tecumseh recruited heavily in an effort to create a pan-Indian force to oppose any further American land demands, violently if necessary. At the same time, the Delawares sought to curry favor with the Americans by serving as intermediaries and negotiators, hoping, in the process, to somehow forestall or avert a war that was not of their making. During a secluded meeting in May, several Indian nations, including the Delawares, rejected overtures from the Prophet to join his militant followers. Indeed, the White River Delawares staunchly opposed a war against the United States. In their estimation, it was a battle that would end badly for all Indians, not just the militants. To that end, the Delawares delivered a message from Governor Harrison warning that all Indians would be imperiled if war erupted, as the American militia would be unable to differentiate between hostile and peaceful Indians. It was perhaps a hollow threat, but it underscored the Delawares' conviction that the policies of Teskwatawa and Tecumseh endangered all Indians in the region.[31]

That fear substantially increased over the course of the following year. As tensions between Governor Harrison and the Shawnee brothers mounted, the Delawares struggled to remain neutral. Neither side made it easy for them. In July 1810 warriors from Prophetstown stole horses and slaughtered livestock belonging to newly settled American farmers along the Wabash and White rivers. This directly imperiled the Delawares, who were the closest Indian nation to the American settlements. During the summer of 1811 Governor Harrison reminded the Indian nations in Indiana of the pledges made at the Treaty of Greenville, in which the assembled Indians had promised to obstruct the efforts of Indians that fomented war against the United States. The Delawares, bound by the agreement, once again adopted the role of messengers and intermediaries. As Harrison prepared an assault against

Prophetstown, which he timed to coincide with the absence of Tecumseh, he dispatched a group of Delawares to the White River to warn friendly Indian nations to stay clear of the army's approach. The governor then asked the Delawares to join a delegation of Miamis who were traveling to the Prophet to deliver an ultimatum and outline Harrison's terms for peace. A party of Tenkswatawa's warriors captured the Delaware chiefs en route and took them under guard to Prophetstown, where Tenskwatawa belittled the Delawares for their refusal to join his cause. Confident of victory, the Prophet boasted that he would roast the Americans in fire, but he allowed the Delawares to depart under promises that they would remain neutral in the coming fight. While a scattering of warriors had already joined the militants, the majority of the Delawares retired to their villages and observed their official position of neutrality, although they must have waited anxiously for news of the outcome of the conflict.[32]

Delaware neutrality appeared to pay off. On 7 November 1811 Harrison's army defeated the Prophet's followers at the Battle of Tippecanoe Creek. It was a serious blow for the militants' cause, but hardly the end of tension along the frontier. But for the Delawares it provided a chance to breathe. The American victory and the Delawares' refusal to side with the militants ensured that their government annuities, valued at $1,600–$1,800 per year after the 1809 Treaty of Fort Wayne, would continue to be paid without interruption. But danger still abounded. In 1812 the conflict between Harrison and Tenskwatawa and Tecumseh became part of a larger dispute between Great Britain and the United States. During the War of 1812, Tecumseh, emboldened by British promises of assistance, renewed his call for war. Again the Delawares refused. In May 1812, during a multitribal conference along the Mississinewa River in eastern Indiana, the Delawares rebuked Tecumseh, telling the Shawnee leader that "we have not met at this place to hear such words."[33] Over the next two years, as the war intensified along the frontier, many Delawares left the White River and relocated to western Ohio in order to safeguard themselves from Tecumseh's warriors, as well as American militia that might mistake them for enemies. Those who remained along the White River did so at their own peril, although Harrison made at least some effort to protect them. He specifically ordered his troops not to attack Delaware villages during a campaign against the Miamis during the winter of 1812–13. Following the attack on the Miamis, some additional Delaware warriors joined Tecumseh's ranks, but American success in the Battle of Lake Erie undercut their support. Indeed, the Delawares appear to have been among those Indians who defected from the cause just prior to Tecumseh's defeat at the Battle of the Thames in October 1813. By the following summer the war on the frontier was essentially over. In July 1814 Harrison negotiated a peace treaty with the defeated militants, now nominally led by Teskwatawa. In the treaty proceedings, the Delawares, lauded for having "preserved their fidelity to the United States throughout the war," were named a partner of the United States in the granting of peace.[34]

Much like they had done during the Revolutionary era, the Delawares had employed a strategy of self-interested neutrality during the twenty years between the Treaty of Greenville and the end of the War of 1812. The Delawares had shifted their allegiance in order to attain the best terms for themselves. At the end of the War of 1812, it seemed as though their strategy had been successful. The Delawares believed themselves to be allies and partners with the United States. But it was only an illusion. Years of war and pan-Indian resistance had created a mind-set among Americans that would not allow any form of partnership with native peoples. The period from the onset of the French and Indian War through the end of the War of 1812 was in many regards a single, sustained war between westward-moving Americans and native peoples focused on maintaining their cultural and territorial autonomy. It was a struggle often characterized by brutal and merciless tactics, with both sides participating in gruesome atrocities intended to terrorize the enemy into submission. By the conclusion of the War of 1812, the Americans had emerged as the victors of this long struggle. But preconditioned by decades of conflict to distrust and hate Indians, the Americans were not inclined to offer the Delawares a place in the emerging national landscape. Rather, they had come to embrace the policies of Thomas Jefferson, who believed that Indians, even those who had not directly opposed American interests, had to be removed in order for American destiny to be fulfilled. Thus, within three years, the American government coerced the Delawares into ceding their remaining lands in Indiana. Under the terms of the 1818 Treaty of St. Mary's, the Delawares surrendered their lands along the White River and agreed to relocate west of the Mississippi River. It was a bitter pill for the Delawares to swallow. William Anderson, still principal chief of the Delawares, summarized Delaware sentiments after the treaty:

> A little more than a year ago the United States agent advised us to adopt the habits of civilized life. At that time his word was very good . . . [but] scarcely had we commenced this course, when we were asked to cede our lands to the

> white people. Something of this has been done; the white people now claim our country, and desire that we should leave it—and now we know not what to do. I think that the men who made this bargain with us have done wrong.[35]

In November 1820 American agents at Kaskaskia, Illinois, reported that 1,346 Delawares, along with 1,499 horses, had crossed the Mississippi en route to Cape Girardeau in Missouri territory. The Delawares' long struggle for autonomy and security in the East was over, ended by the American victory at the Battle of Lake Erie and the frontier triumph it helped to secure for the United States during the War of 1812. The Delawares sought to avoid the loss of their lands by remaining apart from the fighting and, in some regards, by aiding the American cause. Neither would win them favor, in the East or in the West. Anderson hoped that at long last that the United States government would "send me a paper that will give us sure title to the land to which we are going, so that the white people may no more disturb us." Such would not be the case. The Delawares would eventually settle along the James Fork of the White River in southwest Missouri before relocating again to Kansas territory in 1829. Additional removals and migrations would follow. Their long ordeal in the East had ended, but the Delawares would continue to face challenges to their autonomy amid a difficult contest for survival in the trans-Mississippi West.[36]

NOTES

1. Donald R. Hickey, *The War of 1812: A Forgotten Conflict* (Urbana: University of Illinois Press, 1989), 130–39; John Sugden, *Tecumseh: A Life* (New York: Henry Holt, 1997), 354–60.

2. C. A. Weslager, *The Delaware Indians: A History* (New Brunswick, NJ: Rutgers University Press, 1972), 31–76; Stephen Craig Harper, *Promised Land: Penn's Holy Experiment, the Walking Purchase, and the Dispossession of the Delawares, 1600–1763* (Bethlehem, PA: Lehigh University Press, 2006), 13–17; Amy C. Schutt, *People of the River Valleys: The Odyssey of the Delaware Indians* (Philadelphia: University of Pennsylvania Press, 2007), 7–59.

3. Harper, *Promised Land,* 46–101; Daniel P. Barr, "A Road for Warriors: The Western Delawares and the Seven years' War in Pennsylvania," *Pennsylvania History: A Journal of Mid-Atlantic Studies* 73 (Winter 2006): 1–7.

4. Barr, "A Road for Warriors," 8–36; Daniel P. Barr, ed., *The Boundaries Between Us: Natives and Newcomers Along the Frontiers of the Old Northwest Territory, 1750–1850* (Kent, OH: Kent State University Press, 2006), 25–43.

5. Colin G. Calloway, *The Scratch of a Pen: 1763 and the Transformation of North America* (New York: Oxford University Press, 2006), 47–91. For a more detailed examination of Delaware participation in Pontiac's War, see Gregory Evans Dowd, *War Under Heaven: Pontiac, the Indian Nations, and the British Empire* (Baltimore: John Hopkins University Press, 2002); and

David Dixon, *Never Come to Peace Again: Pontiac's Uprising and the fate of the British Empire in North America* (Norman: University of Oklahoma Press, 2005).

6. Weslager, *Delaware Indians,* 282–316. For a first-person assessment of White Eyes' efforts to Christianize and westernize the Delawares, see Hermann Wellenreuther and Carola Wessel, eds., *The Moravian Mission Diaries of David Zeisberger, 1772–1781* (University Park: Penn State Press, 2005). For Gnadenhutten, see Leonard Sadosky, "Rethinking the Gnadenhutten Massacre: The Contest for Power in the Public World of the Revolutionary Pennsylvania Frontier," in *The Sixty Years War for the Great Lakes,* ed. David Curtis Skaggs and Larry L. Nelson (East Lansing: Michigan State University Press, 2001), 187–214.

7. Weslager, *Delaware Indians,* 317–22, 330; Wiley Sword, *President Washington's Indian War: The Struggle for the Old Northwest, 1790–1795* (Norman: University of Oklahoma Press, 1985), 324–31; Richard White, *The Middle Ground: Indians, Empires, and Republics in the Great Lakes Region, 1650–1815* (New York: Cambridge University Press, 1991), 413–68. For a detailed accounting of the Delawares' involvement in the Northwest Indian Wars of the 1790s, particularly the role of Buckongahelas, see John Sugden, *Blue Jacket: Warrior of the Shawnees* (Lincoln: University of Nebraska Press, 2000).

8. Weslager, *Delaware Indians,* 333–36; Lawrence Henry Gipson, ed., *The Moravian Indian Mission on the White River: Diaries and Letters, May 5, 1799–November 12, 1806* (Indianapolis: Indiana Historical Bureau, 1938), 107–8, 166–67; Earl P. Olmstead, *Blackcoats Among the Delaware: David Zeisberger on the Ohio Frontier* (Kent, OH: Kent State University Press, 1991), 114–16; Andrew R. L. Cayton, *Frontier Indiana* (Bloomington: Indiana University Press, 1996), 197–98.

9. Gipson, *Moravian Indian Mission,* 297, 484; Weslager, *Delaware Indians,* 336–38; Cayton, *Frontier Indiana,* 200.

10. Gipson, *Moravian Indian Mission,* 141, 155, 406, 436; Weslager, *Delaware Indians,* 342.

11. Gipson, *Moravian Indian Mission,* 346, 356; Robert M. Owens, *Mr. Jefferson's Hammer: William Henry Harrison and the Origins of American Indian Policy* (Norman: University of Oklahoma Press, 2007), 119. For an excellent assessment of the impact of the Gnadenhutten massacre on Moravian missionary efforts in Ohio and Canada, see John P. Bowes, "The Gnadenhutten Effect: Moravian Converts and the Search for Safety on the Canadian Borderlands," *Michigan Historical Review* 34 (Spring 2008): 101–18.

12. Gipson, *Moravian Indian Mission,* 346, 359–62, 381–82; Sugden, *Tecumseh,* 109–10.

13. Sugden, *Tecumseh,* 106; Owens, *Mr. Jefferson's Hammer,* 78–79.

14. Logan Esarey, ed., *Messages and Letters of William Henry Harrison,* 2 vols. (Indianapolis: Indiana Historical Commission, 1922), 1:141, 147, 161, 164; Charles J. Kappler, ed., *Indian Treaties 1778–1883* (New York: Interland Publishing, 1972), 72, 80–81; Gipson, *Moravian Indian Mission,* 328–29, 379, 385; Owens, *Mr. Jefferson's Hammer,* 84–85, 100–105.

15. Gipson, *Moravian Indian Mission,* 262; Cayton, *Frontier Indiana,* 205; Owens, *Mr. Jefferson's Hammer,* 120.

16. Gipson, *Moravian Indian Mission,* 333–35, 339–40, 354–55; Sugden, *Tecumseh,* 114; Owens, *Mr. Jefferson's Hammer,* 120.

17. Gipson, *Moravian Indian Mission,* 402.

18. Ibid., 339–40.

19. Ibid., 256; Sugden, *Tecumseh,* 109–10; Owens, *Mr. Jefferson's Hammer,* 123.

20. Gipson, *Moravian Indian Mission,* 339–40.

21. Ibid., 111, 357–58, 394–95; Esarey, *Messages and Letters,* 1:117–18, 121–23; Owens, *Mr. Jefferson's Hammer,* 123; White, *The Middle Ground,* 501.

22. Gipson, *Moravian Indian Mission,* 621.

23. R. David Edmunds, *The Shawnee Prophet* (Lincoln: University of Nebraska Press, 1983), 28–41; Cayton, *Frontier Indiana,* 205–8.

24. Gipson, *Moravian Indian Mission,* 618, 621; Edmunds, *The Shawnee Prophet,* 43; Olmstead, *Blackcoats Among the Delaware,* 181–84; Sugden, *Tecumseh,* 122–23.

25. Gipson, *Moravian Indian Mission,* 414–16, 557–610; John Heckewelder, *A Narrative of the Mission of the United Brethren Among the Delaware and Mohegan Indians, from Its Commencement in the Year 1740 to the Close of the Year 1808* (New York: Arno Press, 1971), 410–15; Harry Emilius Stocker, *A History of the Moravian Mission Among the Indians on the White River in Indiana* (Bethlehem, PA: Times Publishing, 1917), 115; Edmunds, *The Shawnee Prophet,* 43–45.

26. Gipson, *Moravian Indian Mission,* 420; Stocker, *History of the Moravian Mission,* 115–16; Edmunds, *The Shawnee Prophet,* 45–46.

27. Esarey, *Messages and Letters of Harrison,* 1:182–84; Gipson, *Moravian Indian Mission,* 421–22, 623; Edmunds, *The Shawnee Prophet,* 47–48.

28. Clarence E. Carter, ed., *The Territorial Papers of the United States,* 28 vols. (Washington, DC: Government Printing Office, 1934–75), 7:558–60; Esarey, *Messages and Letters of Harrison,* 1:290–91; Edmunds, *The Shawnee Prophet,* 69–70, 75.

29. Esarey, *Messages and Letters of Harrison,* 1:362–78; Kappler, *Indian Treaties,* 101–2; Edmunds, *The Shawnee Prophet,* 80–81; Sugden, *Tecumseh,* 183–84.

30. Esarey, *Messages and Letters of Harrison,* 1:387–91, 422–30. For the reaction of Tenskwatawa and Tecumseh to the 1809 Fort Wayne Treaty, see Edmunds, *The Shawnee Prophet,* 81–93; and Sugden, *Tecumseh,* 185–90, 209. My interpretation of the 1810 witch crisis generally follows Sugden, *Tecumseh,* 436–37n13. More detailed records for other Indian nations who also experienced similar witch crises in 1809–10 suggest that the majority of these nations were opposed to Tenskwatawa and Tecumseh. Sugden believes the witch crises were rooted in illness and suffering rather than the influence of the Prophet, but it seems at least equally likely that they were influenced by political discord. In most cases, antiwar factions conducted the trials and imposed the death sentences, perhaps in an effort to destroy any vestiges of support for the war in their communities.

31. Esarey, *Messages and Letters of Harrison,* 1:433–36, 438; Edmunds, *The Shawnee Prophet,* 82; Sugden, *Tecumseh,* 195.

32. Esarey, *Messages and Letters of Harrison,* 1:589–92, 599–603; Weslager, *Delaware Indians,* 344–45; Edmunds, *The Shawnee Prophet,* 105–6; Sugden, *Tecumseh,* 228–30. Weslager cites a report that the Delawares promised to send thirty warriors to support the American army during the battle, but there is no reliable evidence that any Delawares fought with Harrison's forces. See Weslager, *Delaware Indians,* 345.

33. Esarey, *Messages and Letters of Harrison,* 2:50–53; Edmunds, *The Shawnee Prophet,* 122–23.

34. Kappler, *Indian Treaties,* 105–7; Weslager, *Delaware Indians,* 345–46, 357n26; Edmunds, *The Shawnee Prophet,* 133, 140; Owens, *Mr. Jefferson's Hammer,* 235–38.

35. Isaac McCoy, *History of the Baptist Indian Missions* (Washington, DC: William M. Morrison, 1840), 52–54; Herbert C. Kraft, *The Lenape: Archeology, History, and Ethnography* (Newark: New Jersey Historical Society, 1986), 236–37; Cayton, *Frontier Indiana,* 263–64. The development of anti-Indian sentiments in the late eighteenth and early nineteenth centuries has been thoroughly investigated in recent scholarship. See, for example, Daniel K. Richter, *Facing East from Indian Country: A Native History of Early America* (Cambridge, MA: Harvard University Press, 2001), esp. 189–253; Patrick Griffin, *American Leviathan: Empire, Nation, and the Revolutionary Frontier* (New York: Hill & Wang, 2007), esp. 152–80; and Peter Silver, *Our Savage Neighbors: How Indian War Transformed Early America* (New York: W. W. Norton, 2008).

36. McCoy, *Baptist Indian Missions,* 59; Kraft, *Lenape,* 236–37. For a detailed examination of Delaware struggles in the trans-Mississippi West, see John P. Bowes, *Exiles and Pioneers: Eastern Indians in the Trans-Mississippi West* (New York: Cambridge University Press, 2007).

"The Disagreeablest Night I Ever Saw"

John Tipton, Tippecanoe, and the Dissolution of the Middle Ground

GINETTE ALEY

For twenty-five-year-old ensign John Tipton and the rest of Indiana Territory's Harrison County volunteer mounted riflemen, the campaign had already been especially grueling and tedious by the time they came within a mile of their Prophetstown target on 6 November 1811. His militia company, the Yellow Jackets, captained by Spier Spencer (his friend as well as the county's sheriff), had commenced the northerly march from southern Indiana on 12 September at Governor William Henry Harrison's request. Since then, Tipton's duties consisted of scouting, repairing guns, marching in deteriorating weather, standing guard, working on the building of Fort Harrison along the way, and tracking lost horses (which, according to his journal, was a problem that directly corresponded to the amount of drinking he and the men did). Tipton even had been mistakenly put under guard and taken to Governor Harrison for discipline but then let go. Tipton's company passed fleeting moments in amusements like shooting contests, card playing, and wrestling and other time hunting and fishing to supplement the woefully insufficient provisions. While whisky by the quart seemed always at hand, real sustenance was not. Five weeks into the campaign he noted that "we Supt last night on a bit of Bread about as big as a mans [two] fingers." By this time, men were murmuring about the conditions and impending Indian fight, and some had deserted. By 19 October Tipton was certainly miserable too. The rain that had consistently dogged them fell even harder and then, accompanied by strong winds, turned to snow. "It was," he wrote, "the Disagreeablest night I ever Saw."[1]

Tipton and the Yellow Jackets were part of a combined force of Indiana and Kentucky militias and more than 300 U.S. Army regulars, totaling about

1,000 men, charged with dispersing the supporters of the Shawnee Prophet and his brother, Tecumseh, whose presence and activities in and around Prophetstown on the Tippecanoe River created a great deal of anxiety among the American settlers. And with good reason. Although Harrison's detractors (including some scholars) contended that this show of American military force was unnecessary and motivated solely by his political ambition, it cannot be denied that many settlers and others believed that a coordinated Indian attack, egged on and perhaps supported by certain British agents, was imminent. Tense native-white relations had been the rule for the better part of a decade, if not much longer; indeed, one historian asserts that outbreaks of war and raiding in the Ohio Valley region were more the norm for at least the three generations leading up to the War of 1812. As for the Prophetstown campaign specifically, one of the Kentucky volunteers insisted that it was necessary because the "Shawnee Proffet . . . [and his followers] have been threatening us with ware & have carried matters to such lengths" as to require some action. True or not, this was a widely shared sentiment among American settlers, and one with some basis in actual lived experiences.[2]

The current hostilities stemmed from Governor Harrison's heavy-handed style, in large part encouraged by President Thomas Jefferson, in concluding a swift series of major land cession treaties in the Indiana Territory between 1803 and 1809. The most egregious of these was the 1809 Treaty of Fort Wayne in which Harrison pressured leaders of the Delawares, Miamis, Eel River Miamis, and Potawatomis to cede claims to yet another 2.5 million acres of land in southern Indiana and Illinois in return for an increase in annuities and more trade goods. Indianans and American expansionists welcomed the treaty as "good news"; the Prophet, Tecumseh, and their supporters vehemently did not. In fact, the bad faith way in which Harrison manipulated the various chiefs into signing away even more of a drastically shrinking land base prompted the angry and energized response that ultimately brought him and Tipton to Prophetstown two years later. They had come ostensibly to put down the spread of a pan-Indian movement that some believed was further enticed by the British (however covertly) to halt or impede American expansion any further into the Ohio Valley.[3]

Historian Richard White interprets this pan-Indian movement as a purposeful attempt to reassert "middle ground" dynamics with the Americans by which more accommodation and less usurpation would occur. But, unfortunately for Native American interests, larger, more complicated forces were now in play that diminished the utility of the middle ground, at least from the perspective of the Americans. For all intents and purposes any traditional middle ground context was gone. At this point the Old Northwest looked more like a borderland of hotly contested ground, or perhaps Michael McConnell's "a country between," than a middle ground of accommodation. Harrison's and Tipton's experiences in the ensuing Battle of Tippecanoe and the aftermath of the War of 1812 would translate into career currency and opportunities for both men, as one would expect in the context of an era that typically esteemed a man's character by his participation in military (i.e., militia) obligations as a great service to the republic. Tipton's extensive correspondence with his peers makes this point self-evident. It is also true that Tipton and his generation would exploit the failure of Tecumseh's efforts into an opportunity to expand white settlement into the upper Wabash Valley. If, as Harrison biographer Robert M. Owens argues, Harrison was Jefferson's hammer, then certainly Tipton was one of the nails used in Jeffersonian empire building in the Old Northwest. For Tipton, Tippecanoe reached beyond the political and military arenas and became an event that never really left him. Nor would he allow the memory or meaning of that tragic November morning be buried with the bones of dead comrades-in-arms.[4]

Accounts from both sides characterize the battle as having come on too quickly. In order to strike while the skilled and charismatic warrior Tecumseh was away (and in so doing hopefully thwart the pan-Indian confederacy's spread), Harrison had pushed his men north to Prophetstown. From Tipton's perspective, their approach on 6 November was greeted with consternation, pleading for peace, and a constant "hollowing" (hollering), as if they had disrupted plans, although perhaps the greatest source of confusion was the absence of Tecumseh's leadership in the face of Harrison's army. While the Prophet's agents had professed a desire for peace and for both parties to break for the evening and delay parlaying until the next day, Harrison's men had more than an inkling of what to expect. As it turned out, a good deal of the Indians' consternation was genuine. An Ottawa named Shabonee who was close to Tecumseh said afterward that "our people were more surprised than yours." They had misjudged the Americans on several accounts, he acknowledged, including how they would initially approach Prophetstown, despite having scouted them, as well as assumptions about the Americans' level of fatigue from the hard march. In getting Harrison to agree to break for the night, the Prophet was buying time for the warriors; but one of the

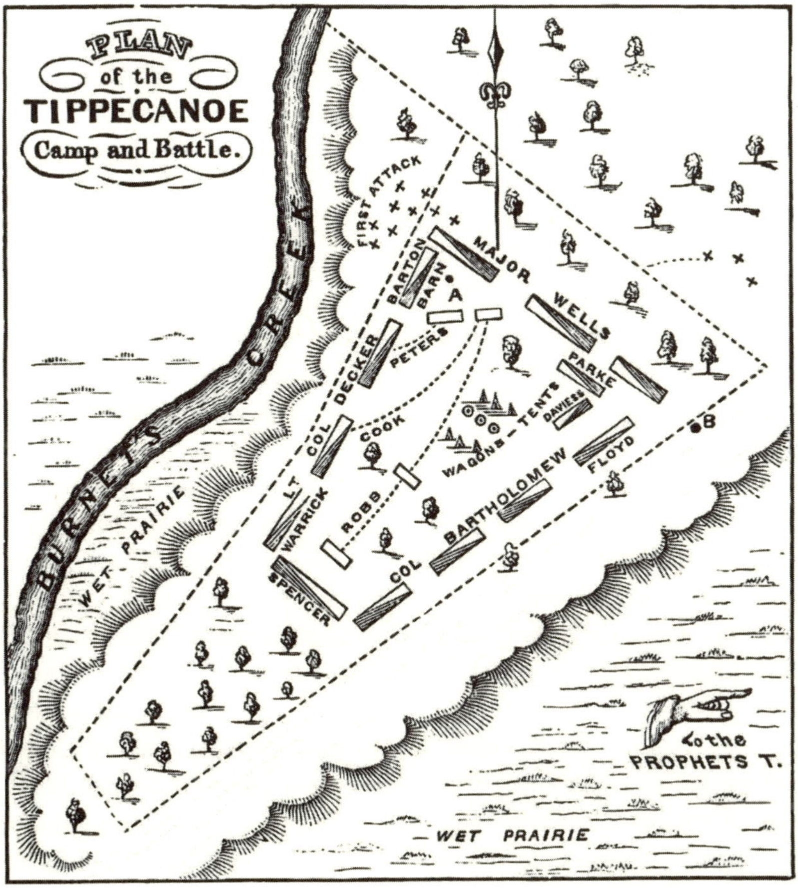

The Battle of Tippecanoe. Reprinted from Benson J. Lossing, *Pictorial Field-Book of the War of 1812* (New York: Harper Brothers, 1869), as modified by Bill Nelson Maps.

oldest maxims in fighting against Native Americans is to expect the surprise attack. Harrison's men were ready—mostly.[5]

Around 4:30 A.M. the Prophet's fighting force of about 500 warriors dramatically descended close in on Harrison's men, who on his orders the previous evening had lain down at arms to be prepared. Yet, apparently Harrison had failed to fortify the camp area, and this would cost him dearly in men and reputation. A failure to fortify the camp probably accounts for Tipton's (and others') description the morning of 7 November of the sudden "firring of guns and the Shawnies Brakeng into our tents." Without protective support,

Harrison's men had little time to react or seek cover, which generated some initial confusion, possibly even a friendly fire scenario. According to Tipton, the fierce and bloody combat kept up for two hours and twenty minutes. When it was over he recorded that 179 of their men had been killed or wounded, including a very high casualty rate among the officers. Although he believed that their Indian opponents lost a higher number, scholars tend to put that number at about fifty warriors. Regardless, Tipton wrote that "no Companey suffered like ours." When they held elections to replace the officers killed, Tipton was elected captain in the place of his dead friend, Spier Spencer, the first of many such opportunities that came out of Tippecanoe. His company finished the day burying the dead, caring for the wounded, building a breastwork, scrounging for provisions (netting only some whisky), and bracing for another possible night attack. The next day Harrison's men raided and burned the near-deserted Prophetstown, and the following day the victors began their slow, anguished march home.[6]

Two decades later, Tipton, as something of a self-appointed historian and memory keeper of the battle, was still publicly defending Harrison, correcting misinformation, and finding meaning in that campaign. In October 1833 Tipton chided the *Vincennes Gazette* for publishing what he called an erroneous account of the battle, particularly in the matter of the decision not to fortify the camp and the resulting loss of so many men. While something had been said the day before the attack about building a breastwork, he recalled, axes were scarce, and, considering this, "the prevalent opinion [was] that it was unnecessary." Moreover, he pointed out, Harrison was forced to take "a due regard to the exhausted condition of the soldiers, owing to forced marches on a reduced ration." And Tipton dismissed those who diminished either the battle's participants or its consequences. He asserted that the meaning was found in the events that followed in the War of 1812 and in the continued disintegration of the middle ground: "It has always been believed by those qualified to judge that this victory had much influence in shortening the war that commenced the ensuing spring and in saving many lives of the people of the Territory." This was true, he continued, because it was quite plausible that Prophetstown would have otherwise persisted as an influential "rallying point." The fact that the followers of the Prophet and Tecumseh were also "beaten upon their own ground with the advantage of their favorite mode of attack" (the surprise attack) had perhaps a greater meaning in the context of defeating Indian resistance than contemporaries realized. Tippecanoe was not merely a turning point for Tipton but for all those who lived in the region.[7]

American victory at Tippecanoe opened the door to linking the Old Northwest to the larger national conflict with the British and the War of 1812. Many Ohio Valley Native Americans decided to take their chances with the British after Tippecanoe and sided against the Americans, which led to a frightening number of raids and counterraids. Having established himself at Tippecanoe, Tipton saw his star rise quickly in the 5th Regiment of the Indiana Militia as the Territory clearly needed his military skills to protect the settlers during the war years. Beginning in May of 1812 with a commission to major, he was promoted on a yearly basis, being made colonel in April of 1814. He was gaining in public roles and authority, too, as he was made the deputy sheriff in Harrison County in June 1812 and four years later the sheriff, thus, once again, filling the job once held by Spier Spencer, his slain friend and captain at Tippecanoe. What is especially significant about his public roles in Harrison County is that the territorial capital had been moved there, to the county seat of Corydon, during the frenzy of the War of 1812. This and his participation in Masonry kept Tipton in the sphere of political activity, where he was increasingly comfortable and frequently sought out for commissions. His personal life and family dynamics changed as well, representing another of the consequences of Tippecanoe. In April of 1817, the same year he was commissioned brigadier general of the Third Brigade of the Indiana Militia, Tipton filed for divorce from his wife, Matty, essentially because she had already left him for another man and vowed not to return. He was granted the divorce and custody of their surviving three children, Joshua, Matilda, and Spier. The next year he was made guardian of the five children of a fellow soldier who had died at Tippecanoe.[8]

But the militia duty that kept Tipton busy as the War of 1812 played out was in many ways a continuation of a role that was familiar to him, that of protector. His orders were to protect the settlers on the frontiers of Harrison and Clark counties from Indian attacks, which included the building of blockhouses. As he did in the Prophetstown campaign, he kept detailed journals of the expeditions he undertook. Little out of the ordinary transpired during Tipton's expedition of May 1812, other than the men being warmly received by the residents and greatly tormented by the "muskeeters." In June, settlers on the Driftwood fork of the White River wrote asking for protection as well as the privilege of hosting a Fourth of July dinner for the men. The militia came and stayed so that some in the company could guard while others helped the settlers in their agricultural labors, including pulling flax. Compared to other campaigns, this was a very relaxed if not amusing expedition that Tipton described as involving a great deal of whisky drinking and hilarity and, after twenty days, having done "no good after indians." Indeed, Indianans in that part of the territory would recall this false sense of relative security, even against a backdrop of war, especially nearby Scott County residents. In the late afternoon on 3 September, a small party of Indians (supposedly Shawnees) came into the Pigeon Roost settlement and instigated a horrifying attack on unprotected families that left nine adults (reportedly eight of these were women) and fifteen children dead. The Territory was now at war. Hundreds of militia were called in to track down the offenders, and one of the survivors, John Kimberlin, gave provisions and forage to pursuing militia. (Years later Kimberlin petitioned the U.S. government for reimbursement, and it was Tipton who wrote the letter in support of a $150 payment.[9])

The Pigeon Roost attack ushered in a period of widespread fear in the Territory. In a letter to his wife in the attack's aftermath, Bourbon County, Kentucky, volunteer Captain Robert Hamilton observed that "the people in this country is all livig [*sic*] in forts except the Town[.] the Indians is very troublesome now." Men who were serving outside their counties petitioned their officers, who then petitioned Acting Territorial Governor John Gibson to be allowed to do their tour of duty closer to home. Residents of Clark County, home of the Pigeon Roost attack, petitioned President Madison to get Acting Governor Gibson to reinstate their local militia and to not ignore "the serious evil that will be produced by leaving our frontiers at this season of the year, unprotected." Indeed, with so many men called out to serve, western women, families, and communities were particularly vulnerable during the War of 1812, and the attack on Pigeon Roost proved that the vulnerability was real. As one would expect, Tipton's descriptions of his next Indian expedition, in March 1813, took on a far more serious tone as he now believed "that protection consists in offensive warfare." He recounted coming on a group of Indians who were constructing rafts presumably in preparation of another attack on nearby settlers. Tipton's men engaged them in a fierce twenty-minute skirmish that left one of their opponents dead and most of the rest apparently wounded. In April Tipton wrote to Acting Governor Gibson about "these rascals" the Delawares, who seemed to be harboring or enabling various raiding parties to "do mischief" and menace the settlers. He urged the governor for more protection for Clark and Harrison counties, as "our case is a dangerous one." He said that the settlers were "living between hope and despair, waiting to know their doom."[10]

The fears, alarms, and uncertainties in the Indiana Territory would fade as the intensity and hot spots of the War of 1812 in the Old Northwest shifted northward and essentially concluded in October 1813 with American victory at the Battle of the Thames. For Tipton and his contemporaries, the Battle of Lake Erie and its consequences opened a new world of change and opportunities. To Tipton's generation of westerners, these intermittent periods of tense native-white relations represented an all-too-familiar world. Family histories were often told by way of noting in which Indian wars male relatives had participated—but *not* as an illustration of the "backcountry" Indian-hating that Richard White links especially to Americans' incursions into the middle ground. What seems missing in that characterization is a degree of differentiation as well as a recognition that men like Tipton responded to their government's call to protect the settlers, the families and communities already at risk for (legally) inhabiting sparsely settled areas like the Indiana Territory, as opposed to the shear renegades acting out of an obvious deep-seated, race-based hatred. Tipton grew up understanding the weight of duty and the role of protector—and living in the West, he pushed the meanings of these terms beyond the common gendered expectations. He was a boy not yet seven years old in Sevier County, Tennessee, when his father was killed by warring Cherokees in 1793. Fourteen years later, in 1807, he migrated to the Indiana Territory with his mother and her family and continued living in a world in which tensions between Indians and whites occasionally flared.[11]

In this regard, the postwar Old Northwest was a different place. Scholars generally agree that Native American strength and influence in the interior declined drastically with the defeat of their British allies. They were less a conquered people than a people lodged in between their past and the dreaded road ahead. Indian removal west of the Mississippi, for example, was not an uncommon idea or prospect. The United States was rapidly moving toward the point when, according to historian James Merrell, by 1840, "widespread face-to-face contacts between Natives and whites were a thing of the past; never again would Indians occupy so central a place in American life." Instead of fighting Indians, men like Tipton became preoccupied with nailing down the boundaries of and seeking opportunities in the new state of Indiana (as of

1816). Although these were "peace times," as one of his correspondents put it, militia service was still expected, and he continued to advance. As primarily a well-connected county sheriff, reappointed to a second two-year term in 1818, Tipton still served as a protector of citizens, although not without controversy, the effects of the Panic of 1819, and some bad press. But his ambitions and reputation fostered an ironic dimension to his interactions with Indiana's native peoples and his role as protector. Tipton emerged as a man caught between his empathy for the Native Americans' circumstances and his own desire to encourage, even profit from, the expansion of white settlement.[12]

These were busy years for Tipton as well as for the new state of Indiana. As he was considering various paths to a career as a public official, he was repeatedly commissioned to assist the state in formalizing its identity because of his intimate knowledge of the area. In 1818 and 1819 he affixed the locations of the Warrick and Owen county seats (the latter county's citizens gave him the honor of naming the county seat, which he did in memory of a fallen Tippecanoe comrade). While he was unsuccessful in seeking land office appointments, he and several other Indiana officials enjoyed the privilege of dining with President James Monroe and General Andrew Jackson as they stopped in Corydon on a tour of the West in June 1819 and even toasted William Henry Harrison as "the hero of Tippecanoe." In May 1820 Tipton published his candidacy for representative in the general assembly and left Corydon as one of those commissioned to locate a new seat of government for the state in the future city of Indianapolis.[13]

A few months shy of his thirty-fourth birthday, Tipton found much to contemplate during this expedition about his life and changes in native-white relations since Tippecanoe and the War of 1812. Like many western men of his generation, these two factors were inextricably linked. Within the first week he made a number of observations about how circumstances were different now: it was the first time since 1814 that he had slept in a tent or killed a deer; he had found a tree on which he had carved his name and the date, 19 June 1813; and their interactions with Indians along the way were markedly different. Often Tipton's party stayed over in Indian towns or camps and was extended hospitality that included wood, shelter, bark to sleep on, food, and playing games. But he also noted seeing "drunk Indians this morning." The tragic irony of the situation struck him that, altogether, these were "altereded times Since 1813 when I was last here hunting the Indians with whom we now eat Drink and Sleep." More than this, he noted, "they have sold thier land for a Trifle and [are] prepareing to leave the Country where the[y] have laid their fathers and relatives," this same place where the commissioners sought to build a new state capital. Tipton and his fellow commissioners were merely following through on the American victory years earlier in asserting a new identity for this place despite any reservations they may have had about the consequences. Indeed, on 7 June they agreed on the location and told their clerk to draw up the papers. That evening Tipton noticed a small ferry with a canoe tied alongside approaching the site, both loaded with the household goods of two immigrant families. As they were unloading, he bought some corn and whisky from them. Given the decisions of that day, he believed this to be a symbolically important moment: "at 45 p[ast] 6 the first Boat landed that ever was Seen at the seat of Government."[14]

While Tipton appeared to grasp his significance in Indiana's early history and the transformation of Indiana's identity from middle ground or borderland to American state, he was also acutely aware that financial rewards would have to come from some other source. Careful recorder that he was, Tipton concluded his journal of the expedition by stating that his absence of twenty-seven days resulted in being paid $2 for every twenty-five miles traveled, plus $2 for each day spent carrying out his duty, for a total of $58. This represented "not half what I could have made in my office [as sheriff]" and was thus "a very poor compensation." However, a few months later Tipton learned that he had won the representative election (by a considerable margin over the other candidates) and was also elected Grand Master of the Grand Lodge of Masons in Indiana. In April 1821 he was again appointed to act as a commissioner on behalf of the state, this time to "adjust, run, and mark" the boundary line separating Indiana from Illinois (which had become a state at the end of 1818). This responsibility took him back to the Tippecanoe battleground within four months of the tenth anniversary of the battle, and not for the last time.[15]

Even more than during the previous expedition, Tipton's party encountered numerous friendly Indians who offered hospitality, valuable information, and their services as guides and more. Their aggravations, however, were considerable: mosquitoes ("verry plenty and Large"), tedious and dangerous swamps, and grass higher than their heads. Fort Dearborn, on the western shore of Lake Michigan, was far more impressive to Tipton, with its "comfortable Barracks and Rooms for soldiers & officers," than was Chicago, which was no more than a village "of about 9 or 10 houses & families[,] mostly French Trader[s] without any kind of civil government." This area, too, was part of the landscape of the War of 1812. Not far from the fort they came on the site, including human bones, of the infamous August 1812 attack and massacre of soldiers and families evacuating to Fort Wayne by a force of some 500 Potawatomis, Winnebagos, Kickapoos, Chippewas, and other native peoples. The commissioners and their crew moved on, and, a week later, on 7 July, Tipton faced the ghosts of Tippecanoe and was profoundly affected by what he encountered. He remarked that Prophetstown possessed "little appearance of having once been a large Town." As for the former battlefield, he wrote that "my feeling is easier concieved [*sic*] than described." In an obviously disconcerting manner, the quarter-mile stretch leading to the site was littered with both human and horse skeletal remains, "bleching together whither our men or Indian it is unknown." It appeared as if at least eight graves had been dug up. The importance of the battle and what had actually been a long, fierce fight for control of the region was now overshadowed by randomness, neglect, and desecration. What was clearly missing, he observed, was a marble monument to mark this spot. It would be several years before he could act on this sentiment; but in the meantime, within a few months, a company of men from Terre Haute came to collect the bones and temporarily buried them, marking the spot with a large stone.[16]

On his return to Harrison County, Tipton learned that he was reelected to a second term as representative. In less than two years, in March 1823, he finally attained the public role he had been seeking—that of federal Indian agent at the Fort Wayne agency in northern Indiana. Here, initially, he found himself walking a fine—and disputatious—line between the goals of the federal government and the wants and expectations of the Indian groups he served. Increasingly, however, the citizens of Indiana also called on him to account for his handling of awarding the local contracts that translated into much-needed cash. And there were other constituents as well, such as the white settlers near the agency who occasionally had disputes with agency Indians. He made few people happy, and he thought it a thankless position. Being a federal Indian agent required that Tipton regulate the trade and intercourse between the Indians and whites at the agency, which included licensing and monitoring the traders, many of whom raised his suspicions. Having been county sheriff served him well in this position, as did his penchant for details and keeping records, because his biggest duty revolved around distributing annuity payments, settling debts, and making reports.

Additional responsibilities included overseeing expenditures related to the "civilization" of the Indians, especially in promoting their cultivation of fields and building of log homes.[17]

In this position, Tipton could satisfy the two most familiar roles he had known since Tippecanoe: man of duty and protector. Immediately on his appointment and throughout, he pledged his fidelity to the government and his country. But a perceptive and fair-minded person like Tipton might be tempted to question whose interests he, as federal Indian agent, was supposed to protect first under these circumstances. From his vantage point, the agency Indians were being victimized by the traders under his purview who, among other things, were violating the antiliquor rules; and very early on he was troubled by the government's apparent lack of interest in fulfilling treaty stipulations. Soon after he arrived at Fort Wayne, he was confronted by several Miami chiefs who wanted to know why they had not yet received a gunsmith and blacksmith per the terms of the 1818 Treaty of St. Mary's. They were also entitled to a saw mill and grist mill, and the mill dam was in need of repair.

Tipton brought this to the attention of his supervisor, Michigan Territory governor Lewis Cass, whose reply essentially set the tone for how these matters would be addressed—and reveals much about the nature of U.S. Indian policy. Cass did not believe that the United States was under any obligation, "conventional or moral," to spend any more money on the mills, and he further wondered aloud if their request derived from "ignorance, bad advice or some worse motive" to pursue this matter. While he would authorize a small sum to deal with this, there would be no money forthcoming for a gunsmith. Tipton's instructions were clear: "the Chiefs must distinctly understand, that this is the last expense the United States will incur in relation to this subject, and that they consider the stipulation of the treaty of St. Mary's for the building of the mills fairly and faithfully executed." And so it went.[18]

In five years' time, however, the abuses against the agency Indians had reached a point where Tipton felt compelled to make a decision that he knew would earn him scathing criticism, particularly among those who saw their financial opportunities threatened. In April 1828 he relocated the Indian agency further into Indian country to the Miami Reserve, opposite the mouth of the Eel River. He explained his actions a few months later at the payment of annuities to the Miami, when he detailed his duties and responsibilities as an agent of the U.S. government, including the settling of *legitimate* claims against both the government and agency Indians. "But," he emphasized, "it is painful to me to see claims presented against the Indians that has no colour of Justice in them. if I were base enough to compell or even stand by and suffer the Indians to pay them I would be unworthy of the office I now hold." They needed to be protected from unlawful activities. Tipton's sharpest words were aimed at the traders who violated the rules against making alcohol available during trades with Native Americans ("wretched beings," "dirty villains"), whose behavior forced him to move the agency out of their reach and begin paying Miami annuities in Miami country. For Tipton, native-white relations now turned on a smaller scale, one of settling claims and protecting them from abuse. But that would change one final time.[19]

Tippecanoe had receded into the past, but Tipton was still determined to memorialize the event. In November 1829 he purchased a 156¾-acre tract at the Crawfordsville Land Office that included the battleground. He later told Governor Noah Noble that his sole motivation in buying the land was "to preserve the bones of my companions in arms who fell there." Eleven months later Tipton organized a formal ceremony around the reinterment of the bones he had found while surveying for the state of Indiana in 1821. It was attended by a number of Tippecanoe survivors and relatives from several states, although William Henry Harrison was unable to attend. With Tipton's election to the U.S. Senate to fill a vacancy caused by James Noble's death in December 1831, and then reelected on his own in December of 1832, further action on memorializing Tippecanoe was postponed several years. But on 7 November 1836, the twenty-fifth anniversary of the battle, he deeded the sixteen-acre site to Indiana free of cost. One month later he forwarded to Governor Noble his plans for a monument, although one would not be erected until 1908.[20]

Due in large part to the passage of the Indian Removal Act in 1830, Indian affairs continued to dominate Tipton's public life (although he was also heavily involved in the internal improvement movement for his part of the state). There was a considerable degree of finality when one talked about native-white relations and the sense of a forceful tide sweeping eastern Indians westward. Even as Tipton was in the process of turning over Tippecanoe to the state, he was about to confront the military dynamic again. By the summer of 1838, talk of Indian "emigration" enveloped Indiana, especially with regards to groups like the Potawatomis, who were clearly not making plans to leave despite pressure from the U.S. government. Not surprisingly, the more pressure that was asserted, the greater the resistance and hostility toward whites. Tipton received numerous letters urging him to oversee the

Potawatomis' emigration in hopes of achieving a peaceful end. As senator and Indiana statesmen, Tipton still assumed the roles of dutiful citizen and protector, but his constituency had changed again, and he was now being asked to give primacy to the citizens of Indiana. He did not wish to meddle, but given the increasing tension he agreed to visit with several Potawatomis. He found most of them in a bad temper and indicating their intent to stay. Tipton had come to believe they needed to leave and warned a correspondent, "Do not be surprised if strong measures are taken."[21]

On 27 August 1838 Indiana governor David Wallace authorized Tipton to organize a company of 100 armed and equipped volunteers "for the purpose of preventing serious difficulty" in completing the emigration. Tipton agreed, but only on the condition that he not be paid, which is an indication of his discomfort with the job he was asked to do. Nevertheless, within a week he had enrolled some 750 Potawatomi men, women, and children for removal. Another 100 were soon added. However, once the westward journey began, the entire process broke down due to a lack of food and wagons and the "miserably poor" condition of the Indians, who lacked sufficient clothing and blankets. Again Tipton took charge, obtained what was needed, and completed his part of what he repeatedly called "this unpleasant business," which was to accompany the emigrants as far as Danville, Illinois. In his report to Governor Wallace, Tipton described being conflicted over what had just happened and not feeling authorized "to drive these poor degraded beings from our State, but to remove them from the reserve, and to give peace and security to our own citizens." He appeared to rationalize his role as a performing a duty to his country and serving as a protector of the state's citizens. Like so many of his contemporaries, he became committed to his prejudices and to the idea that no other option existed and then resigned himself to wrestling with his conscience later.

Tipton's long drive to memorialize Tippecanoe may have resulted in an unintended consequence—preserving the stark history of native-white relations and setting in stone the hostility that once characterized them. To a generation that grew up in this context, this kind of memorializing privileged the limitations over the possibilities. Yet, it reflects one of the many important contests that shaped the regional identity of the early Midwest.[22]

NOTES

1. "Journal of Tippecanoe Expedition, 12 September to 24 November 1811," Nellie Armstrong Robertson and Dorothy Riker, eds., *The John Tipton Papers,* vol. 1: *1809–1827* (Indianapolis: Indiana Historical Bureau, 1942), 62–83; for background see Ginette Aley, "Westward Expansion, John Tipton, and the Emergence of the American Midwest, 1800–1839" (Ph.D. diss., Iowa State University, 2005); William Frederick Collins, "John Tipton and the Indians of the Old Northwest" (Ph.D. diss., Purdue University, 1997); and John D. Barnhart and Dorothy L. Riker, *Indiana to 1816: The Colonial Period,* vol. 1: *The History of Indiana* (1971; repr., Indianapolis: Indiana Historical Society, 1994).

2. "Journal of Tippecanoe Expedition." For a sense of the anxiety over the Prophet and his followers, see various official correspondence to and from William Henry Harrison in Logan Esarey, ed., *Messages and Letters of William Henry Harrison,* vol. 1 (New York: Arno Press, 1975), 239–43, 243–45, 249–51; John A. Jakle, *Images of the Ohio Valley: A Historical Geography of Travel, 1740 to 1860* (New York: Oxford University Press, 1977), 94; Robert M. Owens, *Mr. Jefferson's Hammer: William Henry Harrison and the Origins of American Indian Policy* (Norman: University of Oklahoma Press, 2007), 215, chap. 7; Barnhart and Riker, *Indiana to 1816,* chap. 11; Patrick Bottiger, "Prophetstown for Their Own Purposes: The French Miamis and Cultural Identities in the Wabash-Miami Valley," *Journal of the Early Republic* 33 (Spring 2013): 29–60.

3. On the Fort Wayne treaty proceedings and reactions to them, including Tecumseh's grievance, see Robert M. Owens, "Jeffersonian Benevolence on the Ground: The Indian Land Cession Treaties of William Henry Harrison," *Journal of the Early Republic* 22 (Fall 2002): 405–35. see Esarey, *Messages and Letters,* 358–78, 387–91, 396–98, 417–19, 463–69; on the treaty particulars see Charles J. Kappler, *Indian Affairs. Laws and Treaties,* vol. 2, *Treaties,* (Washington: GPO, 1904), 101–5; Andrew R. L. Cayton, *Frontier Indiana* (Bloomington: Indiana University Press, 1996), chap. 8; Gregory Evans Dowd, *A Spirited Resistance: The North American Indian Struggle for Unity, 1745–1815* (Baltimore: Johns Hopkins University Press, 1992), 139–47; see also Anthony F. C. Wallace, *Jefferson and the Indians: The Tragic Fate of the First Americans* (Cambridge, MA: Belknap Press, 1999), and R. David Edmunds, *Tecumseh and the Quest for Indian Leadership* (Boston: Little, Brown, 1984), chap. 5.

4. Richard White, *The Middle Ground: Indians, Empires, and Republics in the Great Lakes Region, 1650–1815* (Cambridge: Cambridge University Press, 1991), chap. 11; Michael N. McConnell, *A Country Between: The Upper Ohio Valley and Its Peoples, 1724–1774* (Lincoln: University of Nebraska Press, 1992).

5. "Journal of the Tippecanoe Expedition," 6 Nov. 1811, 77; J. Wesley Whickar, ed., "Shabonee's Account of Tippecanoe," *Indiana Magazine of History* 17 (Dec. 1921): 355–57.

6. Along with Tipton's account, see Harrison's official correspondence in Esarey, *Messages and Letters,* 608–15, 618–30; Richard G. Carlson, ed., "George P. Peters' Version of the Battle of Tippecanoe," *Vermont History* 45 (Winter 1977): 38–43. For an insightful perspective on the Tippecanoe campaign and why Indian fighting was different than other kinds from a first lieutenant of the Fourth U.S. Infantry, which accompanied Harrison, see Florence G. Watts, ed., "Lieutenant Charles Larrabee's Account of the Battle of Tippecanoe, 1811," *Indiana Magazine of History* 57 (Sept. 1961): 225–47. For details on how Spencer's Yellow Jackets fared in the war, see "Spier Spencer's Company: Pay Roll, 12 September to 23 November 1811," Robertson and Riker, *John Tipton Papers,* 1:84–88.

7. "A Volunteer [John Tipton] to the Editor," *Vincennes Gazette,* Sept. 1833, Nellie Armstrong Robertson and Dorothy Riker, eds., *The John Tipton Papers,* vol. 2, *1828–1833,* ed. Nellie Armstrong Robertson and Dorothy Riker (Indianapolis: Indiana Historical Bureau, 1942), 829, 830, 832. Watts, "Lieutenant Charles Larrabee's Account," 225, notes that eleven counties bear

names of participants in the battle, as well as the battle itself (Harrison, Spencer, Tipton, Bartholomew, Daviess, Floyd, Parke, Randolph, Warrick, Dubois, and Tippecanoe), which suggests the importance of the event to Indiana's early identity. Not surprisingly, Tipton was a founding signer of the state constitution and a member of Indiana's historical society in December 1830, as noted in "Minutes of the Indiana Historical Society," *Proceedings of the Indiana Historical Society, 1830–1886* (Indianapolis: Bowen-Merrill, 1897), 9–13. He also continued to seek out reports about Tippecanoe to donate to the society, as seen in his 1832 letter to Secretary of War Lewis Cass, Robertson and Riker, *John Tipton Papers,* 2:619–20, 620n86.

8. Dowd, *Spirited Resistance,* chap. 9, esp. 183–85; Barnhart and Riker, *Indiana to 1816,* 395–411. Tipton's commissions and appointments mentioned here are reprinted in Robertson and Riker, *John Tipton Papers,* 1:89–90, 94, 109, 112–13, 119–20, 175n.22; for reference to his guardianship of the Berry children, see ibid., 215n97. It is revealing that two of Tipton's sons from his first marriage were named William Henry Harrison Tipton and Spear (or Spier) Spencer Tipton, as noted on the Tipton family genealogy tree, ibid., xvii. Research on Tipton's divorce and his years as sheriff of Harrison County is found in Ginette Aley, "Sheriff Tipton and Susan, a Woman of Color: Race and Gender Borderlands in the Ohio Valley During the Early Republic," in *North American Borderlands,* ed. Glenn Crothers (Athens: Ohio University Press, forthcoming).

9. "Journal of Expedition to Frontiers, 19–31 May 1812 and 30 June–22 July 1812," Robertson and Riker, *John Tipton Papers,* 1:91–93, 94–97; John Gibson, General Orders, 9 Feb. 1813, ibid., 103–4. On what has come to be called the Pigeon Roost Massacre, see Gerald O. Haffner, ed., "The Pigeon Roost Massacre: An Eyewitness Account," *Indiana History Bulletin* 53 (Nov.–Dec. 1976): 158–61; Aaron Wood, *Sketches of Things and People in Indiana* (Indianapolis: J. M. Olcott Publishers, 1883), 13–14; Isaac Naylor, "An Account of Pigeon Roost Massacre" and A. W. Tobias, "Pigeon-Roost Massacre," in *Lougherys Defeat and Pigeon Roost Massacre,* ed. Charles Martindale (Indianapolis: Bowen-Merrill, 1888), 128–31, 132–34; "Minutes of the Indiana Historical Society," 51–54; Roy H. Beldon, *The Collings Story of Pigeon Roost Massacre* (Crothersville, IN, n.d.), 4–15.

10. R. Hamilton to Polly Hamilton, 30 Sept. 1812, "The Expeditions of Major-General Samuel Hopkins up the Wabash, 1812: The Letters of Captain Robert Hamilton," *Indiana Magazine of History* 43 (Dec. 1947): 395; "George Beck et al to the Governor of Indiana Territory," Sept. 1812, *The First American West: The Ohio River Valley, 1750–1820,* Library of Congress, http://memory.loc.gov/ammem/award99/icuhtml/fawhome.html; "Joseph Bartholomew et al [the citizens of Clark County, Indiana Territory] to President James Madison," 13 Apr. 1813, ibid.; Tipton to Robert M. Evans, 26 Mar. 1813, and Tipton to John Gibson, April 1813, Robertson and Riker, *John Tipton Papers,* 1:105–6, 107–8.

11. Tipton to Lyman Draper, 22 Jan. 1839, Robertson and Riker, *John Tipton Papers,* 1:802–4, 57n.1; White, *The Middle Ground,* 384, chap. 9. White's misleading generalizations about Indian haters and frontier people include: "The backcountry declared its own Indian policy in blood." One is tempted to ask, Who, specifically, in the backcountry? Such simplifications as White's suggest that all in the backcountry/frontier are bound to the actions and hatred of the genuine renegade Indian haters.

12. White, *The Middle Ground,* 517; James H. Merrell, "American Nations, Old and New: Reflections on Indians and the Early Republic," in *Native Americans and the Early Republic,* ed. Frederick E. Hoxie, Ronald Hoffman, and Peter J. Albert (Charlottesville: University Press of Virginia, 1999), 338. A detailed assessment of Tipton's role as Harrison County Sheriff is found in Aley, "Westward Expansion," chap. 3. Joseph Bartholomew to Tipton, 27 Jan. 1820, Robertson and Riker, *John Tipton Papers,* 1:175–78.

13. Robertson and Riker, *John Tipton Papers,* 1:xv-xvi; "To Locate Seat of Justice, Owen County, 3–15 February 1820," ibid., 179–84; "Candidacy for Legislature, 17 May 1820," ibid., 194–95. Tipton wrote two journals on the expedition to select a new state capital, both of which are reprinted in ibid., 195–215.

14. See ibid., 200, 209.

15. Ibid., 210. For election results see ibid., 218n3. A chronology listing his appointments and elections is in ibid., xv–xvi. Examples of Tipton's Masonic leadership and responsibilities are in ibid., 229–33, 235–36, 239, 242–43, 243–44. Tipton's boundary commissioner appointment is reprinted in ibid., 241.

16. "Indiana-Illinois Boundary, 15 May–30 July 1821," journal, ibid., 244–80. For the Fort Dearborn massacre, see James E. Davis, *Frontier Illinois* (Bloomington: Indiana University Press, 1998), 144–46; "Account of Battle of Tippecanoe, September 1833," Robertson and Riker, *John Tipton Papers,* 2:833.

17. For Tipton's appointment see John C. Calhoun to Tipton, 28 Mar. 1823, Robertson and Riker, *John Tipton Papers,* 1:300–302.

18. Tipton to John C. Calhoun, 30 Aug. 1823; Tipton to Lewis Cass, 19 Oct. 1823; Lewis Cass to Tipton, 22 Oct. 1823; Tipton to Lewis Cass, 31 Oct. 1823, Robertson and Riker, *John Tipton Papers,* 1:315, 320–21, 321–22, 325–25.

19. "Address at Miami Payment, 30[?] August 1828," Robertson and Riker, *John Tipton Papers,* 2:86–88.

20. "Account of the Battle of Tippecanoe, September 1833," ibid., 825–33; Tipton to Noah Noble, 7 Nov. 1834, in The John Tipton Papers, vol. 3, *1834–1839,* ed. Nellie Armstrong Robertson and Dorothy Riker (Indianapolis: Indiana Historical Bureau, 1942), 81, 196n65, 332. The Tippecanoe Battlefield was designated a National Historic Landmark in 1963.

21. Letters urging Tipton to take over the situation are reprinted in *John Tipton Papers,* 3:660–62; Tipton to Carey A. Harris, 21 Aug. 1838, ibid., 667.

22. David Wallace to Tipton, 27 Aug. 1838; Tipton to David Wallace, 27 Aug. 1838; Tipton to Carey A. Harris, 2 Sept. 1838; Tipton to David Wallace, 16 Sept. 1838, ibid., 675, 676, 685–86, 713–14.

The Late War

Black Hawk and the Legacies of Violence in the Great Lakes Region

JOHN P. BOWES

The Battle of Lake Erie, in which the American fleet led by Master Commandant Oliver Perry defeated the British naval force under the command of Captain Robert Barclay, lasted only a couple of hours on 10 September 1813. Yet it turned the tide of American fortunes in the western Great Lakes. American domination of the lake waters meant control over the transport of goods and people. The British force under Major General Henry Procter had to surrender its position at Detroit. They crossed the border to Amherstburg and in short order began a retreat up the Thames River through Upper Canada. General William Henry Harrison and his army were not very far behind. On 5 October, at the Battle of the Thames, Harrison and his men routed the British forces and secured their hold on the region. Much has been made of these events. Procter is lambasted for his retreat, and the Shawnee warrior and British ally Tecumseh is praised for his desire and willingness to make a stand, even though it meant his life.[1]

Tecumseh's death on the Thames River appeared to end Indian resistance to American expansion in the Old Northwest. Yet the perceived threat of a pan-Indian uprising endured in the very person of his brother Tenskwatawa, also known as the Prophet. The Prophet had fled after the initial American charge at the Battle of the Thames and therefore did not learn of his brother's death until later. He spent the remainder of the war trying to stay out of harm's way, and at war's end was living near Amherstburg on the Canadian side of the border. For the next five years, Tenskwatawa attempted to retain a measure of influence and made several weak attempts to revive what had been a powerful Indian confederacy. American officials at Detroit and British officials across the river at Amherstburg did their best to keep track of his actions and those of his small band of followers. By the mid-1820s, however, the Shawnee Prophet had become relatively harmless in the eyes of American officials like the governor of the Michigan Territory, Lewis Cass. The aging visionary no longer had the religious power or authority to influence or attract Indians in the region.[2]

Yet even Tenskwatawa's weakened influence could not erase the memory of a British-Indian alliance, and, as evidenced by events surrounding the Black Hawk War, the strength of that ongoing concern endured into the early 1830s. Despite a host of factors leading to the outbreak of violence in 1832, American citizens and officials in the Old Northwest Territory could not free themselves from the assumption of British involvement. At the centers of power in London and Washington, British and American officials may have distanced themselves from talk of British interference in Indian affairs in the decades after the War of 1812, but this did not alter regional prejudices. Consequently, American agents and residents placed any and all Indian activity in the western Great Lakes in the 1830s within a framework that had existed for decades.[3]

From the perspective of American officials and citizens in the early republic, Indians often worked within the context of a British alliance or a pan-Indian confederacy to undermine the interests of the young United States. In the long list of grievances that comprised the Declaration of Independence, there appeared the accusation that King George "has endeavoured to bring on the inhabitants of our frontiers, the merciless Indian Savages, whose known rule of warfare, is an undistinguished destruction of all ages, sexes and condition." At the outbreak of war in 1812, Americans identified British interests in the confederacy built by Tecumseh and the Prophet. And in the summer of 1832, American citizens in northern Illinois saw a familiar danger in every Indian face. They asserted that the local Potawatomis and Ho Chunks had "about as much friendship for us now, as they had during the late war with Great Britain." Thus, the Black Hawk War proved to be only the most recent in a string of conflicts encompassing more than five decades sparked by British interference and Indian violence.[4]

Warfare marked the people and places of the western Great Lakes region. From the 1750s to the 1830s, violence under the auspices of multiple imperial struggles shaped the physical landscape. It drew, erased, and imposed political borders in territories more naturally delineated by rivers, portages, and lakes. The passage of time witnessed the transformation of the *pays d'en haut* into the Old Northwest Territory and finally into the states of Ohio, Indiana, Illinois, Michigan, and Wisconsin. But perception shaped the landscape of American-Indian relations just as powerfully. As a result, even as the threat of Sauk violence diminished with the destruction of Black Hawks' band on the Bad Axe River in early August 1832, the ghosts of other traditional opponents refused to disappear. From the 1810s to the 1830s, the memories of the late war and the specter of British influence over the Indians in the western Great Lakes haunted the thoughts and shaped the actions of American citizens and officials in that region.

From June 1812 to January 1815, Indian residents of the western Great Lakes region were caught in the middle of a conflict they did not start or want. This was particularly true for the Moravian Munsee and Delaware Indians who had lived at their town of Fairfield on the Thames River in Upper Canada since 1792. Most Fairfield residents were Indians seeking to escape the violence that enveloped the Ohio Valley from the 1750s through the 1780s. In fact, the core of the community was men and women who fled the Ohio Country in the aftermath of the Gnadenhutten massacre. The death of ninety-six Moravian converts at the hands of American militiamen under the command of Lieutenant Colonel David Williamson in March 1782 sparked a series of migrations that ended on the banks of the Thames. The Moravian missionaries and their native followers put their faith in God and the British government.[5]

Yet, the onset of the War of 1812 eliminated any notion that the boundary line between Canada and the United States could protect them from circumstances similar to those that had turned Ohio into a battleground. In July 1812 the Moravians learned of the declaration of war. Only a few weeks later, just the rumor of an American expedition into Upper Canada awakened fears of another Gnadenhutten and sent dozens of Moravian Indians fleeing into the woods near Fairfield. By the end of the summer, parties of Mingoes, Munsees, and Ojibwes passed through Fairfield on their way to Malden to join the British cause, and in early 1813 the British attempted to enlist more Indians from the Thames River villages.[6]

The Battle of Lake Erie raised concerns throughout Upper Canada about the British ability to maintain its hold on the region. But word of the evacuation of Malden and Detroit transformed concern to fear. Procter quickly gave ground, and fleeing British soldiers turned Fairfield into a field hospital. The

Moravian Indians panicked. "All Indian brethren left Fairfield and took their cattle with them," missionary Christian Denke wrote in his diary entry for 4 October. Events unfolded rapidly once Harrison defeated Procter only two miles downstream and to the west of Fairfield. Tecumseh died as he attempted to maintain the integrity of his portion of the British line. His death and the failure of the British troops to hold back Harrison's men left Fairfield and the surrounding region at the mercy of the Americans. As the Moravian Indians left Fairfield and retreated into the woods, Brother John Schnall and his fellow missionaries sought to appease the invading force. But the American soldiers did not see neutrality in the Moravians' actions. They accused Schnall and his compatriots of hiding British soldiers and provisions. Only two days after the battle had ended, Harrison's men began ransacking the town. Another two days later the Americans torched Fairfield and left it in ashes.[7]

Although Harrison and his army did not stay in Upper Canada for the duration of the war, the destruction of Fairfield scattered the Moravian community. Schnall and his family ended up in eastern Pennsylvania. Most of the Indian members of the congregation traveled east with Brother Denke to Niagara. Fewer than two months after Fairfield burned, 160 men, women, and children found refuge at Dundas, more than 100 miles to the northeast. Only when the war ended did the Moravian missionaries and their Indian converts return to the Thames River.[8]

Neutrality would have been a difficult position for anyone to assume in the vicinity of Detroit and Amherstburg. Circumstances had placed the Moravian Indians of Fairfield at the epicenter of military campaigns in 1812 and 1813. But more than geography complicated matters. Their identity as Indians hampered their ability to operate without external interference. The British and Americans viewed Indians as both valuable allies and dangerous enemies in the War of 1812. Particularly for Americans, however, the war and its legacy constantly reminded them of the threat posed by British support of Indian interests.

The Treaty of Ghent officially ended the War of 1812, but it provided little comfort to Americans living in the western Great Lakes region. Agents in the field and territorial governors saw the British around every corner and viewed any contact between Indian tribes as the foundation of a militant confederacy that would carry on the work of Tecumseh and the Prophet. American citizens also tended to lump Indians into a single group and seldom distinguished between tribes or bands. Even into the 1830s Americans defined some Indian communities and individuals by their actions in the late war; most expected Indians in the western Great Lakes to be faithless and easily swayed by British temptations.

The American government sought to reestablish order in Indian affairs as soon as possible after the war ended. In the summer of 1815 treaty commissioners held councils at Portage des Sioux, Detroit, and other northern locales to formalize peaceful relations with those Indian nations that had allied with the British. Government agents also received specific instructions. Acting Secretary of War A. J. Dallas informed the new agent for the Illinois Territory, Richard Graham, that he was to execute his duties according to guidelines laid out in the Trade and Intercourse Act of 1799. Graham would particularly need to be on the alert for any individual "among the Indians attempting to mislead them, or to inspire them with distrust in the U. States." Within a year of his appointment, Graham found reason to appreciate that warning. "The British traders will have to be watched very close," he wrote to his superiors in July 1816, "those who have been trading on the waters of the Mississippi have used all their influence, which is very considerable to excite distrust among the Indians." The agent feared the economic hold of foreign traders and the ease with which they appeared to manipulate the minds of their Indian customers.[9]

Border permeability exacerbated American anxieties. The Treaty of Ghent had not ended a decades-long relationship between local Indians and their British father, and agents at Fort Malden distributed clothing, weapons, and ammunition annually to those Indians who visited their outpost. From his office in Detroit, Lewis Cass argued that it was absolutely necessary for the U.S. government to respond to this trade. More than economics underscored his opinion. The trade spawned violence against American settlers. "In nine cases out of ten," Cass asserted, "the Indians, who are guilty of these aggressions are on their return from Malden, carrying with them British presents and British counsels." Secretary of War John C. Calhoun hastened to reassure American agents in the Old Northwest, writing, "Efficient measures will be taken by the Government, as soon as practicable, to prevent the Indians from crossing into Canada." But from Cass's position in Detroit, government efforts would have little impact. Indians moved through the region in large numbers through the early 1820s. Although it is an admittedly inexact measure, the numbers of Indians crossing over the Raisin and Huron rivers in southern Michigan provide some sense of how many were heading north to Detroit and Fort Malden: from March 1822 to April 1823, approximately 2,000 Indians used the bridge over the River Raisin, while nearly as many used a similar span that crossed the Huron River.[10]

The Senecas, Delawares, Wyandots, Shawnees, Potawatomis, Sauks, and Ottawas who crossed those bridges were not necessarily heading directly to Malden. Detroit was the headquarters of the Michigan Superintendency and therefore served as the location of American annuity distributions. Nevertheless, the distance between the two settlements made it impossible to limit travel between them, and the records of British agents underscore the ongoing relations. According to Captain Billy Caldwell of the British Indian Department, a total of 1,166 men, women, and children of eight different tribes visited Amherstburg on 15 August 1816. Caldwell's report described these visitors as "Dependent Indians." The description mattered, for it designated those Indians who were expected as opposed to the twenty-two who visited on 14 August and labeled "Strangers." Multiple sources confirmed that Indians continued to deal with the British in large numbers.[11]

British infiltration and influence spanned a vast stretch of the Canadian border, and the geography of the Great Lakes played a crucial role in the manner in which Indians maintained or developed relationships with the British and Americans in the decades after the War of 1812. As historian Timothy Willig has illustrated, for the thirty-year period leading up to 1815, the strength of British diplomacy was not evenly spread, and by the War of 1812 the strongest ties between Indians and the British rested northwest of the Detroit-Amherstburg corridor. It should not have been surprising, then, for Americans to see signs of British influence along the shores of Lake Superior and the present-day Upper Peninsula of Michigan. On 16 June 1820, Cass held a council with the Ojibwe bands living near Sault Ste. Marie. He was in the midst of an expedition designed to introduce Indians in the far northwestern reaches of his jurisdiction to the reach and measures of American policy. Henry Rowe Schoolcraft was a member of the expedition, officially appointed as its geologist. His observations of the Ojibwe delegates at the 16 June council are telling. Schoolcraft explained their resistance to American authority by noting the "costly broadcloths, feathers, epaulets, medals, and silverwares, of British fabric" worn by the chiefs. And only moments after the Ojibwe delegation literally kicked aside the presents brought by the Cass expedition and left the council meeting, they "hoisted the British flag in the midst of their encampment." Schoolcraft had no doubt that the British bore responsibility for this belligerence.[12]

Similar warnings about British influence filled the letters and reports of Indian agents into the 1820s, and these men did not hesitate to point out the relationship between potentially dangerous Indians and the War of 1812. The lead up to the Black Hawk War demonstrates this tendency perfectly. Tensions first began to rise in northern Illinois over the movement of Sauks and Mesquakies on both sides of the Mississippi River in the late 1820s and early 1830s. The Sauks had never been satisfied with an 1804 treaty that obligated them to move from their lands east of the Mississippi when the federal government deemed it necessary. The history of that accord was rife with fraud, and the warrior Black Hawk was one of many Sauks who refused to accept its terms. But the situation came to a head in the early 1830s when the federal government chose to enforce the terms of the treaty. Under the auspices of that agreement, American citizens began to move into the territory still claimed by the Sauks. When Black Hawk and the members of the British Band protested, their intransigence made American agents and military officers in the region nervous.[13]

The very designation of the British Band referred to the fact that Black Hawk and other Sauk warriors had allied with the British in the War of 1812. Nearly twenty years later, this affiliation was used to distinguish them from the "friendly" Sauks under Keokuk who had moved west of the Mississippi River and accepted the terms of the 1804 treaty. Dangerous affiliations were not limited to the Sauks, however. Captain Richard Bell praised the decorum and peaceful intentions of the Ho Chunk, Menominee, Ojibwe, and Potawatomi Indians of northern Illinois and southern Wisconsin but still expressed some doubts about some of their chiefs. Black Eagle, a Ho Chunk headman, was of particular concern. "Black Eagle fought with Tecumsee, was a principal councilor of his," Bell informed his superior, "and is under British influence with his followers and receive annual stipends or presents from the British at Drummonds Island." Guilt by previous and present association mattered more to Bell in 1831 than apparent peaceful intentions.[14]

In the shape of the Black Hawk War, then, the traditional threats of confederacy and foreign influence returned to a region that only two decades earlier had experienced firsthand the damage done by a British-Indian alliance. Clearly, the Black Hawk War was far more complicated than presented by this narrative. Indeed, as historian John Hall has recently argued, those Indians who allied with the United States during the conflict did so for reasons that had nothing to do with American or British interests. But alternative perspectives like that presented by Hall do not alter the fact that the hostilities marked a revival of long-standing fears regarding the relationship between the British and the Indians in the western Great Lakes region. Though few could point to British responsibility in the Ho Chunk attacks in the lead mining region of southern Wisconsin in 1826 and 1827, in Black Hawk and the British Band Americans had a recognizable target. American officials were quick to revive the accusations and actions of the past. In the process they stoked the fires of rumor and panic as they painted a picture of Indian traitors working in concert with the British to once again assault the lives and interests of the United States in general and American settlers specifically.[15]

For a year before Black Hawk and his band crossed the Mississippi River in April 1832 and sparked a substantial uproar, American officials saw the British everywhere they looked. From his position as Superintendent of Indian Affairs for the St. Louis superintendency, William Clark noted in the late spring of 1831 that the British Band have "been for many years in the habit of making annual visits at Malden in U. Canada." They went for the presents, but also to talk. It was because of these ongoing conversations, Clark argued, "that so little influence has been acquired over them by the U. States Agents." American officials even put in writing their determination to sever relations between the British Band and the British agents. On 30 June 1831, at a council held at Rock Island, Illinois, Major General Edmund Gaines confronted the Sauks regarding their unwillingness to surrender land officially ceded in the 1804 treaty. To record their official recognition of the terms, he had the Indians sign articles of "Agreement and Capitulation." The fourth article specifically required the Indians "to abandon all communication, &cease to hold any intercourse, with any British Post, Garrison, or Town." The American government refused to tolerate any more meddling.[16]

Fears of a potential pan-Indian uprising also grew in size and scope once the British Band crossed the Mississippi River and headed northeast up the Rock River through northern Illinois in early April 1832. Three men informed Governor John Reynolds on 20 April that they were confident "that the pottawattimes will join the Sacs & have little doubt that if their first effort should not prove disastrous the Winnebagoes will unite their forces with others." Within a month of that letter, Reynolds himself believed he had the information necessary to declare in a statewide announcement that the Potawatomis and Ho Chunks were now allied in full with the British Band. Even as agents like Thomas Owen of the Chicago agency counteracted such statements with a more knowledgeable assessment of the Potawatomi bands with whom he interacted, the fears of confederacy would not disappear.[17]

American officials and citizens throughout the western Great Lakes asserted that Indians in their vicinity could not be trusted. An American soldier named George McCall combined a number of these notions when he spoke about the hostility of the Sauks and Mesquakies in northern Illinois in the summer of 1831. In council with General Edmund Gaines, the Sauks professed their desire to be at peace. According to McCall, however, that was simply "Indian talk." McCall explained that the Sauks "are perhaps the most warlike and the fiercest as well as the most determined Indians in our country, as their conduct during the last war exemplified." McCall, like Reynolds and others, saw the War of 1812 as a critical point of reference.[18]

References to the late war often included testaments to the faithfulness, or lack thereof, of the Indians, and the fever created by the movements of the British Band thus placed the Potawatomis of northern Illinois in a difficult position. Like other Indians in the region, they were guilty until proven innocent. But the guilt of May 1832 was based in part on the events of August 1812. In the early stages of the late war a wagon train of American men, women, and children left Fort Dearborn under an armed escort. Only a mile and a half east of the fort, nearly 500 Potawatomi warriors under the leadership of Blackbird and Mad Sturgeon assaulted the American column. More than fifty Americans died, and the Potawatomis killed some of the prisoners after herding them back to Fort Dearborn. The incident became known as the Fort Dearborn massacre, and it scarred Potawatomi-American relations.[19]

In the spring of 1832, every mile the British Band advanced brought them closer to Potawatomi villages on the Rock, Kishwaukee, and Fox rivers. Then, on the night of 17 May, a runner from either Shabonee's or Asiminekon's Potawatomi village arrived at Fort Dearborn to notify Indian Agent Thomas Owen that a skirmish had occurred between the Sauks and a scouting party of Illinois militia. The skirmish at Stillman's Run marked the first shots of the Black Hawk War, and word of that fight sent hundreds of American settlers fleeing to the relative safety of Fort Dearborn. It also forced the Potawatomis of northern Illinois and southern Wisconsin into a defensive posture. The same runner informed Owen that the Potawatomis had tried to "persuade them [the Sauks] from their contemplated designs," but with no success. Although Owen was "pleased to see, that the Indians of this Agency have fully evinced their determination to render no aid to the Sacs whatever," the Potawatomis knew that most citizens did not share Owen's calm demeanor. In early June, as the British Band hid in the marshes north of Lake Koshkonong in southern Wisconsin, a Potawatomi headman named Big Foot sent a belt of white wampum and a message to Black Hawk. Big Foot wanted the British Band "to leave the Country, that the Potawatomies might return with safety to their respective Villages and plant corn before the season was too far advanced." Similar to the other Potawatomi headmen who moved their people closer to Fort Dearborn during the conflict, Big Foot knew that even friendly Indians were in danger as long as the Sauks continued their hostilities.[20]

The Potawatomis of northern Illinois also sought to dissuade Black Hawk from his notions that the British would come to his aid. Only hours before the firefight at Stillman's Run, a delegation of Potawatomis had met with the Sauks near the village of Kishkawaka at the juncture of the Rock and Kishwaukee rivers. At a public council the Potawatomis informed the Sauks that they could not supply them with any corn. But a more important session with Black Hawk occurred in his lodge in the dead of night. While the other Sauks slept, Black Hawk asked his visitors if they had "received any news from the lake from the British?" When the Potawatomis said no, Black Hawk pressed them further. "I inquired if they had heard that a chief of our British father was coming to Mil-wâ-kee," the Sauk warrior remembered, "to bring us guns, ammunition, goods and provisions?" Once again the reply was no.[21]

This admission by Black Hawk illustrates that American officials did not invent a possible British-Sauk connection. Indeed, some actions of the British Band in the early 1830s fueled such speculation. In the summer of 1830 Black Hawk visited Fort Malden to ask the British about their perspective on American land policies. The British advised him to stay at peace and trust the Americans. But American officials only knew that Black Hawk had visited Malden. In the spring of 1831 members of the British Band once again made their annual pilgrimage to Canada. American general Edmund Gaines reported that according to the Indians, the British were less neutral this time around. "Their English friends, they say, have spoken to them of an intended war with us," Gaines reported. "These speculations will serve to shew their continued, deep rooted infatuation towards England, & relentless enmity towards the United States." The news of British hostility, however, came from the Sauks, who may have hoped it was true. At no time did British officials make a move to assist the Sauks.[22]

Yet when the violence on the Bad Axe ended and Black Hawk had been captured, American officials still tried to uncover insidious connections and confederacies. On 13 August, eleven days after the bloodshed on the Bad Axe, Colonel Samuel Stambaugh turned over seven Sauk prisoners to the commanding officer at Prairie du Chien. One of the prisoners, an elderly woman, had in her possession a letter written by the former governor of Canada, Sir George Prevost, to the Sauk Indians. Stambaugh enclosed this incriminating document in a letter to his superiors but did not describe its contents. The military man believed that the problem was clear. Stambaugh even noted that he explained to the Sauk woman "the injury these papers had done her people." From his perspective, two things made the letter dangerous. First, a powerful British official wrote the missive. Second, and even more important, the letter bore the date of 7 March 1814, which meant it was composed during the War of 1812. American fears simply would not disappear.[23]

A Sauk headman named Taimah may have summed up the problems of the Indians in the western Great Lakes region best in July 1832 when he wrote to William Clark, "You are well aware of the utter impossibility for us to refute even the most glaring falsehoods which malice or ignorance can invent." Like the Moravian Indians at Fairfield during the War of 1812, the Sauks and Mesquakies who had not joined the British Band were caught in the middle of a conflict they did not want or create. "We have from the first to last, done all in our power to prevent the rising storm," Taimah explained, "but to no purpose." The rumors of their involvement continued unabated, and the accusations of their hostility did not go away. Taimah even turned to language he knew the Americans would understand. "I am the same man now that I was in the year 1814," he reminded Clark, "when I took (as it were) my life in my hand to rescue from certain destruction the public property of the Factory." In contrast to the British Band, Taimah had helped the Americans in the late war and even saved an American trading house on the Little Moniteau River in Missouri. Just as the actions of the British Band in the War of 1812 proved their treachery in 1832, Taimah believed his past loyalty should prove his faithfulness in another time of war.[24]

Despite Taimah's eloquence, the Black Hawk War confirmed fears formed among Americans decades earlier and framed within the hallowed words of the Declaration of Independence. Indians could not be trusted, and, just as important, behind most Indian actions were the machinations of devious

British agents and traders. For American officials and citizens in the western Great Lakes region in particular, the British-Indian alliance was an integral factor in diplomatic and economic policy from the 1770s into the 1830s.

And in 1832, for the residents of Indiana, Illinois, and the Michigan Territory especially, it was a very short step from these determinations to the promotion of removal. The U.S. Congress passed the Indian Removal Act in May 1830, two years before the Black Hawk War. The first emigrant trains in both the North and the South had already crossed the Mississippi heading west before the British Band crossed the Mississippi heading east. But it was that eastward crossing that initiated much more substantial efforts to remove Indians throughout the Old Northwest. It made it that much more logical for Governor John Reynolds to connect the two in his address to the Illinois General Assembly in December 1832. After summarizing the efforts taken against the Sauks, Reynolds advocated the removal of the Potawatomis from Illinois. "When they are permitted to remain intermixed with the white population," Reynolds concluded, "it is almost certain that contests, and collisions will arise, and thereby, both parties be injured." Removal would therefore benefit both Indians and Americans by relocating the Indians from desirable lands and preventing future violence.[25]

More importantly, perhaps, removal would also put more distance between the Indians and the British. Neither the passage of time nor the professions of Indian headmen like Taimah could exorcise the ghost that had haunted American minds since the 1770s. And as a result, the decisive military victories of Perry and Harrison in September and October of 1813 ended only a single chapter in a larger narrative. Unlike the forces of Barclay and Procter, the specter of British influence could not be so soundly defeated.

NOTES

1. R. David Edmunds, *The Shawnee Prophet* (Lincoln: University of Nebraska Press, 1983), 137–42; Sandy Antal, *A Wampum Denied: Procter's War of 1812* (East Lansing: Michigan State University Press, 1997), 315–54; Robert S. Quimby, *The U.S. Army in the War of 1812 : An Operational and Command Study,* 2 vols. (East Lansing: Michigan State University Press, 1997), 1:259–300.

2. Edmunds, *The Shawnee Prophet,* 142–64.

3. For discussions of the ongoing concerns about British interference in the region, see Kerry Trask, *Black Hawk: The Battle for the Heart of America* (New York: Henry Holt, 2006), 126–40.

4. "The Declaration of Independence," National Archives, http://www.archives.gov/exhibits/charters/declaration_transcript.html; "Memorial of citizens of Shelbyville, Illinois, July 10, 1832," Letters Received by the Office of Indian Affairs, 1824–1881, roll 132, Record Group 75, M234, National Archives, Washington, DC. Although the quotation refers to Winnebago Indians, I will use Ho Chunk outside of any direct quotes because that is the preferred name in the present day.

5. John P. Bowes, "The Gnadenhutten Effect: Moravian Converts and the Search for Safety in the Canadian Borderlands," *Michigan Historical Review* 34(Spring 2008): 101–8.

6. Linda Sabathy-Judd, ed. and trans., *Moravians in Upper Canada: The Diary of the Indian Mission of Fairfield on the Thames, 1792–1813* (Toronto: Champlain Society, 1999), 481–82, 486, 488–89; Bowes, "The Gnadenhutten Effect," 114.

7. Sabathy-Judd, *Moravians in Upper Canada,* 495, 504–6, 513–20; R. David Edmunds, *Tecumseh and the Quest for Indian Leadership* (New York: Pearson Longman, 2007), 194–212; Henry Procter to de Rottenburg, 23 Oct. 1813, William Wood, ed., *Select British Documents of the Canadian War of 1812,* 3 vols. (Toronto: Champlain Society, 1923), 2:323–27.

8. Sabathy-Judd, *Moravians in Upper Canada,* 506–11.

9. Because the commissioners relied on a template, most of these treaties have the same wording. Examples can be found in Charles Kappler, ed., *Indian Affairs: Laws and Treaties,* 7 vols. (Washington, DC: Government Printing Office, 1904), 2:110–12, 116–69; A. J. Dallas to Richard Graham, 14 July 1815, Clarence Edward Carter and John Porter Bloom, eds., *The Territorial Papers of the United States,* 28 vols. (Washington, DC: Government Printing Office, 1934–75), 17:198–200; Richard Graham to Secretary of War, 8 July 1816, ibid., 359–61. For similar concerns expressed by local officials, see Ninian Edwards to Secretary of State, 3 Mar. 1816, ibid., 308–10; Ninian Edwards to the Secretary of War, 20 Mar. 1816, ibid., 318–19; Ninian Edwards to the Secretary of War, 18 Nov. 1816, ibid., 430–37.

10. Governor Cass to the Secretary of War, 3 Aug. 1819, Carter, *Territorial Papers,* 10:852–55; the Secretary of War to Governor Cass, 11 Feb. 1822, ibid., 11:224–25; Governor Cass to the Secretary of War, with enclosures, 27 June 1823, ibid., 375–80.

11. "Return of Indians Dependent on the Post of Amherstburg 15th August 1816," in "Subsequent Relations, 1816–1819," *Michigan Historical Collections* 16 (1890): 523–25.

12. Timothy D. Willig, *Restoring the Chain of Friendship: British Policy and the Indians of the Great Lakes, 1783–1815* (Lincoln: University of Nebraska Press, 2008), 243–71; Henry Rowe Schoolcraft, *Travels Through the Northwestern Regions of the United States* (1821; repr., Ann Arbor, MI: University Microfilms, 1966), 136–38.

13. For full accounts of the Black Hawk War and its context, see Trask, *Black Hawk;* Patrick J. Jung, *Black Hawk and the War of 1832* (Norman: University of Oklahoma Press, 2008).

14. Richard H. Bell to Alexander Macomb, 16 Aug. 1831, Carter, *Territorial Papers,* 12:332–35.

15. John Hall, *Uncommon Defense: Indian Allies in the Black Hawk War* (Cambridge, MA: Harvard University Press, 2009), 1–12; Lucy Eldersveld Murphy, *A Gathering of Rivers: Indians, Metis, and Mining in the Western Great Lakes, 1737–1832* (Lincoln: University of Nebraska Press, 2000), 113–30.

16. William Clark to Edmund P. Gaines, 28 May 1831, Ellen M. Whitney, ed., *The Black Hawk War 1831–1832*, 3 vols. (Springfield: Illinois State Historical Library, 1973), 2:16–17; "Articles of Agreement and Capitulation between the United States and the Sauk and Fox, June 30, 1831," ibid., 85–88.

17. Richard M. Young, Benjamin Mills, and James M. Strode to John Reynolds, 20 Apr. 1832, ibid., 288–89; "John Reynolds: Proclamation, May 15, 1832," ibid., 373–74; Thomas J. V. Owen to George B. Porter, 18 May 1832, ibid., 383–84; Thomas J. V. Owen to the Public, 5 June 1832, ibid., 527–28. Other warnings about an Indian confederacy can be found in Paul L. Chouteau to William Clark, 27 June 1831, ibid., 78–79; John Reynolds to the Secretary of War, 7 July 1831, ibid., 104–5.

18. George A. McCall to Archibald McCall, 17 June 1831, ibid., 55–58.

19. R. David Edmunds, *The Potawatomis: Keepers of the Fire* (Norman: University of Oklahoma Press, 1978), 186–88;

20. Thomas V. Owen to Steven T. Mason, 3 May 1832, Letters Received by the Office of Indian Affairs, 1824–1881, roll 132; Thomas J. V. Owen to John Reynolds, 12 May 1832, Whitney, *Black Hawk War*, 2:365; Thomas V. Owen to George Porter, 18 May 1832, Letters Received by the Office of Indian Affairs, 1824–1881, roll 132; Thomas V. Owen to Stephen T. Mason, 3 June 1832, Letters Received by the Office of Indian Affairs, 1824–1881, roll 132; Helen Hornbeck Tanner, *Atlas of Great Lakes Indian History* (Norman: University of Oklahoma Press, 1987), 151–53.

21. Edmunds, *The Potawatomis*, 235–37; Donald Jackson, ed., *Black Hawk: An Autobiography* (Urbana: University of Illinois Press, 1987), 121–23; Tanner, *Atlas of Great Lakes Indian History*, 140.

22. Jackson, *Black Hawk*, 105–6; Edmund P. Gaines to Roger Jones, June 1831, Whitney, *Black Hawk War*, 2:47–51.

23. Samuel C. Stambaugh to Winfield Scott, 13 Aug. 1832, in Whitney, *Black Hawk War*, 2:996. For other attempts to connect the British and the Sauk Indians, see Gideon Low to Winfield Scott, 3 Sept. 1832, ibid., 1100–1101; "Minutes of Examination of Prisoners," ibid., 1028–37.

24. Taimah and Apenose to William Clark, 22 July 1832, ibid., 852–54.

25. "John Reynolds: Message to Both Houses of the Illinois General Assembly, December 4, 1832," ibid., 2:1218–22.

The Aftermath of Victory

The Settlement of Fort Wayne, Indiana, and the Surrounding Region

PHYLLIS GERNHARDT

In 1805, just ten years after the Treaty of Greenville had established a fragile peace with the Great Lakes Indian nations, the small number of settlers who lived in the shadow of Fort Wayne turned their attention toward issues that would encourage population growth in the surrounding region. They believed that the conditions were perfect for settlement in the Great Lakes area, yet they were unaware that in just seven years a new war between the young United States and Great Britain would erupt. Their focus was on the present, however, and the two most pressing concerns, they felt, were better transportation and communication with families, friends, and the government in the East. Most significantly, they called for the sale of the public lands. The conditions of transportation and communication posed difficulties. Before the War of 1812, Fort Wayne remained very much an outpost, distant from settlements both in the East and to the South. Transportation routes were primitive. A portage road ran eight miles southwest from the garrison to a tributary of the Wabash River, where for decades traders had landed their goods. Other roadways consisted of traces that led from Fort Wayne to Fort Recovery, into today's Adams County, Ohio, and toward present-day Chicago, as well as following each side of the Maumee River.[1]

The residents of Fort Wayne found the personal inconveniences as well as the military ramifications of unreliable communication disconcerting. In 1807 the population at the fort petitioned the federal government for a mail route to their area. The nearest post office, in Staunton, Ohio, was about 100 miles from the garrison, and their personal mail as well as "publick dispatches of great importance" frequently remained there for months before they reached

Fort Wayne. Inhabitants desired a post road for the "benefit to the Publick and to Individuals." Twenty-two residents signed the petition. It was rejected at the time, but one year later the U.S. government established a post office at Fort Wayne.[2]

From the national government's point of view, their main priority regarding the Great Lakes region focused on establishing routes between the military posts within Indian country rather than routes connecting the frontier to the eastern section of the United States or promoting settlement. In 1803, plans for a fort west of Fort Wayne were under way, and the Secretary of War requested that William Wells, the Indian agent at Fort Wayne, find the most direct path or bridle road from Fort Wayne to this newly established Fort Dearborn. He also requested that a "Mr. Burnet," the only known settler between the posts, supply goods for the new garrison.[3]

The presence of the military post built at the Maumee-Wabash portage in 1794 had brought a sense of peace to the region. As the situation with the natives in the area calmed, the conditions for American settlement improved. As early as 1800, Fort Wayne's Indian agent, William Wells, expected that the garrison would soon be withdrawn. Indeed, plans to sell the government land around the fort were under consideration in 1805. Yet many government officials believed that Fort Wayne still stood too far from compact settlement and that the purchased lands would fall into the hands of unscrupulous traders. These traders, they feared, would create problems with the Indians. Any such conflicts would prove too much for the distant government for the Indiana Territory (established in 1803 and centered at Vincennes) to control effectively. They also expressed concern about the negative impact such instability in the region would have on potential settlers and felt that American farmers would hesitate to settle at Fort Wayne because of its remote location.[4] These conditions needed to be remedied before settlement could move forward in the orderly fashion that the government desired.

Several years later, Fort Wayne residents still urged Washington to establish policies that would bring "actual settlers" to the region. They argued that Americans in the "heart of the Indian Country" would be a sufficient means of controlling the region through its volunteer militia, thus lessening the responsibility of regular troops. They also argued that it would bring the Indians into greater and more intimate contact with Americans, thus forging a stronger bond between the native inhabitants and the American republic and destroying the influence of the British. Their very specific recommendations for accomplishing these measures included allowing settlers to buy land based on credit and for a cheaper price than land sold in Ohio, thus enticing emigrants to look further west. The fort, they believed, was the perfect place to accommodate the land sales.[5] Their hope for a policy supporting increased settlement would be delayed until after the War of 1812, however, as tensions between Indians in the Great Lakes, encouraged by the British as they sought to reclaim part of their empire, would soon erupt into military combat.

Scholarly discussions on the settlement of the U.S. frontiers have largely focused on the tensions between its settlers and the federal government. Francis Paul Prucha, in his classic study *Broadax and Bayonet: The Role of the United States Army in the Development of the Northwest, 1815–1860,* analyzes the relationship between these two groups on the Great Lakes frontier following the War of 1812. His study centers on the role that the military played in the region's development. The military faced difficult circumstances on the frontier, he argues, thwarted by "cunning traders, irresponsible Indians, unsympathetic state and local officials, white settlers hostile to army authority, and the confusion that existed in the interpretation of laws." He concludes that, ultimately, the civilians' struggle to promote their communities won out, but only as a result of the work of the military.[6] His focus on the military, however, leaves out the significant role that the Indian agencies, trading factories, and land offices played in the settlement of the frontier.

Patrick Griffin, in *American Leviathan: Empire, Nation, and Revolutionary Frontier,* studies the role of the frontier in the creation of the American republic. While he, too, focuses on the conflicts between the frontier's settlers and the government's attempts to control them, and thus the region, he argues that the stability on the frontier came about ultimately as a result of the power of the government. By 1795, he argues, the government would meet settlers' demands for protection through Great Britain's guarantee to leave the region and through the implementation of a military presence on the frontier. However, Britain's promise to remove its military presence from the Great Lakes region did not materialize until the United States military forced them out in the War of 1812. Griffin's statement that the frontier process would move forward more readily as a result of a new "federally administered garrison government" that would now control the western frontier does not address the fact that the settlement process following the 1795 Treaty of Greenville in the Great Lakes region would experience the same complexity and uncertainty that plagued the frontier during the Revolutionary era.[7]

In his seminal work on the frontier era in the Great Lakes region, *The Middle Ground: Indians, Empires, and Republics in the Great Lakes Region, 1650–1815*, Richard White analyzes the interplay of Indian and white cultures during this struggle for empire around the Great Lakes. He describes this region as a "middle ground," a place where the social, political, and cultural interactions should be analyzed as a process of "mutual accommodation." Rather than a process of assimilation or acculturation, it was a "joint Indian-white creation," White argues.[8] Many historians have analyzed and tested the validity of the "middle ground" thesis, and this focus has provided an intriguing perspective for studies of the American frontiers. White's focus, however, has largely highlighted the occupants of this middle ground phenomenon. This current look at the settlement at Fort Wayne, however, emphasizes the role of the distant eastern government in relation to this unique frontier accommodation and its interaction with the settlers on the frontier. White describes the government's relationship to the middle ground as one that had many of the characteristics of "imperialism," yet, it was one "that weakens at its periphery. At the center are hands on the levers of power, but the cables have, in a sense, been badly frayed or even cut. It is a world system in which minor agents, allies, and even subjects at the periphery often guide the course of empires."[9] As the young United States government sought to hold and strengthen its governing power on its frontier, the administration quite effectively used the unique skills of the occupants of the middle ground to achieve its goals.

The story of the Great Lakes region prior to and after the War of 1812 reveals that the relationship between settlers and government during the settlement process was complex in nature. Although largely defined by historians as a process marked with tensions as settlers struck out on their own into the frontier regions and as federal officials sought to rein them in, it was also often a cooperative venture, one in which a mutually benefiting relationship emerged. Even as settlers often stridently called for government action to protect them and promote the settlement process, they just as readily protested the enacted policies as too restrictive in nature; yet, they enjoyed the profits gained from government contracts and the military's success in bringing peace to the region through its victories over the British and the Indians. Policy makers, however, sought to restrain settlers' actions in dealing with the native nations of the region, fearing that they might spark further military conflicts on the frontier; yet, they did not hesitate to use the settlers' knowledge of the frontier and its native inhabitants to achieve their policy goals.

Through an accommodation of its own, then, the federal government created and implemented military strategies, Indian polices, and, ultimately, the sale of the public lands to a responsible citizenry. Adapting to the unique conditions of the middle ground, the government thus extended the "cables" of administrative control. Before this could successfully occur, however, the new nation had to reaffirm its control over the Great Lakes region through the military confrontation with both the British and the Indians in the middle ground. Ultimately, both the settlers and the American government achieved their goals. Those who lost out in the process, however, were the Indians and British, whose detrimental effects on settling the frontier were greatly diminished as a result of the War of 1812.

In the struggle of empires for the New World, the 1783 Treaty of Paris brought the Americans' Revolutionary War to an end and marked Great Britain's recognition of the United States, but it did little to end the conflict in the Great Lakes region. The newly formed American government had several issues with which to contend on this middle ground. Britain refused to surrender the post at Detroit as well as others throughout the Great Lakes. Americans were illegally settling along the Ohio River, and Indians of the region had formed a confederation to try to stop this invasion of their territory.[10] The secretary of war kept the president updated on the "murders . . . lately committed on the inhabitants" of the frontier.[11] Miamitown, the Indian villages at today's Fort Wayne, Indiana, was at the center of this problem. In 1786, at least twenty-six war parties left Miamitown over a six-month period. Raids resulted in the deaths of many American settlers, sometimes numbering close to forty in each raid. Just as frequently, Indians took Americans as prisoners, occasionally allowing them to return to their homes in exchange for information about the white settlements and after requiring them to work as manual laborers during their captivity. The Indians also adopted many into their nations, including William Wells.[12] The leaders of the early republic made the conquest of Miamitown their priority, for control of this center of Indian activity at the confluence of the St. Mary's, St. Joseph, and Maumee rivers meant security for the entire region.

Compounding the problems with the Indians experienced by Americans, the U.S. government received evidence that the British were supplying the Indians in the Great Lakes region. Although the extent of British involvement was unknown, reports such as Thomas Rhea's in 1790 were common. Indians arrived at Detroit, he reported, in "parties of one, two, three, four and five hundred at a time, from different quarters" and received from the British agent "clothing, arms, ammunition, provisions, &c." The Indians would then travel to Miamitown, and from there they supplied much more distant nations.[13] British Indian agents like Alexander McKee at Detroit and the Girty brothers—Simon, James, and George, who lived near Miamitown—kept the British well informed of the strength and movements of the American forces and encouraged Indian raids into Kentucky and Ohio settlements.[14] Miamitown served as a central provision and information center for the Indians of the Great Lakes and thus became the focal point for American control.

In addition to stopping the raiding activities of the Great Lakes Indians, American officials wished to exert their political control over citizens settling the frontier. National leaders believed it was necessary to emphasize to western settlers that "the Government of the United States was not a mere shadow" and that Americans' independent retaliatory raids against the Indians were in direct opposition to government policy. Northwest Territory governor Arthur St. Clair feared that the settlers' rash initiatives to solve the problems of the raiding Indians on their own would destroy the territorial government.[15] The federal government needed to subdue both the Indians and control the westward-moving emigrants. Not willing to lose the Great Lakes region, the new administration attempted to give direction to the settlement of the frontier. The Ordinance of 1787 declared that no Indian lands would be taken without the Indians' consent, and an army went west to evict squatters from Ohio. The job, however, was too big to be done effectively by so young a government.[16]

American leaders continued to favor peaceful negotiations, and government officials negotiated treaties throughout the 1780s. Yet, the treaties resolved very little. The Shawnee and Miami nations based at Miamitown, which had not attended negotiations or the signing, remained hostile.[17]

By the summer of 1790, federal officials realized the need for armed forces to back their authority and raised an army with the purpose of controlling both the Indians and the western emigrants.[18] In 1791 an American army attacked the thriving Indian villages at today's Fort Wayne, thus beginning a four-year U.S. military campaign for control of the headwaters of the Maumee. This campaign ended with Anthony Wayne's victory over the Great Lakes native nations at the Battle of Fallen Timbers in 1794.[19]

With Wayne's victory and the subsequent Treaty of Greenville in 1795, the United States gained an area of six square miles around the newly established fort at the former Miamitown for use as a military reservation, free use of the Maumee-Wabash portage, and an area of two square miles at the Wabash end of the portage. The United States also gained access to the roads leading to Fort Wayne from Defiance to the northeast and Piqua to the southeast. The Greenville agreement established a boundary line at the Cuyahoga River and approximately 150 miles north of the Ohio River.[20]

The campaign of the 1790s moved the military frontier further north and west. Fort Wayne, established in 1794, was soon joined by Fort Dearborn in 1803, when American troops built the additional fort on the site of today's Chicago. Fort Madison was established in present-day Iowa five years later, in 1808. Both fortifications received their supplies and mail via Fort Wayne, which stood as a critical outpost in the territory northwest of the Ohio River.[21] From this vantage point the United States stood guard over the Indian country, seeking to control native activities in the region and countering the presence of the British in the Great Lakes region. The extension of government control into the middle ground had begun.

In addition to maintaining peace on the middle ground, the military attempted to exert federal control over the inhabitants of the fort's reservation and the troops of the garrison. These residents included the contractor's agents, the sutlers who traded with the garrison and the nearby Indians, the settlers on the public grounds, and the families and slaves of the garrison. Officers worked to control this civilian population mainly through regulating their business with the soldiers and the Indians who visited the fort.[22] With the promise of a federal post, early residents of Fort Wayne agreed to submit to the discipline of the U.S. military. These relationships were central to the middle ground during its formative years.

Garrison orders from Fort Wayne occasionally referred to another village beyond the walls of the fort that also provided services to the military. French Town stood on the site of trading villages that flourished at Miamitown prior to 1790.[23] Following the U.S. victory at the Battle of Fallen Timbers, military officials encouraged the engagement of "some of the principal French traders" and the "most influential Characters among them" so that the U.S. government could make use of their connections with the native tribes of the region.[24] Military officials gained the cooperation of these French traders in January 1795 when several of them returned to Fort Wayne, bringing many of the Miamis with them, along with a large quantity of goods to trade. There they informed the post's commander of their hopes to work with the United States.[25] The post even supplied the French traders with the necessary men needed to build their trading house near the garrison.[26]

Just two months later the U.S. government issued an order granting these traders official licenses. In exchange for the right to continue their trade under American governance, they were to abide by the prices and rules established by a board of officers. This licensed position put these French traders under the political jurisdiction of the United States while allowing federal officials to benefit from the traders' knowledge and intimacy with the native nations of the Great Lakes region.[27] Cooperation with the federal government proved economically beneficial to them, and the inhabitants of French Town seized the opportunities presented and forged alliances with the American military forces. During this time, the political relationship between the U.S. government and the French in the region was one of peaceful coexistence and cooperation.

Because the United States military had less control over the French community than it did the American settlers who lived near the fort, the army restricted contact with the residents at French Town. Time limitations for visits to this community, for example, varied according to the individual commander or Indian activities in the region. In 1803 and 1804, those associated with the post were not allowed to visit either homes or stores "before Troop beating, in the Morning or after retreat Beat in the evening." Yet three years later, when Indian unrest was becoming a problem, the restrictions were even more stringent, allowing members of the garrison to visit the village between 11:00 a.m. and 1:00 P.M., and then only with permission from the commanding officer. Violators received fifteen lashes.[28]

In addition to establishing a military presence in the middle ground, the United States implemented Indian policies that they hoped would maintain peaceful conditions on the frontier. In doing so, Congress passed a series of commerce or trading laws that outlawed the purchase of Indian lands by individual settlers and outlined punishments for those who committed crimes against the Indians. These Indian policies sought to control the behavior of American settlers as well as limit their numbers on the frontier until after the War of 1812.[29]

In the very earliest years of the new nation, the government considered the country large enough for both U.S. citizens and the native inhabitants. Its first regulations called for boundary lines and forbade Americans from hunting or settling within the Indian country, allowing them to enter only if engaged in government-approved business. Settlers were strictly prohibited from buying or trading for Indian lands. Government administrators especially feared unscrupulous traders. The government hoped to prevent the frontier from being "over run with Land Jobbers, Speculators, and Monopolisers or even with scatter'd setlers." This "parcel of Banditti" would selfishly profit from the trade at the expense of the nation, perhaps even inciting war. Thus, policies were established requiring a license in order to trade with the Indians and outlining specific rules and regulations. Failure to adhere to these could result in the loss of one's license.[30]

Simultaneously, the administration set up a series of government trading factories. The Fort Wayne factory was one of the twenty-eight government trading stores that operated between the years 1796–1822.[31] The factory engaged in a large trade with the Indians of the Great Lakes until the War of 1812, exchanging manufactured goods for pelts and furs.[32] By trading directly with the Indians, the government limited the number of private traders on the frontier, thus attempting to rid the middle ground "of this pest without giving offence or umbrage to the Indians."[33]

The government did, however, allow the traders, including the French, who had lived and traded with the Indians prior to Wayne's conquest in 1794, to continue their economic activities in the Fort Wayne region. It actively sought to tie these members of the middle ground to the young republic's interests, allowing them to continue in the profitable trade and licensing them under the new factory system.[34] Doing so, officials believed, would strengthen any allegiance the traders might have with the American government rather than risk a shift in their loyalties to the British, the ever-present rival for the Great Lakes region.[35] In addition to using their influence, this licensed position put these traders under the political jurisdiction of the United States. Controlling the activities of these individuals and limiting their numbers on the frontier was essential to the extension of Washington's control into the middle ground. In this way the factory limited American access to Fort Wayne's frontier region prior to the War of 1812 and thereby maintained peace with the original inhabitants. Peace was tenuous, however, and would not be fully secured until the British and their Indian allies in the Great Lakes were defeated.

But by 1807 relations between the Great Lakes Indians and the United States were once again troubled. Just two years after Wells had expressed the belief that the military was no longer necessary at the forks of the Maumee and the settlers at the post called for an emphasis on attracting a civilian population, he wrote of the difficulties of settling the region. The disruptions caused by the "Shawnee Prophet," who struggled to unite the Indians in a single force against American encroachments, upset the peaceful conditions. Restless Indians assembled at Fort Wayne and caused "a great stagnation to the population of the frontiers," Wells reported.[36] Settlers at Fort Wayne expressed their fears of Indian depredations and requested that Wells intercede on their behalf. They asked that the government remove the Indians by force, if necessary, in order to calm the fears of the pioneers, many of whom were fleeing because of the Prophet's message.[37] Suddenly, conditions for settlement once again looked difficult, and they would remain so until after the War of 1812.

The increasing numbers of the Prophet's followers concerned Wells. Beginning in 1807, his reports focused on the growing number of Indians within this territory that the native nations had ceded at the Treaty of Greenville in 1795. In answer to the Americans' request, Wells worked to keep the Indians from gathering at Greenville, where he believed the Prophet encouraged anti-American sentiments. The agent then turned his attention to calming the fears of the frontier settlers. Although Wells believed the Indians meant the settlers no harm, the Indians' presence disturbed the orderly settlement so desired by the government. Indeed, by 1808 Wells estimated that as many as 20,000 Americans had been discouraged from settling in northwestern Ohio because of the situation at Greenville.[38]

From its strategic position in the middle of Indian territory, the small outpost at Fort Wayne played an important part in the events preceding the War of 1812. From Fort Wayne, Wells remained well informed of the Indians' movements and plans and kept the secretary of war notified of the Shawnee Prophet's growing influence. Large numbers of Indians had passed by Fort Wayne, and Wells estimated that at least 1,500 had gone to meet with the Prophet at Greenville and that many more were expected in the months to come. News of the communications between the Indians and the British agents at Malden created even greater anxiety.[39]

During the summer of 1811, the population at Fort Wayne was anxious. Rumor had reached them that Harrison's troops had been defeated at Tippecanoe. And as posts on the northwestern frontier came under attack, the inhabitants of Fort Dearborn received orders to evacuate their garrison and take refuge at Fort Wayne. Many, including William Wells, who had organized a relief expedition to Fort Dearborn, were killed as they left the post. John Johnston at Piqua, Ohio, reported to the secretary of war that the inhabitants of the frontier were "flying in every direction" for fear of attack from the Indians. The women and children from Fort Wayne took refuge in Ohio.[40] Some remained at the post during the war, staying in their homes outside the fort, continuing a limited trade and communication with the native nations of the region, and attempting to mediate terms of peace between the two forces.[41]

Those who remained played an important role in the events surrounding the post during the War of 1812. As the federal government had anticipated, the traders at Fort Wayne worked within the policies established on the frontier. Their relationships with the Indians as economic partners in trade and, for some, as members of their tribes through marriage gave them tremendous influence with the Indians of the region. With this bond of friendship and the economic ties that the traders had with the military post and the Indian agencies at Fort Wayne, this population played a significant role as cultural mediators, promoting the defense of the garrison against attack.

Regardless of their efforts, in August and September of 1812, the fort was under siege. Robert B. McAfee, who served with Harrison's volunteers, related in his history of the War of 1812 that the "handsome little village" at Fort Wayne now lay "in ruin," reduced by the ravages of war. Help came as Harrison and his army made their way to Fort Wayne with the aid of volunteers. During the remainder of the War of 1812, Fort Wayne served as a supply center. Good news for the settlers came late in 1813 with the death of Tecumseh, the Prophet's brother and the dynamic leader of the Indian confederacy, in the Battle of the Thames in October. Unofficially, the war came to a close the following year.[42]

At Fort Wayne, the Indian factory did not resume business. The buildings had been destroyed during the siege, partly by the American troops in an effort to protect the fort. The Indian agent remained the sole representative of the federal government at Fort Wayne along with the army troops garrisoned there until 1819. Yet the lack of clarity regarding policies and the strategies to achieve those goals continued to plague the outpost in this middle ground.[43] Frontier conditions required policies that would adapt to the unique conditions of the region.

The residents of Fort Wayne, whose numbers increased after 1814, when former settlers returned and newcomers arrived, lived with an ever-present awareness that further attack was possible, even though the danger had greatly diminished. Still remote from compact settlement, Fort Wayne continued as an outpost of defense in the Great Lakes region. The closest settlement was St. Mary's in Ohio, and other than the inhabitants of the posts at Fort Wayne and Fort Dearborn, only one known American settler, Indian trader Joseph Bartrand, lived in the middle of Indian country.[44] Federal troops took every precaution against further attack, relying on civilian residents such as Bartrand, who signed an affidavit swearing his "faith and allegiance" to the commanding officer at Fort Wayne. He promised to inform either post of any news he might gain regarding a potential uprising. In preparation for such an event, Fort Wayne's commander requested more troops or permission to reconstruct the fort. It was rebuilt in the fall of 1815, during which time Indians continued to congregate at the fort to trade and receive their annuities.[45]

Additional changes affected the region. In 1816 Indiana became a state and territorial government ended. The Treaty of 1818 gave the United States title to the territory south of the Maumee and Wabash rivers, and it was expected that these new public lands would soon be opened for settlement. The military's frontier was moving, and the need for federal troops was lessened as the Indians north and west of the Ohio River suffered defeat on the battlefield during the War of 1812 and lost their lands at the treaty table. Still, the northern third of the state, in which Fort Wayne was the only white settlement of any size, remained Indian country.

The small number of settlers who had found protection at the garrison remained far within the frontier.[46] Visitors to the region noted little "more than 40 families of 'Squatters' and traders," a settlement of about thirty log cabins and two farm houses, as well as the Indian agent, a Baptist missionary, and some private families who still lived in the military barracks. The Indians were still the majority. In 1822 Peter Kiser recalled that on his first trip to Fort Wayne there were at least forty Indians to every white person.[47] Still, the residents remained hopeful that settlement of the region would become a priority for their national government.

In April 1819, four years after the War of 1812 ended, the post at Fort Wayne was permanently evacuated. The prediction that "compact settlement" would soon occur in northeastern Indiana, which the U.S. garrison had conquered and protected for twenty-five years, would soon be a reality.[48] With the promise of peace and stability now more certain with the threat of the British gone and the power of the native nations diminished, the federal government hoped to sell off the public lands around the fort. In 1819 it sent civil engineer James Riley to survey the area in preparation for the sale of a portion of the military reservation. Its fertility and prime location impressed Riley, who noted, "Here will arise a town of great importance which must become a depot of immense trade. The fort is now only a small stockade, no troops are stationed here, and less than thirty dwelling houses occupied by French and American families form the whole settlement."[49]

When he returned a year later, at a time that apparently coincided with the distribution of annuities and cash payments to the Indians of the region, he called for action from the federal government to promote controlled settlement. The main threat to stability now came from an unruly citizenry. Riley noted many young men, "each with his bundle or ship, of goods and trinkets," who had set up trade at the former military post and reported that temporary residents were destroying the government's property. They seemingly had no intention of settling in the area. All were "depradating on the public lands," using timber for their homes and stores as well as for firewood. This unauthorized use of resources on lands intended for settlers destroyed the property and lessened its value to potential purchasers.[50]

This was an issue that concerned the local Indian agent as well. Federal agents at Fort Wayne noted that it attracted a rowdy element and that "drunkenness and other irregularities of the Indians proceeding from the unrestrained conduct of the Traders" made the outpost "a very uncomfortable residence" and "a resort for discharged soldiers and others of the refuse of the human race."[51] Trying to control the "rambling white people" on the frontier, particularly on the public reserves surrounding the garrison, proved to be more difficult than dealing with the Indians, agents bewailed. The settlers who lived on the borders of U.S. land and Indian country were also difficult to control. The greatest problem Indian agents encountered, he argued, came for "a want of information or disposition in our citizens to support the policy of the Government."[52] Obviously, the need for controlled settlement was necessary.

For Riley, the solution required the "speedy survey and sale" of public lands, which would attract "a cordon of hardy and respectable settlers." He noted that Fort Wayne, "if laid out as a town and sold by the government, would bring a large sum of money. The St. Mary's has been covered with boats, every freshet, for several years past. This is a central spot, combining more natural advantages to build up and support a town of importance, as a place of deposit and trade . . . than any point I have yet seen in the western country."[53] This goal would only be achieved, however, with the enforcement of policies that would maintain peace with the Indians and with their removal from the region. This required close regulation of the traders on the middle ground and negotiations with the native nations of northern Indiana to cede their remaining land to the federal government.

The most significant change in policies following the War of 1812 came when government administrators reassessed the Indian trade on the frontier. Following the demise of the trading factory after the siege of Fort Wayne, the government no longer traded directly with the native nations of the region, and now they considered lessening the restrictions on the private traders. Some officials still opposed the use of the traders entirely, arguing that it was in the government's best interest to monopolize the Indian trade. Private traders were notorious for taking advantage of the Indians and were detrimental to the government policy of maintaining a peaceful relationship with its native population. Their concerns seemed to have been justified, as descriptions of Fort Wayne and the character of its populace revealed the very type of settlement that the federal government hoped to prevent as it settled the nation's frontiers. In spite of these arguments, in 1818 the government decided to allow private individuals to trade with the Indians, although federal regulation provided some amount of government control. In order to achieve some balance, federal officials set the required minimum amount of capital at the high rate of $5,000, thus limiting the number of traders who could qualify and allowing the government to monitor their activities with greater ease.[54]

These changes coincided with an increased demand by Americans for the reduction of Indian lands in northern Indiana. The number of Indians in this middle ground was also declining. In 1823 there were only 2,441 Miami, Potawatomi, and Eel River Indians left in the territory covered by the Fort Wayne agency. Though their numbers were dwindling, they still claimed over 6.37 million acres of land in northern Indiana.[55] Pressure for land sales and another cession of land, this time in the northern portion of Indiana grew, and as a result of the U.S. victory in the War of 1812, that goal was met with relative ease.

The establishment of the Fort Wayne land office in 1822 began the final stage of settling this part of the middle ground. Congress created the Fort Wayne Land District in May of that year in order to control the sale and distribution of land in the northeastern section of the state.[56] In that same year a report by Secretary of War Lewis Cass reaffirmed the decision to no longer house troops at Fort Wayne.[57] Lasting peace seemed assured, and settlement and development moved forward at a rapid pace.

Great care was taken that the most desirable situation for a site be found in order to attract settlers. At Fort Wayne, the post and thirty acres of land adjoining it were reserved from public sale either for defense purposes or for the Indian Department with the proviso that this would not interfere with the "proper location of a village."[58] The success of land sales depended on the peoples' interest in the region and the strategic layout of a well-planned town center. Finally, a proclamation by President James Monroe announced the sale of lands at the Fort Wayne district that would take place on the third Monday in October 1823.[59]

Pressured by the Indiana legislature and anxious to open northern Indiana to settlement and development, John Tipton, the Indian agent at Fort Wayne, arranged for treaty negotiations with the Potawatomis and Miamis in October 1826. To induce the Indians to cede the land needed for internal improvements and settlement, the commissioners distributed more than $31,000 worth of goods before negotiating. In the treaty that followed, the Miami ceded all their land north and west of the Wabash and Miami rivers, about 1.5 million acres: The Miamis were now entirely restricted to reservations. That year the Potawatomis also surrendered a strip of land along the north bank of the Wabash.[60]

Two years later the Indian agency, which had been headquartered at Fort Wayne since its creation, was removed from northern Indiana. The residents at Fort Wayne feared that this would have a negative impact on the settlement there and, most significantly, on their personal economies. Merchants were making a handsome profit in their dealings with the Indians; as long as the Indian agency remained at Fort Wayne, they profited. Of the fifty to 100 families living there, more than two-thirds were Indian traders.[61] Despite settlers' protests, the agency was relocated to Logansport, along the Wabash and Eel rivers near the great Miami reservation.[62] The land office remained the only federal agency centered at Fort Wayne.

At the height of the land business in 1837, the federal government administered sixty-two offices throughout the nation. The first Indiana land office, established in 1804, was in Vincennes. By 1840 six offices in the state handled the sale of the 21,637,760 acres of public domain. During the 1830s an increase and shift in migration occurred as settlers poured into the newly acquired 1826 treaty lands in northern Indiana, which finally opened up the northern third of the state to settlement. From 1830 to 1837, Indianapolis almost doubled its land sales to about 1.5 million acres, as did Crawfordsville with sales of 1,686,708 acres. Fort Wayne's increase was even more astonishing, totaling 2,377,837 acres. In 1836 alone the Fort Wayne land office distributed half of that amount—1,294,356 acres—for $1,620,617.34.[63]

Northern Indiana developed rapidly in the decade following the 1826 treaty. Settlers north of the Wabash River increased from 3,380 to 65,897, while the native nations decreased to about 800 Miamis. The Indian land base had also diminished to approximately 30,000 acres. By 1840 the Miamis finally gave in to the pressures of westward-driving pioneers and the decline of their economic situation. With the 1840 treaty the Miamis forfeited their claim to remaining lands in Indiana and agreed to move west of the Mississippi within five years.[64]

With these changes, the U.S. government, as well as the early residents on the Great Lakes frontier, realized their goals for this middle ground. Prior to the War of 1812, settlement at Fort Wayne and its surrounding region had failed to materialize as conditions of peace and stability were threatened by the native nations' resistance to settlers and the continued hostile presence of the British. As a result of the U.S. military victory in the Great Lakes during the War of 1812, this outside threat to settlement was diminished. The complex process of settling the frontier was thus achieved, and, as a result, a tense but ultimately mutually beneficial relationship between the federal government and the frontier residents emerged. This relationship was often characterized by rowdy behavior and resistance on the part of the settlers and reactive restraints and regulations on the part of the federal government; yet, together they created the compact settlement so desired by the federal government.

After the War of 1812, the conditions that characterized the middle ground no longer existed. Four years after the war ended, the U.S. government removed the military troops from Fort Wayne and three years later established a regional land office in the former military structure. Peaceful conditions reigned. The nation soon realized its ultimate goal of settling and developing the region. The compact settlement that government officials had worked to create on the frontier now existed as the settlers that the residents had called for in 1808 filled the region. Through accommodations of its own, the U.S. government established policies unique to the middle ground and thus extended its cables of empire in the Great Lakes region following the War of 1812.

NOTES

1. Shirley S. McCord, comp., *Travel Accounts of Indiana, 1679–1961* (Indianapolis: Indiana Historical Bureau, 1970), 41; Wallace A. Brice, *History of Fort Wayne, from the Earliest Known Accounts of this Point, to the Present Period* (Fort Wayne: D. W. Jones & Son, 1868), 287.

2. "Petition to the Postmaster General by Residents at Fort Wayne, October 1, 1807," Clarence E. Carter, ed., *The Territorial Papers of the United States,* 27 vols. (Washington, DC: Government Printing Office, 1934–), 7:477–78; Charles R. Poinsatte, *Outpost in the Wilderness: Fort Wayne, 1706–1828* (Fort Wayne, IN: Allen County-Fort Wayne Historical Society, 1976), 89.

3. Secretary of War to William Wells, 26 May 1803, Carter, *Territorial Papers,* 7:115.

4. Logan Esarey, *Messages and Letters of William Henry Harrison,* 2 vols. (Indianapolis: Indiana Historical Commission, 1922), 7:149.

5. John Johnston to the Secretary of War, 25 May 1808, Letters Received by the Secretary of War, Unregistered Series (M222), Records of the Office of the Secretary of War, Record Group 107, National Archives, Washington, DC.

6. Francis Paul Prucha, *Broadax and Bayonet: The Role of the United States Army in the Development of the Northwest, 1815–1860* (1953; repr., Lincoln: University of Nebraska Press, 1994), 59, 103. For a further look at the policies that regulated the distribution and use of the lands on the frontier and the difficulty that policy makers had controlling the settlers on the frontier, see Paul Wallace Gates, *History of Public Land Law Development,* Management of Public Lands U.S. Series (Washington, DC: Wm. W. Gaunt & Sons, 1987).

7. Patrick Griffin, *American Leviathan: Empire, Nation, and Revolutionary Frontier* (New York: Hill & Wang, 2007), 14–15, 205.

8. Richard White, *The Middle Ground: Indians, Empires, and Republics in the Great Lakes Region, 1650–1815* (New York: Cambridge University Press, 1991), x.

9. Ibid., xi.

10. Andrew R. L. Cayton, *Frontier Indiana* (Indianapolis: Indiana University Press, 1996), 89; "Journal of Henry Hay," ed. Milo M. Quaife, reprinted as *Fort Wayne in 1790* (Fort Wayne, IN: Public Library of Fort Wayne and Allen County, 1955), 4, 6, 21–22, 25–26, 54.

11. Secretary of War Henry Knox to George Washington, 15 June 1789, Brice, *History of Fort Wayne,* 112–13.

12. White, *Middle Ground,* 452; Poinsatte, *Outpost,* 17; Hay, *Fort Wayne in 1790,* 73, 18, 15, 57. William Wells, taken captive in a 1784 raid, was the fourteen-year-old orphaned son of settlers near today's Louisville, Kentucky. He was brought north to the villages along the Eel River, where the village chief, Porcupine, and his wife adopted him, naming him Apkonit, or wild carrot, well befitting his freckled complexion and red hair. Wells later married Little Turtle's daughter, Sweet Breeze, and served as a Miami warrior. He played a significant role as a cultural mediator, a true symbol of the middle ground, working for the United States as a Miami interpreter, army scout, and Indian agent among the Miamis. For an excellent look at Wells, see Paul A. Hutton, "William Wells: Frontier Scout and Indian Agent," *Indiana Magazine of History* 74 (September 1978): 183–222.

13. Certificate of Thomas Rhea, 1790, Brice, *History of Fort Wayne,* 123–24.

14. Cayton, *Frontier Indiana,* 88; Poinsatte, *Outpost,* 22; Harvey Lewis Carter, *The Life and Times of Little Turtle: First Sagamore of the Wabash* (Urbana: University of Illinois Press, 1987), 58.

15. Henry Knox to St. Clair, 19 Dec. 1789, and Arthur St. Clair to George Washington, August 1789, Carter, *Territorial Papers,* 2:225, 212; Governor Arthur St. Clair to George Washington, 14 Sept. 1789, Brice, *History of Fort Wayne,* 113–14.

16. Carter, *Little Turtle,* 60–61; Stewart Rafert, *The Miami Indians of Indiana: A Persistent People, 1654–1994* (Indianapolis: Indiana Historical Society, 1996), 45.

17. "Instructions to the Governor of the Territory of the United States Northwest of the River Ohio," William Henry Smith, ed., *The St. Clair Papers: The Life and Public Services of Arthur St. Clair,* 2 vols. (Cincinnati: R. Clarke & Co., 1882), 2:2, 37; Arthur St. Clair to George Washington, 14 Sept. 1789, Brice, *History of Fort Wayne,* 113–14; Andrew R. L. Cayton, *The Frontier Republic: Ideology and Politics in the Ohio Country, 1780–1825* (Kent, OH: Kent State University Press, 1986), 38.

18. Cayton, *Frontier Republic,* 38; Wiley Sword, *President Washington's Indian War: The Struggle for the Old Northwest, 1790–1795* (Norman: University of Oklahoma Press, 1985), 87.

19. Paul Woehrmann, *At the Headwaters of the Maumee: A History of the Forts of Fort Wayne* (Indianapolis: Indiana Historical Society, 1971), 31; Carter, *Little Turtle,* 89–90.

20. Horace S. Knapp, *History of the Maumee Valley* (Toledo, OH: Blade Mammoth, 1871), 357; Cayton, *Frontier Republic,* 39.

21. Francis Paul Prucha, *The Sword of the Republic: The United States Army on the Frontier, 1783–1846* (Lincoln: University of Nebraska Press, 1969), 40; Francis Paul Prucha, *A Guide to the Military Posts of the United States, 1789–1895* (Madison: State Historical of Wisconsin, 1964), 2, 4.

22. Bert J. Griswold, ed., *Fort Wayne, Gateway of the West, 1802–1813* (Indianapolis: Indiana Historical Bureau, 1927), 136n; Woehrmann, *At the Headwaters,* 61.

23. Griswold, *Fort Wayne, Gateway,* 173–74n.

24. J. F. Hamtramck to Wayne, 15 Jan. 1795, *Wayne Papers,* 52 vols., transcribed by Richard C. Knopf (Columbus: Anthony Wayne Parkway Board, 1952–56), 39:15; Wayne to Hamtramck, 25 Feb. 1795, *Wayne Papers;* Walter Font, ed., *A Garrison at Miami Town: Fort Wayne, October 1794–June 1795* (Fort Wayne, IN; Allen Country-Fort Wayne Historical Society, 1994), 49n–50n.

25. Antoine Laselle to Jacques Laselle, 31 Jan. 1795, E. A. Cruikshank, ed., *The Correspondence of Lieut. Governor John Graves Simcoe,* 3 vols. (Toronto: Ontario Historical Society, 1925), 3:281; J. F. Hamtramck to Wayne, 15 Jan. 1795, *Wayne Papers,* 39:15.

26. George Ironside to Alexander McKee, 10 Feb. 1795, Cruikshank, *Simcoe Correspondence,* 3:294–95.

27. J. F. Hamtramck to Wayne, 15 Jan. 1795, *Wayne Papers,* 39:15; Font, *A Garrison,* 49n–50n. For further information of the French during this frontier era, see Jay Gitlin, *Bourgeois Frontier: French Towns, French Traders and American Expansion* (New Haven, CT: Yale University Press, 2010), 56–82.

28. Garrison Orders, 4 Nov. 1803, Bert J. Griswold, ed., "Garrison Orderly Book," in *Fort Wayne, Gateway of the West, 1802–1813* (Indianapolis: Indiana Historical Bureau, 1927), 150; Garrison Orders, April 1807, ibid., 251; 28 July1807, ibid., 255; Garrison Orders, April 1807, ibid., 251; After Orders, 8 Jan. 1809, ibid., 281.

29. "Report of Henry Knox on the Northwestern Indians," 15 June 1789, in Francis Paul Prucha, ed., *Documents of the United States Indian Policy* (Lincoln: University of Nebraska Press), 12.

30. George Washington to James Duane, 7 Sept. 1783, ibid., 1–2; "President Washington on Government Trading Houses," 3 Dec. 1793, ibid., 16; "Report of Henry Knox on the Northwestern Indians," 15 June 1789, ibid., 12.

31. Woehrmann, *At the Headwaters,* 86–87; Prucha, *Documents,* 33.

32. Indent Books, vol. 8, Records of the Bureau of Indian Affairs, Record Group 75, National Archives.

33. Proclamation of the Continental Congress, 22 Sept. 1783, Prucha, *Documents,* 3; George Washington to James Duane, 7 Sept. 1783, ibid., 2; Trade and Intercourse Act, 22 July 1790, ibid., 14–15; Woehrmann, *At the Headwaters,* 83; Leonard White, *The Federalists: A Study in*

Administrative History (New York: Macmillan, 1940), 380; "President Jefferson on Indian Trading Houses," 18 Jan., 1801, Prucha, *Documents,* 21–22; President Jefferson to William Henry Harrison, 27 Feb., 1803, ibid., 22–23.

34. Walter Font, ed., *A Garrison at Miamitown: Fort Wayne, October 1794–June 1795* (Fort Wayne, IN: Allen County-Fort Wayne Historical Society, 1994), 46n, 60n; Brice, *History of Fort Wayne,* 15.

35. Font, *A Garrison at Miamitown,* 40n, 49n–50n.

36. William Wells to the Secretary of War, 26 May 1808, Letters Received by the Secretary of War, Unregistered Series.

37. William Wells to the Secretary of War, Fort Wayne, 31 Mar. 1807, and Petition to Wells from citizens of Staunton, Miami County, Ohio, 8 July 1807, Letters Received by the Secretary of War, Registered Series, M221, Records of the Office of the Secretary of War.

38. William Wells to the Secretary of War, Fort Wayne, 19 Apr. 1807; William Wells to Henry Dearborn, Fort Wayne, 25 Apr. 1807, 7, 23 Jan., and 6 Mar. 1808, Letters Received by the Secretary of War, Registered Series.

39. Esarey, *Messages and Letters of William Henry Harrison,* 7:223, 242; William Wells to Henry Dearborn, 19 and 25 Apr. 1807, Letters Received by the Secretary of War, Registered Series; William Wells to the Secretary of War, 5 Dec. 1807, Carter, *Territorial Papers,* 7:498; William Wells to Henry Dearborn, 31 Dec. 1807, Letters Received by the Secretary of War, Registered Series.

40. Johnston to Eustis, 26 Aug. 1812, Richard C. Knopf, ed., *Anthony Wayne: A Name in Arms* (Pittsburgh: University of Pittsburgh Press, 1949), 6:73; Woehrmann, *At the Headwaters,* 233; Griswold, *Fort Wayne, Gateway,* 54.

41. Bert J. Griswold, *A Pictorial History of Fort Wayne, Indiana* (Chicago: Robert O. Law Co., 1917), 2:176–79.

42. Robert B. McAfee, *History of the Late War in the Western Country* (Lexington, KY: Worsley & Smith, 1816), 123; Donald Hickey, *The War of 1812: A Forgotten Conflict* (Urbana: University of Illinois Press, 1989).

43. Benjamin Stickney to William Crawford, 1 Oct. 1815, Gayle Thornbrough, ed., *Letter Book of the Indian Agency of Fort Wayne, 1809–1815* (Indianapolis: Indiana Historical Society, 1961), 230–34.

44. Brice, *History of Fort Wayne,* 283; Poinsatte, *Outpost,* 79.

45. Joseph Bartrand to Daniel Curtis, 12 Dec. 1814, Letters Received by the Secretary of War, Unregistered Series; Brice, *History of Fort Wayne,* 281.

46. Charles J. Kappler, *Indian Affairs: Laws and Treaties,* 2 vols. (Washington, DC: Government Printing Office, 1904) 2:169–72; Rafert, *Miami Indians,* 85.

47. Poinsatte, *Outpost,* 83–85; Thomas Scattergood Teas, "Journal of a Tour to Fort Wayne and the Adjacent Country, in the Year 1821," in *Indiana as Seen by Early Travelers: A Collection of Reprints from Books of Travel, Letters and Diaries Prior to 1830,* ed. Harlow Lindley (Indianapolis: Indiana Historical Commission, 1916), 250; Woodworth, *Reminiscences,* 21.

48. Poinsatte, *Outpost,* 82; Cass to Calhoun, 17 July 1822, and 5 June 1823, and Calhoun to Josiah Meigs, 27 Aug. 1822, Abandoned Military Reservations, Records of the Bureau of Land Management, Record Group 49, National Archives; Woehrmann, *At the Headwaters,* 273.

49. Poinsatte, *Outpost,* 83–84.

50. Ibid., 84–85.

51. Benjamin Stickney to Lewis Cass, December 1817, Thornbrough, *Letter Book,* 242.

52. Stickney to Cass, 6 Oct. 1815, and Stickney to Cass, 1 May 1816, Records of the Michigan Superintendency of Indian Affairs, Records of the Bureau of Indian Affairs.

53. Poinsatte, *Outpost,* 84; Teas, "Journal," 251.

54. Poinsatte, *Outpost,* 84–85; Secretary of War Calhoun on Indian Trade, 5 Dec. 1818, Prucha, *Documents,* 31–33.

55. Poinsatte, *Outpost,* 92; Rafert, *Miami Indians,* 88; Population Figures, 1800–1853, Records of the Civilization Division, Bureau of Indian Affairs; Tipton to Thomas L. McKenney, 13 Nov. 1824, Glen A. Blackburn, ed., *The John Tipton Papers,* 3 vols. (Indianapolis: Indiana Historical Bureau, 1942), 1:408.

56. "A Bill for Attaching Certain lands in the State of Indiana ceded to the United States by the Miami Indians to the Adjacent Land Districts," HR27A-G20.4, Committee on Public Lands, Various Subjects, Petitions or Memorials, Record Group 223, National Archives; Robert Robertson, *Valley of the Upper Maumee River: With Historical Account of Allen County and the City of Fort Wayne, Indiana* (Madison, WI: Brant & Fuller, 1889), 1:198–99.

57. Cass to Calhoun, 17 July 1822 and 5 June 1823, and Calhoun to Josiah Meigs, 27 Aug. 1822, Abandoned Military Reservations, Bureau of Land Management; Woehrmann, *At the Headwaters,* 273.

58. "Josiah Meigs, Treasury Department, General Land Office, to Edward Tiffin, Surveyor General," 28 Aug. 1822, and Josiah Meigs to Edward Tiffin, 29 June 1822, Letters Received by the Surveyor General of the Territory Northwest of the River Ohio, 1797–1856, M479, Bureau of Land Management.

59. John McLean to Edward Tiffin, 23 June 1823; James Milroy to Governor Tiffin, 17 Oct. 1822; and John McLean to Edward Tiffin, 23 June 1823, Letters Received by the Surveyor General of the Territory Northwest of the River Ohio, 1797–1856; Robertson, *Valley of the Upper Maumee,* 1:198–99.

60. *Indianapolis Gazette,* 26 Oct. 1826; Kappler, *Indian Affairs,* 2:278; Rafert, *Miami Indians,* 91.

61. William Suttenfield to Oliver H. Smith, 2 Feb. 1828; John Tipton to [the Secretary of War], 7 Feb. 1827; W. G. and G. W. Ewing to Oliver H. Smith, 4 Feb. 1828, Letters Received by the Office of Indian Affairs, 1824–1881, M234, Bureau of Indian Affairs.

62. John Tipton to Col. McKenney, 14 July 1828, Letters Received by the Office of Indian Affairs, 1824–1881; Darwin Kelley, "Securing the Land: John Tipton and the Miami Indians," *Old Fort News* 25 (1962).

63. Malcolm Rohrbough, "The Land Office Business in Indiana," *This Land of Ours: The Acquisition and Disposition of the Public Domain* (Indianapolis: Indiana Historical Society, 1978), 39, 48, 50–52.

64. Rafert, *Miami Indians,* 95; Kappler, *Indian Affairs,* 2:531–32.

"A Gallant and Valuable Officer"

The Naval Career of Thomas Holdup Stevens, 1809–1841

CHARLES E. BRODINE JR.

On 13 September 1813, three days after securing a bloody, hard-fought victory over the British fleet on Lake Erie, Oliver Hazard Perry sat down to compose a detailed after-action report to Secretary of the Navy William Jones. In this report, meant for public as well as official consumption, Perry vividly described how the two opposing squadrons had fought for supremacy in the waters off Put-in-Bay.[1] Before concluding his letter, Perry singled out eighteen officers whose gallant behavior had contributed to the American triumph. Tellingly, he withheld mention of the four officers who had commanded the vessels at the rear of his battle line, among them Lieutenant Thomas Holdup, captain of the one-gun sloop *Trippe*. For Holdup, Perry's silence was particularly mortifying, as he had performed well in the battle, aggressively bringing his little sloop into action against the two largest ships in the British squadron, the *Detroit* and the *Queen Charlotte*, and later overhauling and capturing the fleeing sloop *Little Belt* at the contest's close.[2]

Through the intercession of senior squadron officers, Perry soon discovered that he had erred in failing to praise Holdup in his 13 September report. To make amends, the commodore promised to give his young subordinate "every justice" on visiting Navy Department officials in Washington.[3] While Perry honored his pledge to Holdup, even becoming the latter's short-lived patron, this episode is emblematic of how Holdup's meritorious wartime services have failed to receive the recognition they deserve. Only recently have historians begun to detail his contributions to the 1813 Erie campaign, though his spirited conduct in operations on the Niagara River in 1812 and on Lake Huron in 1814 remain largely untold.[4] This essay is a contribution toward telling that story and giving Thomas Holdup, who later took the name Thomas Holdup Stevens, the recognition due him.

Thomas Holdup Stevens's naval services before and after the War of 1812 are equally deserving of treatment. These include enforcing the nation's maritime laws, surveying harbors and coastlines, fighting pirates in the West Indies, assisting diplomatic missions in the Mediterranean, supervising recruiting stations, and administering major shore installations. Taken in their entirety, these services illustrate the wide range of challenging duties U.S. naval officers performed in the early nineteenth century. Sketching Thomas Holdup's career not only highlights the accomplishments of this 1812 sailor but also reveals how the navy defended and advanced American interests in the first decades of the new republic.

The information on Stevens's early life is scarce and sometimes conflicting. In all likelihood he was born in Charleston, South Carolina, the city in which he was raised. The date most frequently given for his birth is 22 February 1795, though strong evidence exists that he was born in 1794.[5] Stevens first appears in the historical record as "Thomas Holdrupe," an eight-year-old inmate of the Charleston poor house who was bound over to the city orphanage on 24 November 1803. As two other poor house boys bearing the surname Holdrupe entered the Orphan House at or near this time, it seems reasonable to conclude that Stevens had two brothers, both younger, with whom he was institutionalized.[6]

What tragic family event left the Holdup boys parentless and wards of the city is unknown. In all probability, both mother and father died after contracting one of the more virulent diseases—yellow fever, smallpox, cholera—that struck down Charlestonians in large numbers in the eighteenth and nineteenth centuries. The city's poor and indigent classes, to whom the Holdups doubtless belonged, were especially vulnerable to such health threats.[7]

The Holdup children were fortunate to find asylum at the Charleston Orphan House. Established by the Charleston City Council in October 1790, the Orphan House was the first publicly funded institution of its kind in the United States. It "provided a safe, structured environment for abandoned, orphaned, or needy children."[8] A council-appointed board of commissioners oversaw the Orphan House's management while a small staff of administrators, instructors, and custodians tended to the children's day-to-day needs. Children were maintained and educated until they were old enough to be apprenticed to a trade, usually at age thirteen for girls and fourteen for boys.[9]

Thomas Holdup spent just over five years at the Charleston Orphan House. The full dimensions of how this experience affected him as he grew into adolescence can only be guessed at. More easily discerned are the ways in which the Orphan House made possible his subsequent navy career. Perhaps the most fundamental of these was the provision of an education. Orphan House boys received thirty hours of classroom instruction a week.[10] Based on the evidence of Holdup's earliest letters, illiteracy would never prove a bar to his naval ambitions. His correspondence is legibly written in a clear, thoughtful, and grammatically correct prose. Indeed, a brother officer would later eulogize Thomas Holdup Stevens as a man who possessed "literary talents . . . of a high order."[11]

Certainly growing up in an institution whose governing principles (discipline, order, respect for authority) mirrored those of a man-of-war helped prepare Holdup psychologically for a naval life, as did the challenge of sharing work and living quarters with a large community of people.[12] Likewise, the religious schooling he received at the orphanage instilled in him ideals that were integral to the ethos of a successful naval officer—honor, duty, cooperation, and submission to superiors.[13]

While these attainments may have qualified Holdup for a midshipman's warrant in the U.S. Navy, they meant little without a politically influential sponsor to promote his candidacy. Such support was a necessity in the pre-1815 navy, where the number of aspirants for midshipmen's places far exceeded the number of available billets.[14] Fortunately for Holdup, he had the patronage of two of Charleston's leading politicians, Langdon Cheves and Colonel Daniel Stevens, both of whom were members of the Orphan House's Board of Commissioners. Cheves was South Carolina's attorney general and destined to hold several powerful congressional posts during the War of 1812, including Speaker of the House.[15] Stevens was a Revolutionary War veteran and a city councilman who had held elective and appointive offices at the local, state, and federal levels.[16] Both he and Cheves used their influence and political connections to secure Holdup's entry into the navy.

Daniel Stevens's support of Holdup, in fact, went well beyond endorsing his name to the Navy Department, and despite the seeming disparities in their backgrounds, Stevens became the youth's mentor—guiding, advising, and encouraging Holdup in his new profession as a naval officer.[17] Over time, Stevens and Holdup grew closer, their relationship becoming more that of father and son than of adviser and protégé. The two men would legally formalize their ties in 1815 when Holdup adopted the surname Stevens and the elder Stevens named the young naval officer as one of his legatees.[18]

To champion Holdup's naval appointment in Washington, Cheves and Stevens turned to their state's senators, Thomas Sumter and John Gaillard. In early April 1808, the two Carolina lawmakers spoke with Secretary of the Navy Robert Smith about a warrant for Holdup. While amenable to granting the senators' request, Smith was unable to oblige as there were no vacancies "in the corps of Midshipmen" at that time. The navy secretary assured the legislators that Holdup's application would be kept on file at the department and given respectful consideration when new openings for midshipmen occurred.[19]

That opening came in January of the following year when Congress authorized the president to increase the number of commissioned vessels in active service to assist in enforcing the embargo.[20] This naval mobilization created an immediate need for midshipmen in the newly enlarged fleet. Casting his eye over the list of deserving applicants in department files, Secretary Smith saw that he now had the opportunity to satisfy the request of Senators Sumter and Gaillard. On 8 February 1809 he made good his promise to them, appointing Thomas Holdup a midshipman in the United States Navy with orders to report to Master Commandant John H. Dent, captain of the U.S. brig *Hornet* and commanding officer of the Charleston Station.[21] Since Holdup had already been acting as a midshipman in the *Hornet* since 4 February, Smith's letter of appointment officially confirmed what had already taken place.[22]

How did Thomas Holdup compare with his fellow midshipmen at the time he entered service? His youth, while not exceptional, was noteworthy. At fourteen, he was one to four years younger than at least half of the young gentlemen appointed midshipmen before 1815. He likewise stood out as an officer from the Deep South, with only 10 percent of the corps hailing from that region. As a resident of a maritime community, however, he shared a common background with the majority of his brother officers. Holdup may himself have been surprised to discover that a significant number of midshipmen knew something of an orphan's pain, as nearly a third of all new officers came "from homes in which the biological father had died."[23]

The day Thomas Holdup was appointed an acting midshipman in the *Hornet* marked the beginning of his apprenticeship as a naval officer. In the months to come, he acquired the skills and knowledge and developed the talents and abilities that one day enabled him to command both men and ships. The process by which novice midshipmen such as Holdup learned to become competent and professional sea officers has been ably described elsewhere.[24] What follows will instead highlight those experiences that shaped the contours and affected the quality of Holdup's early naval education.

The most important experience of Holdup's first years in the navy was the opportunity to serve in a succession of medium- to large-sized warships "actively cruising at sea" under experienced commanders. Navy leaders agreed that it was this type of assignment that offered "the best possible place to learn officership."[25] In this regard Holdup was blessed four times over; he was assigned, in turn, to the 16-gun brig *Hornet* (February–December 1809), the 44-gun frigates *Constitution* (December 1809–June 1810) and *President* (June–October 1810), and the 24-gun frigate *John Adams* (November 1810–September 1812). Each of these postings contributed to Holdup's knowledge of seamanship as he learned the management of square-rigged vessels in all types of weather and seas. He also became familiar with the particular sailing qualities of individual as well as classes of ships in the fleet. After serving only seventeen months in uniform, Holdup was confident enough in his own knowledge of seamanship to offer a detailed opinion on the superiority of the *President* over the *Constitution* in point of rigging and sailing.[26]

Holdup's early service also gave him the opportunity to participate in some of the more important national missions the navy performed before 1812. For example, in his inaugural cruise in the *Hornet,* he had the notable experience of assisting in the transport of General James Wilkinson and his military embassy from Charleston to New Orleans, with diplomatic stops along the way at Havana, Cuba, and Pensacola, Spanish West Florida.[27] One of the more controversial and unpopular duties the navy performed at this time was the enforcement of the nation's trade laws. In 1810, as a crewman in the *Constitution,* Holdup helped seize and send in for adjudication a number of ships suspected of violating these laws.[28]

Another, more unusual, service the navy provided from time to time was the testing of new technology that might have military and naval applications. Before he left the *President* in October 1810, Holdup saw his commanding officer, John Rodgers manage several experiments involving Robert Fulton's torpedoes (exploding mines).[29] A longstanding mission performed by the navy was the transport of diplomatic dispatches and personnel overseas, and in 1811 the *John Adams* transported several diplomats to their posts in France and England. The voyage proved memorable to Holdup both for the crowded and uncomfortable living conditions aboard and the fact that it was his first transatlantic voyage.[30]

As a new midshipman, Thomas Holdup could not have asked for a better role model to serve under than John Rodgers, his commanding officer first in the *Constitution* and then in the *President.* As the navy's senior officer afloat and its recognized professional head, Rodgers "took very seriously his responsibility . . . to train and mold junior officers."[31] He had a special interest in educating his midshipmen, and in February 1810 Rodgers arranged for Chaplain Robert Thompson to teach navigational science to the young "reefers" in the *Constitution.*[32] In addition to being an educator, Rodgers was also a tough disciplinarian who ran a taut, well-ordered ship.

The most meaningful shipboard relationship Holdup developed during this phase of his career was the friendship he forged with Ralph Izard Jr. A fellow Charlestonian and son and namesake of a wealthy U.S. politician, Izard served as first lieutenant in Holdup's first two ships, the *Hornet* and the *Constitution.* Although Izard resigned his commission in 1810, he and Holdup remained fast friends. The half dozen or so letters Holdup wrote to Izard between 1810 and 1814 represent the largest cache of his letters for this period and the only known collection of his personal correspondence. Holdup's salutary greeting to Izard in all of these letters—"Dear Father"—suggests the closeness of their relationship.[33] Collectively, the letters reveal Holdup as a modest and conscientious officer eager to rise in his profession.

When the United States declared war against Great Britain in June of 1812, Thomas Holdup was stationed at New York, where his ship, the *John Adams,* was undergoing repairs. As the weeks of inactivity passed, Holdup grew increasingly anxious over his bleak prospects of getting to sea and into the fight against England. In early September he wrote to Secretary of the Navy Paul Hamilton requesting a transfer from the *John Adams* to the frigate *Constitution.*[34] Holdup's benefactor, Daniel Stevens, wrote a similar letter to Hamilton soliciting an active, seagoing assignment for his young friend. Stevens pointed out that Holdup stood high in the estimation of his superiors for "his Seamanship, industry, activity in his profession, and strict obedience to orders, and his manliness, courage, and integrity." Such a meritorious officer deserved "an Opportunity to distinguish himself in the Service of his Country."[35] The looked-for reply from the Navy Department never came. But it did not matter, for soon the opportunity for naval glory presented itself in another quarter.

About the time Holdup was penning his transfer request to Hamilton, a confidential letter from the navy secretary to Isaac Chauncey, commandant of the New York Navy Yard, was making its way through the mail. The secretary charged Chauncey with building a naval force on the northern frontier strong enough "to obtain command of . . . Lakes Erie & Ontario."[36] On receiving these orders, Chauncey made immediate preparations for sending men, supplies, and armaments to both lakes. The commandant canvassed the officers and sailors attached to the navy yard for volunteers to accompany him northward on his "secret mission." According to Holdup, nearly the entire crew of the *John Adams* enthusiastically stepped forward to answer Chauncey's call to arms.[37]

On 24 September, Isaac Chauncey and his contingent headed for the Great Lakes via Albany, Schenectady, and the Mohawk River. At Utica he divided his force between men going north to the naval station at Sackets Harbor on Lake Ontario and those going west to the navy yard Lieutenant Jesse Duncan Elliott was establishing at Black Rock on the Niagara River.[38] Holdup was attached to this latter party along with Surgeon's Mate Usher Parsons, with whom he would form a lifelong friendship. Holdup was excited at the prospect of going into combat and wrote Izard that he soon hoped to see "some hard fighting." The small detachment of American sailors arrived at Black Rock on 16 October "worn out with fatigue" from their three-week journey.[39]

Despite their weariness, Holdup and the other new arrivals volunteered to help salvage the wreck of the brig *Detroit,* one of the enemy vessels Elliott had cut out and scuttled on 8 October.[40] Under cover of darkness, Holdup and the other volunteers managed to recover four 12-pounder guns, 680 rounds of grape and round shot, and assorted naval stores.[41] The operation reunited Holdup and Elliott, who had briefly been shipmates in the *John Adams.* The midshipman's performance may have impressed Elliott enough to request Holdup as his first lieutenant in the *Niagara* in 1813.

In mid-October Commodore Chauncey recalled Elliott to Sackets Harbor and directed Lieutenant Samuel Angus to assume command of the facility at Black Rock. Angus, who had served with Holdup in the *Constitution,* arrived at his new post on 19 October and immediately set about superintending the construction of two 400-ton vessels and eight gunboats for use on Lake Erie, as well as new barracks to house his command. He also supervised the men's training in the use of "musket, pistol, cutlass, & pike."[42] Owing to the armistice that was then in force along the Niagara, Angus's men had few opportunities to practice their combat skills against the enemy, the one exception being a failed open-boat pursuit of the *Queen Charlotte* up the Niagara River on 28 October.[43]

Angus and his men got their chance to engage the British foe on 28 November when they participated in a cross-river assault on enemy batteries opposite Black Rock. The American attack force totaled 180 men, soldiers, and sailors divided among ten boats. Angus and his officers had charge of the boats, which were organized into four divisions. The American boats shoved off from the east shore of the Niagara around 2:00 A.M. When the little flotilla came within a quarter mile of the Canadian shore, the British batteries and soldiery unleashed a fusillade of shot, canister, and musketry, creating havoc among the U.S. forces. As casualties mounted, some of the boats began to drop back and out of the fight. To encourage his comrades, Angus made "a desperate push" with the first boat division and, on nearing shore, plunged into the water beckoning his "Officers and Sailors to follow" him.

With only two boats ashore at this point, Angus had but two dozen officers and sailors to press home the attack, among them Thomas Holdup. Undaunted, Angus ordered his men on an uphill charge against the enemy batteries. The American tars, "armed [only] with Pikes, Cuttlasses and Boarding axes," scattered the British defenders, spiked the guns, and rolled the caissons into the river. When the retreating redcoats attempted to rally at their barracks, Angus's force, now strengthened by the addition of two more boat crews and a score of U.S. soldiers, drove them out of the building and set it on fire.[44]

But just when the American assault seemed on the verge of success, it faltered and collapsed in disorder. In part, this was because the small landing party had already sustained heavy casualties. Half of the men in Angus's first two boat crews were killed or wounded before day's end. The U.S. forces were also scattered and under no effective command and control, leading to confusion among soldiers and sailors. "By some means [or] other," reported Holdup, "the word *Retreat* was sounded & men & the greater part of the Office[rs] returned to our Shore." Angus himself barely escaped capture after being cut off when his men set off for the beaches.

As Holdup was returning to the beach, he came across "the brave Sai[ling Master] Watts lying wounded on the ground." In the act of assisting his fallen comrade, Holdup "received a [musket] Ball in" his "right Hand" that entered "under the Thumb" and exited "at the Ring finger." Though he did not realize it at the time, this wound left his right hand totally disabled. Nearly a quarter-century after the event, Holdup applied for and received a navy pension based on this disability.[45]

In his after-action report to navy secretary Hamilton, Angus heaped praise on his officers and men. Of Holdup he wrote, "The truly brave Holdup . . . behaved himself like a Gallant and valuable Officer."[46] As to Holdup's own assessment of his performance on the 28th, he wrote a friend, "I have no business to say any thing but I will say this that a clear conscience is the greatest blessing a man can feel."[47] Commodore Chauncey was impressed enough with Holdup's performance to appoint the seventeen-year-old midshipman acting lieutenant on 7 January 1813, a promotion that the Navy Department later confirmed on 24 July.[48]

Commodore Chauncey's arrest of Samuel Angus in the waning days of 1812 for disobeying orders temporarily threw U.S. naval affairs on Lake Erie into upheaval.[49] The assumption of the Erie command in March 1813 by Master Commandant Oliver Hazard Perry restored purpose, direction, and vigor to American operations in that theater.[50] It is likely that Thomas Holdup had already met Perry when both were stationed in vessels attached to John Rodgers's squadron at New York.[51] For Holdup, the bond formed with Perry during the spring and summer of 1813 proved to be the most influential professional relationship of his career.

Perry soon put the energetic Holdup to work providing logistical support to shipbuilders constructing the new brigs and gunboats at Erie.[52] Over the months of April and May, Holdup transported critical naval stores and ordnance from Black Rock and Buffalo to Erie.[53] In June Perry gave Holdup charge of the sloop *Trippe*, one of five squadron vessels at Black Rock, during the commodore's daring move to unite his entire fleet at Erie.[54] From mid-July to early August, Holdup acted as first lieutenant in the *Niagara* and then the *Lawrence*.[55] On 10 August, at the insistence of Jesse Duncan Elliott, he shifted his berth back to the *Niagara* to serve as first lieutenant. However, an "altercation" between the two men, the details of which are unknown, soon led to Holdup's transfer to the command of the *Trippe*.[56] The dispute with Elliott had momentous consequences for Holdup. As captain of his own vessel, he now had the means by which he might clearly distinguish himself in battle. He had also made a powerful enemy in the person of Jesse Duncan Elliott.

The sixty-three-ton sloop Thomas Holdup would take into combat on 10 September was one of the smaller vessels in Perry's squadron. It was "quite a good sailor in a strong breeze," and being a fore-and-aft rigged craft it could sail and maneuver closer to the wind than the squadron's square-rigged brigs.[57] In the event of light or negligible winds, long-oared sweeps powered the sloop through the water. The *Trippe*'s crew numbered thirty-five, only eleven of whom were sailors. The rest were an eclectic assortment of infantrymen, artillerists, militiamen, and volunteers, giving Holdup, in the words of one student of the battle, "the greatest diversity of men" in the American fleet.[58] The *Trippe*'s main firepower consisted of a 24-pounder long gun capable of delivering round shot on target from up to 1,200 yards away. Small arms fire provided additional killing force in close-quarters fighting with the enemy.

Perry's tactical plan for engaging the British squadron, finalized on 4 September, called for the *Trippe* to take station as the lead ship in the American order of sail. The commodore's last-minute reshuffling of this arrangement on the day of the fight resulted in the little sloop being shifted from the front to the rear-most position of the U.S. battle line. The light and baffling winds that prevailed off Put-in-Bay on the morning of the 10th proved especially challenging to the *Trippe* and the other three gunboats bringing up the American line—the *Somers, Porcupine,* and *Tigress.* Lacking the superior equipment and loftier sails that enabled the five larger vessels of the squadron to achieve headway and maneuverability under sail, the *Trippe* and its consorts were reduced to using sweeps to power themselves through Erie's waters. As a consequence of this differential in sailing capability, an ever-widening gap developed between the front and rear of Perry's battle line as his squadron slowly bore down on the British fleet. By 11:45 A.M., the time the action commenced, the *Trippe* and the other gunboats trailed the rest of the American squadron by more than a mile. It would take a further hour and a quarter before the lagging gunboats could close to effective cannon range with the enemy.[59]

Though latecomers to the action, the *Trippe* and the other gunboats moved aggressively to engage the enemy. Holdup's own narrative of the fight, written shortly before his death in 1841, offers fresh details on the contributions these plucky vessels made to the American victory that day. According to him, the *Trippe* and the other gunboats supported the brig *Caledonia* in "keeping up a heavy and well-directed fire at the *Lady Prevost, Hunter,* and *Little Belt,* occasionally firing into the heavy ships." The *Trippe* also furnished the *Caledonia* with gun cartridges on three separate occasions after the rapidly firing brig had exhausted its own supplies of ammunition. Toward the end of the battle, Holdup directed a raking fire against the *Queen Charlotte* that was so obstinate and unremitting its commander believed *Trippe* "meant to sink him," even though he had struck his colors. And once the firing between squadrons had ceased, an alert Holdup moved in concert with the *Caledonia* and *Scorpion* to snap up enemy vessels attempting to flee the battle scene. In company with the *Scorpion,* the *Trippe* pursued and overhauled the sloop *Little Belt.*[60]

Lieutenant Thomas Holdup Stevens. This photograph of a painting is the property of the Naval History and Heritage Command, Washington, DC. The provenance of the original painting is unknown.

Holdup's direction of the *Trippe* during the Battle of Lake Erie revealed his talent for managing men under fire. William P. Brady, a purser's steward in the *Trippe,* recalled that Holdup warned his crew of incoming cannon fire by yelling "squat," at which command the men would "dodge behind the Low Bulworks" to protect themselves "from the canister shot which the Enemy were firing."[61] This tactic may have been the reason why only two of the *Trippe*'s four casualties resulted from enemy gunfire.[62] Holdup also demonstrated that he had something of a reckless streak, at times exposing his ship and crew to needless jeopardy. On being ordered by Elliott to close to within "half pistol-shot" of the enemy, Holdup maneuvered the *Trippe* between the *Caledonia* and the enemy squadron. When the *Caledonia*'s commander, Daniel Turner, ordered Holdup to shift the *Trippe*'s position, the South Carolinian refused. When Turner then threatened to fire through the *Trippe,* Holdup replied, "fire away." A broadside from the *Caledonia* quickly ripped through the sloop's jib nearly carrying the whole away.[63]

Considering his youth, his complete lack of command experience afloat, the quality of his crew, and the short time he and his men had trained together, Holdup's performance in the *Trippe* was extraordinary. Knowing that this achievement would be shared with friends through Commodore Perry's publicized after-action report must have cheered Holdup considerably. In a letter to Daniel Stevens written four days after the battle, Holdup resisted the urge to brag about his contribution to the American victory. "I shall not attempt to describe the actions of any officer," he declared. "The Commodore, no doubt, will give them all the justice in his power."[64]

This expectation was shattered when Perry's report of 13 September appeared in print. "You'll observe" he wrote to his friend Ralph Izard Jr., "that I am not at all mentioned" in Captain Perry's official dispatch. "You may depend," he admitted, "I felt no little mortification at this circumstance."[65] Holdup's friends were no less troubled by Perry's oversight and wrote "anxious letters" to the commodore requesting a confirmation of Thomas's good character. Daniel Turner, among others, assured Perry that Holdup "had brought his vessel into action with special gallantry."[66] At the encouragement of his "Brother Officers," Holdup sought out Perry for an explanation. In the ensuing conversation, the young lieutenant learned that his name had been left out of official dispatches at the request of Jesse Duncan Elliott, who still bore a grudge against Holdup from his days in the *Niagara.* Perry affirmed his high regard for Holdup and vowed to have him as an officer in his next command.[67]

In the weeks following the Battle of Lake Erie, Perry's squadron actively supported the operations of Major General William Henry Harrison's North Western Army to recapture Detroit and invade Upper Canada. American warships ferried troops, transported food and supplies, and provided gunfire support for Harrison's force. The brig *Caledonia,* now under the command of Thomas Holdup, was one of the squadron vessels supporting army operations at this time. During the Thames River campaign, Perry charged Holdup with closely shadowing the movements of the army in the provisions-ladened *Caledonia.* Navy support of these operations proved instrumental to Harrison's 5 October victory over British forces at the Battle of the Thames.[68] In the space of four weeks, Holdup had participated in the two most pivotal military operations of the war in the Old Northwest.

With the departure of Perry for Newport, Rhode Island, in October 1813, Jesse Duncan Elliott assumed direction of the Lake Erie Squadron. The winter of 1813–14 was a particularly difficult one for Holdup and the men of the Erie Squadron, because the feud that divided Perry and Elliott now poisoned relations between their subordinates.[69] Elliott singled out known Perry supporters for retribution, assigning them particularly onerous duties.

Such treatment, however, did not extend to Holdup. "Since Elliott has had the command," Holdup wrote his friend Izard, "he has treated me extremely well." But, the wary lieutenant added, "I see through his designs & shall avoid being ensnared."[70] The arrival of Arthur Sinclair in April 1814 to assume command of the Erie Station spelled professional relief for Holdup, offering the South Carolinian another opportunity to signalize himself in combat.

In the spring of 1814, the Navy Department began to contemplate an expedition to recapture Fort Michilimackinac on Lake Huron.[71] The mere prospect of such a campaign was enough to prompt Holdup to write Izard excitedly, "It would please you, to see little Tom Holdup dashing through the straits of Erie with an Expedition" in command "of a 14 gun Brig"—a reference to the captured brig *Lady Prevost.*[72] By June the government had finalized its plans, and a joint army-navy force entered Lake Huron on 13 July.[73] Holdup served during the expedition not as the *Lady Prevost*'s captain but as the first lieutenant in the brig *Niagara,* Sinclair's flagship.[74] While the expedition failed in its main objective, the recapture of Michilimackinac, it did manage to capture two North West Company schooners, the *Mink* and the *Perseverance,* and to destroy the British schooner *Nancy* in the Nottawasaga River. Thomas Holdup commanded a mobile shore battery that destroyed the *Nancy* and the blockhouse guarding it.[75]

On returning home to Erie in September, an arsonist set fire to the brig *Caledonia,* nearly destroying Holdup's last command on Lake Erie. On shore at the time of the incident, Holdup had to swim out to the *Caledonia* in order to fight the blaze before it reached the brig's powder room. In a letter to Secretary of the Navy William Jones, Sinclair lauded his quick-thinking subordinate's brave conduct, writing, "Much praise is due to Lieut. Holdup who left a sick bed and swam off to her just in time to save her [from] exploding." He added, "It must have required considerable enterprise and exertion to have extinguished the flames while they were at such a hight, and separated from the powder only by a thin Bulk head."[76]

On 11 November the Erie Station's routine was interrupted by the execution of three servicemen for desertion. Two of the men, marines James Bird and James Rankin, were shot to death, while the third, Seaman Henry Davidson, was killed by hanging. Thomas Holdup served on Davidson's court-martial, so one wonders what thoughts must have been going through his mind as he witnessed the sentence being carried out that day on board the *Niagara.* Davidson's was one of two courts Holdup served on in 1814 that meted out death sentences, a rarity in the early sailing navy.[77] Two of the six officers who sat on each these courts opposed the capital sentences that were ultimately handed down, and it is possible that Holdup may have been one of those who argued for leniency. The court records are silent on this point, but it is tempting to speculate that this was the case based on the charity that others had shown Holdup in his childhood. Whatever the case, these courts-martial were Thomas Holdup's first official participation in the harsh disciplinary system that governed naval personnel.

By the fall of 1814, Holdup eagerly sought a furlough from the Lake Erie Station. Two years of active campaigning on the upper Great Lakes had undermined his health and left him with a disabling wound. To improve his chances of securing a leave of absence from the Navy Department, Holdup made his appeal through Langdon Cheves, his former political sponsor and now Speaker of the House of Representatives.[78] But before Cheves could even petition the Navy Department on Holdup's behalf, Secretary Jones had already issued orders of a different sort that would deliver that officer from the Erie Station. These instructions, which arrived on 2 December, directed Holdup to "repair to Baltimore" and report himself "to Captain O. H. Perry, for duty in the frigate *Java*."[79] Usher Parsons and Thomas Breese received orders identical to Holdup's the same day. The phrase "High glee," which appears in Parsons' diary entry for the 2nd, captures the jubilant and celebratory mood of the three officers that day.[80]

On 9 December Thomas Holdup and Usher Parsons set out for New York City en route to their new assignment. Surely the two men, now fast friends, must have reflected on all that they had seen and experienced over the past two years as they retraced, in reverse fashion, the route they had followed from New York to Black Rock in 1812.[81]

The precise date that Holdup reported for duty in Baltimore is unknown. The *Java*'s earliest surviving muster rolls document that he commenced service in the frigate on 21 July 1815.[82] How, then, does one account for the seven months that intervened between Holdup's departure from Presque Isle and his arrival at Baltimore? Perhaps, like Parsons, he enjoyed a brief furlough with family and friends before reporting for duty.[83] More likely, this was the time that he met, courted, and became engaged to Elizabeth (Eliza) Read Sage of Middletown, Connecticut.[84] The couple wed in December of that year, and their marriage shaped the remainder of Thomas Holdup's naval career.

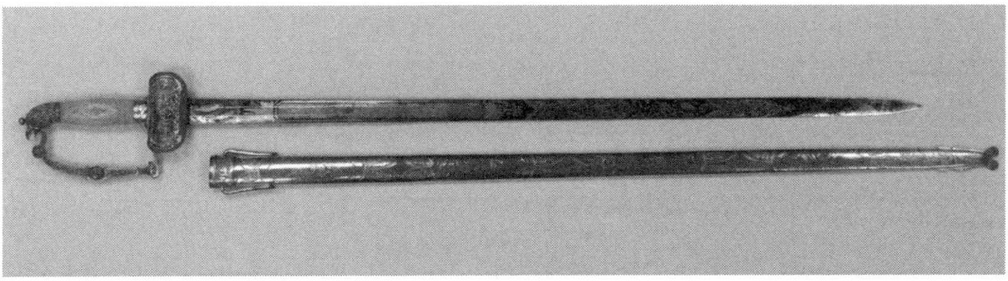

Presentation sword given by the citizens of Charleston, SC, to Lieutenant Thomas Holdup. Courtesy of the Naval History and Heritage Command, Washington, DC.

For all the elation that Holdup felt at being reunited with his Erie shipmates under Perry's command, his stay in the *Java* was short-lived, lasting less than five months—just long enough to sail with the ship to New York to help oversee the frigate's initial repair and outfit.[85] On 16 November, in the midst of this work, a four-man committee, led by Daniel Stevens, came aboard the *Java* and presented Holdup with an honorary sword the people of Charleston had voted for him to receive for his gallant conduct at the Battle of Lake Erie.[86] The richly detailed blue, gold, and silver blade bore the inscription: "The Citizens of CHARLESTON to Lieut. THOMAS HOLDUP. He was in the Battle of LAKE ERIE."[87] Such a public display of appreciation before his own peers surely filled Holdup with great pride.

In the afterglow of this presentation, Holdup and Eliza Sage prepared for their nuptials. The two married on 3 December 1815.[88] He was twenty years old at the time; she twenty-five. The pair now bore Thomas's new surname of Stevens.[89] Based on the testimony of Daniel Stevens, it is clear that both families embraced the union and that Thomas and Eliza were a well-matched couple.[90] With a three-month furlough in hand, Thomas and his new bride set up housekeeping in Middletown, where they lived until near the end of Stevens's naval career.[91]

As Thomas Holdup Stevens looked ahead to the new year, he had every reason to feel optimistic about his future. He had emerged from the war with Great Britain with command experience, a promotion, honors, and prize money.[92] He had secured a billet in a frigate bound for the Mediterranean, "one of the best naval schools in the world."[93] He had allied himself with one of the great captains in the U.S. Navy. And he had found someone with whom he could begin his own family. But the sailing of the *Java* in late

January 1816, before he could rejoin it, dealt his professional ambitions, if not his private ones, a major setback.

Except for a brief stint inspecting swords manufactured by a navy contractor, Stevens spent the next eighteen months on half pay in Middletown.[94] His repeated appeals to the navy secretary for active duty went unfulfilled. A 16 May petition stressed the "pecuniary concerns" that necessitated full-time employment—a reference to his new family obligations.[95] Others emphasized more professional worries. "I need not inform you," he wrote one Navy Department official, "how detrimental to an Officer, and a young one too, such a relaxation from duty is."[96] But because the postwar fleet had far more officers to place than vacant billets in which to put them, the secretary of the navy was unable "to find employment" for every officer in the corps. The best that he could do was to offer each man a "turn of active duty" as his name came up in rotation.[97]

The return home of Commodore Perry from his Mediterranean cruise in March 1817 revived Steven's spirits and his hopes for a seagoing assignment. Perry immediately extended an invitation to his former lieutenant to rejoin the *Java,* which Stevens gladly accepted.[98] In June Stevens requested and received permission to accompany Perry on a coastal survey the commodore was conducting as part of a congressionally mandated study of the nation's maritime defenses.[99] Stevens viewed the survey as an opportunity "to derive considerable information in one branch of my profession, in which I am little acquainted."[100] Stevens spent the summer months with Perry surveying the eastern entrance to Long Island Sound and Newport Harbor to determine the best possible locations for a naval depot and military fortifications. Perry submitted his findings to the secretary of the navy on 30 October.[101]

The year 1818 was a memorable one for Stevens on several accounts. First, he was given charge of the U.S. storeship *Alert* on 6 January.[102] Though not a man-of-war, it was Stevens's first independent command in four years. The converted 1812 prize ship carried naval stores between Norfolk and other navy yards on the eastern seaboard.[103] Second, Eliza Stevens delivered the couple's first child, Frederick, born on the fifth anniversary of the Battle of Lake Erie![104] To paraphrase Perry, it was a "Signal Birth!" And third, Stevens provided Perry with an affidavit that validated the commodore's "version of what happened on 10 September 1813." The subsequent publication of this affidavit following the commodore's death, along with those of Perry's other

Lake Erie subordinates, embroiled Stevens and his shipmates in continued controversy with Jesse Duncan Elliott and his partisans.[105]

On being relieved of command of the *Alert* in November 1818, Stevens returned home to Middletown, where he remained for the next seven months. On 27 May 1819 Eliza gave birth to the couple's second son, Thomas Holdup Stevens Jr. Like his father, Thomas Jr. went on to join the navy, achieving the rank of rear admiral before he retired and, also like his father, fight in a historic naval battle, Mobile Bay, under a great squadron commander, David Glasgow Farragut.[106]

The next three and a half years constituted a professional low point for Thomas Holdup Stevens, highlighted by mediocre shore postings.[107] The event that plunged his career in the doldrums, at least in Stevens's estimation, was the unexpected death of his patron, Oliver Hazard Perry.[108] Without a respected senior officer to advance his professional claims, Stevens saw little possibility of obtaining the type of command he merited. "I now have no naval friends to intercede on my behalf," he wrote Secretary of the Navy Smith Thompson. "Those who could have given you my character, (Comdr. Decater & Comdr. Perry) are now in their Graves."[109] In multiple letters to the Navy Department, Stevens vented his frustrations at being passed over for command by more junior officers. "The state of idleness, I have endured for some time past," he fumed, "has been most galling to my feelings, & those of my friends."[110] There is no doubt that his complaints regarding seniority were well justified. In 1821, for example, the schooners *Grampus* and *Porpoise* were commanded by officers who were junior to Stevens by eleven and seventeen months respectively.[111]

The decision of the Monroe administration in 1822 to create a special naval squadron to suppress piracy in the West Indies finally thrust Stevens back into the role he performed best, that of combat commander. On 20 December the Navy Department ordered Stevens to Norfolk to assume command of one of eight recently purchased schooners for the West India Squadron.[112] These swift-sailing, shallow-draft vessels were ideal craft for operations against West Indian pirates who preferred to strike their quarry from close inshore rather than on the open seas.[113] Commodore David Porter, the squadron commander, assigned Stevens to command the schooner *Jackall.*

The squadron departed Norfolk the last week of February 1823 and arrived in the Caribbean the first week of March. Porter deployed the majority of his command on systematic patrols off the coasts of southern Florida, Cuba, and

Puerto Rico, the most notorious areas of piratical activity. He detached other ships to perform convoy duty, escorting American merchantmen safely in and out of the Cuban ports of Matanzas and Havana. Duty in the squadron was physically and psychologically taxing. "The service we are employed on," Porter informed Secretary Thompson, "is a very harassing one, and, if it should not occasion much waste of life, it will, at least, try the strength of our constitutions, and our capacity for the endurance of fatigue and privations."[114]

Between March and June Stevens operated largely in Cuban waters, convoying merchantmen, cruising singly on patrol, and participating in offensive operations against pirates along the island's northwestern coast.[115] During the middle weeks of April, the *Jackall* sailed in a five-vessel task force of schooners and barges under the command of Master Commandant Stephen Cassin. Cruising east to west, Cassin's detachment carefully worked the waters and coastline between Havana and Cape San Antonio, seizing a schooner, a sloop boat, and a felucca. In capturing the felucca, the Americans engaged in a running firefight with the pirate defenders ashore, driving them off into the bushes, after which they destroyed five of the buccaneers' huts. In his official report to Porter, Cassin praised the contribution of his officers, including Stevens, to a successful cruise.[116] The seizure of the felucca earned Stephens and his fellow captors $2,000 in prize moneys, though it took the government more than eleven years to award it.[117]

On 18 June Stevens sailed for Washington to exchange the *Jackall* for another command.[118] After taking a brief leave of absence in Middletown, he received orders to assume command of the schooner *Shark* at New York.[119] His next mission was prompted by a medical crisis on Thompson's Island (Key West), the site of the West India Squadron's rendezvous in the Florida Keys. Many of the squadron's officers and men had contracted yellow fever, including David Porter, and the death toll was rising.[120] At the request of the Navy Department, Navy Board of Commissioners president John Rodgers and a team of senior surgeons agreed to visit the island and investigate the situation there. They sailed in the *Shark* on 6 October, arriving at Key West on the 23rd. Though they found the situation at Key West grim, neither Rodgers nor his medical advisers thought the island uninhabitable and made recommendations that they believed would reduce the mortality rate at the island naval base.[121] After spending less than a fortnight at Key West, Stevens transported his passengers back to Norfolk, where they arrived on 16 November.

On 31 December Stevens departed Norfolk on his last cruise in the *Shark*. He had on board agents from the Bank of the United States, whom he was carrying to Alvarado, Mexico. After landing his passengers on 28 January 1824, Stevens anchored the *Shark* at nearby Antón Lizardo. On the afternoon of 11 February, while returning to the schooner in an open boat, a powerful storm with gale-force winds broke in full fury on Stevens and his boat crew. The only hope for the American commander and his men lay in scudding along under bare poles back to Alvarado Harbor. But as the seas began to rise ever higher, threatening to swamp his craft, Stevens found it necessary to set sail in order to drive the boat through the water faster than the waves that were trailing it. Against all odds, Stevens and his passengers made it safely to Alvarado Harbor. It was an amazing and daring bit of seamanship conducted with "the most perfect order and self-possession."[122]

When Stevens rejoined the *Shark*, he learned that fourteen of his men had perished when the launch they were in capsized while trying to render assistance to a British vessel.[123] He remained stationed off the Mexican coast until the second week of April, when he left for Key West and then New York, where he arrived on 14 May. One month later Stevens requested permission to resign command of the *Shark* in favor of a shore assignment.[124] From this point in his career forward, Stevens never solicited another active seagoing command; he always requested duty ashore.

Given Stevens's repeated and impassioned pleas for sea duty prior to his West Indian service, the shift in career focus is striking. The reason for the change was twofold: family and finances. Eliza Stevens had just delivered their third child (of seven), Eliza Augusta.[125] With a growing family, Steven's desire to be more home-centered increased. As someone who was raised an orphan, Stevens was keenly aware of what the absence of a parent meant to a child. Perhaps his near-fatal experience in the hurricane off Alvarado drove this point home even harder.

Finances also loomed large in Stevens's career calculations at this time, and they continued to dominate his thoughts for years to come. Supporting a family on a lieutenant's pay was extremely challenging.[126] Thus, Stevens sought assignments whose positions brought extra pay and benefits. "In my letter to the Secretary," he wrote John Rodgers, "I have solicited command of the Receiving ship at Boston . . . My large family, renders the emoluments of Lieut. Comdt. important to me at this moment."[127] He also realized by this time that he was unlikely to receive anything from his adoptive father Daniel

Stevens's estate. "My prospects at the South," he confessed to navy secretary Samuel L. Southard, "'tho not entirely blasted afford but a feeble hope that I shall be able to realize any thing from my Father's property."[128] Deprived of this anticipated legacy, Stevens's family became solely dependent on his naval salary for its well-being.

In 1825 Stevens received some relief from his financial concerns with a promotion to the rank of master commandant. The top seven senior lieutenants in the service (Stevens being seventh) were elevated to that rank on 3 March, with their order of precedence as lieutenants being preserved as master commandants.[129] Earlier in the year Stevens had been concerned enough about the possibility of being passed over for promotion that he wrote to John Rodgers for support.[130] Like the other men who were promoted with him, Stevens earned his promotion based on length of service rather than Rodgers's intervention.

On 16 May Stevens performed his first official duty as a master commandant in giving testimony at Commodore David Porter's court of inquiry.[131] The court was investigating "two particular matters: the rectitude of Porter's landing at Fajardo [Puerto Rico], and whether he had neglected his duties as Commodore of the West India Squadron in order to carry specie."[132] The Navy Department had given Porter permission to engage in this practice as long as it did not interfere with his squadron's central mission of fighting pirates. As ship commanders were allowed to charge as freightage a small percentage of the value of specie carried, the temptation to ignore the suppression of piracy in favor of private gain was obvious. Stevens himself had transported specie valued at $163,000, charging a freightage of between 1.5 percent and 2.5 percent.[133] While charges of peculation against Porter went unproven, the 1812 hero was found guilty of more serious charges and suspended from service, a verdict that led to his resignation from the navy.[134]

Except for a brief stint as commander of the receiving ship *Fulton*, Stevens spent his next two years of naval service unemployed.[135] He returned to active duty once again in the spring of 1827 as second-in-command to Thomas Tingey at the Washington Navy Yard.[136] One of the chief functions of the yard at this time was as a shipbuilding and repair facility. Three major warships under construction there were the frigates *Columbia* and *Potomac* and the sloop of war *St. Louis*. Another important function of the yard was as a manufacturer of naval stores, such as blocks and ship fittings, for the rest of the fleet. The administrative duties associated with running the yard were formidable and included purchasing of stores, letting contracts, managing the labor force, maintaining all accounts, and corresponding with the Navy Board of Commissioners.[137]

Tingey must have surely welcomed the assistance of an energetic and intelligent deputy such as Stevens, who relieved the septuagenarian commandant of much of the day-to-day burden of running the yard. On two occasions Tingey left for a month or longer and Stevens filled in capably.[138] On 23 February 1829 Thomas Tingey died, leaving Thomas Holdup Stevens as acting commandant of the Washington Navy Yard, a duty he performed until 11 April when he was relieved by Isaac Hull.[139] Stevens successfully petitioned the Navy Department for the additional pay he was due for performing the duties of a navy yard commandant for more than six weeks.[140]

On 12 June Secretary of the Navy John Branch ordered Stevens to New York to assume command of the sloop of war *Ontario*.[141] The American warship was slated to join the Mediterranean Squadron under Commodore James Biddle, who was undertaking a diplomatic mission to the Ottoman Empire.[142] It is unlikely that Stevens solicited this command, since he only asked for assignments ashore or in stationary vessels. Moreover, he was involved in a pay dispute with the Treasury Department's navy auditor that left in doubt whether his family would be provided for while he was away.[143] On the eve of the *Ontario*'s sailing, it might be fair to characterize Stevens as a reluctant, if willing, commander.

On 22 August the *Ontario* set sail from New York for the Mediterranean. Less than three weeks out, a hurricane slammed into the sloop, knocking the vessel on its beam ends. Water poured down the hatchways and the crew struggled to stay upright as the *Ontario* inclined at a near forty-five-degree angle. Only the quick response of Stevens and his officers kept the vessel from foundering. The experience of fighting the storm left one midshipman so bone-weary that he fell asleep in steerage in knee-deep water.[144] Stevens later reported that the storm exceeded in "violence . . . any thing I believe ever witnessed by the oldest seaman on board."[145]

The *Ontario* arrived at Gibraltar on 17 September. Over the next twenty-one months, the ship patrolled largely in the western Mediterranean, making regular stops at Algiers, Gibraltar, Barcelona, Marseilles, and Port Mahon, sometimes transporting U.S. and foreign diplomats along the way. The sloop made a single trip to the eastern Mediterranean in November 1830, lying off Smyrna for over two months. Shortly after arriving at this port, an Austrian admiral visited the *Ontario.* Through a mishap, one of the saluting guns was inadvertently left loaded with shot. When fired off, the cannon sent a missile that passed "through the Main Boom of a Dutch Brig of War, Cut away the main lift and brace of a French Brig of War, and lodged in the hold of an Austrian merchant Brig."[146]

According to John Dahlgren, a midshipman in the *Ontario* (and a future Civil War admiral), the sloop of war was a well-run and orderly vessel with a spirited crew. "Duty was done with exactitude," he recalled with pride, "but in a dashing manner." Reflective of this high morale was the sloop's handsome, sailorly appearance: "Nothing could be more perfect than the order and high finish of the 'Ontario.' The nautical critic could not detect a slack rope, or a mast of a line, or an unsquared yard, and her light, graceful hull shone in polished black." Perhaps the ship's company took its cue from Stevens, whom Dahlgren described as "a handsome, open-hearted sailor, with a friend in every man on board."[147]

Dahlgren's testimony notwithstanding, the *Ontario* had its share of crewmen whose disruptive and disobedient behavior tested Stevens's ability to maintain discipline in the sloop. Alcohol abuse fueled much of this delinquent behavior, both among the enlisted and the officer ranks. Stevens punished *Ontario* sailors guilty of drunkenness with six to twelve lashes from a colt or cat-o'-nine-tails, while officers who made a habit of being intoxicated he placed under arrest.[148] Infighting among the sloop's cadre of midshipmen posed yet another kind of threat to shipboard discipline in the *Ontario.* Young, often reckless, and possessing outsized notions of personal honor, midshipmen "were the chief duelists of the Old Navy."[149] Doubtless influenced by his mentor Perry's views on the subject, as well as his own experiences on the Lake Erie station, Stevens opposed dueling. On learning that two of his midshipmen, John Dahlgren and Henry Walke, planned to settle their differences by fighting a duel, Stevens intervened promptly and quashed the combat, an action that preserved order in his vessel and the lives of two future flag officers of note.[150]

Despite the fact that service in the squadron was considered desirable duty, Stevens yearned to be with his family again. After only a year of service in the Mediterranean Squadron, he applied for permission to return home[151] The Navy Department delayed authorizing his return until the spring of 1831. On 15 June of that year, Stevens surrendered his ship to Master Commandant William L. Gordon.

Captain Thomas Holdup Stevens. Reprinted from Benson J. Lossing, *Pictorial Field-Book of the War of 1812* (New York: Harper Brothers, 1869).

Although Stevens arrived home in early September, he had to wait until January of the following year to receive a new assignment, a posting as second-in-command at the Pensacola Navy Yard. Stevens asked to be released from these orders owing to the heavy expense and great inconvenience entailed in moving his family "to so distant a Station," as well as the "impracticability of educating" his children there. The department thoughtfully rescinded these orders and issued a new set directing Stevens to report to Commodore Charles Morris at Boston "for command of the Rendezvous on that station."[152] As Stevens had repeatedly angled for duty in Boston since mid-1824, the prospect of serving in the Bay State capital was a pleasant one. Had he known that within a year of his arrival at Charlestown, Jesse Duncan Elliott would assume command of that navy yard, he might have declined the appointment.[153]

Stevens commanded the Boston rendezvous—the nineteenth-century equivalent of today's navy recruiting station—for nearly four years. In this post he oversaw the enlistment of able-bodied men and boys into naval service. Since low pay, the use of corporal punishment, and abuses in enlistment and discharges had made service in the navy unattractive to Americans, it was a challenging assignment.[154] This difficulty in securing men was reflected in Stevens's correspondence with Washington. For example, when asked to recruit men for the ship of the line *Delaware,* Stevens sought to temper department expectations for ample recruits. "The scarcity of seamen and the high wages given in the Merchant Service," he warned, " . . . has operated as a strong inducement on them to prefer that service to our own, and we have consequently been unable to ship but very few men."[155]

Elliott's arrival at Charlestown in May 1833 revived angry and painful memories of Lake Erie days for Stevens. These found vent in the local republication of his 1818 affidavit impugning Elliott's conduct in the Battle of Lake Erie. "It was the general opinion of the officers and men of the squadron," declared Stevens, "that Captain Elliott did not do his duty in the action of the 10th of Sept.; and that had he been impelled by a becoming bravery, he would have made greater exertions to have taken an active part in the fight." In a mocking swipe at his old shipmate, Stevens repeated the following piece of squadron gossip: "It was reported he [Elliott] beat the Captain of the gun [in *Somers*] very severely with a speaking trumpet, for having laughed at his dodging a shot which passed over him from the enemy."[156] Elliott replied to Stevens's charges through an anonymous proxy who attacked in print the commander of the *Trippe* and his fellow Perry partisans.[157] These were but the opening salvos in a renewed war of words that raged on well after Stevens had died.

In March 1836 Stevens received word that he had been detached from the Boston rendezvous and granted a three-month leave of absence.[158] He began his furlough on a high note, with a newly signed captain's commission in hand.[159] It had taken him twenty-seven years to reach the navy's highest rank. As no navy assignments were forthcoming over the next four years, Stevens focused his time and energies on family and business matters. One of his primary concerns was finding positions in the military for sons Frederick, age eighteen, and Thomas Jr., age seventeen. He succeeded in securing an acting midshipman's appointment for Thomas Jr. but failed to obtain a coveted marine lieutenancy for Frederick.[160] Though his father would not live to see it, Frederick ultimately received a purser's commission from the Navy Department after the commissioners of the Charleston Orphan House lobbied navy officials on his behalf.[161]

One of the more obscure activities Stevens was involved in while on furlough involved travel to the Great Lakes. Between June of 1836 and 1837, he visited Detroit and Chicago on "business of importance."[162] What this business may have involved is suggested by a letter Stevens wrote to Congressman James D. Doty in 1840 supporting a plan to construct harbors along the Wisconsin shore of Lake Michigan from Manitowac to Racine.[163] Given Doty's heavy involvement in the purchase and commercial development of public lands in Wisconsin, it would be interesting to know if Stevens's endorsement of the harbor plan was motivated by public-spiritedness or other considerations.[164]

From 1837 to 1840 Stevens appeared on Navy Registers as "Waiting orders." During this period he applied repeatedly for assignment to a number of stations, including Pensacola, Charleston, and Philadelphia. The Navy Department was not indifferent to Stevens's requests; they simply lacked a vacant billet in which to place him. A comparison between the Navy Registers for 1820 and 1840 is illustrative of the department's dilemma. In 1820 the navy carried thirty-four captains on its rolls, all but one of whom were employed on duty. In 1840, the year Stevens returned to service, the number of captains on navy rolls had increased to fifty-five, but only twenty-nine of these held active posts. In two decades the navy had lost the ability to find meaningful work for nearly half of its highest-ranking officers, a situation that was reflected in lower ranks as well.[165] Thus, just as when he was a lieutenant impatient for assignment, Stevens had to wait his turn for a captain's billet to come open.

The death of Washington Navy Yard commandant Daniel T. Patterson in August 1839 created the opening that led to Stevens's return to service. On 26 February 1840 Secretary of the Navy James K. Paulding appointed Stevens to fill the Washington yard's vacant command.[166] A local newspaper opined that Stevens's appointment could not but be "otherwise than acceptable to the inhabitants of Washington," as it brought "amongst them again, as a resident, a gentleman so favorably known to them during his former service at that Yard."[167] Stevens assumed command of the Washington Navy Yard on 5 March as its fifth commandant and held the post until his death eleven months later.

The Washington establishment of which Stevens assumed command was in a state of transition. Shipbuilding, an important operation since the yard's early days, had ceased to be a major activity at the facility. Instead, its primary mission had become the manufacture of equipment and machinery for outfitting the fleet. As one 1840 visitor summarized, "In this yard are manufactured all the tanks and cambooses, blocks and brass work, now used in our navy."[168] Another indication of the yard's changing character was the addition of steam-powered machinery to its manufacturing plants.[169] Recognizing the importance of this new technology entering the fleet, Stevens petitioned Secretary Paulding for books "on the Steam Engine, & Steam Navigation" with which to instruct midshipmen attached to the yard.[170] The parsimonious Paulding balked at purchasing expensive textbooks, suggesting instead that Stevens's "young gentlemen" gain their knowledge of steam engines through hands-on experience.[171]

On the morning of 20 January 1841, Stevens visited navy yard surgeon David S. Edwards complaining of stomach distress. Edwards dosed Stevens with Seidlitz powder (a cathartic) and magnesium carbonate (a laxative) to help relieve the commandant's symptoms. By four in the afternoon, Stevens reported that he was free of abdominal pain but told Edwards he had "a soreness across the muscles of the chest." The surgeon then prescribed a treatment that included mint tea, a warm foot bath, and mustard plaster wraps. When he called on Stevens later that evening, Edwards was told that his patient "had gone to bed and was very comfortable." Shortly after midnight on the 21st, Eliza Stevens awoke to her husband's loud and labored breathing. Despite her best efforts to rouse him, Stevens failed to regain consciousness "and in a few minutes expired."[172] Edwards speculated that Stevens died due to "the rupture of a blood vessel, or scrous effusion in the brain."[173]

On learning of Stevens's death, Secretary Paulding immediately directed a month-long, servicewide display of mourning "as a mark of respect" to the 1812 veteran's memory.[174] Much of official Washington turned out for Stevens's funeral on the 23rd, including members of Congress, the war and navy secretaries, and the commissioners of the Navy Board. Washington citizens of a humbler standing also attended the funeral in large numbers. One city newspaper noted the presence of "the great body of mechanics, and others attached to the Navy [Yard]," who came to demonstrate "their sincere and cordial respect for the memory and character of the late Commodore Stevens." The funeral service opened at the Washington Navy Yard and concluded at the Congressional Cemetery, where Stevens's remains were interred. At the close of the ceremonies, "the usual military honors were paid by the Marine Corps to the departed Commodore."[175]

Washington's *Daily National Intelligencer* published a eulogy of Stevens that was reprinted widely throughout the country. It spoke of Stevens's youth when he entered the navy, of his gallant service as one of Perry's ship commanders, and of how "he had distinguished himself in the war of 1812, even before Perry's brilliant victory on Lake Erie." The most striking feature of this tribute was its praise of Stevens's character: "Open-hearted, frank, and generous, we knew not a man who made his way so directly to the affections of all to whom he became known as this gallant and lamented officer."[176]

Stevens's passing led a New Hampshire newspaper to wonder how many ship commanders "who shed so much lustre upon our national flag in the last war" were yet living. Their tally showed nine of twenty-two 1812 commanders still alive, including three from Perry's squadron.[177] One remembrance, published eighteen years after his death, would have had special meaning to Stevens. It appeared in an article paying tribute to the work of the Charleston Orphan House. The piece celebrated Stevens's "distinguished" and intrepid service in Commodore Perry's fleet in the Battle of Lake Erie.[178]

Thomas Holdup Stevens's life was one that defied the odds. That he could overcome the disadvantages of an impoverished, parentless childhood to forge a distinguished naval career for himself is truly quite remarkable—a testament not only to his character, intelligence, and fortitude but to his sheer good luck. That he is not better remembered today for what he accomplished, particularly during the War of 1812, is unfortunate, though not surprising. For one thing, Stevens left a very light footprint in the documentary record. Not only did he leave few personal papers to posterity, but his surviving official correspondence is exceedingly thin in quantity and quality. Never a self-promoter of the Jesse Duncan Elliott stripe, Stevens preferred to let his deeds speak for themselves. Hence, he left no written or published record of any kind highlighting his career.

But Thomas Holdup Stevens does deserve our attention, and his career is noteworthy for several reasons. First, Stevens's life casts in bold relief some of the more important issues that characterized and defined naval service in the antebellum navy. Stevens's oft-articulated concerns regarding salary and personal finances reflect a corpswide disgruntlement with a navy pay structure that remained fundamentally unchanged until 1835. Stevens was only one of a number of officers who agitated for better pay and compensation with the Navy Department and Congress.[179] A more powerful frustration, perhaps, was the Navy Department's inability to find meaningful employment for all of its commissioned and warranted officers in the decades following the War of 1812. With too few billets, too many officers, and no mechanism for forced retirement, many officers were compelled to endure long periods of administrative idleness before returning to duty. Finally, Stevens's involvement in the Perry-Elliott controversy reveals how easily personality disputes disrupted relations within the early officer corps. As the experience of the Erie Station shows, such quarrels were productive of great mischief, often leading to physical violence and sometimes bloodshed. It is ironic that Stevens, a man known for his genial manner and lack of animus, became embroiled in a destructive personal feud with other officers.

As an 1812 figure, Thomas Holdup Stevens should be remembered for his contributions to the navy's war effort on the upper Great Lakes between 1812 and 1814. As an officer he was loyal and devoted; as a fighter he was brave and relentless; as a commander he was fearless and resolute. Oliver Hazard Perry had need of such men in the spring and summer of 1813, for without them victory on Lake Erie would not have been possible. Indeed, the presence of so many junior officers like Stevens throughout the American fleet goes far in explaining why the U.S. Navy performed so brilliantly against the Royal Navy in the War of 1812.

As a figure of the early sailing navy, Stevens should be remembered for the many and varied naval services he so ably performed over the course of his thirty-two-year career, including protecting the nation's commerce, surveying its coasts, fighting its enemies, and advancing its diplomatic interests. These duties were typically demanding, sometimes mundane, and often hazardous. The navy had need of men such as Stevens, whose quiet, steady professionalism enabled them to execute successfully the hard but necessary work of a peacetime service.

NOTES

1. See Perry to Jones, 13 Sept. 1813, in William S. Dudley and Michael J. Crawford, eds., *The Naval War of 1812: A Documentary History,* 3 vols. (Washington, DC: Naval Historical Center, 1982–), 2:557–59.

2. Usher Parsons identifies the *Little Belt* as the ship that the *Trippe* overhauled and captured. See Usher Parsons to the Committee of Arrangements at the Inauguration of the Perry Statute, n.d., Stevens Family Papers, MSS 53082, Library of Congress, Washington, DC.

3. On the intercession of squadron officers on Holdup's behalf, see Alexander Slidell Mackenzie, *The Life of Commodore Oliver Hazard Perry,* 2 vols. (New York: Harper & Brothers, 1843), 1:276. Thomas Holdup to Ralph Izard Jr., 14 Apr. 1814, Stevens Family Papers. The abbreviations TH and THS are used in the notes for references to Thomas Holdup Stevens.

4. For the fullest treatment of Holdup's 1813 service on Lake Erie, see David Curtis Skaggs and Gerard T. Altoff, *A Signal Victory: The Lake Erie Campaign, 1812–1813* (Annapolis, MD: Naval Institute Press, 1997). Two classic naval histories of the War of 1812, Alfred Thayer Mahan's *Sea Power in Its Relations to the War of 1812* (Boston: Little, Brown, 1905) and Theodore Roosevelt's *The Naval War of 1812* (New York: G. P. Putnam Son's, 1882), mention Holdup either not at all (in the case of Mahan) or simply as the commander of the *Trippe* (in the case of Roosevelt).

5. Stevens's date of birth was not reported in local obituaries. What gives credence to 22 February 1795 as the date of his birth is that it appeared in a publication to which his son, Rear Admiral Thomas Holdup Stevens Jr., was a contributor. See *A Naval Encyclopaedia: Comprising a Dictionary*

of Nautical Words and Phrases . . . (Philadelphia: L. R. Hamersly & Co., 1881), 777. This date was likewise given by Allan Westcott, whose entry on Stevens in Allen Johnson and Dumas Malone, eds., *The Dictionary of American Biography*, 20 vols. (New York: Charles Scribner's Sons, 1928–36) was vetted by that officer's great-granddaughter, Mrs. Fred C. Hicks. See Westcott to Hicks, 6 May 1932, Stevens Family Papers. The 1794 birth date is inscribed on Stevens's headstones at the Congressional Cemetery where he was originally buried and at Arlington National Cemetery, where his remains were reinterred in 1905. Images of these headstones may be viewed at http://www.arlingtoncemetery.net/thsteven.htm. Since Charleston Orphan House records describe Thomas Holdup as being eight years old in 1803, an age that corresponds with a birth year of 1795, this narrative calculates Thomas's age based on a birth date of 22 February 1795.

6. Six-year-old George Holdrupe was admitted to the Orphan House the same day as Thomas, while James Holdrupe was admitted on 21 October 1805 (two years later) at age five. See the entries for all three Holdup boys in Susan L. King, *History and Records of the Charleston Orphan House, 1790–1860* (Easley, SC: Southern Historical Press, 1984), 42. King's data is abstracted from the manuscript records of the Charleston Orphan House, Record Group 001277, South Carolina Department of Archives and History, Columbia. It is possible they hold more detailed information on Thomas and his family.

7. The distressing and unhealthy living conditions of Charleston's poor are described in Barbara L. Bellows, *Benevolence Among Slaveholders: Assisting the Poor in Charleston, 1670–1860* (Baton Rouge: Louisiana State University Press, 1993), esp. chap. 3; and in Walter J. Fraser, *Charleston! Charleston! The History of a Southern City* (Columbia: University of South Carolina Press, 1991), 174–75, 189–90. For a contemporary view of the effects of disease on Carolinians, see David Ramsay, *Ramsay's History of South Carolina, from Its First Settlement in 1670 to the Year 1808*, 2 vols. (Newberry, SC: W. J. Duffie, 1858), 2:42–59.

8. Quoted text from Walter B. Edgar, *South Carolina: A History* (Columbia: University of South Carolina Press, 1998), 297. The ordinance establishing the Orphan House, dated 18 October 1790, is published in *Ordinances of the City Council of Charleston, in the State of South-Carolina, Passed since the Incorporation of the City . . .* (Charleston, SC: William P. Young, 1802), 82–85. For the history of the Orphan House, see Alan Keith-Lucas, *A Legacy of Caring: The Charleston Orphan House, 1790–1990* (Charleston, SC: Charleston Orphan House, 1991).

9. John E. Murray details the operation and management of the Charleston Orphan house in "Fates of Orphans: Poor Children in Antebellum Charleston," *Journal of Interdisciplinary History* 33 (Spring 2003): 519–45, and "Mothers and Children in and out of the Charleston Orphan House," in *Children Bound to Labor: The Pauper Apprentice System in Early America*, ed. Ruth Wallis Herndon and John E. Murray (Ithaca, NY: Cornell University Press, 2009), 102–18.

10. On classroom activities and instruction at the Orphan House, see John E. Murray, "Literacy Acquisition in an Orphanage: A Historical-Longitudinal Case Study," *American Journal of Education* 110 (Feb. 2004): 180–82. Murray concludes that the Orphan House was more successful at producing literate pupils than were the city's free or charity schools, largely because it was able to enforce compulsory attendance.

11. Usher Parsons, *Brief Sketches of the Officers Who Were in the Battle of Lake Erie* (Albany, NY: J. Munsell, 1862), 13.

12. Between 1794 and 1860 the Charleston Orphan House cared for more than 2,000 children, with boys outnumbering girls as inmates by a factor of two to one. On average, children resided at the Orphan House five and a half years and were seven and a half years old on entering. During Thomas's stay at the orphanage (November 1803–February 1809), the approximate population of inmates ranged from 140 to 160 children. See Murray, "Fates of Orphans," 523–24, 531.

13. For the promulgation of such ideals to Orphan House children, see George Buist, *An Oration Delivered at the Orphan-House of Charleston, South-Carolina, October 18th, 1795; Being the Sixth Anniversary of the Institution* (Charleston: Markland & M'Iver, 1795), 18–22; and

Thomas Smyth, *Oration Delivered on the Forty-Eighth Anniversary of the Orphan House, in Charleston, S.C., October 18th, 1837* (Charleston: J. S. Burges, 1837), 16–21.

14. On the link between political patronage and officer appointments in the early navy's officer corps, see Christopher McKee's pathbreaking study, *A Gentlemanly and Honorable Profession: The Creation of the U.S. Naval Officer Corps, 1794–1815* (Annapolis, MD: Naval Institute Press, 1991), esp. chap. 4.

15. For evidence of Cheves's role in Thomas Holdup's naval appointment, see TH to Langdon Cheves, 15 Nov. 1814, Letters Received by the Secretary of the Navy from Commissioned Officers below the Rank of Commander and from Warrant Officers, Naval Records Collection of the Office of Naval Records and Library, Record Group 45, M148, roll 13, National Archives, Washington, DC. In this letter Thomas wrote: "I am the same person, whom your bounty, Sir! and that of the Commissioners of the Orphan House in Charleston, placed in the Navy as a Midshipman."

16. For a listing of the elective and appointive offices Daniel Stevens held, see Emily Bellinger Reynolds and Joan Reynolds Faunt, comps., *Biographical Directory of the Senate of the State of South Carolina, 1776–1964* (Columbia: South Carolina Archives Department, 1964), 315. See also Daniel Stevens, "Autobiography of Daniel Stevens, 1746–1835," *South Carolina Historical Magazine* 58 (Jan. 1957): 16–17.

17. Daniel Stevens did have two important things in common with his young friend. One, he had spent part of his childhood in an orphanage. And two, he had suffered significant family loss, including the deaths of two wives and six children. On Stevens's experience in an orphanage, see Stevens, "Autobiography of Daniel Stevens," 2–3; and Edward J. Cashin, *Beloved Bethesda: A History of George Whitefield's Home for Boys, 1740–2000* (Macon, GA: Mercer University Press, 2001), 96–97. On the deaths of Stevens's wives and children, see Stevens, "Autobiography of Daniel Stevens," 4, 6–7.

18. Holdup changed his name in South Carolina's Court of Equity sometime before 7 December 1815. See THS to Benjamin W. Crowninshield, 7 Dec. 1815, Letters Received by the Secretary of the Navy from Commissioned Officers below the Rank of Commander and from Warrant Officers, roll 15. According to Usher Parsons, Daniel Stevens offered a share in his estate to Thomas as an inducement "to adopt the name Stevens." See Parsons, "Brief Sketches," 13.

19. Robert Smith to Thomas Sumter and John Gaillard, 8 Apr. 1808, Miscellaneous Letters Sent by the Secretary of the Navy, Naval Records Collection, M209, roll 3. This letter should be read in conjunction with Smith to John H. Dent, 16 May 1808, Letters Sent by the Secretary of the Navy to Officers, Naval Records Collection, M149, roll 8.

20. See "An Act authorizing the employment of an additional naval force," passed 31 Jan. 1809, Richard Peters, ed., *The Public Statutes at Large of the United States of America from the Organization of the Government in 1789, to March 3, 1845*, 8 vols. (Boston: Charles C. Little and James Brown, 1845–67), 2:514. Though not specified in its language, the purpose of this law was to enable a more rigorous naval enforcement of U.S. trade laws.

21. Robert Smith to TH, 8 Feb. 1809, Letters Sent by the Secretary of the Navy to Officers, roll 8. Holdup's warrant was dated 16 January 1809.

22. In his letter of acceptance Holdup states that he "was appointed an acting Midshipman in the *Hornet* on the 7th" of February. See TH to Robert Smith, 21 Feb. 1809, Letters of Acceptance, 1804–23, G–N, Naval Records Collection, T829, roll 368. But according to the brig's muster roll, Thomas's service in the *Hornet* commenced 4 February. See entry 10, page 22, *Hornet* Muster Roll, 1809–10, Muster Rolls and Payrolls for U.S. Navy Vessels, Naval Records Collection, T829, roll 99. On 15 February John H. Dent reported to Smith: "I have recd. on board the *Hornet* Mdn. Forrest & Holdup under the assurances that they would be appointed as soon as vacancy's might offer." Dent to Smith, 15 Feb. 1809, Letters Received by the Secretary of the Navy from Commanders, Naval Records Collection, M147, roll 3.

23. This paragraph draws on Christopher McKee's insightful analysis of the backgrounds of pre-1815 midshipmen in *Gentlemanly and Honorable Profession,* esp. chaps. 5–7: for data on ages, see 68–69; on southern officers, 59; on maritime communities, 66; quotation on loss of fathers, 75.

24. Ibid., esp. chaps. 15–19.

25. Ibid., 156.

26. TH to Ralph Izard Jr., 19 July 1810, Stevens Family Papers.

27. For the events of this voyage, see 14 March–10 June 1809, USS *Hornet* Logbook, Logs of U.S. Naval Ships and Stations, Records of the Bureau of Naval Personnel, RG 24, M1030a, roll 2.

28. For example, on 2 May 1810 the *Constitution* sent in two American merchantmen, *Goleonda* and *Rose,* for "violation of the non intercourse Law." See Rodgers to Paul Hamilton, 13 and 14 May 1810, Letters Received by the Secretary of the Navy from Captains, Naval Records Collection, M125, roll 19.

29. Documents relating to Fulton's torpedoes are published in *American State Papers,* class 6, *Naval Affairs,* 4 vols. (Washington, DC: Gales & Seaton, 1834–61), 1:211–26, 234–45. On John Rodgers and the torpedo experiments, see John H. Schroeder, *Commodore John Rodgers: Paragon of the Early Navy* (Gainesville: University Press of Florida, 2006), 79–84.

30. For the events of this voyage, see 18 March–28 August 1810, USS *John Adams* Logbook, Logs of U.S. Naval Ships and Stations, roll 3.

31. Schroeder, *Commodore John Rodgers,* 71.

32. On Thompson's teaching navigation in the *Constitution* and other ships in the fleet, see John Rodgers to Robert Thompson, 23 May 1810, Letters and Orders, 22 July 1808–30 December 1810, container 37, Part 3, Rodgers Family Papers, MSS 38125, Library of Congress. For a sketch of Thompson's career as a teacher, see McKee, *Gentlemanly and Honorable Profession,* 203–5. For Rodgers's efforts to make his young officers familiar with the navigation of New York Bay, see Rodgers to Hamilton, 22 Mar. 1810, Letters Received by the Secretary of the Navy from Captains, M125, roll 18.

33. In one letter Thomas styles himself Izard's protégé. See TH to Ralph Izard Jr., 10 Apr. 1814, Stevens Family Papers.

34. TH to Paul Hamilton, 3 Sept. 1812, Letters Received by the Secretary of the Navy from Commissioned Officers below the Rank of Commander and from Warrant Officers, roll 10.

35. Daniel Stevens to Paul Hamilton, 2 Sept. 1812, Miscellaneous Letters Received by the Secretary of the Navy, Naval Records Collection, M124, roll 51.

36. See Paul Hamilton to Isaac Chauncey, 31 Aug. 1812, Dudley and Crawford, *Naval War of 1812,* 1:297–301.

37. TH to Ralph Izard Jr., 29 Sept. 1812, Stevens Family Papers. For another description of Chauncey's visit to *John Adams,* see Usher Parsons, *Surgeon of the Lakes: The Diary of Dr. Usher Parsons, 1812–1814,* ed. John D. Fredriksen (Erie, PA: Erie County Historical Society, 2000), 1.

38. Lieutenant John Pettigrew was in charge of the detachment travelling to Black Rock. See Chauncey to Pettigrew, 24 Sept. 1812, Isaac Chauncey Letter Books, William L. Clements Library, University of Michigan, Ann Arbor.

39. TH to Ralph Izard Jr., 29 Sept. 1812, Stevens Family Papers; TH to Izard, 11 Jan. 1813, Dudley and Crawford, *Naval War of 1812,* 2:414. Both letters provide details of the trek from New York to Black Rock. For another description see Parsons, *Surgeon of the Lakes,* 1–11.

40. For details of this operation, see Jesse D. Elliott to Paul Hamilton, 9 Oct. 1812, Dudley and Crawford, *Naval War of 1812,* 1:328–31.

41. TH to Ralph Izard Jr., 11 Jan. 1813, Dudley and Crawford, *Naval War of 1812,* 2:414. The salvage operation occurred on 17 October according to Parsons, *Surgeon of the Lakes,* 12.

42. Chauncey to Samuel Angus, 8 Oct. 1812, Chauncey Letter Books. The ten vessels whose

construction Chauncey ordered Angus to superintend were never built at Black Rock. By year's end the navy's leadership had determined that Erie was the best site for building the American fleet.

43. The British and American commanders agreed to an armistice following the Battle of Queenston Heights on 13 October. The cease-fire remained in place until 20 November. On the chase of the *Queen Charlotte,* see TH to Ralph Izard Jr., 11 Jan. 1813, Dudley and Crawford, *Naval War of 1812,* 2:414. Holdup wrote that had the American boats caught up with the *Queen Charlotte,* she would have given her pursuers "a Queenly reception." See also Parsons, *Surgeon of the Lakes,* 13.

44. This narrative draws on Samuel Angus's after-action report to the Navy Department. See Angus to Hamilton, 1 Dec. 1812, Dudley and Crawford, *Naval War of 1812,* 1:356, 359.

45. TH to Ralph Izard Jr., 11 Jan. 1813, ibid., 2:412, 413. The government awarded Thomas Holdup Stevens a monthly pension of $7.12½ on 29 March 1837, with payments retroactive to the date of his injury. The retroactive payment alone totaled nearly $2,000. See Thomas Holdup Stevens Pension Application, File No. 1462, War of 1812 Series, Pension Application Files, RG 15, National Archives.

46. Angus to Hamilton, 1 Dec. 1812, Dudley and Crawford, *Naval War of 1812,* 1:356.

47. TH to Izard, 11 Jan. 1813, ibid., 2:413.

48. For Holdup's appointment as acting lieutenant, see notation following Chauncey to James A. Dudley, 24 Dec. 1812, Chauncey Letter Books; and Chauncey to Hamilton, 25 Dec. 1812, Letters Received by the Secretary of the Navy from Captains, M125, roll 25. For his promotion to lieutenant, see William Jones to TH, 3 Aug. 1813, Letters to Commissioned and Warrant Officers Transmitting Appointments and Orders and Accepting Resignations, Naval Records Collection, T829, roll 382.

49. For documents related to the Chauncey-Angus feud, see Dudley and Crawford, *Naval War of 1812,* 1:371–74. See also Harold D. Langley, "Respect for Civilian Authority: The Tragic Career of Samuel Angus," *American Neptune* 40 (Jan. 1980): 23–37.

50. For background on Perry's appointment to the Erie command, see David C. Skaggs, *Oliver Hazard Perry: Honor, Courage, and Patriotism in the Early U.S. Navy* (Annapolis, MD: Naval Institute Press, 2006), 45–48.

51. Perry's service on a court-martial convened on board the *Hornet* on 12 December 1809 may have provided one such opportunity for an encounter between the two men. Lieutenant John Trippe, the namesake of Holdup's sloop in the Battle of Lake Erie, also served on this court. See John Rodgers to Theodore Hunt, 10 Dec. 1809, Letters and Orders, 22 July 1808–30 December 1810, container 37, part 3, Rodgers Family Papers.

52. For two excellent treatments of the building of the Lake Erie squadron, see Skaggs, *Oliver Hazard Perry,* chap. 3; and Skaggs and Altoff, *A Signal Victory,* chap. 3.

53. See Perry's letters to Holdup: 28 Apr. and 9, 17, 23 May 1813, Perry Letter Book, 1813, Oliver Hazard Perry Papers, William L. Clements Library, University of Michigan. For additional documentation of Holdup's movements while performing logistical duties, see Parsons, *Surgeon of the Lakes,* 31, 34, 35.

54. For a detailed description of this movement, see Skaggs, *Oliver Hazard Perry,* 69–71. Usher Parsons credits Holdup with being in command of the *Trippe* when the five vessels left Black Rock. Parsons, *Surgeon of the Lakes,* 38.

55. Captain's Clerk Thomas L. Breese addresses Holdup as a lieutenant in the *Niagara* in Breese to TH and Daniel Turner, 19 July 1813, Order Book, Perry Papers. Parsons mentions losing Holdup as a messmate in the *Lawrence* on 10 August. Parsons, *Surgeon of the Lakes,* 44.

56. Holdup references his quarrel with Elliott in TH to Ralph Izard Jr., 14 Apr. 1814, Stevens Family Papers. For Holdup's transfer order to the *Trippe,* see Perry to TH, 2 Sept. 1813, Order Book, Perry Papers.

57. William W. Dobbins, *History of the Battle of Lake Erie (September 10, 1813) and Reminiscences of the Flagships Lawrence and Niagara* (1876; rpr., Erie, PA: Ashby Printing Co., 1913), n.p.

58. Gerard T. Altoff, *Deep Water Sailors, Shallow Water Soldiers: Manning the United States Fleet on Lake Erie, 1813* (Put-in-Bay, OH: The Perry Group, 1993), 33.

59. For a more detailed analysis of the battle, see David Skaggs's and Mike Palmer's essays in this collection.

60. Stevens likely composed his battle narrative in 1840. For the full text of this document, see Mackenzie, *Commodore Oliver Hazard Perry,* 2:272–75.

61. William P. Brady Memorial to Congress, 19 Nov. 1847, William P. Brady Pension Application, File No. 3069, Old Wars Series, Pension Application Files.

62. Soldiers Isaac Green and John Nailes were the two crewman wounded by gunfire. *American State Papers,* 1:296. The *Trippe*'s pilot, Patrick FitzPatrick, and Purser's steward, William P. Brady, were the other two casualties.

63. Mackenzie, *Commodore Oliver Hazard Perry,* 2:274.

64. TH to Daniel Stevens, 14 Sept. 1813, *Charleston Courier,* 30 Sept. 1813.

65. TH to Ralph Izard Jr., 10 Apr. 1814, Stevens Family Papers.

66. Mackenzie, *Commodore Oliver Hazard Perry,* 1:276.

67. TH to Izard, 10 Apr. 1814, Stevens Family Papers.

68. See Perry to TH, 16 Sept. 1813, and Perry to TH, 2 Oct. 1813, Perry Papers. See also David C. Skaggs, "Joint Operations during the Detroit-Erie Campaign, 1813," in *New Interpretations in Naval History: Selected Papers from the Eighth Naval History Symposium,* ed. William B. Cogar (Annapolis, MD: Naval Institute Press, 1989), 121–38. Naval documents relating to the Thames River campaign are published in Dudley and Crawford, *Naval War of 1812,* 2:565–76.

69. On the difficult winter at Erie, see Skaggs and Altoff, *A Signal Victory,* 167–70. Much ink has been spilled over the Perry-Elliott feud. One essay that provides a unique perspective is Lawrence J. Friedman and David Curtis Skaggs, "Jesse Duncan Elliott and the Battle of Lake Erie: The Issue of Mental Stability," *Journal of the Early Republic* 10 (Winter 1990): 493–516.

70. TH to Izard, 10 Apr. 1814, Stevens Family Papers.

71. See Dudley and Crawford, *Naval War of 1812,* 3:417–24.

72. TH to Izard, 10 Apr. 1814, Stevens Family Papers.

73. For additional documents relating to the planning, objectives, and launch of this expedition, see Dudley and Crawford, *Naval War of 1812,* 3:458–63, 512–18. For documents on the expedition, see ibid., 557–72. See also Barry Gough, *Fighting Sail on Lake Huron and Georgian Bay: The War of 1812 and Its Aftermath* (Annapolis, MD: Naval Institute Press, 2002), chap. 5.

74. Holdup is identified as first lieutenant of the *Niagara* in *Hallowell* (ME) *Gazette,* 5 Oct. 1814.

75. See Arthur Sinclair to William Jones, 3 Sept. 1814, Dudley and Crawford, *Naval War of 1812,* 3:572–73. On the *Nancy*'s career, see Barry Gough, *Through Fire and Ice: Schooner Nancy of the War of 1812* (Toronto: Dundurn Group, 2006).

76. Sinclair to William Jones, 21 Oct. 1814, Dudley and Crawford, *Naval War of 1812,* 3:603. See also, TH to Sinclair, 6 Sept. 1814, ibid., 3:602.

77. See court-martial of Seaman Henry Davidson, 25 and 28 June 1814, No. 167, Records of General Courts-Martial and Courts of Inquiry of the Navy Department, Records of the Office of the Judge Advocate General, RG125, M273, roll 7, National Archives; and court-martial of marine privates William Burnett and John Monroe, 28 Oct. 1814, No. 178, Records of General Courts-Martial and Courts of Inquiry of the Navy Department, roll 7. The executions carried out on 11 November are mentioned in Parsons, *Surgeon of the Lakes,* 104. Shortly before departing the Erie Station, Holdup served on the naval court that tried Surgeon Joseph G. Roberts for embezzlement, neglecting his patients, and unofficer-like conduct. See Dudley and Crawford, *Naval War of 1812,* 3:675–80.

78. TH to Langdon Cheves, 15 Nov. 1814, Letters Received by the Secretary of the Navy from Commissioned Officers below the Rank of Commander and from Warrant Officers, roll 13.

79. William Jones to TH, 19 November 1814, Letters to Commissioned and Warrant Officers Transmitting Appointments and Orders and Accepting Resignations, T829, roll 382.

80. Parsons, *Surgeon of the Lakes,* 107.

81. On the date of departure, see ibid., 107. See also UP to W. W. Dobbin, 3 Sept. 1860, Stevens Family Papers, in which Parsons writes: "I have not the pleasure of knowing T. H. Stevens Esqr. of Erie personally, but I have passed many pleasant days & months with his lamented father—walked with him from Albany to Buffalo in 1812, and rode with him from Erie to New York, when we were both ordered from Erie to join the U.S. Frigate *Java* in Baltimore under Com: Perry."

82. See entry 5, page 1, *Java* Muster Roll, 1815–16, Muster Rolls and Payrolls for U.S. Navy Vessels, roll 107.

83. Seebert J. Goldowsky, *Yankee Surgeon: The Life and Times of Usher Parsons, 1788–1868* (Boston: Francis A. Countway Library of Medicine and Rhode Island Historical Society, 1988), 89.

84. Elizabeth was the daughter of Ebenezer and Sarah Sage. Ebenezer was a merchant, ship owner, and local justice of the peace who had served in the Continental Navy frigate *Trumbull* during the Revolutionary War. See H. Franklin Andrews, ed., *The Hamlin Family: A Genealogy of Capt. Giles Hamlin of Middletown, Connecticut, 1654–1900* (Exira, IA, 1900), 115, 160. For documentation on Ebenezer's service in the *Trumbull,* see Henry P. Johnston, ed., *The Record of Connecticut Men in the Military and Naval Service during the War of the Revolution, 1775–1783* (Hartford: Case, Lockwood & Brainard, 1889), 599.

85. On the *Java*'s preparations for overseas duty, see Skaggs, *Oliver Hazard Perry,* 164–67.

86. For the Charleston committee's testimonial letter to Holdup and his reply, both dated 16 Nov. 1815, see the *Telescope* (Columbia, SC), 9 Jan. 1816. That the presentation took place aboard the *Java* and was witnessed publicly by the crew seems a reasonable surmise.

87. This beautiful presentation sword is held by the Curator Branch of the Naval History and Heritage Command in Washington, DC, accession number 82–65-C.

88. Eliza gives 3 December 1815 as the date of her marriage to Thomas Holdup Stevens. See Eliza R. Stevens to Commissioner of Pensions, 22 Mar. 1843, File No. 1133, Old Wars Series, Pension Application Files. This letter is part of the documentation Eliza filed to collect her widow's pension.

89. Four days after his wedding, Thomas informed the Navy Department that he had legally taken the surname Stevens. See THS to Benjamin W. Crowninshield, 7 Dec. 1815, Letters Received by the Secretary of the Navy from Commissioned Officers below the Rank of Commander and from Warrant Officers, roll 15. The timing of these two legal events, one a marriage and the other a name change, occurred so close together as to suggest a connection. It is possible that Daniel Stevens adopted the orphan Thomas in order to remove any doubts in the minds of the elder Sages about his financial suitability as a spouse for Eliza.

90. See Daniel Stevens to Ebenezer Sage, 20 Mar. 1816, Stevens Family Papers. This letter speaks of the esteem the Sage's feel for Thomas, the "parental warmth" and "friendship" Daniel Stevens feels for Eliza, and of the mutual affection the newlyweds feel for one another.

91. Secretary Benjamin W. Crowninshield granted Stevens a furlough on 13 December with instructions to return to duty in the *Java* after three months. See Crowninshield to THS, 13 Dec. 1815, Letters to Commissioned and Warrant Officers Transmitting Appointments and Orders Accepting Resignations, RG 45, T829, 383.

92. On 6 January 1814 Congress authorized the striking of gold medals for presentation to Perry and Elliott in recognition of their victory on Lake Erie. The remaining commissioned officers were to receive silver medals, while midshipmen were to be given presentation swords. *Statutes at Large,* 3:141. On 18 April 1814 Congress also voted $250,000 for distribution among

the officers and crew of Perry's squadron. *Statutes at Large,* 3:130. Thomas Holdup's share of prize moneys came to $2,293, nearly five times the $480 base pay given to lieutenants. *American State Papers,* 1:568. For the annual compensation of navy officers in 1814, see McKee, *Gentlemanly and Honorable Profession,* 490–91 (table 29).

93. Daniel Stevens to Ebenezer Sage, 20 Mar. 1816, Stevens Family Papers.

94. For correspondence relating to this assignment, see John Rodgers to THS, 12 Aug. 1816, Letters Sent by the Board of Navy Commissioners to Naval Officers, Naval Records Collection, T829, roll 287; and THS to JR, 12 Nov. 1816, Letters Received by the Board of Navy Commissioners from Naval Officers, 5 September 1814–5 July 1842, vol. 2, Records of Boards and Commissions, Naval Records Collection.

95. THS to Benjamin W. Crowninshield, 26 May 1816, Letters Received by the Secretary of the Navy from Commissioned Officers below the Rank of Commander and from Warrant Officers, roll 16.

96. THS to Benjamin Homans, 13 Jan. 1817, and THS to Crowninshield, 13 Jan. 1817, Letters Received by the Secretary of the Navy from Commissioned Officers below the Rank of Commander and from Warrant Officers, roll 18.

97. Crowninshield to THS, 31 Jan. 1817, Letters Sent by the Secretary of the Navy to Officers, roll 12. This letter replied to THS to Crowninshield, 13 Jan. 1817, Letters Received by the Scretary of the Navy from Commissioned Officers below the Rank of Commander and from Warrant Officers, roll 18.

98. Perry's letter to Stevens inviting him to rejoin the *Java* is referenced in THS to Crowninshield, 16 Mar. 1817, Letters Received by the Secretary of the Navy from Commissioned Officers below the Rank of Commander and from Warrant Officers, roll 18. The *Java*'s payroll lists Stevens as being attached to the ship from 18 March to 31 August 1817. See entry 5, page 1, *Java* Payroll, 1815–17, Muster Rolls and Payrolls for U.S. Navy Vessels, roll 107.

99. The Board of Navy Commissioners ordered Perry on coastal survey duty on 29 May 1817. Captain Samuel Evans and two Army Corps of Engineers officers accompanied him on this duty. See John Rodgers to Oliver H. Perry, 29 May 1817, Letters Sent by the Board of Navy Commissioners to Naval Officers, roll 287. The board ordered other pairs of naval officers to conduct identical surveys along other sections of the nation's coastal waters. For printed documents relating to these surveys, see *American State Papers,* 1:434–43, 486–92.

100. THS to Oliver H. Perry, 8 June 1817, Letters Received by the Secretary of the Navy from Commissioned Officers below the Rank of Commander and from Warrant Officers, roll 18. The Navy Department ordered Stevens to report to Perry "for duty on the Surveys of the Coast" on 24 June. See Benjamin Homans to THS, 24 June 1817, Letters to Commissioned and Warrant Officers Transmitting Appointments and Orders and Accepting Resignations, roll 383.

101. For Perry's report, see *American State Papers,* 1:490–92.

102. For Steven's orders to the *Alert,* see Benjamin W. Crowninshield to THS, 6 Jan. 1818, Letters to Commissioned and Warrant Officers Transmitting Appointments and Orders and Accepting Resignations, roll 383. According to the *Alert*'s muster roll, Stevens remained in command of the storeship until 28 November. See entry 1, page 21, *Alert* Muster Roll, 16 January–28 November 1817, Muster Rolls and Payrolls for U.S. Navy Vessels, roll 21.

103. For a short history of this ship, see http://www.history.navy.mil/danfs/a6/alert-i.htm

104. Frederick Stevens was born on 10 September 1817. He was commissioned a purser in the navy on 13 September 1841. He died at Nassau, New Providence, on 14 July 1843 while serving in the U.S. brig *Boxer.* Alfred Johnson, "Burial Records and Inscriptions at Nassau, New Providence," *New England Historical and Genealogical Register* 68 (July 1914): 242; Edward W. Callahan, ed., *List of Officers of the Navy of the United States and of the Marine Corps from 1775 to 1900* (1901; rpr., New York: Haskell House, 1969), 520.

105. For discussion of this phase of the Perry-Elliott controversy, see Skaggs, *Oliver Hazard Perry,* 191–98. Quotation is from p. 194 of this title. The original of Stevens's affidavit is in the Perry Papers; a published version appears in *Documents in Relation to the Differences which Subsisted between the Late Commodore O. H. Perry and Captain J. D. Elliott* (Boston, 1834), 25–26.

106. For a detailed summary of Thomas Holdup Stevens Jr.'s naval career, see William B. Cogar, ed., *Dictionary of Admirals of the U.S. Navy,* 2 vols. (Annapolis, MD: Naval Institute Press, 1989), 1:180–81.

107. Stevens was attached as a supernumerary lieutenant in the *Constellation* from 6 July 1819 to 30 June 1820. See Benjamin Homans to THS, 6 July 1819, Letters to Commissioned and Warrant Officers Transmitting Appointments and Orders and Accepting Resignations, roll 383. On 1 September 1820 the Navy Department ordered Stevens to report to Commodore Isaac Chauncey "for duty on the [New York] Station." See Smith Thompson to THS, 1 Sept. 1820, Letters to Commissioned and Warrant Officers Transmitting Appointments and Orders and Accepting Resignations, roll 383.

108. Perry died of yellow fever on 23 August 1819 while on a diplomatic mission to Venezuela. See Skaggs, *Oliver Hazard Perry,* 207–10.

109. THS to Smith Thompson, 12 June 1821, and THS to Thompson, 23 Aug. 1822, Letters Received by the Secretary of the Navy from Commissioned Officers below the Rank of Commander and from Warrant Officers, rolls 26 and 29.

110. THS to Thompson, 29 Jan. 1822, Letters Received by the Secretary of the Navy from Commissioned Officers below the Rank of Commander and from Warrant Officers, roll 28.

111. Francis H. Gregory, commander of the *Grampus,* was commissioned a lieutenant on 18 June 1814; James Ramage, commander of the *Porpoise,* was commissioned a lieutenant on 9 December 1814; Stevens was commissioned a lieutenant on 24 July 1813. *Register of the Commission and Warrant Officers of the Navy of the United States; Including Officers of the Marine Corps* (n.p.: Metropolitan Press, 1821), 5–6.

112. Smith Thompson to THS, 20 Dec. 1822, Letters to Commissioned and Warrant Officers Transmitting Appointments and Orders and Accepting Resignations, roll 384.

113. Commodore David Porter purchased these schooners in Baltimore for $10,190. They were "known as 'bay boats,' . . . averaged a little more than 50 tons and each one mounted three guns and carried thirty-one men." David F Long, *Nothing Too Daring: A Biography of Commodore David Porter, 1783–1843* (Annapolis, MD: Naval Institute Press, 1981), 210.

114. Quotation from *Minutes of Proceedings of the Courts of Inquiry and Court Martial in Relation to Captain David Porter: Convened at Washington, D.C. on Thursday, the 7th Day of July, A.D. 1825. Printed by Authority from the Official Records* (Washington, DC: Davis & Force, 1825), 207. On Porter's command of the West India Squadron, see Long, *Nothing Too Daring,* chapters 8 and 9.

115. For Stevens's own summary of his service in *Jackall* at this time, see *Proceedings of the Courts of Inquiry,* 65–66.

116. For Stevens's account of this mission, see ibid., 66. For Stephen Cassin's after-action reports detailing this mission, see ibid., 236–39.

117. See "An ACT for the relief of Thomas Holdup Stevens, and others," in Acts Passed in the First Session of the Twenty-Second Congress of the United States (Washington, DC: Francis Preston Blair, 1832), 220. For legal questions raised over how prize shares were to be distributed to Stevens and his fellow captors, see B. F. Butler to Levi Woodbury, 4 Mar. and 6 July 1834, folder 2, box XZ, Subject File, Naval Records Collection.

118. For David Porter's orders to Stevens on this head, see *Proceedings of the Courts of Inquiry,* 254–55.

119. See Smith Thompson to THS, 29 July 1824, Letters to Commissioned and Warrant Officers Transmitting Appointments and Orders and Accepting Resignations, roll 384.

120. An officers' obituary report for 1823 lists twenty-two out of forty-six officers as having died at Thompson's Island. See *American State Papers,* 1:1098.

121. On yellow fever at Key West, see Long, *Nothing Too Daring,* 215–17; and Schroeder, *Commodore John Rodgers,* 161–62. For the findings of Rodgers and his team, see *American State Papers,* 1:1119–20, 1121.

122. This account draws on George Coggeshall, *Thirty-Six Voyages to Various Parts of the World, Made between the Years 1799 and 1841,* 3rd ed. (New York, 1858), 399–402. Coggeshall was at Alvarado at the time and "had many conversations with Captain Stevens on the subject of his miraculous escape." For Stevens's own brief account, see *Proceedings of the Courts of Inquiry,* 67. Stevens described the storm as a "tornado." See THS to Samuel Evans, 15 May 1825, Letters Received by the Secretary of the Navy from Commissioned Officers below the Rank of Commander and from Warrant Officers, roll 35. This letter also lists the damage the *Shark* sustained in the storm.

123. See *Niles' Weekly Register,* 20 Mar. 1824, 48. The *Daily National Intelligencer,* 24 Mar. 1824, published the names of thirteen of the victims. The fourteenth victim was Luke Cavener. For all names, see the *Shark*'s Muster Roll, 1821–35, 40–43, Muster Rolls and Payrolls for U.S. Navy Vessels, roll 76.

124. THS to Samuel L. Southard, 10 June 1824, Letters Received by the Secretary of the Navy from Commissioned Officers below the Rank of Commander and from Warrant Officers, roll 35.

125. Eliza Augusta is not listed in Eliza Stevens's family genealogy. Andrews, *Hamlin Family,* 160. Eliza Augusta died on 18 March 1826 at the age of twenty-two months. *Middlesex Gazette,* 22 Mar. 1826. Based on this information, Eliza Augusta was most likely born in mid-May 1824, around the time Thomas Holdup Stevens arrived at New York in the *Shark.* The remaining Stevens children were Catherine, Emma Maria, Virginia, and Eben.

126. On the financial difficulties naval officers faced in supporting their families on government pay, see McKee, *Gentlemanly and Honorable Profession,* chap. 27.

127. THS to John Rodgers, 10 June 1824, container 4, part 3, Rodgers Family Papers.

128. THS to Southard, 24 Sept. 1824, Letters Received by the Secretary of the Navy from Commissioned Officers below the Rank of Commander and from Warrant Officers, roll 37. See also THS to Southard, 10 June 1824, Letters Received by the Secretary of the Navy from Commissioned Officers below the Rank of Commander and from Warrant Officers, roll 35, in which Stevens writes, "I am apprehensive, that the prospect once anticipated, of receiving a property equal to all my wants, may never be realized." According to Usher Parsons, Daniel Stevens "lived to see his fortune exhausted." Parsons, *Brief Sketches,* 13. What caused the elder Stevens's financial ruin is unknown. He died on 20 March 1835.

129. Samuel L. Southard to THS, 20–25 Apr. 1825, Letters to Commissioned and Warrant Officers Transmitting Appointments and Orders and Accepting Resignations, roll 384. See also *Commission and Warrant Officers of the Navy* for 1825, p. 4, and for 1826, p. 4, to compare ordering of seniority.

130. THS to John Rodgers, 26 Jan. 1825, container 5, part 3, Rodgers Family Papers.

131. See Samuel L. Southard to THS, 26 Apr. 1825, Letters to Commissioned and Warrant Officers Transmitting Appointments and Orders and Accepting Resignations, roll 384.

132. Long, *Nothing Too Daring,* 237.

133. See Stevens's testimony on this question in *Proceedings of the Courts of Inquiry,* 68. Porter testified that Stevens carried only $102,000 at 1.25 percent freightage. Ibid., 225.

134. On Porter's court of inquiry and court-martial, see Long, *Nothing Too Daring,* chap. 9.

135. Stevens commanded the *Fulton* from mid-August to mid-November 1826. See Samuel L. Southard to THS, 22 July 1826, Letters to Commissioned and Warrant Officers Transmitting Appointments and Orders and Accepting Resignations, roll 384; and THS to Southard, 19 Nov. 1826, Letters Received by the Secretary of the Navy from Commanders, roll 12.

136. Southard to THS, 26 Apr. 1827, Letters to Commissioned and Warrant Officers Transmitting Appointments and Orders and Accepting Resignations, roll 384.

137. The standard history of the Washington Navy Yard is Taylor Peck, *Round-Shot to Rockets: A History of the Washington Navy Yard and U.S. Naval Gun Factory* (Annapolis, MD: Naval Institute Press, 1949). See also Henry B. Hibban, *Navy-Yard, Washington: History from Organization, 1799 to Present Date* (Washington, DC: Government Printing Office, 1890).

138. Based on an examination of yard correspondence, Stevens had acting command of the Washington facility 2–29 October 1828 and again 17 February–10 April 1829. The bulk of Stevens's yard correspondence for this time may be found in vols. 81–83, Letters, Proposals, Reports, and Estimates Received from Commandants of Navy Yards and Naval Stations, Mar. 1814–July 1842, Records of Boards and Commissions, 1812–90, Naval Records Collection.

139. THS to Samuel L. Southard, 23 Feb. 1829, Letters Received by the Secretary of the Navy from Commanders, roll 15.

140. THS to John Branch, 11 July 1829, Letters Received by the Secretary of the Navy from Commanders, roll 15.

141. Branch to THS, 12 June 1829, Letters to Commissioned and Warrant Officers Transmitting Appointments and Orders and Accepting Resignations, roll 391.

142. For Biddle's tenure as Mediterranean Squadron commander, see David F. Long, *Sailor-Diplomat: A Biography of Commodore James Biddle, 1783–1848* (Boston: Northeastern University Press, 1983), chap. 8.

143. See THS to Branch, 7 Aug. 1829, Letters Received by the Secretary of the Navy from Commanders, roll 15.

144. See John Dahlgren's memorable description in Madeleine Vinton Dahlgren, *Memoir of John A. Dahlgren, Rear-Admiral United States Navy* (Boston: James R. Osgood & Co., 1882), 47–48.

145. THS to Branch, 18 Sept. 1829, Letters Received by the Secretary of the Navy from Commanders, roll 15. The *Ontario*'s log records "a Tremendous Squall struck the Ship and buried the Guns under Water." See entry for 8 Sept. 1829, vol. 5, USS *Ontario* Logbook, Logs of U.S. Naval Ships and Stations.

146. Entry for 31 Nov. 1830, USS *Ontario* Logbook.

147. Dahlgren, *Memoir of John A. Dahlgren,* 42.

148. For examples of *Ontario* sailors punished for drunkenness, see entries for 8 Dec. 1829 and 27 Jan. 1830, USS *Ontario* Logbook. For mention of officers arrested for drunkenness, see John A. B. Dahlgren, undated memorandum, box 1, John Adolphus Bernard Dahlgren Papers, MSS 17624, Library of Congress. A note signed by Surgeon J. W. Plummer dated 25 Aug. 1831 appears at the bottom of this memo. Stevens stripped Acting Carpenter John Deacon of his appointment for "habits of intemperance." Stevens to James Biddle, 18 Sept. 1830, Letters Received by the Secretary of the Navy from Commanders, reel 15. For a discussion of intemperance in Biddle's squadron, see Long, *Sailor Diplomat,* 148–49.

149. Charles Oscar Paullin, "Dueling in the Old Navy," *United States Naval Institute Proceedings,* vol. 35 (1909): 1156.

150. On Stevens's intervention in this affair, see Dahlgren to Henry Walke, 14 Sept. 1831, box 1, John A. B. Dahlgren Papers. In a note appended below this letter, Dahlgren states that Walke claimed to have "promised Captain Stevens upon leaving the *Ontario,* to prosecute the affair no further (which he says he was obliged to do before he would be permitted to leave the said Ship)." On Perry's views on dueling and his own duel with marine captain John Heath, see Skaggs, *Oliver Hazard Perry,* 188–90. For a contemporary description of duels between midshipmen in Biddle's squadron, see E. C. Wines, *Two Years and a Half in the Navy: or, Journal of a Cruise in the Mediterranean and Levant, on Board of the U.S. Frigate Constellation, in the Years 1829, 1830, and 1831* (Philadelphia: Carey & Lea, 1832), 1:153–54.

151. This request is referenced in THS to Branch, 4 May 1831, Letters Received by the Secretary of the Navy from Commanders, roll 16.

152. For this series of orders and replies, see Levi Woodbury to THS, 31 Jan. 1832, Letters to Commissioned and Warrant Officers Transmitting Appointments and Orders and Accepting Resignations, roll 392; THS to Woodbury, 14 Feb. 1832, Letters Received by the Secretary of the Navy from Commanders, roll 17; Woodbury to THS, 14 Feb. 1832, and Woodbury to THS, 26 Apr. 1832, Letters to Commissioned and Warrant Officers Transmitting Appointments and Orders Accepting Resignations, roll 392; and THS to Woodbury, 29 Apr. 1832, Letters Received by the Secretary of the Navy from Commanders, roll 17.

153. William Bainbridge replaced Charles Morris as commandant at Charlestown on the latter's elevation to the Navy Board of Commissioners. Rapidly declining health prompted Bainbridge to resign his command in April 1832. He was replaced by Elliott, who assumed direction of the navy yard on 12 May 1832. For a history of the Charlestown Navy Yard during Elliott's tenure as commandant, see Edwin C. Bearss, *Charlestown Navy Yard, 1800–1842: Boston National Historical Park, Massachusetts,* 2 vols. (Washington, DC: U.S. Department of the Interior/National Park Service, 1984), 2:625–753.

154. For a contemporary articulation of the recruiting problem, see Samuel L. Southard to Samuel Smith, 23 May 1828, K. Jack Bauer, ed., *The New American State Papers: Naval Affairs* (Wilmington, DE: Scholarly Resources, 1981), 7:41–44. For a modern treatment, see Harold D. Langley, *Social Reform in the United States Navy, 1798–1862* (Urbana: University of Illinois Press, 1967), esp. chaps. 4–6.

155. THS to John Boyle, 8 May 1833, Letters Received by the Secretary of the Navy from Commanders, roll 18.

156. *Documents in Relation to the Differences,* 26, 27. The 1821 edition of this publication left out Stevens's affidavit; but for an earlier printed copy of this document, see *New-York Evening Post,* 17 Apr. 1821.

157. See *A Biographical Notice of Com. Jesse D. Elliott . . .* (Philadelphia, 1835). It is presumed that Elliott had New York journalist Russell Jarvis write this 450-page book. For more on the Perry-Elliott controversy, see Skaggs, *Oliver Hazard Perry,* 218–44.

158. Mahlon Dickerson to THS, 15 Mar. 1836, Letters to Commissioned and Warrant Officers Transmitting Appointments and Orders and Accepting Resignations, roll 392.

159. Dickerson to THS, 12 Mar. 1836, Letters to Commissioned and Warrant Officers Transmitting Appointments and Orders and Accepting Resignations, roll 392.

160. Thomas Holdup Stevens Jr. was appointed an acting midshipman on 14 December 1836. See Mahlon Dickerson to Thomas Holdup Stevens Jr., 14 Dec. 1836, Letters to Commissioned and Warrant Officers Transmitting Appointments and Orders and Accepting Resignations, roll 393; and, Callahan, *List of Officers,* 521. On Frederick's applications for a marine lieutenancy, see James Kirke Paulding to THS, 14 July 1838; Paulding to THS, 12 Feb. 1839; and Paulding to THS, 10 Oct. 1839, Letters Sent by the Secretary of the Navy to Officers, rolls 27, 28, and 30.

161. Frederick Stevens was commissioned a purser on 13 September 1841. See John D. Simms to Frederick Stevens, 18 Sept. 1840, Letters to Commissioned and Warrant Officers Transmitting Appointments and Orders and Accepting Resignations, roll 395. On the role of the Commissioners of the Charleston Orphan House, see King, *Records of the Charleston Orphan House,* 42; Callahan, *List of Officers,* 521; and Johnson, "Burial Records," 242.

162. See THS (in Detroit) to Dickerson, 13 June 1836; THS (in Chicago) to Dickerson, 2 July 1836; and THS (in Philadelphia) to Dickerson, 30 June 1837, Letters Received by the Secretary of the Navy from Captains, rolls 216, 218, 228.

163. THS to J. D. Doty, June 1840, *Public Documents Presented by Order of the Senate of the United States, during the First Session of the Twenty-Sixth Congress, Begun and Held at the City of Washington, December 2, 1839,* 8 vols. (Washington, DC: Blair & Rives, 1840), 8:1–2 (doc. 564).

164. For a brief sketch of Doty and information on his private papers held by the Wisconsin Historical Society, see http://www.wisconsinhistory.org/dictionary/index.asp?action=view&term_id=2448&search_term=doty.

165. On the early navy's flawed and unwieldy personnel system, see Donald Chisholm, *Waiting for Dead Men's Shoes: Origins and Development of the U.S. Navy Officer Personnel System, 1793–1941* (Palo Alto, CA: Stanford University Press, 2001), chaps. 6–10.

166. James Kirke Paulding to THS, 26 Feb. 1840, Letters to Commissioned and Warrant Officers Transmitting Appointments and Orders and Accepting Resignations, roll 394. Stevens assumed command of the Washington Navy Yard on 5 March 1840.

167. *Daily National Intelligencer,* 30 Mar. 1840.

168. *The Sun* (Baltimore), 7 Sept. 1840.

169. This steam engine is briefly described in ibid.

170. See THS to Paulding, 2 Oct. 1840, and, THS to Paulding, 23 Oct. 1840, Letters Received by the Secretary of the Navy from Captains, roll 268. The bulk of Stevens's yard correspondence for this time will be found in vols. 231–35, Letters, Proposals and Estimates Received from Commandants of Navy Yards and Naval Stations, Mar. 1814–July 1842.

171. Paulding to THS, 27 Oct. 1840, Letters Sent by the Secretary of the Navy to Officers, roll 32.

172. Excerpt from the journal of Surgeon David S. Edwards, 20–21 Jan. 1841, Eliza Stevens and Eben W. Sage Pension Application, File No. 1133, Old Wars Series, Pension Application Files.

173. Surgeon David S. Edwards, Death Certificate of Thomas Holdup Stevens, 18 March 1843, Eliza Stevens and Eben W. Sage Pension Application, File No. 1133, Old Wars Series, Pension Application Files. According to Edwards, "No examination to ascertain the precise character of the disease would be permitted by the family." Excerpt from the Journal of Surgeon David S. Edwards, 20–21 Jan. 1841, Eliza Stevens and Eben W. Sage Pension Application File No. 1133. Old Wars Series, Pension Application Files.

174. See James K. Paulding, General Order, 22 Jan. 1841, Navy Department General Orders and Circulars, Naval Records Collection, M977, roll 1. Servicewide displays of mourning included gun salutes, flying of flags at half mast, and the wearing of crepe arm bands by U.S. Navy and Marine Corps officers.

175. *Daily National Intelligencer,* 25 Jan. 1841. For notices directing army, navy, and marine officers to attend Stevens's funeral, see ibid., 23 Jan. 1841. The Anacostia Fire Company tolled its fire bell during the funeral procession in tribute to "the disinterested kindness" Stevens had always shown that organization.

176. *Daily National Intelligencer,* 22 Jan. 1841. Contemporaries of Stevens who left impressions of that naval officer invariably spoke of his "rare social gifts." He had a common touch with people. *Naval Encyclopaedia,* 778.

177. *New-Hampshire Patriot and State Gazette* (Concord), 7 May 1841. The three Perry squadron officers mentioned are Jesse D. Elliott, Daniel Turner, and Stephen Champlin. Elliott died in 1845, Turner 1850, and Champlin 1870. See Callahan, *List of Officers,* 108, 181, 553.

178. *Charleston* (SC) *Mercury,* 15 June 1859.

179. See, for example, THS et al. to Congress, 7 Dec. 1828, *American State Papers,* 3:240–41. This memorial articulates many of the pay issues troubling members of the officer corps.

PART III

Memory

Not Pretty, but Beautiful

Oliver Hazard Perry's Battle Flag

DEBORAH LEE TRUPIN AND J. SCOTT HARMON

In a central area of the newly renovated Naval Academy Museum is displayed a flag familiar to Americans, especially those interested in the naval aspects of the War of 1812. It bears the dying words, or reasonable facsimile thereof, of Captain James Lawrence, who was mortally wounded on board his ship the U.S. frigate *Chesapeake* while engaged with the British frigate *Shannon.* While the flag may be familiar—we know the size, shape, wording, and its general history—there are many aspects of the flag that are curious and may forever remain mysteries.

The story begins with Captain Lawrence. Born in 1781, he received his warrant as midshipman in 1798 and served in the *Ganges* and *Adams* during the Quasi-War with France. As a lieutenant in the conflicts with the Barbary Wars, he was second-in-command to Stephen Decatur Jr. in the expedition to burn the captured frigate *Philadelphia.* Promoted to master commandant in 1810, Lawrence was given command of brig-rigged sloop of war the *Hornet.* With the declaration of war against England, the *Hornet,* by this time converted to a ship, cruised off the coast of Brazil, blockading the British sloop *Bonne Citoyenne,* capturing several merchant vessels, and then sinking the brig-sloop *Peacock* in a battle that lasted less than fifteen minutes.[1]

Lawrence returned to New York in the *Hornet* in March and learned that he had been promoted to captain. In May he took command of the *Chesapeake,* then fitting out in Boston. Off shore, the 38-gun British frigate *Shannon* patrolled the harbor entrance, a taunting and unspoken challenge to the Americans to come out and fight. Three weeks later Lawrence answered the challenge; pitting his untested crew against a Royal Navy crew that, for seven years under the command of Captain Philip Bowes Vere Broke, had trained almost daily on the great guns. Broke also encouraged marksmanship with rifles rather than the usual muskets, his mantra being, "Kill the men and the ship is ours."

On 1 June 1813 the *Chesapeake,* followed by a fleet of sightseers, stood out of Boston Harbor to face the *Shannon.* The battle began at about 4:00 P.M. and was over in about fifteen minutes. The *Shannon*'s first broadsides shot away the *Chesapeake*'s headsails and spanker. Marksmen cleared the *Chesapeake*'s decks, concentrating on officers and the helmsmen. Every officer but one was killed or wounded, including Captain Lawrence. As the captain was carried below, he repeated, "Don't give up the ship, don't give up the ship." Nevertheless, the *Chesapeake* was overwhelmed, the American survivors were secured below deck, and the ship was taken as a prize to Halifax.[2]

About the time Master Commandant Oliver Hazard Perry arrived at Presque Isle, he learned that James Lawrence had been killed on board the *Chesapeake.* Determined to memorialize his good friend, Perry ordered one of the brigs to be named the *Lawrence.* He also approved the making of a battle flag bearing Lawrence's dying words. Purser Samuel Hambleton hired Margaret Foster Steuart, of Erie, Pennsylvania, to make the flag. Mrs. Steuart enlisted the help of her two daughters, three of her brothers' daughters, and a cousin. The flag was completed in a few days.[3]

The evening before the battle, Perry met with the commanders of the vessels in his squadron. Just before the meeting broke up, at about 10:00, Perry pulled a dark flag from a chest and laid it out on his cabin table. On it were Lawrence's words, "Dont Give Up the Ship." Perry told his commanders that when they saw this flag hoisted to the main royal masthead, it would be the signal to begin action.[4] (The use of an apostrophe in contractions was uncommon in the early nineteenth century.)

In the battle, the *Lawrence* was the focus of British attention, and by 2:30 it was a floating wreck. When Perry left the *Lawrence* and was rowed to the *Niagara,* his battle flag was hauled down and Seaman Hosea Sargeant handed the flag to Perry, who hoisted it in the *Niagara* and rejoined the action.

"Dear Gen'l. We have met the enemy and they are ours, two ships, two brigs, one schooner and one sloop. Yours with great respect and esteem. O. H. Perry." With a succinct after-action report, Perry announced his victory over the British squadron to Major General William Henry Harrison. Perry followed up his report, sending Lieutenant Dulaney Forrest with additional dispatches and all the flags and pennants captured from the British ships to General Harrison. Forrest then carried the flags on to Washington. It is presumed that Perry's battle flag was among those taken to the capital, but that cannot be confirmed.

On 18 April 1814 Congress passed a statute requiring the secretary of the navy to collect in Washington all flags, standards, and colors taken by the navy from enemies. The navy was already collecting such war trophies; the oldest flag in the Naval Academy's Trophy Flag Collection is from the French frigate *L'Insurgente,* captured by the USS *Constellation* in February 1799 during the Quasi-War with France.

There is no evidence of where the flags resided or to what use they were put from the time they arrived in Washington in 1814 until they were transferred to the Naval School (as the Naval Academy was originally named) in 1849.[5] However, on 9 February 1849, on the conclusion of the war with Mexico and the acquisition of additional trophy flags, President James K. Polk issued an executive order directing the secretary of the navy to deposit the flags with the superintendent of the Naval School for care and use. The flags were delivered to Chaplain George Jones, who was in charge of the Naval School Lyceum. We know that the Perry flag was among those delivered to Chaplain Jones; on 13 June 1849 the *Niles National Register* provided an inventory of the flags under the title "National Trophies":

> The room in the Naval School Institution at Annapolis, Md., recently fitted up for the reception of articles of interest is now open, and among other objects the following may be seen there. The list is deserving of preservation for its chronological information . . .
>
> "Perry's Flag," worn at his mast-head, during his engagement on Lake Erie, and carried under his arm when he removed from the Lawrence to the Niagara. It is black, (the death color,) with Lawrence's last words "Don't give up the ship,[*sic*] inscribed on it in white letters.[6]

On delivery to the Naval School in 1849, the flags were probably displayed in the Lyceum on the second floor of the new midshipmen's mess hall on Stribling Row. In 1862, with the threat of military action around Annapolis, the Academy moved to Newport, Rhode Island. There, Perry's flag was displayed in the lobby of the Atlantic Hotel, which was used as a dormitory and classrooms for midshipmen. In early 1864 the flag was loaned for display at the Great Sanitary Fair in New York. In the earliest depiction of the full flag, Benson Lossing shows it as it appeared displayed in the trophy room at the fair.[7]

Following the Civil War, the Academy—and Perry's flag—returned to Annapolis. Under the vigorous administration of its superintendant, Rear Admiral David Dixon Porter, the Academy was revitalized and a new chapel was built. The old chapel on Stribling Row was converted to the Lyceum.[8] Inventories of flags displayed in the Lyceum (variously called the Gunnery Room and Naval Institute Hall) indicate that the "Dont Give Up the Ship" flag was displayed there for most of the period from the Civil War to the construction of the New Naval Academy at the turn of the twentieth century. The earliest photograph of the flag, draped over the Gunnery Room balcony, appears in a book of 1876, although the author describes the flag as a red banner, probably a misinterpretation of the color.[9]

Following the Spanish-American War, the Naval Academy received a complete makeover; a new dormitory, chapel, classroom buildings, administrative building, officer housing, and auditorium were built. As construction progressed, the old buildings from the Fort Severn era were demolished. The new academic group of buildings, consisting of Sampson, Maury, and Mahan halls, the last housing the Auditorium and Library, were completed in 1907. There are references to the Perry flag being displayed in the ceiling of the Auditorium, but just when it was placed there is uncertain.

The pending observance of the centennial of the Battle of Lake Erie generated considerable interest in the battle flag. An examination made of the trophy flags in the Academy's collection in 1912 found the flags in need of extensive conservation treatment. Through the efforts of Commander William C. Cole, the senior member of the Committee on Memorials and Exhibits at the Naval Academy, Perry's flag was taken to Washington and exhibited before the House of Representatives. Cole's efforts persuaded Congress to appropriate $30,000 for treatment of the 170 trophy flags in the collection and for construction of display cases. Amelia Fowler was contracted to do the preservation work. She hired thirty seamstresses, and they completed the work by 16 May 1913. A letter from Lieuenant Commander R. L. Berry, the officer in charge of buildings and grounds at the Naval Academy, indicates that by that time the "Dont Give Up the Ship" flag was already in the ceiling of the Auditorium.[10]

In January 1913 James Cooke Mills, a writer from Saginaw, Michigan, wrote to the Naval Academy requesting to use an image of the flag that he had seen in a booklet by Annette P. Ward, librarian of the Western Reserve Historical Society in Cleveland. Mills was planning a book on Oliver Hazard Perry and wanted to borrow a copy of the image for the book.[11] On 10 February 1913 Lieutenant Commander Berry sent a photograph of the flag and an interesting descriptive letter, including a reference to the "chain stitch" that held the flag to the backing of "heavy flax canvas," obviously the Fowler treatment. The last paragraph of the letter states that originally the inscription was on a black flag "but that later on when blue bunting did become available, it was applied over the original black flag" and that a careful examination of the image will reveal areas where the black fabric can be seen.[12] The image in the Ward booklet does not show evidence of the Fowler treatment, but it does appear to show the blue bunting.[13] The image shows that the flag and the blue bunting had a great deal of wear and deterioration.

Lieutenant Commander Berry's letter to Austin crossed paths with another chain of correspondence that would lead to the flag's temporary removal from the Auditorium. On 27 January 1913 George W. Stevens, director of the Toledo Museum of Art, wrote to the secretary of the Naval Institute requesting the loan of the John Wesley Jarvis portrait of Oliver Hazard Perry. Ralph Earle, the Institute's secretary and treasurer, forwarded the letter to the appropriate Naval Academy officer, Lieutenant Commander Berry, since the portrait was owned by the Academy and was displayed in Bancroft Hall. Acceptance of this request by the Naval Academy perhaps led Stevens to make a further request—how about Perry's flag? On 14 April 1913 Captain John H. Gibbons, superintendent of the Academy, endorsed the proposal in a memo to the secretary of the navy. By 2 May the secretary had approved the loan on the condition that the flag would not be removed until after commissioning exercises in June and that the flag was not to be entrusted to express companies for transportation, only to a special courier from the museum. On 10 June 1913 Almon C. Whiting, curator of the Toledo Museum of Art, received the flag. It was returned to the Academy following the September observance of the battle and re-placed in the ceiling of the Mahan Hall Auditorium.[14]

In about 1920 the flag was removed from the Mahan Hall Auditorium because it interfered with acoustics. There was some talk of placing it in the Chapel, but by 1930 it had found a new home in Memorial Hall. Initially, the flag hung in a lunette above the doors that look out of the hall onto Chesapeake Bay. This location had many problems, the gravest of which were not recognized at the time. The east-facing doors allowed sunlight to stream in, blinding those who might see the flag as they approached the grand staircase leading into Memorial Hall. And if the sunlight did not obscure the flag, the lighting of the hall itself reflected off the glass of the case. The flag was barely noticeable at any time.

In 1948 the Academy once more loaned the flag for a special exhibition, Your Navy at the Metropolitan Museum of Art in New York City. This provided an opportunity to revisit the display case. In January 1947 Captain Harry A. Baldridge, director of the Naval Academy Museum, wrote to W. F. Davidson of the Knoedler Galleries in New York City about the reflection problem. Davidson felt that the "non-reflecting plate glass recently invented . . . would do the trick."[15] On its return, the flag was remounted, again in the lunette above the doors, but this time in a case that answered some of the viewing problems. Apparently, the environmental conditions to which the historic flag was subjected were not a consideration; Memorial Hall was not air conditioned and there was significant temperature instability.

The environmental threats to the flag were exacerbated when, in 1958, a bronze panel honoring Naval Academy alumni killed in action was installed in Memorial Hall. The center of the three doors facing seaward was closed and the space used for the memorial panel. The flag was placed in the transom window above the former door, where it remained until the restoration of Memorial Hall began in 2002.

As planning for the restoration work in Memorial Hall began, the Naval Academy contracted with New York State Office of Parks, Recreation and Historic Preservation (OPRHP) textile conservator Deborah Trupin to examine the flag and advise on its preservation needs during and after the room's restoration. Trupin first examined the flag in December 2001 in situ from scaffolding, so full details of its construction and condition could not be determined. The most visible aspect of the flag was the grid work of stitching from the Fowler treatment. Areas of stitching had discolored, leaving paler bands that were visible even from the floor. Examination from the scaffolding showed that some areas of the flag and stitching had been overpainted and that the flag was folded back on the top and bottom. It was not apparent how the flag was affixed either to the mount or the wall. The on-site examination also showed that the blue fabric was not directly attached to the letters, indicating that it, like the grid work of stitches, was a previous treatment. Trupin was quite relieved to learn from Naval Academy Museum files that the staff was aware of this.

Following the on-site examination and discussions with Scott Harmon, Naval Academy Museum director, Trupin prepared a condition report and an initial treatment proposal. Harmon and Trupin agreed that the flag must be removed from Memorial Hall during building restoration and that this was an appropriate time to provide conservation treatment. The request to the conservators was to treat the flag and work with the Naval Academy's exhibit design consultants to develop a new mounting system to reinstall the flag in Memorial Hall.

For the initial treatment, the Naval Academy contracted with OPRHP textile conservators to assist in removing the flag from Memorial Hall. The Academy had the flag transported to OPRHP's textile conservation lab at Peebles Island in Waterford, New York, where the conservators could perform more complete examination, analysis, and documentation to develop full treatment proposals.

"DONT GIVE UP THE SHIP" flag—before treatment, fully opened. Most of the visible ground is the blue overlay fabric. Light areas are faded areas of Fowler stitching. (Photograph by Rich Clauss, New York State Office of Parks, Recreation and Historic Preservation.)

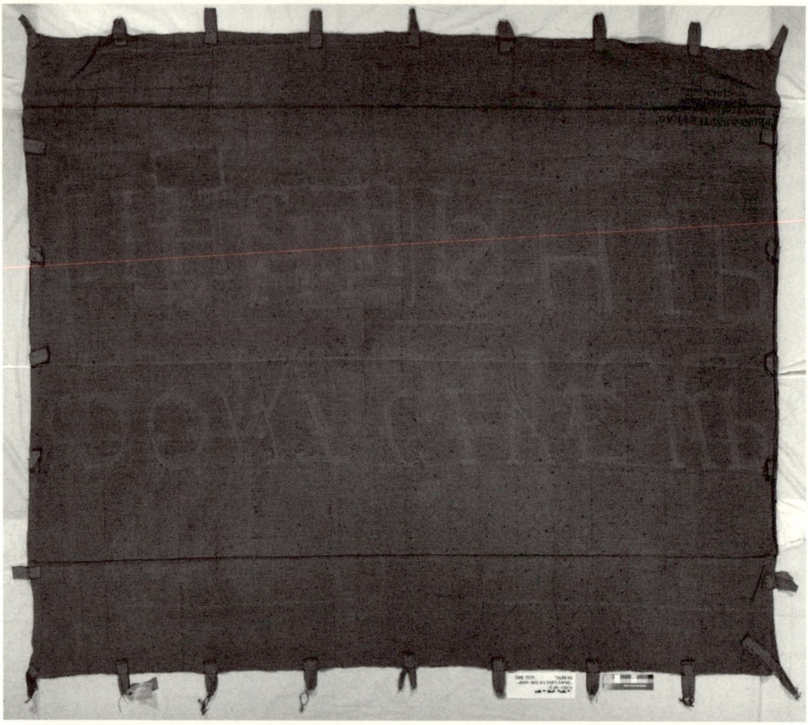

"DONT GIVE UP THE SHIP" flag—before treatment, fully opened. Fabric visible on this side is the linen lining applied by Amelia Bold Fowler and staff in 1912. (Photograph by Rich Clauss, New York State Office of Parks, Recreation and Historic Preservation.)

Removal of the flag from Memorial Hall was harrowing but successful, thanks to the excellent work of Artex Fine Arts Movers, Inc., and United Rigging of Beltsville, Maryland. During removal, the poor environment for the flag in Memorial Hall was confirmed and the mounting mechanism determined. The flag had been nailed around its perimeter to a plywood backing. The plywood had rested directly in the former window and, during the removal in August 2002, was quite warm to the touch.

Artex delivered the flag to Peebles Island, where the textile conservators documented and removed the modern mounting materials. For the Memorial Hall display, the flag had been stitched to a heavy cotton canvas. Between the flag and the canvas was a layer of thick cotton batting, which gave the flag the appearance of a quilt. About 18 inches on the top and 10 inches on the bottom of the flag had been folded back; removal of the canvas and batting permitted the flag to be opened to its full size (about 98" x 105") for the first time since 1958. Sharp crease lines remained where the flag had been folded.

The conservators performed a more detailed examination of the flag from the reverse, through the Fowler lining, using transmitted light. In a few small areas, they selectively clipped the Fowler stitches and support fabric.

This examination confirmed that the blue bunting forming the visual ground of the flag was an overlay. From the quality of the fabric and the type and placement of the stitches securing it to the flag, Trupin guessed that the blue fabric had been applied in the mid-to-late nineteenth century; the documents cited above show that the bunting was applied between 1876 and 1912. Thus, for nearly 150 years the letters had been the only visible part of the original flag.

The original flag ground fabric, largely obscured by the blue overlay fabric, appeared to be black or dark brown, which raised the question of why a blue fabric was used and gave rise to the question of whether the brown flag fabric had originally been blue. This seemed unlikely, as the most likely blue dye in the early nineteenth century was indigo, which normally does not shift color or fade significantly. To be certain, however, the conservators commissioned Ina Vanden Berghe of the Royal Institute for Cultural Heritage (Institut Royal du Patrimoine Artistique/Koninklijk Instituut voor het Kunstpatrimonium) in Brussels, Belgium, to perform dye analysis on the flag fibers. The analysis showed no indigotin, the color compound found in indigo-dyed fibers. Vanden Berghe suggested that the "Dont Give up the Ship" flag fabric may have been woven from wool from black sheep, which is actually a very dark brown.[16] As of current understanding, this seems to be the most likely case, although it leaves open the question of why a blue overlay fabric was used.

The detailed examination also revealed two different fabrics, both of which seemed to be original ground fabrics, each quite different from the other. This led the conservators to think that the flag was originally two-sided, that it was made from two different fabrics, each with an applied set of letters. With most of the Fowler treatment in place, however, it was not possible to confirm whether the flag was two-sided nor to determine the extent of losses in the fabrics, which conservators presumed had suffered moderate to extreme losses.

As examination of the flag progressed, the conservators had increasing doubts about the wisdom of reinstalling the flag in Memorial Hall. They prepared a menu of treatment options and noted that their treatment of choice was to remove the two previous treatments (the Fowler treatment and the blue overlay), to conserve whatever remained of the original flag, and to prepare the flag for display in the Naval Academy Museum, where it could be provided with a more preservation-friendly environment. They recommended that the Naval Academy commission a reproduction flag to be placed in the frame in Memorial Hall.

In September 2002 the museum director traveled to Peebles Island to view the flag and discuss the treatment options. He agreed with the conservators' treatment of choice but noted that he would need approval from his superiors at the Naval Academy. With that approval, the restored Memorial Hall opened in May 2003 with a reproduction of the "Dont Give up the Ship" flag installed in the frame where the original had been. Funds for the reproduction flag were contributed by Robert F. Sumrall, a retired navy chief petty officer and longtime curator of ship models for the museum.[17]

Treatment of the original flag began shortly thereafter. The treatment plan was to remove both the Fowler treatment and the blue overlay, clean the flag as safely as possible, and then prepare it for display by stitching first the blue overlay and then the flag itself to a lining fabric. The lined flag would then be secured to a rigid mount for display in a custom-made case in the Academy Museum.

The first step in treatment was the removal of the 1912 Fowler treatment. As they had done with 170 flags at the Naval Academy, Mrs. Fowler and her staff had stitched the flag to a heavy linen fabric with a one-inch grid of interlocking buttonhole stitches in heavy linen thread. The removal of the Fowler stitches and lining was straightforward but nerve-racking, and it required time, focus, and precision.

In removing the Fowler lining, the conservators exposed the side of the flag to which the lining had been stitched (deemed the obverse, as the hoist rope is at the viewer's left) for the first time since 1912. The obverse featured a second set of letters, as had been glimpsed previously. These letters were not exact copies of those on the reverse (the side that had been exposed). The differences in the letters and their placement gave a human touch to the flag; one could imagine Mrs. Steuart and her family stitching the flag under less-than-ideal conditions.

More significantly, removal of the Fowler lining showed that the flag was originally made of only one layer of ground fabric with two sets of letters. The original ground fabric is a fine, very dark brown wool. It is more like a dress

"DONT GIVE UP THE SHIP" flag—original reverse, after removal of Fowler treatment. The blue overlay fabric is still in place. This side was displayed as obverse for more than 100 years. (Photograph by Rich Clauss, New York State Office of Parks, Recreation and Historic Preservation.)

fabric than the wool bunting (a more open weave made from more loosely spun yarns) that was typically used for flags in the early nineteenth century. The fabric that the conservators had thought was the second ground fabric seems instead to be an early repair fabric. This fabric, however, is not stitched to the original ground fabric, so its origin and purpose remain unclear.

Removal of the Fowler treatment also exposed a history of repairs to the flag:

1. The earliest repairs seemed to be some sewn repairs and the above-mentioned fabric thought to have been a second ground fabric.
2. Later, several patches were inset. At least some of these patches were most likely done by Annapolis sailmaker Henry T. Stocker.[18] The inset patches strongly resemble the patching technique still used by sailmakers.
3. Then, between about 1876 and 1912, the blue overlay fabric was placed

"DONT GIVE UP THE SHIP" flag—original obverse, after removal of Fowler treatment. The blue overlay fabric, visible through some losses, is below the flag. (Photograph by Rich Clauss, New York State Office of Parks, Recreation and Historic Preservation.)

on the reverse of the flag, making that side serve as the obverse for about 100 years.

4. All of these repairs were in place by 1912, when Mrs. Fowler applied her treatment.

Removal of the blue overlay fabric was the next treatment step in the conservation process. Before removing the blue overlay fabric, conservators made a template of it, since it would be displayed with the flag. With the removal of the overlay, the original reverse of the flag was visible for the first time in more than 100 years.

Once the original flag was exposed, conservators performed tests to evaluate cleaning options. The flag was quite soiled from its years of display. Of greater concern, however, were the low pH (4.5–5.0) levels of the wool ground and the extremely low pH (3.6–4.6) of the cotton letters. (These low pH readings meant the fabrics were acidic, a dangerous condition for fabrics, especially cotton.)

They first vacuumed the entire flag to remove as much particulate soil as possible. This did remove particulate soils, but it produced no visible changes (nor did it affect pH). After testing several cleaning approaches, Trupin and her colleagues determined that wet cleaning the flag in a water bath with a mild, non-ionic detergent would be the best approach. Wet cleaning would remove more soils, improve the pH of the flag (i.e., reduce the acidity), and reduce fabric distortion caused by the Fowler stitches and the creases from the mounting in Memorial Hall.

Excessive movement from the flag "swimming" in the bath seemed to pose the biggest risk in wet cleaning. To minimize movement, the textile conservators designed a special wet cleaning support system so that the flag could be immersed in a bath without moving.

"DONT GIVE UP THE SHIP" flag—original obverse, after wet cleaning, ready for mounting. (Photograph by Rich Clauss, New York State Office of Parks, Recreation and Historic Preservation.)

The Peebles Island conservators wet cleaned the flag in December 2004 and the blue overlay fabric about two weeks later. The flag benefited tremendously from the wet cleaning. The pH rose from 3.2 to 3.6 in the letters and from 4.5 in the ground fabric to about 7.5 in all parts. (It is understood that the final pH reading reflects to a certain extent the water pH.) The flag is noticeably brighter. The color of a few letters was measured using the Munsell system, before and after treatment. The change in color in the letters reflects more the removal of dirt (blackness, or value change) than the removal of yellow degradation products. The holes and puckering (quilted appearance) from the Fowler treatment disappeared. This not only improved the appearance of the flag, but it is a sign that the fabrics still retain some suppleness.

The removal of soils revealed the extent of fading. The location of the hems around the letters in the blue overlay fabric can be easily seen by the color change between the exposed areas and the folded-back hem areas. Both the flag and the blue overlay fabric have distinctly less faded areas along the top and bottom where the flag (and blue overlay) was folded back. It is sobering to realize the extent of light damage incurred over the last forty or so years.

After wet cleaning, conservators rolled the flag and the blue overlay separately on wide-diameter acid-free tubes to await further treatment. Treatment of the flag resumed in the summer of 2009 in preparation for its exhibition in the newly remodeled Naval Academy Museum. At the beginning of the treatment, the museum staff and the textile conservators agreed that the flag should be displayed with its original obverse up—with the hoist at the viewer's left. They also decided that the flag would be mounted on top of the blue previous-overlay fabric, which would show through some of the losses in the flag fabric to make the connection between the original dark-brown flag and the blue flag that people had seen for so many years. The flag would show its history.

To achieve this, the conservators stretched a neutral-colored, washed, cotton mounting fabric on a temporary stretcher. They positioned the blue previous-overlay fabric on the mounting fabric and stitched it on. They then unrolled the flag itself and carefully positioned it over the blue fabric and stitched through to the mounting fabric. Because of the size and fragility of the flag, it was kept horizontal for the stitching, with one conservator working below the flag and passing the needle to a second conservator suspended on a "bridge" above the flag.

Once the flag was stitched to the mounting fabric, the conservators placed a Small Corp. aluminum honeycomb panel, lightly padded with polyester batting, below the mounting fabric. They then secured the mounting fabric to the wooden perimeter of the mounting panel. After being photographed, the flag was wrapped for transport to Annapolis.

In July 2009 a team from Artex delivered the flag to its new home in the renovated Naval Academy Museum. The mounted flag was placed on a custom-made iron support frame in a custom-made case. What the visitor now sees is the original flag, its dark-brown fabric unevenly faded, and the tears, holes, and wear marks of nearly 200 years of hard use clearly visible. It is a flag that is not pretty, but in terms of character and history, as expressed in wear and tear,

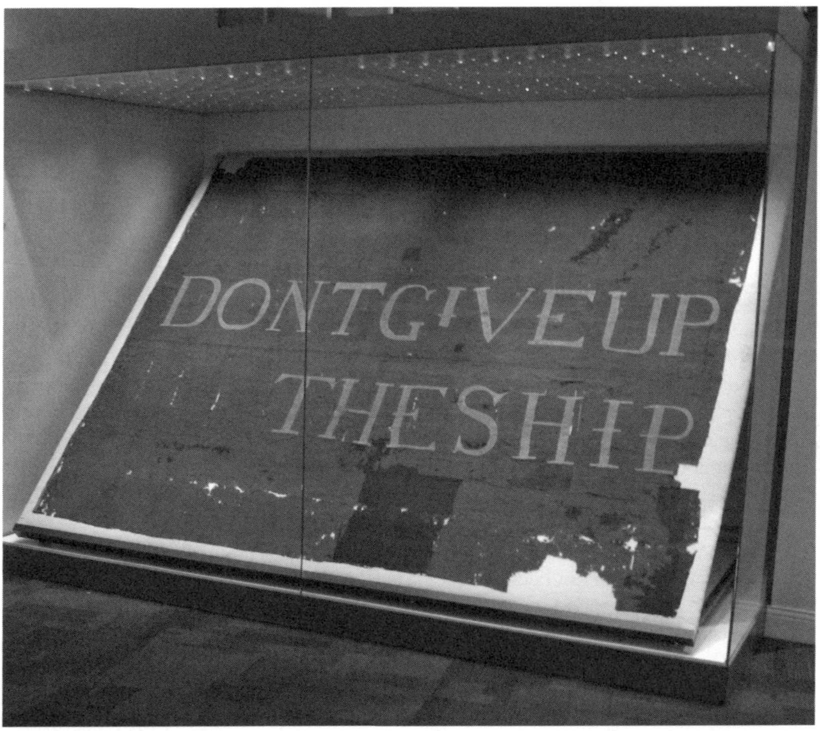

"DONT GIVE UP THE SHIP" flag—after treatment, installed in United States Naval Academy Museum. This lighting in this image is deceiving; to help preserve the flag, lighting is kept at a very low level, about five foot-candles. (Photograph by Deborah Trupin, New York State Office of Parks, Recreation and Historic Preservation.)

it is indeed beautiful. In the museum, under optimal environmental conditions and low light levels, the flag is on its way to serving as an inspiration to midshipmen and visitors from around the world for another 200 years.

To Americans, James Lawrence died a hero, regardless of the fact that he may have been a foolish hero. His words, however, live on. Ironically, according to Captain Edward Beach, who writes that "even his poignant last words, feverishly and obsessively repeated during the four days it took him to die from his wounds, are hardly a battle cry, though, thanks to Oliver Hazard Perry, we have made them into one."[19] The motto, Captain Lawrence's dying words expressed on this historic flag now displayed in the Naval Academy Museum, speaks to the U.S. Navy and Marine Corps of perseverance and dedication; and it speaks to midshipmen of the values expressed in the mission of the Naval Academy: duty, honor, loyalty.

NOTES

1. Naval History Division, *Dictionary of American Naval Fighting Ships*, vol. 4 (Washington, DC: Government Printing Office, 1969), 68.

2. There are many descriptions of the battle. See, for example, Theodore Roosevelt, *The Naval War of 1812* (New York: Modern Library, 1902), 179–96; C. S. Forester, *The Age of Fighting Sail: The Story of the Naval War of 1812* (Garden City, NY: Doubleday, 1956), 160–66; Ian W. Toll, *Six Frigates: The Epic History of the Founding of the U.S. Navy* (New York: W. W. Norton, 2006), 404–17; and David Curtis Skaggs and Gerard T. Altoff, *A Signal Victory: The Lake Erie Campaign, 1812–1813* (Annapolis, MD: Naval Institute Press, 1997), 118–48.

3. Emily Pritchard Cary, "The Flag That Helped Captain Perry Win the Battle of Lake Erie in 1813," *Pennsylvania Magazine* 7, no. 4 (1988): 62. A letter dated 21 January 1976 from Edward E. Wheeler of the Erie County Historical Society identifies eight women who worked on the flag. Found in the Curatorial Records, U.S. Naval Academy Museum, Annapolis, MD.

4. The seamstress, following early-nineteenth-century custom, did not insert an apostrophe in "don't." Charles J. Dutton, *Oliver Hazard Perry* (New York: Longmans, Green, 1935), 142; Skaggs and Altoff, *Signal Victory*, 115.

5. Memoranda dated 17 and 19 December 1936 from E. Craven to Captain Dudley W. Knox, Officer in Charge of the Navy Department's Office of Naval Records and Library, indicate that a thorough search was made of all relevant official letters of Superintendents Franklin Buchanan, George P. Upshur, and Cornelius K. Stribling and that "nothing has been found in manuscript relating to the banner either immediately after the battle or in or about 1849." File copies in Curatorial Records.

6. *Niles National Register*, 75, no. 24 (13 June 1849): 370.

7. Benjamin J. Lossing, *The Pictorial Field-Book of the War of 1812* (New York: Harper & Brothers, 1868), 519.

8. James W. Cheevers, "Curatorial Notes: USNA 1849.001.012 Don't Give up the Ship flag," May 1968, revised 1999, Curatorial Records.

9. James Russell Soley, *Historical Sketch of the United States Naval Academy* (Washington, DC: Government Printing Office, 1876), 219.

10. Lt. Commander R. L. Berry to Thos. L. Austin, Curator, Public Museum, Erie, PA, 8 Mar. 1913, Curatorial Records. In response to Austin's request for measurements of the flag, Berry states that the flag has been placed in the ceiling of the Auditorium and that it would be necessary to "build a large amount of scaffolding, and since this scaffolding has been removed I have no means of taking the measurements."

11. James Cooke Mills to Commander W. C. Cole, 21 Jan. 1913, Curatorial Records.

12. R. L. Berry to James Cooke Mills, 10 Feb. 1913, Curatorial Records.

13. Annette P. Ward, *"Lest We Forget." Oliver Hazard Perry, the War of 1812, the Battle of Lake Erie* (Cleveland, 1912), 11.

14. At this time, no information or photos are known that describe how the flag was mounted in the Auditorium. There were tabs sewn around the periphery of the canvas backing applied by Amelia Fowler, and they may have been used, with lanyards to suspension points, to stretch the flag and hold it in place.

15. Captain H. A. Baldridge to Rear Adm S. H. Ingersoll, 8 Feb. 1947, Curatorial Records.

16. Ina Vanden Berghe, "Natural Dye Analysis Report, IRPA/KIK project 2005.08601," 2005,Textile Conservation Laboratory, NYSOPRPH Peebles Island Resource Center, Waterford, NY.

17. The reproduction flag was made by Steve Hill of DuPage Military Flag Company. Hill worked from the before-treatment photo of the flag, with the blue overlay fabric in place, so the reproduction is also blue.

18. G. S. Blake, 2 May 1864, *Letters Sent by the Superintendent of the U.S. Naval Academy Feb.1, 1864–Oct. 20, 1864*, Records of the U.S. Naval Academy, Record Group 405, National Archives–Affiliated Archives, on deposit at U.S. Naval Academy Archives, Annapolis, MD.

19. Edward L. Beach, *The United States Navy: 200 Years* (New York: Henry Holt, 1986), 112.

Observations on the Sailing Characteristics of the U.S. Brig *Niagara*

WALTER P. RYBKA

In the constant search for a more accurate understanding of history, I intend this essay to better acquaint the reader with the shipboard environment, particularly the performance capabilities of the sailing warships of the Lake Erie squadrons, and how these factors affected the commanders' choices. My observations are based on experience sailing in command of the present-day reconstruction of the U.S. Brig *Niagara*, which has conducted sail training cruises every summer since 1991.[1]

The present *Niagara* is the fourth version of this ship. The first, built in Erie in 1813, was scuttled in Misery Bay (within Erie's harbor) in 1820. What was left was raised and rebuilt in 1913 for the centennial of the Battle of Lake Erie under the direction of navy lieutenant William L. Morrison.

After being towed on a commemorative tour of Great Lakes ports, the ship was allowed to decay for many years. Another rebuilding was sporadically funded, partially as a Works Progress Administration project between 1933 and 1943. The latter stages were supervised by Howard I. Chapelle. This vessel was dry berthed as an exhibit until advancing decay led to the research, design, and building of the present ship by Melbourne Smith between 1987 and 1990. Sixty frame futtocks from the original ship are incorporated in approximately their original positions, but only as a symbolic presence rather than as structural members.[2] Some of the light joiner work in the wardroom is from original timbers re-sawn. As a practical matter, the *Niagara* is a new ship.

What is original is the process by which we sail it, albeit with some different circumstances. The overall dimensions and shape of the lower hull were derived from the wreck of the original ship, raised in 1913. The known features—rake (angle off plumb) of stem and sternpost, keel assembly (backbone of the ship), and hull structure out to turn of bilge, mast steps, and height of deck, bulwarks, gunports—allowed projections to be made, filling in the missing pieces. The rest is based on Smith's research into other ships by Noah Brown, the original builder, and U.S. Navy practice of the period.

The *Niagara* and the *Lawrence* were very similar in length and breadth to oceangoing sloops of war carrying the same armament. What was very different about them was their need for shallow draft, both to get over the bar at the entrance to Erie and because the intended area of operation was known to have many shoals. The dominant characteristics of this configuration were greater speed in light air due to less wetted surface, but, at the same time, it had poor windward ability due to the hull form having inadequate lateral resistance. No ship can sail directly into the wind, but it can be sailed to get upwind (windward) of the starting position by steering far enough away from the wind direction that the sails, configured for this condition, stay full, keeping the wind on one side. Getting to windward depends on how close to the wind direction the ship can be made to point and still make forward progress. Shape of the hull is also part of the story, the type of rig and sail configuration being equally important.

The shoal draft hull also has a lower range of stability than would a deeper vessel intended for ocean service. The result was greater vulnerability to heavy weather, requiring sails to be shortened earlier than was the case in standard-construction naval vessels. Another characteristic of a shallow hull girder is that the vessel is more subject to wracking, twisting, and bending strains in rough seas that loosen the hull structure and result in heavy leaking.

The *Niagara* has a lot of deadrise (the angle of the bottom rising outboard from the keel; a deep V-shaped hull would be described as high deadrise, while a flat-bottomed vessel has no deadrise) and a slack turn of the bilge (a large radius curve between bottom planking and topsides). The keel only projected seventeen inches below the garboard. Heeling her over 20 degrees would rotate the keel up and the bilge down to the point of shadowing the keel and thus helping the ship skate to leeward. A square rigger is rarely sailed at more than 10–15 degrees of heel, for beyond that it is very difficult for the crew to keep their feet or get much purchase on a line. Yet in heavy weather the only way to get the ship to windward under sail is to have enough sail on to generate enough power to overcome the windage (drag of all surface area of the hull, masts, and rigging that the wind can act against) and drive the vessel through the seas. This ship, if driven, will gain little benefit from its keel.

A valuable guide to the operations of 1813 is the log of the *Lawrence*, kept by Sailing Master William V. Taylor.[3] On 5 August 1813, when sailing by the wind, Taylor recorded the "leeway" (sideslip) of the shallow hulled vessel as 1.75 points (compass circle of 360 degrees in this period was divided into 32 points of 11.25 degrees). In the example quoted, 1.75 points converts to 18 degrees. A ship of this type configured to sail as close to the direction the wind was coming from (windward) as possible would point approximately 65 degrees off the wind. When the excessive leeway is factored in, the actual track over the sea bottom (course made good) is 83 degrees away from the wind. That is only 7 degrees above merely sailing across the wind. In 1991 the *Niagara* did not yet have an external ballast keel. A measure of the validity of Melbourne Smith's interpretation was confirmed in 1991 when we recorded exactly the same miserable performance on several occasions.

In 1992, as part of the auxiliary power installation, twenty-five tons of internal lead ballast had to be removed to make room for fuel tanks, engine foundations, shaft alleys, etc. It was recast and bolted on below the keel, which now gives the ship thirty inches below the garboard planks and a much improved grip on the water, cutting the leeway down to about six degrees. Lowering the center of gravity also improved stability.

The present *Niagara* is true to period in that the rig has hardly any iron in it, only the chain plates and deadeye straps. In 1813 both standing (keep the masts in column) and running (control the sails) rigging were of fiber rope. The standing rigging was heavily tarred hemp to preserve it from rot; the running rigging was untarred hemp so that it could run freely over sheaves. Today's standing rigging is Kevlar, a low-stretch synthetic fiber that holds adjustment better than a hemp rig. Impervious to fungal decay, the Kevlar standing rigging is still tarred both for correct appearance and to preserve it from ultraviolet degradation. Today's running rigging is mostly Manila, a plant fiber similar to hemp. The present-day Niagara has synthetic sailcloth, which is stronger and holds shape better than natural-fiber sails. The original sails were most likely flax, and therefore almost inherently baggy, but could be made to stand well by the bowlines (light running rigging leading from the edges of the square sails to some point far enough forward to allow for pulling the bag out of the sails). The synthetic sailcloth stands flatter, so bowlines are not needed. Today's *Niagara* has never rigged bowlines because our present crew size is so much smaller than the original. It is very desirable to limit the number of lines that must be handled simultaneously during maneuvers.

The primary reason for use of synthetics is to lower the maintenance burden, given our reduced crew. Natural-fiber sails required constant attention to airing and drying to avoid mildew and rot. Hemp rigging, even heavily tarred, required much more frequent tuning. Ironically, all of this stronger synthetic material elevates the level of risk in shifting the "weak link" from sails to sheets or to the spars. Historically, a blown-out sail, while an expensive loss, relieved strain on the rest of the rig. Parting a sheet can be worse if an intact sail violently flogs and causes a spar to break.

The present crew (forty versus 140) is the principal reason why even with stronger and better-shaped sails, combined with external ballast, we have resisted the temptation to drive the ship hard. The first rule of sail-carrying is if you can't get it in quickly, don't set it. Our all hands at general quarters is still a full third smaller than the watch on deck would have been in 1813, which raises the question of how the present-day crew compares to the original. People now average about 20 percent more body mass, as reflected in recent regulatory changes increasing the assumed average weight per passenger from 150 to 170 pounds on commercial aircraft and small passenger vessels.[4] In calculating the heft of the naval crew, the increased mass of the men today is balanced out somewhat because about a third of today's crew are women. Today's crew benefits from a healthier diet and overall better hygiene and therefore, in all probability, loses fewer days to illness. One admitted intangible factor is that the 1813 crowd was likely a lot tougher, having grown up in a world of hard work. Yet whether they were large or small, exhausted or brimming with vitality, the fact that the 1813 crew members were three to four times as numerous meant many more operations could be going on simultaneously. The greater vulnerability of the ship was somewhat mitigated by the alacrity with which changes in configuration could be made.

From the first log raft used to cross a river up to the present-day supertankers, the most efficient way to move anything, or at least anything heavy, has been to float it. Waterborne transport has the lowest energy cost per ton per mile. What is less apparent to today's reader is that, until the development of railroads in the middle decades of the nineteenth century, the sailing ship was the fastest form of transport on the planet, at least for distances greater than a day's ride. Living as we do in the age of jet aircraft, high-speed rail, and interstate highway systems, we think of even 25-knot (the rate of nautical miles per hour: land mile x 1.15 = nautical mile) container ships as being slow. We look at a sailing ship, which can very rarely get above 10–12 knots, as being inherently slow—especially when the average speed throughout the age of sail was 4.5 knots.[5] This is the point-to-point average, including time becalmed, time blown off course by adverse weather, and all conditions in between.

How can this be considered fast? Multiply by 24 and then consider the alternatives. A sailing ship on open water could sail around the clock day after day at an average of 108 nautical miles, or 124 land miles per day. What was the competition? A cavalry charge might top 30 miles per hour, but only for the mile or so of life-and-death stakes. Cavalry on patrol planned on 35 miles a day if the horses were expected to remain sound for an extensive campaign.[6] They might do 50–70 miles a day at need, but if they kept at it several days running, most of the horses would be lame, if not dead. Infantry might march 20–25 miles a day for fit troops on good roads, and maybe half that distance in mountainous terrain. Finally, considering the mobility of the supply train, which governs the speed of an advance, heavily loaded wagons would maybe, at best, do the same 20 miles per day as the men on foot, if the ground was firm—which was a pretty big if. While sailing ships might be windbound (prevented from leaving a given harbor by wind direction) or becalmed (no wind to move them) for days on end, the baggage train ashore was just as dependent on weather. Days of heavy rains guaranteed that the heaviest wagons sank into mud. When the storm cleared they often waited days for the ground to dry out and firm up. Or there might be delays finding enough forage and water for the draft animals. For these reasons, schedules did not come into use until the railroads. The speed and carrying capacity of ships stood out even more prominently on the Great Lakes in the War of 1812 because the land was largely a roadless wilderness.[7]

One place the army commander had a planning advantage over his naval contemporaries was with geography, which did not fundamentally change under his feet; high and low ground retained their relationship. For the sailor, the dominant fact of life is that you cannot sail directly into the wind. A sailing vessel must turn away enough for the wind to fill the sails from one side and move the hull. For a square-rigged ship, this angle is about 65–70 degrees on either side of the wind's eye (the direction the wind is coming from). The exact degree will vary from ship to ship, and circumstances of loading, trim, and leeway (sideslip) will make the average closer to 75 degrees off the wind for course made good.

For any given wind, there is an arc of about 150 degrees, or 40 percent of the horizon, that the ship cannot sail directly into but, instead, must sail back and forth slowly gaining ground to windward, if the destination lies that way. Think of going to windward as going uphill, up a mountain road full of switchbacks to lessen the slope. At best, a sailing ship will cover about 4.5 miles over the ground for every mile gained to windward. Add to that shifty winds, rough seas, old sails, or green helmsman, and the ratio may well be 5 or 6 or 7 to 1. In the case of the original *Niagara,* the leeway was known to be excessive due to the shallow hull. The land commander knew he wanted to occupy the high ground and generally knew where it was and that it wasn't moving. The naval commander wanted the same relative advantage of the upwind position, called the "weather gage," but the difference was that the direction of this desirable position could change in a heartbeat, often without notice.

The advantages of the weather gage were many. In maneuvering terms, the windward ship was in undisturbed air and better able to hold its position. At the same time, it retains the option of running at speed if needed. There were several important structural reasons for seeking the weather gage.

- The fire and smoke of the guns of both antagonists would be blown onto the leeward vessel, depriving them of visibility.
- In close-quarters action, the volume of smoke would slow down the leeward ship's gunners due to smoke inhalation and impaired aerobic function.
- The weather vessel is firing from its own lee side. The ship is heeling, to some extent, and the gun's recoil is more readily checked rolling "uphill," and once reloaded it is far easier to run out to the gunport, being a "downhill" roll.
- The opposite case afflicts the leeward vessel. They are firing from a heeling deck that allows the gun to come back hard on the breech rope, and once reloaded their gun must be hauled "uphill" to get out of the gunport again.
- The weather vessel, if heeling at all, is showing less topsides, whereas the leeward vessel may even be exposing bottom planking in the troughs of the waves.

For all of these reasons, the weather gage was worth having. Naval commanders were conditioned to seek it the same way the infantry heads for the heights and fighter pilots crave altitude.

The broadside guns of a sailing warship were typically located 10–12 feet between muzzles. Field artillery lined up axle to axle might achieve a similar density, but not usually with anything heavier than a 12-pounder, versus naval guns, which were up to 32-pounders. A heavily armed naval vessel, especially a ship of the line with multiple decks of closely spaced heavy guns, was the highest concentration of lethal force available at the time.

This level of force was approached by the large vessels built on Lake Ontario but not those built on Lake Erie. One of the crucial decisions to make at the outset of establishing a naval force is the trade-off between having a few ships of great power and many vessels of smaller force. There were two military advantages to many small units, the foremost being that, for reconnaissance purposes, a lot more area could be covered at the same time by multiple units. Secondly, in a hazardous environment, such as uncharted Lake Erie, with its numerous rocks and shoals, smaller shallow-draft vessels were often more survivable and, if lost, easier to replace.

Yet, for projecting offensive power, all the advantages lay with size. A larger hull was inherently more stable than a small one due to the law of spherical volume. The practical expression of this law is that one only has to increase the dimensions (length, breadth, depth) of a hull by 25 percent to double its internal volume. This means much more buoyancy is available to support heavier, stronger structure; there's more ballast and more stores for longer missions; and, of course, a much heavier armament can be carried on a steadier gun platform. While the hull volume increased in three dimensions, the sail area of the rig only increased in a two-dimensional linear relationship. The practical result is that the larger vessel can carry sail much longer because there is so much reserve capacity for both ballast and buoyancy. Also, the larger vessel was burdened less by its armament, especially in rougher sea conditions. What would physically fit along the perimeter of the deck was a smaller percentage of the vessel's weight-carrying capacity.[8]

The percentage of displacement devoted to armament can be approximated by calculation. In this case, the weights of guns and carriages are the average among the as-built weights of the *Niagara*'s present battery, Spencer Tucker's tables in *Arming the Fleet,* and William Brady's tables in *The Kedge Anchor.* Perusal of other sources such as Brian Lavery and Adrian Caruana shows no two in agreement but all within a 15 percent range. Displacement is also an approximation. Even if calculated from a reliable line drawing, there is uncertainty as to loading in terms of consumable stores. And even if the weights are known, the centers of gravity would depend on stowage and remain conjectural.[9]

The tactical point is that armament, a concentrated weight well above waterline, is a much larger percentage of displacement on the smaller warship, which has inherently less stability than a large warship to begin with. The smaller ship will be a much less steady gun platform. Ironically, the Battle of Lake Erie was fought on a light-air day with minimal wave action, the one circumstance under which the heavy guns could be effective from such a small platform.

As might be expected, any complex machine that offered long-range, high-speed, and great offensive power was a major investment. There is a very naive idea regarding sailing that "the wind is free." It is, in that its use is open to all without need of rights to the real estate or fees. But harnessing the wind to do work requires a large investment in rope and canvas, which wear out quickly, and an even larger investment in the crew required to perform all of the myriad tasks. Sailing ships got around the planet without burning hydrocarbons, but they ate men, rope, and canvas in what added up to a high fuel bill.

The *Niagara* carries a large sail area on a small displacement, which is to say a high power to weight ratio. It is at its best in light air and with winds under 15 knots—an important mean number, since it represents the average strength of wind over most of the world's oceans most of the time.[10] The majority of sailing ships carry their full sail plan through at least 15 knots before shortening down. Yet, by the time the wind is up to 20 knots, the dividing line emerges between what is considered "light air" versus "heavy weather" ships, the latter being those that can romp on longer before being shortened down. But somewhere before encountering 30 knots of wind, the upper sails are off of any ship. The best codification of this relationship is seen in the original Beaufort scale, which graded wind force levels by the sails that could be carried by a ship of the line. This level of sail carrying for large heavy-displacement ships could not be emulated, at least not without grave risk, by smaller vessels.[11]

Onboard the *Niagara,* we have learned to start taking in sail about the time whitecaps are consistently seen, or at about 10–12 knots. First in is the main topgallant staysail. In wind over 10 knots it is adding more to heeling and weather helm than to forward drive. Next in are the flying jib and royals. The flying jibboom is so frail the fear is that it will break the stick rather than threaten stability. The royals place bending strain on the thin upper poles of their masts, but it is more the effect on stability that sends them down to deck.

The full mainsail and full spanker are only rarely seen together, perhaps in a beam wind of 5–8 knots. Above this range, the spanker and mainsail become an either-or choice. If well off the wind, take in the spanker; if on the wind, the spanker is much more useful and the mainsail is taken in to avoid backwinding the spanker. The full spanker can be carried in wind velocities in the upper teens, but it is meant to be balanced by the flying jib. Once that forward sail is taken in, the helm balance is much improved by tucking the first reef in the spanker.

Now that the light sails, or "kites," and the mainsail are in, and the spanker reefed, the *Niagara* can carry on until it blows around 20 knots, at which point the ship is sailing at 9 knots and only heeling about 5 degrees. But a sudden gust could threaten the topgallant masts or spanker boom. Also, on the wind the sea state will build, and the motion aloft will increase greatly.

Before the wind is over 20 knots, and the sea state over four feet, is the time to get the second reef in the spanker. If off the wind, the spanker will likely come in altogether, but it is wise to put the second reef in before stowing it. The reason is that if the ship must suddenly be put on the wind, and the wind has piped up a little more in the meantime, it will be ready with a second reef.

Then the choice is to take in the topgallants and furl them or leave them in their gear temporarily while taking a first reef in the topsails before resetting topgallants over it. The topgallants will set well over a first reefed topsail with the sheets started about nine inches. This is a very good combination for winds in the mid-20s range on the *Niagara,* because it lowers the center of effort by the depth of the first reef, allowing the topgallant to be carried a little longer. If the wind rises suddenly, the topgallants can be quickly doused, and then the topsail already has a reef in it.

Somewhere around 25 knots of wind, perhaps a little higher if under a weather shore or the wind is steady and perhaps a little lower if the sea is rough, it is time to get the jib in, perhaps reef the foresail as well, and take in the main topmast staysail. Above 25 knots it is definitely time to get the second reefs in the topsails, if working to windward. By the time the wind is up to 30 knots on the *Niagara,* it is time for the third reef in the topsails and to take in the spanker. Sail can be carried longer if running downwind, but only at the risk of being caught overcanvassed if the wind shifts quickly or if the ship needs to make a course change to come on the wind.

What action to take next is highly dependent on circumstances. Is this rising wind a passing squall line, or is it a deepening storm? Is sheltered water close at hand, or are you in open water where the fetch will build large waves in the near future? If facing the latter condition, a deepening storm, the sea state will be as much a factor as the wind. The *Niagara* pounding into heavy seas will need to have its upper spars sent down. The start of this process is the topgallant yards (the royal yards come down with the sail every time) and the flying jibboom. The topgallant yards are more an issue of stability, reducing the weight and windage high aloft. The flying jibboom is low enough that its heeling moment is not great. The primary reason for housing it is structural, to avoid snapping it off pounding into a heavy sea.

At anything over 30 knots of wind, unless under a weather shore, the *Niagara* is down to close reefed topsails and lower staysails. At 35 knots of wind it can hang on to close reefed topsails if off the wind; but if on the wind, it might be better off motor sailing under lower fore and aft sails. This last was not an option for Perry.

The Battle of Lake Erie was characterized by very light air sailing conditions. Sailing the *Niagara* in these conditions today, we find that the time it takes to tack varies greatly with the wind velocity but that the ship nearly always comes about. We have tacked with less than 1 knot of headway, but it took close to twenty minutes. With 3 knots or more of wind, the *Niagara* generally tacks in about six minutes.

In the Battle of Lake Erie, the ships on both sides were locally built, inherent in a landlocked system, and of limited seaworthiness in terms of their relatively shallow hulls that did not have to carry stores for long passages. The *Lawrence* and *Niagara* were at their best in light air and at their worst working to windward. Light air, to the point of calm, dominated 10 September 1813, which was good for the Americans. If Robert Barclay had had a little more wind overnight, at dawn he may have been just at the harbor mouth at Put-in-Bay, ready to sweep through the anchorage and pour close-range fire into Perry's ships. Considering the preponderance of soldiers on the British crews and the heavier armament of the American squadron, Barclay's best bet would probably have been to come alongside and attempt to take the American ships by boarding. Due to the lightness of the wind, the British squadron was ten miles short of its goal at dawn, but at least it had the weather gage.[12]

Over the next four hours, the American squadron was severely handicapped by the poor windward performance of the two largest brigs. While Perry's men became fatigued short tacking to get clear of the harbor, Barclay was free to sail on and simply wait for the range to close. The windshift that occurred around ten in the morning was the best luck Perry could have had.[13] If the winds had not shifted, he would have been in a perilous position: Barclay would have soon been able to sail in line across the harbor entrance, and Perry's ships would have been at odd angles and masking each other's fire.

After this shift, sailing ability was no longer much of a factor for the British line. Barclay wanted to get the battle over with and hove to to await the Americans. To maintain station, his ships needed slight speed to make the rudders effective, but even a knot would do. This defensive position made it easy for the British to maintain a compact line for mutual support. After the wind shift, Perry no longer had to worry about getting to windward. In the chase that followed, however, the light air speed of his two large brigs was not a decisive asset because there was such a large performance gap with the smaller gunboats.

Large sailing vessels are inherently faster than small ones for three reasons. As previously mentioned, the larger vessel has more stability and thus can carry sail longer in strong winds (this was not a factor at the Battle of Lake Erie). Also, the longer the waterline length, the higher the potential speed. Last, on hot summer days of light wind there is often wind aloft when there is barely any at surface level. I have seen this last phenomenon many times sailing the *Niagara* on the Great Lakes. Perry had the stronger squadron, with nine vessels to Barclay's six, and, more importantly, he outgunned the British in weight of shot for both long guns and carronades. His problem was firepower distribution, the heaviest long guns being on the smaller vessels, which lagged behind.[14] The gunboats had limited deck space and could only carry one or two guns, so the thought was that they might as well give them the heaviest they could carry.

At the head of the American line the schooners *Scorpion* and *Ariel* were able to keep station with the *Lawrence* because they had longer hulls and, more importantly, had been built with much sharper lines, giving them greater speed for their size. The *Caledonia,* stationed between the *Lawrence* and *Niagara,* was smaller and slower, to the extent that Elliott claimed he needed to shorten sail to avoid running into her. The *Caledonia* was a brig and as such carried a better rig for downwind performance than a schooner, and this is probably why it was able to stay within range throughout the battle, although lagging behind the *Lawrence.* In fact, since the *Caledonia* was armed with 24-pounder long guns and its designated adversary was the *Queen Charlotte,* armed with 24-pounder carronades, it made perfect sense for Lieutenant Turner to keep the *Caledonia* at long range where his long 24-pounders were effective but the *Queen Charlotte*'s carronades would fall short.

The four gunboats that lagged astern for most of the battle were inherently slow. Two of them, the schooner *Somers* and the sloop *Trippe*, were converted merchant vessels with full-ended hulls designed for cargo capacity rather than speed. The other pair, the *Tigress* and *Porcupine*, were the gunboats deemed too small for effective service when inspected by Isaac Chauncey and Henry Eckford. The combination of small hulls and shorter rigs put these vessels at a severe disadvantage.

If the vessels at the head of the squadron and the large brigs were described as having a "three knot breeze" during the morning's chase, the smaller ones were likely doing only two knots, which in the two hours between 10:00 A.M. and noon would leave them about two miles astern and completely out of range.[15] When the breeze again filled in at about 2:30, it was still from the southeast. This wind would have reached these four gunboats first and moved them along before it got to the ships closely engaged. On sultry summer days, the afternoon breeze is typically stronger than the morning breeze. Getting it first, and having undamaged rigging and sails, allowed these small but heavily armed vessels to finally join the climax of the battle.

Thus, the reconstructed *Niagara* allows modern North Americans to better understand the sailing capabilities and the interaction of various vessels of the two squadrons and provides us with a workshop into the world of fighting sail that would otherwise be lost. It is an appropriate memorial to the officers and men of the U.S. Navy and the Royal Navy who risked their lives that September day 200 years ago on the freshwater sea we know as Lake Erie.

NOTES

1. Pennsylvania Historical and Museum Commission (PHMC) refers to the *Niagara* as a "reconstruction," the term used by preservationists to describe historic structures that are mostly new material but on the same foundations as the original and that have documentation as to the appearance of missing elements. The present ship incorporates all the knowledge gleaned from the original structure. For the *Niagara*, the primary source was the wreck of the original and documentation of contemporary practice for missing elements. "Replica" or "reproduction" imply an entirely new structure that represents the old but with little known about the original. "Restoration" implies the repair and refinishing of an entire structure that is extant.

2. U.S. Brig Niagara Chronology 1908–1988, PHMC unpublished manuscript by Commander Robert Eaton, USN retired,Erie Maritime Museum and PHMC, Harrisburg, PA.

3. Journal of Sailing Master Taylor, original log, Rhode Island Historical Society, Providence; typescript generated by Robert Eaton, Erie Maritime Museum.

4. In 2008 the U.S. Coast Guard, after extensive study, changed the assumed average passenger weight used for simplified stability calculations from 140 pounds to 170 pounds. Code of Federal Regulations (CFR) 46 Shipping, part 178.330 (a) (4) (ii).

5. This average speed of 4.5 knots for sailing vessels is the planning norm in use to this day for sail training vessels planning passage times to be made under sail rather than with power assist.

6. The 35-mile day was indicated by Leonard Allen, who served in the U.S. Cavalry in the 1930s. The longer distances of over 50 miles are ridden today in competitive endurance riding by lightly loaded horses, and they are not expected to repeat the feat without several rest days.

7. The primary problem for both sides in this war was consistently underestimating the difficulty of moving masses of men and materials in a wilderness. The absence of good roads and the ease of interdiction by the Indians were what made the Great Lakes so strategically crucial. Reginald Horsman stresses this factor most eloquently in *The War of 1812* (New York: Knopf, 1969), 29–32.

8. Howard I. Chapelle, *History of the American Sailing Navy* (New York: W. W. Norton, ca. 1949), 11–16, gives an excellent summary of the trade-offs involved in warship design.

9. Weight calculation comparison: U.S. Brig *Niagara,* displacement estimated between 277 and 315 long tons, the median being 296 long tons at 2,240 pounds equaling 663,040 pounds. Accepting the weight of a 32-pounder carronade as 2,000 pounds, plus 500 pounds for the carriage and a 12-pound long gun at 3,800 pounds, plus 600 pounds for the carriage, an armament of eighteen carronades and two long guns (with an allowance of another 1,200 pounds for gun tools and tackles) brings the armament total up to 55,000 pounds and 8.3 percent of the displacement. For the large ship example, the USS *Constitution* displaces 2,300 long tons in light sailing trim, as of her 1998 sea trial. Using Brady's tables of allowances for fresh water, provisions, and stores, a maximum displacement could be about 400 tons larger. Let us assume a midcruise displacement of 2,500 long tons, or 5.6 million pounds. The *Constitution* carried 32-pounder carronades, as cited for the *Niagara,* as well as 24-pounder long guns, at 5,800 pounds per gun plus 800 pounds per carriage, or 6,600 pounds per piece. The weight of twenty-four carronades and thirty long guns, with tools and tackle, would be approximately 260,000 pounds and 4.6 percent of the displacement. Thus, the larger vessel, in addition to being a steadier gun platform, is burdened much less by carrying a heavier armament.

10. Pilot charts are published for all oceans by the National Ocean and Atmospheric Administration (NOAA) in the United States and by the Hydrographic Office in the United Kingdom.

11. John Harlan, *Seamanship in the Age of Sail* (Annapolis, MD: Naval Institute Press, 1996), 53. This Beaufort scale (developed by Robert Beaufort, an officer in the Royal Navy, to show what sail large warships were considered capable of carrying) comparison with the *Niagara* gives a tabular summary of contrasting performance capability.

Wind velocity kts	large frigate	*Niagara*
10–15	stunsls	"kites" come in
15–20	all to royals	reefed spanker topgallants over reefed topsails
20–25	topgallants over single-reefed topsails	take in topgallants

Wind velocity kts	large frigate	*Niagara*
25–35	double-reefed topsails	close-reefed topsails
35–40	triple-reefed topsails over courses	
40–45	close-reefed topsails and fore course	storm staysails
45–55	close-reefed main topsail and reefed forecourse	
5–65	storm staysails	
65+	can show no canvas	

12. Statements regarding the battle are from first-person accounts, primarily found in William S. Dudley, ed., *The Naval War of 1812: A Documentary History*, vol. 2 (Washington, DC: Naval Historical Center, Department of the Navy, 1992), 553–65; "Court Martial of RN Commander Robert Heriot Barclay," Sept. 1814, transcript, Naval Historical Center Library, Washington, DC; log of the *Lawrence*, by Sailing Master William V. Taylor, Rhode Island Historical Society, Providence.

13. W. W. Dobbins, *Battle of Lake Erie and Reminiscences of the Flagships Lawrence and Niagara*, 2nd ed. (Erie, PA: Ashby Printing Co., 1913), 74.

14. W. W. Dobbins, *History of the Battle of Lake Erie* (Erie, PA: Ashby Printing Co., 1913), 74.

15. David Curtis Skaggs and Gerard T. Altoff, *A Signal Victory: The Lake Erie Campaign, 1812–1813* (Annapolis, MD: Naval Institute Press, 1997), 104–48.

Bibliography

PRIMARY SOURCES

MANUSCRIPTS

Buffalo Historical Society, Buffalo, NY
  Daniel Dobbins Papers
Erie Maritime Museum, Erie, PA
  Robert Eaton, "U.S. Brig Niagara Chronology, 1908–1988," 1988
Indiana Historical Society, Indianapolis
  Northwest Territory Collection
Library of Congress, Manuscripts Division, Washington, DC
  John Adolphus Bernard Dahlgren Papers (MSS 17624)
  Miscellaneous Manuscripts Collection, Oliver Hazard Perry
  Stevens Family Papers (MSS 53082)
Mackinac State Historic Parks, Mackinac Island, MI
  Michael G. Pratt, "The Battle for Mackinac Island: The Archaeological Survey of the Wawashkamo Golf Course, Mackinac Island, Michigan" [report], December 2002
National Archives and Records Administration, Washington, DC
  Department of the Navy (Record Group 45)
    Captains Letters
    General Orders and Circulars, Naval Records Collection (M977, roll 1)
    Letters from Master Commandants
    Letters from Officers below the Rank of Master Commandant, 1813
      Petitions or Memorials (Record Group 223)
    Letters Received by the Secretary of the Navy from Commissioned Officers below the Rank of Commander and from Warrant Officers (roll 28)
    Letters to Commissioned and Warrant Officers Transmitting Appointments and Orders and Accepting Resignations, Naval Records Collection (T829, rolls 382 and 383)
    Logs of U.S. Naval Ships and Stations, Records of the Bureau of Naval Personnel (Record Group 24)
    Pension Application Files (Record Group 15)
    Records of General Courts-Martial and Courts of Inquiry of the Navy Department, Records of the Office of the Judge Advocate General (Record Group 125. M273, roll 7)
    Washington Navy Yard Letter Books, vols. 231–35

Committee on Public Lands
Establishment of Land Offices or Districts, PM
Various subjects
Records of the Bureau of Indian Affairs (Record Group 75)
Indent Books
Letters Received by the Office of Indian Affairs, 1824–1881 (M234)
Records of the Civilization Division
Records of the Bureau of Land Management (Record Group 49)
Abandoned Military Reservations
Records of the Office of the Secretary of War (Record Group 107)
Letters Received by the Secretary of War, Registered Series (M221)
Letters Received by the Secretary of War, Unregistered Series (M222)
Records of the U.S. Naval Academy (Record Group 405)
Letters Sent by the Superintendent of the U.S. Naval Academy, February 1, 1864–October 20, 1864
National Archives and Records Administration, Great Lakes Region, Chicago
Records of the Bureau of Land Management (Record Group 49)
Letters Received by the Surveyor General of the Territory Northwest of the River Ohio, 1797–1856 (M479)
Records of the Bureau of Indian Affairs (Record Group 75)
Records of the Michigan Superintendency of Indian Affairs (M1)
National Maritime Museum, Greenwich, England
Chesapeake Signal Book
Newport Historical Society, Newport, RI
Log of the *Lawrence*
William V. Taylor Papers
South Carolina Department of Archives and History, Columbia
Charleston Orphan House (Record Group 001277)
U.S. Naval Academy Museum. Annapolis, MD
Curatorial Records
Welsh Regimental Museum, Cardiff Castle, South Wales, UK
James Cochrane, "The War in Canada, 1812–1814," ca. 1840
William L. Clements Library, University of Michigan, Ann Arbor
Perry Papers
Isaac Chauncey Letter Books

PUBLISHED PRIMARY DOCUMENTS

American State Papers. Class 6, *Naval Affairs.* 4 vols. Washington, DC: Gales and Seaton, 1834–61.

"An ACT for the relief of Thomas Holdup Stevens, and Others," in Acts Passed in the First Session of the Twenty-Second Congress of the United States. Washington, DC: Francis Preston Blair, 1832.

Atherton, William. *Narrative of the Suffering and Defeat of the North-Western Army, under General Winchester.* Frankfort, KY: A.G. Hodges, 1842.

Baker, Harrison Scott II, ed. *Journal of William Kennedy Beall: Assistant Quartermaster under General William Hull, War of 1812.* Columbus: Society of the War of 1812 in the State of Ohio, 1999.

Bauer, K. Jack, ed. *The New American State Papers. Naval Affairs*, Vol. 7, *Personnel*. Wilmington, DE: Scholarly Resources, Inc., 1981.

Beard, James Franklin, ed. *The Letters and Journals of James Fenimore Cooper*. 6 vols. Cambridge, MA: Harvard University Press, 1960–68.

Bristol, Mary Ann Brevoort. "Reminiscences of the Northwest." *Wisconsin Historical Collections* 8 (1879): 293–308.

Blackburn, Glen A., ed. *The John Tipton Papers*. 3 vols. Indianapolis: Indiana Historical Bureau, 1942.

Brown, Samuel R. *Views of the Campaigns of the North-Western Army*. Troy, NY: Francis Adancourt, 1814.

[Bulger, Andrew.] *An Autobiographical Sketch of the Services of the Late Captain Andrew Bulger of the Royal Newfoundland Fencible Regiment*. Bangalore, India: Regimental Press, 2nd Battalion, 10th Regiment, 1865.

Bunnell, David C. *The Travels and Adventures of David C. Bunnell During Twenty-three Years of a Sea-faring Life; Containing an Accurate Account of the Battle on Lake Erie, Under the Command of Com. Oliver H. Perry Together with Ten Years' Service in the Navy of the United States Also Service Among the Greeks, Imprisonment Among the Turks, &c. &c.* Palmyra, NY: J. H. Bortles, 1831.

Carlson, Richard G., ed. "George P. Peters' Version of the Battle of Tippecanoe." *Vermont History* 45 (Winter 1977): 38–43.

Carter, Clarence E., and John Porter Bloom, eds. *The Territorial Papers of the United States*. 28 vols. Washington, DC: Government Printing Office, 1934–75.

Crawford, Mary M., ed. "Mrs. Lydia B. Bacon's Journal, 1811–1812." *Indiana Magazine of History* 41 (March 1945): 59–79.

Cruikshank, Ernest A., ed. *The Documentary History of the Campaign Upon the Niagara Frontier*. 9 vols. Welland, Ontario: Lundy's Lane Historical Society, 1896–1908.

———. *Documents Relating to the Invasion of Canada and the Surrender of Detroit, 1812*. Publications of Canadian Archives, No. 7. Ottawa: Government Printing Bureau, 1913.

Darnell, Elias. *A Journal Containing an Accurate and Interesting Account of the Hardships, Suffering, Battles, Defeat, and Captivity of the Kentucky Volunteers and Regulars Commanded by General Winchester in the Years 1812–1813*. Philadelphia: Lippincott & Grambo, 1854.

Dobbins, William W. *History of the Battle of Lake Erie (September 10, 1813) and Reminiscences of the Flagships Lawrence and Niagara*. Erie, PA: Ashby Printing Co., 1913.

Documents in Relation to the Differences which Subsisted between the Late Commodore O. H. Perry and Captain J. D. Elliott. Boston, 1834.

Dudley, William S., and Michael J. Crawford, eds. *The Naval War of 1812: A Documentary History*, 3 vols. Washington, DC: Naval Historical Center, 1985–.

Esarey, Logan. *Messages and Letters of William Henry Harrison*. 2 vols. Indianapolis: Indiana Historical Commission, 1922.

Font, Walter, ed. *A Garrison at Miamitown: Fort Wayne, October 1794–June 1795*. Fort Wayne, IN: Allen County–Fort Wayne Historical Society, 1994.

Fredriksen, John C. *Surgeon of the Lakes: The Diary of Dr. Usher Parsons, 1812–1814*. Erie, PA: Erie County Historical Society, 2000.

Gipson, Lawrence Henry, ed. *The Moravian Indian Mission on the White River: Diaries and Letters, May 5, 1799–November 12, 1806*. Indianapolis: Indiana Historical Bureau, 1938.

Griswold, Bert J., ed. "Garrison Orderly Books." In *Fort Wayne, Gateway of the West, 1802–1813*. Indianapolis: Indiana Historical Bureau, 1927.

Haffner, Gerald O., ed. "The Pigeon Roost Massacre: An Eyewitness Account." *Indiana History Bulletin* 53 (November–December 1976): 158–61.

Hamilton, Robert. "The Expeditions of Major-General Samuel Hopkins up the Wabash, 1812: The Letters of Captain Robert Hamilton." *Indiana Magazine of History* 43 (December 1947): 393–402.

Harrion, Lowell H., ed. "Nat Crain and the Battle of the Thames." *Filson Club History Quarterly* 64 (July 1990): 377–83.

Hay, Henry. "Journal of Henry Hay." In *Fort Wayne in 1790*. Ed. Milo M. Quaife. Reprint. Fort Wayne, IN: Public Library of Fort Wayne and Allen County, 1955.

Heckewelder, John. *A Narrative of the Mission of the United Brethren among the Delaware and Mohegan Indians, from Its Commencement in the Year 1740 to the Close of the Year 1808*. New York: Arno Press, 1971.

Howe, Henry. *Historical Collections of Ohio*. Cincinnati: Bradley & Anthony, 1848.

Hull, William. *Memoirs of the Campaign of the North Western Army of the United States*. Boston: True & Greene, 1824.

Jackson, Donald, ed. *Black Hawk: An Autobiography*. Urbana: University of Illinois Press, 1987.

Kappler, Charles, ed. *Indian Affairs, Laws, and Treaties*. 4 vols. Washington, DC: Government Printing Office, 1904–29.

King, Susan L. *History and Records of the Charleston Orphan House, 1790–1860*. Easley, SC: Southern Historical Press, 1984.

Knopf, Richard C. *Anthony Wayne: A Name in Arms: The Wayne-Knox-Pickering-McHenry Correspondence*. Pittsburgh: University of Pittsburgh Press, 1949.

———, ed. *Document Transcription of the War of 1812 in the Northwest*. 10 vols. Columbus: Ohio Historical Society, 1957–62.

———, ed. *A Short History of the Life of John Anderson*. Columbus, OH: Anthony Wayne Park Way Board, 1956.

Leavitt, Humphrey Howe. *Autobiography of the Hon. Humphrey Howe Leavitt Written for His Family*. New York, 1893.

Lindley, Harlow, ed. *Indiana as Seen by Early Travelers: A Collection of Reprints from Books of Travel, Letters and Diaries Prior to 1830*. Indianapolis: Indiana Historical Commission, 1916.

Martindale, Charles, ed. *Loughery's Defeat and Pigeon Roost Massacre*. Indianapolis: Bowen-Merrill Co., 1888.

McAfee, Robert B. *History of the Late War in the Western Country*. 1816. Bowling Green, OH: Historical Publications Co., 1919.

McCord, Shirley S., comp. *Travel Accounts of Indiana, 1679–1961*. Indianapolis: Indiana Historical Bureau, 1970.

McCoy, Isaac. *History of the Baptist Indian Missions*. Washington, DC: William M. Morrison, 1840.

Michigan Pioneer and Historical Collections. 40 vols. Lansing: Michigan Historical Commission, 1877–1929.

Minutes of Proceedings of the Courts of Inquiry and Court Martial in Relation to Captain David Porter: Convened at Washington, D.C. on Thursday, the 7th Day of July, A.D. 1825. Printed by Authority from the Official Records. Washington, DC: Davis & Force, 1825.

Parsons, Usher. *Battle of Lake Erie: A Discourse.* Providence, RI: Benjamin T. Albro, 1854.

Paullin, Charles Oscar, ed. *The Battle of Lake Erie.* Cleveland: Rowfant Club, 1918.

Peters, Richard, ed. *The Public Statutes at Large of the United States of America from the Organization of the Government in 1789, to March 3, 1845.* 8 vols. Boston: Charles C. Little & James Brown, 1845–67.

Prucha, Francis Paul. *Documents of the United States Indian Policy.* Lincoln: University of Nebraska Press, 1990.

Public Documents Presented by Order of the Senate of the United States, during the First Session of the Twenty-Sixth Congress, Begun and Held at the City of Washington, December 2, 1839. 8 vols. Washington, DC: Blair & Rives, 1840.

Quaife, Milo M., ed. *War on the Detroit: The Chronicles of Thomas Verchères de Boucherville and the Capitulation by an Ohio Volunteer.* Chicago: Lakeside Press, 1940.

———. *The John Askin Papers.* 2 vols. Detroit: Detroit Library Commission, 1931.

Register of the Commission and Warrant Officers of the Navy of the United States; including Officers of the Marine Corps. N.p.: Metropolitan Press, 1821.

The Report of the Loyal and Patriotic Society of Upper Canada, with an Appendix and List of Subscribers and Benefactors. Montreal: William Gray, 1817.

Review of a Pamphlet Purporting to be Documents in Relation to the Differences which Subsisted between the Lake Commodore Oliver H. Perry and Captain Jesse D. Elliott. Boston: H. B. & J. Brewster, 1834.

Reynolds, Catherine. *An Early Canadian Artist in Essex County.* Windsor, Ontario: Willistead Art Gallery, 1967.

Rodgers, John. *Signals to Be Used by the Squadron under the Command of Commodore John Rodgers.* Brooklyn, NY: Thomas Kirk, 1812.

Sabathy-Judd, Linda, ed. and trans. *Moravians in Upper Canada: The Diary of the Indian Mission of Fairfield on the Thames, 1792–1813.* Toronto: Champlain Society, 1999.

Schoolcraft, Henry Rowe. *Travels through the Northwestern Regions of the United States.* 1821. Ann Arbor, MI: University Microfilms, 1966.

"Selections from the Duane Papers," *Historical Magazine* 2nd ser., 4 (1868).

Sketches of the War, Between the United States and the British Isles: Intended as a Faithful History of all the Material Events from the Time of the Declaration in 1812, to and Including the Treaty of Peace in 1815: Interspersed with Geographical Descriptions of Places, and Biographical Notes of Distinguished Military and Naval Commanders. Rutland, VT: Fay & Davison, 1815.

Smith, William Henry, ed. *The St. Clair Papers: The Life and Public Services of Arthur St. Clair.* 2 vols. Cincinnati: R. Clarke & Co., 1882.

Stevens, Daniel. "Autobiography of Daniel Stevens, 1746–1835." *South Carolina Historical Magazine* 58 (January 1957): 16–17.

Talman, James J., ed. *Loyalist Narratives from Upper Canada.* New York: Greenwood Press, 1969.

Thornbrough, Gayle, ed. *Letter Book of the Indian Agency at Fort Wayne, 1809–1815.* Indianapolis: Indiana Historical Society, 1961.

U.S. Department of the Navy. *Signals for the Use of the United States Navy; as Adopted by Order of the Navy Department, August 1813.* Washington, DC: Department of the Navy, 1813.

Watts, Florence G., ed. "Lieutenant Charles Larrabee's Account of the Battle of Tippecanoe, 1811." *Indiana Magazine of History* 57 (September 1961): 225–47.

Wellenreuther, Hermann, and Carola Wessel, eds. *The Moravian Mission Diaries of David Zeisberger, 1772–1781.* University Park: Pennsylvania State University Press, 2005.

Wesley, Edgar B., ed. "A Letter from Colonel John Allen to Judge William Logan, October 2, 1812." *Ohio State Archaeological and Historical Quarterly* 36 (July 1927): 332–39.

Whickar, J. Wesley, ed. "Shabonee's Account of Tippecanoe." *Indiana Magazine of History* 17 (December 1921): 353–63.

Whitney, Ellen M., ed. *The Black Hawk War 1831–1832.* 3 vols. Springfield: Illinois State Historical Library, 1973.

Wood, Aaron. *Sketches of Things and People in Indiana.* Indianapolis: J. M. Olcott, 1883.

Wood, Eleazer. "Journal of the Northwestern Campaign of 1812–13." In *Campaigns of the War of 1812–15.* Ed. George W. Cullum. New York: James Miller, 1879. 362–412.

Wood, William, ed. *Select British Documents of the Canadian War of 1812.* 3 vols. Toronto: Champlain Society, 1923.

Woodworth, Laura Case, et al. *Reminiscences of Old Fort Wayne.* Fort Wayne, IN: Allen County Public Library, 1906.

NEWSPAPERS

Charleston (SC) *Courier*
Charleston (SC) *Mercury*
Columbian Sentinel, Boston
Daily National Intelligencer, Washington, DC
Hallowell (ME) *Gazette*
Indianapolis Gazette
Fort Wayne Sentinel
Fort Wayne Times
Middlesex Gazette (Middletown, CT)
New-Hampshire Patriot and State Gazette, Concord
Niles Weekly Register, Baltimore
Philadelphia Aurora
Plattsburgh (NY) *Republican*
The Sun, Baltimore
Telescope (Columbia, SC)

SECONDARY SOURCES

Aley, Ginette. "Sheriff Tipton and Susan, a Woman of Color: Race and Gender Borderlands in the Ohio Valley during the Early Republic." In Glenn Crothers, ed., *North American Borderlands.* Athens: Ohio University Press (forthcoming).

———. "Westward Expansion, John Tipton, and the Emergence of the American Midwest, 1800–1839." Ph.D. dissertation, Iowa State University, 2005.

Andrews, H. Franklin, ed. *The Hamlin Family: A Genealogy of Capt. Giles Hamlin of Middletown, Connecticut, 1654–1900.* Exira, IA, 1900.

Altoff, Gerard T. "The Battle of Lake Erie: A Narrative." In Welsh and Skaggs, eds., *War on the Great Lakes.* 5–16.

———. *Deep Water Sailors, Shallow Water Soldiers: Manning the United States Fleet on Lake Erie, 1813.* Put-in-Bay, OH: Perry Group, 1993.

Andrews, Roger. *Old Fort Mackinac on the Hill of History.* Menominee, MI: Herald-Leader Press, 1938.

Antal, Sandy. *A Wampum Denied: Procter's War of 1812.* Ottawa: Carleton University Press, 1997.

Babcock, Louis L. *The War of 1812 on the Niagara Frontier.* Buffalo: Buffalo Historical Society, 1927.

Barnhart, John D., and Dorothy L. Riker. *Indiana to 1816: The Colonial Period.* Indianapolis: Indiana Historical Society, 1971.

Barr, Daniel P. "A Road for Warriors: The Western Delawares and the Seven Years' War in Pennsylvania." *Pennsylvania History: A Journal of Mid-Atlantic Studies* (Winter 2006): 1–36.

———, ed. *The Boundaries Between Us: Natives and Newcomers Along the Frontiers of the Old Northwest Territory, 1750–1850.* Kent, OH: Kent State University Press, 2006.

Beach, Edward L. *The United States Navy: 200 Years.* New York: Henry Holt, 1986. *A Biographical Notice of Com. Jesse D. Elliott . . .* Philadelphia, 1835.

Bearss, Edwin C. *Charlestown Navy Yard, 1800–1842: Boston National Historical Park, Massachusetts.* 2 vols. N.p.: U.S. Department of the Interior/National Park Service, 1984.

Bellows, Barbara L. *Benevolence Among Slaveholders: Assisting the Poor in Charleston, 1670–1860.* Baton Rouge: Louisiana State University Press, 1993.

Booraem, Hendrik. "William Henry Harrison Comes to Cincinnati." *Queen City Heritage* 45 (Fall 1998): 3–20.

Bottiger, Patrick. "Prophetstown for Their Own Purposes: The French, Miamis, and Cultural Identities in the Wabash-Maumee Valley." *Journal of the Early Republic* 33 (Spring 2013): 29–60.

Bowes, John P. *Exiles and Pioneers: Eastern Indians in the Trans-Mississippi West.* New York: Cambridge University Press, 2007.

———. "The Gnadenhutten Effect: Moravian Converts and the Search for Safety in the Canadian Borderlands." *Michigan Historical Review* 34 (Spring 2008): 101–8.

Bowlus, Bruce. "A 'Signal Victory': The Battle for Fort Stephenson, August 1–2, 1813." *Northwest Ohio Quarterly* 63 (Summer/Autumn 1991): 43–57.

Brice, Wallace A. *History of Fort Wayne, from the Earliest Known Accounts of this Point, to the Present Period.* Fort Wayne, IN: D. W. Jones & Son, 1868.

Brunson, Alfred. *A Western Pioneer.* 2 vols. Cincinnati: Hitchcock & Walden, 1872.

Buist, George. *An Oration Delivered at the Orphan-House of Charleston, South-Carolina, October 18th, 1795; Being the Sixth Anniversary of the Institution.* Charleston, SC: Markland & M'Iver, 1795.

Callahan, Edward W., ed. *List of Officers of the Navy of the United States and of the Marine Corps from 1775 to 1900.* New York: Haskell House, 1969.

Calloway, Colin G. *The Scratch of a Pen: 1763 and the Transformation of North America.* New York: Oxford University Press, 2006.

Carter, Harvey Lewis. *The Life and Times of Little Turtle: First Sagamore of the Wabash.* Urbana: University of Illinois Press, 1987.

Cary, Emily Pritchard. "The Flag That Helped Captain Perry Win the Battle of Lake Erie in 1813." *Pennsylvania Magazine* 7, no. 4 (1988).

Cashin, Edward J. *Beloved Bethesda: A History of George Whitefield's Home for Boys, 1740–2000.* Macon, GA: Mercer University Press, 2001.

Casselman, Alexander Clark, ed. *Richardson's War of 1812, with Notes and a Life of the Author.* Toronto: Historical Publishing Co., 1902.

Cayton, Andrew R. L. *Frontier Indiana*. Indianapolis: Indiana University Press, 1996.

———. *The Frontier Republic: Ideology and Politics in the Ohio Country, 1780–1825*. Kent, OH: Kent State University Press, 1986.

Chapelle, Howard I. *History of the American Sailing Navy*. New York: W. W. Norton, 1935.

Cheevers, James W. "Curatorial Notes: USNA 1849.001.012 Don't Give Up the Ship Flag." Annapolis, MD: U.S. Naval Academy Museum, 1999.

Chisholm, Donald. *Waiting for Dead Men's Shoes: Origins and Development of the U.S. Navy Officer Personnel System, 1793–1941*. Palo Alto, CA: Stanford University Press, 2001

Clift, Garrett Glen. *Remember the Raisin! Kentucky and Kentuckians in the Battles and Massacre at Frenchtown, Michigan Territory, in the War of 1812*. Frankfort: Kentucky Historical Papers, 1961.

Coffin, William F. *1812: The War and Its Morals: A Canadian Chronicle*. Montreal: John Lovell, 1864.

Cogar, William B., ed. *Dictionary of Admirals of the U.S. Navy*. 2 vols. Annapolis, MD: Naval Institute Press, 1989.

Coggeshall, George. *Thirty-six Voyages to Various Parts of the World, Made between the Years 1799 and 1841*, 3rd. ed. New York, 1858.

Collins, William Frederick. "John Tipton and the Indians of the Old Northwest." Ph.D. dissertation, Purdue University, 1997.

Cooper, James Fenimore. *History of the Navy of the United States of America*. 2 vols. 3rd ed. Cooperstown, NY: H. & E. Phinney, 1848.

Crisman, Kevin J. *The* Eagle: *An American Brig on Lake Champlain during the War of 1812*. Annapolis, MD: Naval Institute Press, 1977.

Dahlgren, Madeleine Vinton. *Memoir of John A. Dahlgren, Rear-Admiral United States Navy*. Boston: James R. Osgood and Company, 1882.

Davis, James E. *Frontier Illinois*. Bloomington: Indiana University Press, 1998.

The Dictionary of American Biography. New York: Charles Scribner's Sons, 1935.

Dillon, Richard. *We Have Met the Enemy: Oliver Hazard Perry, Wilderness Commodore*. New York: McGraw-Hill, 1978.

Dixon, David. *Never Come to Peace Again: Pontiac's Uprising and the Fate of the British Empire in North America*. Norman: University of Oklahoma Press, 2005.

Dobbins, W. W. *History of the Battle of Lake Erie*. Erie, PA: Ashby Printing Co., 1913.

Douglas, W. A. B. "The Honor of the Flag Had Not Suffered: Robert Heriot Barclay and the Battle of Lake Erie." In Welsh and Skaggs, eds., *War on the Great Lakes*. 30–40.

Dowd, Gregory Evans. *A Spirited Resistance: The North American Indian Struggle for Unity, 1745–1815*. Baltimore: Johns Hopkins University Press, 1992.

———. *War under Heaven: Pontiac, the Indian Nations, and the British Empire*. Baltimore: John Hopkins University Press, 2002.

Drake, Frederick C. "Artillery and Its Influence on Naval Tactics: Reflections on the Battle of Lake Erie." In Welsh and Skaggs, eds., *War on the Great Lakes*. 17–29.

Dudley, William S. "Commodore Isaac Chauncey and U.S. Joint Operations on Lake Ontario, 1813–14." In *New Interpretations in Naval History: Selected papers from the Eighth Naval History Symposium*. Ed. William B. Cogan. Annapolis, MD: Naval Institute Press, 1989. 139–55.

——— and Michael J. Crawford, eds. *The Naval War of 1812: A Documentary History*. 3 vols. Washington, DC: Department of the Navy, 1985–.

Dunnigan, Brian Leigh. "The Battle of Mackinac Island." *Michigan History* 59 (Winter 1975): 239–54.

———. *The British Army at Mackinac, 1812–1815.* Mackinac Island, MI: Mackinac Island State Park Commission, 1980.

———. *Frontier Metropolis: Picturing Early Detroit, 1701–1838.* Detroit: Wayne State University Press, 2001.

———. *A Picturesque Situation: Mackinac before Photography, 1615–1860.* Detroit: Wayne State University Press, 2008.

Dutton, Charles J. *Oliver Hazard Perry.* New York: Longmans, Green, 1935.

Edgar, Walter B. *South Carolina: A History.* Columbia: University of South Carolina Press, 1998.

Edmunds, R. David. *The Potawatomis: Keepers of the Fire.* Norman: University of Oklahoma Press, 1978.

———. *The Shawnee Prophet.* Lincoln: University of Nebraska Press, 1983.

———. *Tecumseh and the Quest for Indian Leadership.* Boston: Little, Brown, 1984.

Ellet, Mrs. E. F. *Pioneer Women of the West.* New York: Charles Scribner, 1856.

Fredriksen, John C., ed. *Surgeon of the Lakes: The Diary of Dr. Usher Parsons, 1812–1814.* Erie, PA: Erie County Historical Society, 2000.

Forester, C. S. *The Age of Fighting Sail: The Story of the Naval War of 1812.* Garden City, NY: Doubleday & Company, 1956.

Fraser, Walter J. *Charleston! Charleston! The History of a Southern City.* Columbia: University of South Carolina Press, 1991.

Friedman, Lawrence J., and David Curtis Skaggs. "Jesse Duncan Elliott and the Battle of Lake Erie: The Issue of Mental Stability." *Journal of the Early Republic* 10 (Winter 1990): 493–516.

Gilpin, Alec R. *The War of 1812 in the Old Northwest.* East Lansing: Michigan State University Press, 1958.

Goldowsky, Seebert J. *Yankee Surgeon: The Life and Times of Usher Parsons, 1788–1868.* Boston: Francis A. Countway Library of Medicine and Rhode Island Historical Society, 1988.

Gough, Barry. *Fighting Sail on Lake Huron and Georgian Bay: The War of 1812 and Its Aftermath.* Annapolis, MD: Naval Institute Press, 2002.

———. *Through Fire and Ice: Schooner Nancy of the War of 1812.* Toronto: Dundurn Group, 2006.

Griswold, Bert. *A Pictorial History of Fort Wayne.* Chicago: Robert O. Law Co., 1917.

Gunderson, Robert G. "A Search for Tip Himself." *Register of the Kentucky Historical Society* 86 (Autumn 1968): 330–51.

———. "William Henry Harrison: Apprentice in Arms." *Northwest Ohio Quarterly* 65 (Winter 1993): 3–29.

Hall, John. *Uncommon Defense: Indian Allies in the Black Hawk War.* Cambridge, MA: Harvard University Press, 2009.

Harlan, John. *Seamanship in the Age of Sail.* Annapolis: Naval Institute Press, 1984.

Harmon, J. Scott. "The Perry Flag." *Shipmate* (September 2005): 18–21.

Harper, Stephen Craig. *Promised Land: Penn's Holy Experiment, the Walking Purchase, and the Dispossession of the Delawares, 1600–1763.* Bethlehem, PA: Lehigh University Press, 2006.

Hatch, William Stanley. *A Chapter of the History of the War of 1812 in the Northwest.* Cincinnati: Miami Printing & Publishing Co., 1872.

Hickey, Donald. *The War of 1812: A Forgotten Conflict.* Urbana: University of Illinois Press, 1989.

Hopkins, Gerard T. *Mission to the Indians from the Indian Committee of Baltimore Yearly Meeting to Fort Wayne in 1804.* Philadelphia: T. Ellwood Zell, 1862.

Horsman, Reginald. *Matthew Elliott, British Indian Agent.* Detroit: Wayne State University Press, 1964.

———. *The War of 1812.* New York: Alfred A. Knopf, 1969.

———. "William Henry Harrison: Virginia Gentleman in the Old Northwest." *Indiana Magazine of History* 96 (June 2000): 125–49

Hutton, Paul. "William Wells: Frontier Scout and Indian Agent." *Indiana Magazine of History* 74 (1978): 183–222.

Jakle, John A. *Images of the Ohio Valley: A Historical Geography of Travel, 1740 to 1860.* New York: Oxford University Press, 1977.

Johnson, Alfred. "Burial Records and Inscriptions at Nassau, New Providence." *New England Historical and Genealogical Register* 68 (July 1914): 238–42.

Johnson, Crisfield. *Centennial History of Erie County, New York: Being Its Annals from the Earliest Recorded Events to the Hundredth Year of American Independence.* Buffalo, NY: Matthews & Warren, 1876.

Johnston, Henry P., ed. *The Record of Connecticut Men in the Military and Naval Service during the War of the Revolution, 1775–1783.* Hartford: Case, Lockwood & Brainard, 1889.

Jung, Patrick J. *Black Hawk and the War of 1832.* Norman: University of Oklahoma Press, 2008.

Keith-Lucas, Alan. *A Legacy of Caring: The Charleston Orphan House, 1790–1990.* Charleston, SC: Charleston Orphan House, 1991.

Kinzie, Mrs. John H. *Wau-Bun: The "Early Day" in the North-West with an Introduction by Milo Milton Quaife.* Chicago: Lakeside Press, 1932.

Knapp, Horace S. *History of the Maumee Valley.* Toledo, OH: Blade Mammoth Printing and Publication, 1871.

Knopf, Richard C., ed. *Document Transcriptions of the War of 1812 in the Northwest.* 10 vols. Columbus: Ohio Historical Society, 1956–62.

Kraft, Herbert C. *The Lenape: Archeology, History, and Ethnography.* Newark: New Jersey Historical Society, 1986.

Langley, Harold D. "Respect for Civilian Authority: The Tragic Career of Samuel Angus." *American Neptune* 40 (January 1980): 23–37.

Long, David F. *Nothing Too Daring: A Biography of Commodore David Porter, 1783–1843.* Annapolis, MD: Naval Institute Press, 1981.

———. *Sailor-Diplomat: A Biography of Commodore James Biddle, 1783–1848.* Boston: Northeastern University Press, 1983.

Lossing, Benson J. *The Pictorial Field-Book of the War of 1812.* New York: Harper & Brothers, 1868.

Mackenzie, Alexander Slidell. *The Life of Commodore Oliver Hazard Perry.* 2 vols. New York: Harper & Brothers, 1843.

Mahan, Alfred Thayer. *Sea Power in Its Relations to the War of 1812.* Boston: Little, Brown, 1905.

Mahon, John K. "Oliver Hazard Perry: Savior of the Northwest." In *Command Under Sail: Makers of the American Naval Tradition, 1775–1850.* Ed. James Bradford. Annapolis, MD: Naval Institute Press, 1985.

———. *The War of 1812*. Gainesville: University Press of Florida, 1972.

Mahon, John K., and Romana Danysh. *Infantry Part I: Regular Army*. Army Lineage Series. Washington, DC: Office of the Chief of Military History, 1972.

Malcomson, Robert. *Historical Dictionary of the War of 1812*. Lanham, MD: Scarecrow Press, 2006.

———. *Warships of the Great Lakes, 1754–1834*. Annapolis, MD: Naval Institute Press, 2001.

Matloff, Maurice, ed. *American Military History*. Washington, DC: Office of the Chief of Military History, 1969.

May, George S. *War 1812: The United States and Great Britain at Mackinac, 1812–1815*. 2nd rev. ed. Mackinac Island, MI: Mackinac State Historic Parks, 2004.

McConnell, Michael N. *A Country Between: The Upper Ohio Valley and Its Peoples, 1724–1774*. Lincoln: University of Nebraska Press, 1992.

McKee, Christopher. *A Gentlemanly and Honorable Profession: The Creation of the U.S. Naval Officer Corps, 1794–1815*. Annapolis, MD: Naval Institute Press, 1991.

Merrell, James H. "American Nations, Old and New: Reflections on Indians and the Early Republic." In *Native Americans and the Early Republic*. Ed. Frederick E. Hoxie, Ronald Hoffman, and Peter J. Albert. Charlottesville: University Press of Virginia, 1999. 333–53.

Murphy, Lucy Eldersveld. *A Gathering of Rivers: Indians, Metis, and Mining in the Western Great Lakes, 1737–1832*. Lincoln: University of Nebraska Press, 2000.

Murray John E. "Fates of Orphans: Poor Children in Antebellum Charleston." *Journal of Interdisciplinary History* 33 (Spring 2003): 519–45.

———. "Literacy Acquisition in an Orphanage: A Historical-Longitudinal Case Study." *American Journal of Education* 110 (Feb. 2004): 180–82.

———. "Mothers and Children in and out of the Charleston Orphan House." In *Children Bound to Labor: The Pauper Apprentice System in Early America*. Ed. Ruth Wallis Herndon and John E. Murray. Ithaca, NY: Cornell University Press, 2009. 102–18.

A Naval Encyclopaedia: Comprising a Dictionary of Nautical Words and Phrases... Philadelphia: L. R. Hamersly & Co., 1881.

Nelson, Larry L. "'A Mysterious and Ambiguous Display of Tactics': The Second Siege of Fort Meigs, July 21–28, 1813." *Ohio History* 120 (2013): 5–28.

Olmstead, Earl P. *Blackcoats Among the Delaware: David Zeisberger on the Ohio Frontier*. Kent, OH: Kent State University Press, 1991.

Ordinances of the City Council of Charleston, in the State of South-Carolina, Passed since the Incorporation of the City... Charleston, SC: William P. Young, 1802.

Owens, Robert M. "Jefferson Benevolence on the Ground: The Indian Land Cession Treaties of William Henry Harrison." *Journal of the Early Republic* 22 (Fall 2002): 405–35.

———. *Mr. Jefferson's Hammer: William Henry Harrison and the Origins of American Indian Policy*. Norman: University of Oklahoma Press, 2007.

Palmer, Michael A. *Command at Sea: Naval Command and Control since the Sixteenth Century*. Cambridge, MA: Harvard University Press, 2005.

———. "A Failure of Command Control, and Communications: Oliver Hazard Perry and the Battle of Lake Erie." *Journal of Erie Studies* 17 (Fall 1988): 7–26.

———. "Lord Nelson: Master of Command." *Naval War College Review* 41 (Winter 1988): 105–16.

———. *Stoddert's War: Naval Operations during the Quasi-War with France, 1798–1801*. 2nd ed. Annapolis, MD: Naval Institute Press, 2000.

Parsons, Usher. *Brief Sketches of the Officers Who Were in the Battle of Lake Erie*. Albany, NY: J. Munsell, 1862.

Poinsatte, Charles R. *Outpost in the Wilderness: Fort Wayne, 1706–1828*. Fort Wayne, IN: Allen County–Fort Wayne Historical Society, 1976.

Prucha, Francis Paul. *A Guide to the Military Posts of the United States, 1789–1895*. Madison: State Historical Society of Wisconsin, 1964.

———. *The Sword of the Republic: The United States Army on the Frontier, 1783–1846*. Lincoln: University of Nebraska Press, 1969.

Ramsay, David. *Ramsay's History of South Carolina, from Its First Settlement in 1670 to the Year 1808*. 2 vols. Newberry, SC: W. J. Duffie, 1858

Quimby, Robert S. *The U.S. Army in the War of 1812: An Operational and Command Study*. 2 vols. East Lansing: Michigan State University Press, 1997.

Rafert, Stewart. *The Miami Indians of Indiana: A Persistent People, 1654–1994*. Indianapolis: Indiana Historical Society, 1996.

Reynolds, Emily Bellinger, and Joan Reynolds Faunt, comps. *Biographical Directory of the Senate of the State of South Carolina, 1776–1964*. Columbia: South Carolina Archives Department, 1964.

Robertson, Robert. *Valley of the Upper Maumee River: With Historical Account of Allen County and the City of Fort Wayne, Indiana*. 2 vols. Madison, WI: Brant & Fuller, 1889.

Rohrbough, Malcolm. "The Land Office Business in Indiana, 1800–1840." In *This Land of Ours: The Acquisition and Disposition of the Public Domain*. Indianapolis: Indiana Historical Society, 1978.

———. *The Land Office Business: The Settlement and Administration of American Public Lands, 1789–1837*. New York: Oxford University Press, 1968.

Roosevelt, Theodore. *The Naval War of 1812*. New York: G. P. Putnam's Sons, 1882.

Scarpitti, Allison. "*Niagara/Lawrence*." *Journal of Erie Studies* 26 (Spring 1997): 68–96

Schroeder, John H. *Commodore John Rodgers: Paragon of the Early Navy*. Gainesville: University Press of Florida, 2006.

Schutt, Amy C. *People of the River Valleys: The Odyssey of the Delaware Indians*. Philadelphia: University of Pennsylvania Press, 2007.

Seiken, Jeff. "'To Obtain Command of the Lakes': The United States and the Contest for Lakes Erie and Ontario, 1812–1815." In Skaggs and Nelson, eds., *The Sixty Years' War for the Great Lakes*. 353–59

Sheldon, Electra. *The Early History of Michigan from the First Settlement to 1815*. New York: A. S. Barnes & Co., 1856.

Skaggs, David Curtis. "Aiming at the Truth: James Fenimore Cooper and the Battle of Lake Erie." *Journal of Military History* 59 (April 1995): 237–56.

———."The Battle of Lake Erie." In Jack Sweetman, ed., *Great American Naval Battles*. 65–84.

———. "Joint Operations during the Detroit-Erie Campaign, 1813." In *New Interpretations in Naval History: Selected Papers from the Eighth Naval History Symposium*. Ed. William B. Cogar. Annapolis, MD: Naval Institute Press, 1989. 121–38.

———. "The Making of a Major General: William Henry Harrison and the Politics of Command, 1812–13." *Ohio Valley History* 10 (Spring 2010): 32–52.

———. *Oliver Hazard Perry: Honor, Courage and Patriotism in the Early U.S. Navy*. Annapolis, MD: Naval Institute Press, 2007.

———. "River Raisin Redeemed: William Henry Harrison, Oliver Hazard Perry, and the Midwestern Campaign, 1813." *Northwest Ohio History* 78 (Spring 2010): 67–83.

———. *Thomas Macdonough: Master of Command in the Early U.S. Navy.* Annapolis, MD: Naval Institute Press, 2003.

——— and Gerard T. Altoff. *A Signal Victory: The Lake Erie Campaign, 1812–1813.* Annapolis, MD: Naval Institute Press, 1997.

——— and Larry L. Nelson, eds. *The Sixty Years' War for the Great Lakes.* East Lansing: Michigan State University Press, 2001.

Slocum, Charles Elihu. *History of the Maumee River Basin.* Defiance, OH: Charles Slocum, 1905.

———. "The Origin, Description, and Service of Fort Winchester, with Mention of Some of the Persons and Events Connected with It." *Ohio Archaeological and Historical Quarterly* 9, no. 1 (1901): 253–77.

Smyth, Thomas. *Oration Delivered on the Forty-Eighth Anniversary of the Orphan House, in Charleston, S.C., October 18th, 1837.* Charleston, SC: J. S. Burges, 1837.

Soley, James Russell. *Historical Sketch of the United States Naval Academy.* Washington, DC: Government Printing Office, 1876.

Stanley, George F. G. *The War of 1812: Land Operations.* Toronto: National Museums of Canada and Macmillan, 1983.

Stocker, Harry Emilius. *A History of the Moravian Mission among the Indians on the White River in Indiana.* Bethlehem, PA: Times Publishing Co., 1917.

Strickland, William P. *Old Mackinaw; or, the Fortress of the Lakes.* Philadelphia: James Challen & Son, 1860.

Sugden, John. *Blue Jacket: Warrior of the Shawnees.* Lincoln: University of Nebraska Press, 2000.

———. *Tecumseh: A Life.* New York: Henry Holt, 1997.

Sweetman, Jack. *Great American Naval Battles.* Annapolis, MD: Naval Institute Press, 1998.

Sword, Wiley. *President Washington's Indian War: The Struggle for the Old Northwest, 1790–1795.* Norman: University of Oklahoma Press, 1985.

Symonds, Craig L. *Decision at Sea: Five Naval Battles that Shaped American History.* New York: Oxford University Press, 2005.

Tanner, Helen Hornbeck. *Atlas of Great Lakes Indian History.* Norman: University of Oklahoma Press, 1987.

Toll, Ian. *Six Frigates: The Epic History of the Founding of the U.S. Navy.* New York: W. W. Norton, 2006.

Trask, Kerry. *Black Hawk: The Battle for the Heart of America.* New York: Henry Holt, 2006.

Trupin, Deborah Lee. "A Tale of Two Flags: How History of Treatment and Ownership Affected Conservation Treatment of Two Early 19th-Century American Flags." *Restauro: Forum für Restauratoren, Konservatoren und Denkmalpfleger* 115, no. 3 (2009): 187–97.

———. "Don't Give Up the Flag: The Conservation of the United States Naval Academy's 1813 'DONT GIVE UP THE SHIP' Flag." In *14th Triennial Meeting, The Hague, 12–16 September 2005: preprints ICOM Committee for Conservation.* Ed. Isabelle Verger. London: Earthscan, 2005. 963–68.

———. "Flag Conservation Then and Now." In *Tales in the Textile: The Conservation of Flags and Other Symbolic Textiles: Preprints: North American Textile Conservation Conference 2003, November 6 To 8, 2003.* Ed. Jan Vuori. Albany: New York State Office of Parks, Recreation, and Historic Preservation and North American Textile Conservation Conference, 2003. 55–62.

———. "Patriotism in Fabric and Stitches: The History of Flag Conservation/Restoration in the United States." In *Past Practice, Future Prospects. Occasional Papers (British Museum).* Vol. 145. Ed. Andrew W. Oddy and Sandra Smith. London: British Museum, 2001.

Tucker, Patrick M. and David M. Stothers. "The Amos Spafford Farm and the War of 1812 in Ohio: A Case of Historic Memory Loss." *Northwest Ohio History* 78 (2010): 17–47.

U.S. Department of the Army. *Operations.* FM 100–5. Washington, DC: Department of the Army, 1976.

U.S. Department of the Army. *Operations.* FM 3–0. Washington, DC: Department of the Army, 2008.

U.S. Department of Defense. *Dictionary of Military and Associated Terms.* Joint Pub 1–02. Washington, DC: Department of Defense, 2001.

U.S. Department of the Navy. *Dictionary of American Naval Fighting Ships.* 8 vols. Washington, DC: Naval Historical Center, 1959–81.

U.S. Library of Congress. *The First American West: The Ohio River Valley, 1750–1820.* http://memory.loc.gov/ammem/award99/icuhtml/fawhome.html.

Vanden Berghe, Ina. *Natural Dye Analysis Report, IRPA/KIK Project 2005.08601.* Waterford, NY: NYSOPRPH Peebles Island Resource Center, 2005.

Walker, Adam. *A Journal of Two Campaigns of the Fourth Regiment of U.S. Infantry in the Michigan and Indiana Territories.* Keene, NH: Sentinel Press, 1816.

Wallace, Anthony F. C. *Jefferson and the Indians: The Tragic Fate of the First Americans.* Cambridge, MA: Belknap Press, 1999.

Ward, Annette P. *"Lest We Forget:" Oliver Hazard Perry, the War of 1812, the Battle of Lake Erie.* Cleveland, 1912.

Watkins, Charles Allan, and Mark Matusiak. "Is This the Real *Niagara?*" 15 *Naval History* (February 2001): 36–40.

Welsh, William Jeffrey, and David Curtis Skaggs, eds. *War on the Great Lakes: Essays Commemorating the 175th Anniversary of the Battle of Lake Erie.* Kent, OH: Kent State University Press, 1991.

Weslager, C. A. *The Delaware Indians: A History.* New Brunswick, NJ: Rutgers University Press, 1972.

White, Leonard. *The Federalists: A Study in Administrative History.* New York: Macmillan, 1940.

White, Richard. *The Middle Ground: Indians, Empires, and Republics in the Great Lakes Region, 1650–1815.* New York: Cambridge University Press, 1991.

Whittlesey, Charles. *Early History of Cleveland, Ohio.* Cleveland: Fairbanks, Benedict, & Co., 1867.

Willig, Timothy D. *Restoring the Chain of Friendship: British Policy and the Indians of the Great Lakes, 1783–1815.* Lincoln: University of Nebraska Press, 2008.

Woehrmann, Paul. *At the Headwaters of the Maumee: A History of the Forts of Fort Wayne.* Indianapolis: Indiana Historical Society, 1971.

Wood, Edwin O. *Historic Mackinac: The Historical, Picturesque and Legendary Features of the Mackinac Country.* 2 vols. New York: Macmillan, 1918.

Yanik, Anthony J. *The Fall and Recapture of Detroit in the War of 1812: In Defense of William Hull.* Detroit: Wayne State University Press, 2011

Contributors

Ginette Aley is currently a Carey Fellow in the Department of History at Kansas State University and an adjunct professor at Washburn University in Topeka. She has also taught at Virginia Tech, Drake University, and the University of Southern Indiana. She specializes in nineteenth-century rural and frontier America and has published numerous articles and book chapters on westward expansion into the Old Northwest, land policies, and, most recently, Civil War home fronts, North and South. Her coedited with J. L. Anderson essay collection, *Union Heartland: The Midwestern Home Front During the Civil War,* is forthcoming from Southern Illinois University Press.

Daniel Barr is professor of history at Robert Morris University in suburban Pittsburgh, where he specializes in colonial and revolutionary America, Pennsylvania history, and American Indian history. Among his publications are *The Boundaries Between Us: Natives and Newcomers in the Old Northwest Territory, 1750–1850* and *Unconquered: The Iroquois League at War in Colonial America.* His most recent project is a study of early southwestern Pennsylvania, titled *A Colony Sprung from Hell: Pittsburgh and the Struggle for Authority on the Western Pennsylvania Frontier, 1744–1794* (forthcoming 2014).

John P. Bowes is an associate professor of history at Eastern Kentucky University. His first book, *Exiles and Pioneers: Eastern Indians in the Trans-Mississippi West* (2007), is in the Cambridge University Press series Studies in North American Indian History. His most recent article, "Transformation and Transition: American Indians and the War of 1812 in the Lower Great Lakes," appeared in the October 2012 issue of the *Journal of Military History.* His current research project, *Northern Indian Removal: An Unfamiliar History,* is under contract with University of Oklahoma Press.

Charles E. Brodine Jr. has served as a historian with the Naval History and Heritage Command, Washington, DC, since 1987. He is coauthor and coeditor of a number of publications on the early sailing navy, including *Interpreting Old Ironsides: An Illustrated Guide to USS Constitution* (2007); *Against All Odds: U.S. Sailors in the War of 1812* (2004); volumes 2 and 3 of *The Naval War of 1812: A Documentary History* (1992, 2002); and volume 10 of *Naval Documents of the American Revolution* (1996). In 2008 Brodine was named a co-recipient of the USS Constitution Museum Foundation's Samuel Eliot Morison Award in recognition of his "superior leadership and thoughtful scholarship" in preserving America's "maritime heritage and the traditions of the USS *Constitution* for future generations."

Brian Leigh Dunnigan is associate director and curator of maps at the William L. Clements Library, University of Michigan, Ann Arbor. He formerly served as executive director of Old Fort Niagara in Youngstown, New York (1979–96), and managing director of Historic Fort Wayne, Indiana. Dunnigan has written extensively on the early history of the Great Lakes, including *A Picturesque Situation: Mackinac before Photography* (2008), *Frontier Metropolis: Picturing Early Detroit* (2001), and *Siege, 1759: The Campaign against Niagara* (1986, 1996).

Phyllis Gernhardt is an associate professor of history at the University of Saint Francis in Fort Wayne, Indiana. In 2008 she received the Teaching Excellence and Campus Leadership Award and is currently updating the university's history. She is the author of "Justice and Public Policy: Indian Trade, Treaties, and Removal from Northern Indiana, 1826–1846," in Daniel Barr's *Boundaries Between Us* (2006), as well as several book reviews, and she has made numerous conference and guest presentations on U.S. frontier policy in the Great Lakes region.

J. Scott Harmon graduated from the U.S. Naval Academy in 1964 and served in destroyers before attending Utah State University and earning his doctorate in history at the College of William and Mary. He served for twenty-four years with the National Park Service as a historian and then as an exhibit planner at Harpers Ferry Center. In the latter role he helped develop exhibits for numerous parks, including Arizona Memorial at Pearl Harbor, Hawaii; Salem Maritime, Massachusetts; Martin Luther King Jr. Visitor Center, Atlanta; National Prisoner of War Museum, Andersonville, Georgia; and Springfield Armory, Massachusetts. Harmon transferred from the Park Service to the Naval Academy, where he was director of the Naval Academy Museum and assistant professor of history.

Larry L. Nelson was site manager at Fort Meigs State Memorial until his retirement from the Ohio Historical Society in 2004. He is currently an adjunct assistant professor of history at Bowling Green State University's Firelands College and the editor of *Northwest Ohio History.* He is the author of *A Man of Distinction Among Them: Alexander McKee and the Ohio Frontier* (1999) and editor of *A History of Jonathan Alder, His Captivity and Life with the Indians* (2002). He is also coeditor, with David C. Skaggs, of *The Sixty Years' War for the Great Lakes, 1754–1814* (2001). Nelson has recently published articles exploring the War of 1812 in the Maumee Valley in *Ohio History* and the *Register of the Kentucky Historical Society.*

Michael A. Palmer is a professor of history at East Carolina University. He served as an interim chair of the Departments of English (2007–9) and Geography (1997–99) and as chair of the Department of History (1999–2007). Between 1983 and 1991, Palmer worked at the Naval Historical Center. In 1988 he worked as a field historian in the Persian Gulf. In 1990 he served on the staff of the Office of the Chief of Naval Operations' Strategic Concepts Group in the Pentagon. Palmer is the author of ten books and a score of articles, including *Command at Sea: Naval Command and Control since the Sixteenth Century* (2007). He received the Department of the Navy's Meritorious Civilian Service Medal, the Samuel Eliot Morison Award for Naval Literature from the Naval Order of the United States, the Moncado Prize from the Society for Military History, and a John A. Adams Center prize from the Virginia Military Institute.

Walter P. Rybka, who developed a fascination with maritime history from frequent boyhood visits to New York Harbor, has divided his career between sailing and ship restoration projects from Mystic Seaport to San Francisco, including service as restoration director for the rebuilding of the 1877 iron barque *Elissa.* He sailed as a deck officer for Sea Education Association's schooner *Westward* and brigantine *Corwith Cramer* and has also served as captain for the schooners *Pioneer* and *Californian,* and, since 1991, the U.S. brig *Niagara.* He has been the director of the Erie Maritime Museum in Erie, Pennsylvania, since 2001. Rybka is the author of *The Lake Erie Campaign of 1813: I Shall Fight Them This Day* (2012). He has a B.A. from Macalester College and a U.S. Coast Guard master's license for 1,600-ton vessels.

David Curtis Skaggs is professor emeritus of history at Bowling Green State University, where he taught from 1965 to 2001. He has held visiting professor positions at the University of Wisconsin–Madison, the Air War College, and East Carolina University. He is the author and editor of fourteen books, including *War on the Great Lakes* (1991), *A Signal Victory: The Lake Erie Campaign, 1812–1813* (1997), *The Sixty Years' War for the Great Lakes, 1754–1814* (2001), *Thomas Macdonough: Master of Command in the Early U.S. Navy* (2003), *Oliver Hazard Perry: Honor, Courage and Patriotism in the Early U.S. Navy* (2006), and *Frontier Warfare in the War of 1812: William Henry Harrison and the Conquest of the Ohio Country* (2013). In 2012 he received the Samuel Eliot Morison Award from the USS *Constitution* Museum Foundation for his "distinguished contributions" to the study of the War of 1812 on North America's inland seas.

Deborah Lee Trupin received her M.A. in art history and a diploma in conservation from the Conservation Center, Institute of Fine Arts, New York University. Since 1986 she has been Textile Conservator for New York State's Bureau of Historic Sites (Peebles Island) in Waterford, where she is responsible for the conservation of the textile and upholstery collections of the thirty-five state-run historic sites. Since 2000 she has also supervised the conservation work for the New York State Battle Flag Preservation Project. Her interest in flag conservation dates to her first exposure to these challenging objects in 1983.

Index